MR. DARLEY'S ARABIAN

MR. DARLEY'S
ARABIAN

HIGH LIFE, LOW LIFE, SPORTING LIFE:
A HISTORY OF RACING IN 25 HORSES

Christopher McGrath

PEGASUS BOOKS
NEW YORK LONDON

Mr. Darley's Arabian

Pegasus Books Ltd
148 West 37th Street, 13th Floor
New York, NY 10018

Copyright © 2017 by Christopher McGrath

First Pegasus Books hardcover edition March 2017

ISBN: 978-1-68177-338-4

10 9 8 7 6 5 4 3 2 1

Printed in the United States of America
Distributed by W. W. Norton & Company, Inc.

In memory of Sean Millar, 1959–2012

Contents

CONTENTS

Timeline

1770   Dennis O'Kelly buys Eclipse

1773   Birth of Pot8os

1776   Founding of the St Leger

1780   Diomed wins first running of the Derby

1787   Death of Dennis O'Kelly

1790   Birth of Waxy

1791   Publication of *General Stud Book*

1793   Waxy wins the Derby

1805   Birth of James Merry

1807   Birth of Whalebone

1809   First running of the 2000 Guineas

1810   Whalebone wins the Derby, one of four sons of Waxy to do so

1821   Tout William Taylor is first man 'warned off' by the Jockey Club

1825   Birth of Hugh Lupus Grosvenor, 1st Duke of Westminster

1826   Birth of Sir Hercules

1826   Egremont wins a record fifth Derby

1833   Birth of Birdcatcher

1837   Death of Egremont

1838   First Derby special from Nine Elms station

1842   Birth of The Baron

1844   Derby winner Running Rein unmasked as an impostor

1845   The Baron gives Ireland a second consecutive St Leger

1846   Leviathan Davies posts a 'list' for cash bets in the Durham Arms

1847   Birth of Archibald Philip Primrose, 5th Earl of Rosebery

1849   **Birth of Stockwell**

1852   Birdcatcher sires the Derby winner and the first three in the Oaks

1865   Birth of Solomon Barnato Joel

1867   Birth of Edward George Villiers Stanley, 17th Earl of Derby

1870   Prince of Wales hissed at Ascot after testifying in a divorce case

1870   **Birth of Doncaster**

1871   Death of John Scott, doyen of Yorkshire trainers

1873   Doncaster wins the Derby

1877   Death of James Merry

1877   **Birth of Bend Or**

1880   Fred Archer wins the Derby on Bend Or

1885   Archer rides a record 246 winners

1886   Suicide of Archer

1889   **Birth of Bona Vista**

1894   Rosebery becomes prime minister and wins Derby with Ladas II

1895   **Birth of Cyllene**

1895   Rosebery wins Derby again with Sir Visto but his ministry falls

1896   Persimmon wins the Derby for the Prince of Wales

1897   Arrival in Newmarket of American jockey Tod Sloan

1898   Death of Mat Dawson, modernising trainer

1899   Cyllene wins the Ascot Gold Cup

1899   Federico Tesio begins a stud by Lake Como

1899	Death of the Duke of Westminster
1900	The Prince of Wales wins the Triple Crown with Diamond Jubilee and the Grand National with Ambush II
1901	E. P. Taylor and Horatio Luro born
1902	**Birth of Polymelus**
1906	Polymelus wins Cambridgeshire Handicap
1908	Cyllene exported to Argentina
1909	Minoru becomes the first Derby winner for a reigning monarch
1913	Death of Sir Charles Rose after an aeroplane flight
1913	**Birth of Phalaris**
1915	First wartime Derby moved to Newmarket
1917	Birth of Vincent O'Brien
1917	Phalaris wins seven races despite a restricted wartime programme
1918	Death in action of Fred Rickaby, jockey of Phalaris
1920	**Birth of Pharos**
1924	Sansovino wins Lord Derby the race that bears his name
1929	Death of Rosebery
1931	Death of Solly Joel
1935	**Birth of Nearco**
1936	E. P. Taylor buys his first racehorses
1937	Horatio Luro sails four horses from Argentina to New York
1938	Nearco wins the Grand Prix de Paris
1940	E. P. Taylor torpedoed in the North Atlantic
1943	Birth of Henry Cecil

1948   Death of Lord Derby

1954   Birth of Nearctic

1955   Vincent O'Brien saddles third consecutive Grand National winner

1960   Legalisation of betting shops

1961   Birth of Northern Dancer

1964   Northern Dancer sets record time in the Kentucky Derby

1969   Birth of Aidan O'Brien

1976   Purchase of Fairy Bridge, future dam of Sadler's Wells, for $40,000

1977   A half-share in The Minstrel, a $200,000 yearling, sold back to E. P. Taylor for $4.5 million

1981   Birth of Sadler's Wells

1983   The Maktoum brothers give $10.2 million for a Northern Dancer colt

1984   Northern Dancer's fee now $500,000

1993   Henry Cecil is champion trainer for the tenth time

1998   Birth of Galileo

2001   Galileo wins the Derby

2003   Bobby Frankel trains a record twenty-five Grade One winners

2008   Birth of Frankel

2009   Death of Vincent O'Brien

2011   Frankel wins 2000 Guineas

2013   Death of Henry Cecil

2016   Frankel's first runners appear on the track

A man ain't so different from a horse or a mule, come long come short, except a mule or a horse has got a little more sense.

William Faulkner

Introduction

The horse waits in the starting gate. Before him stretches a long strip of bright turf, tapering to the horizon. As he nods his head, he sees a slick of sunlight sliding up and down the white plastic rails on either side of the racetrack. Frankel's berth is last on the right; a dozen other three-year-old colts have been loaded into the gates to his left. Several have prolonged the illusion that they could be the best of their generation. That is why they have been brought to Newmarket, on the last day of April 2011, for the first of the five Classics staged every year in England.

As herd animals, horses do not always need to test each other's physical prowess to identify a dominant male. Some sweat cravenly simply escorting a champion through his warm-up jog in the mornings. Any horse good enough to contest the 2000 Guineas is accustomed to preening himself among the others in his own stable. So a creeping unease, a sudden sense of doubt, is an unnerving novelty to Frankel's rivals. Not even Tom Queally, the pale Irishman perched on his back, can sense the intimidation exuded by his mount in the parade ring or loping down to the start. But the signs will be there in the other horses, at some level: a dulling of the eye, a tightening of the gait.

The thousands peering from the crowded grandstands have been captivated by the promise of Frankel's five previous wins, making him the hottest Guineas favourite in thirty-seven years. But only one man has a real inkling of what is about to happen.

At sixty-eight, Henry Cecil is feted as one of the greatest trainers in Turf history. But he does not have much time left. Cecil's illness is well known to the racing public. Throughout Frankel's short career, Cecil has timetabled his chemotherapy to fit in with the horse's exercise roster. However debilitating his treatment, Cecil is always back on the gallops to supervise Frankel's key workouts; to inhale something of the vitality he has never seen in any other thoroughbred.

Six years ago Cecil's career reached a nadir: twelve winners in the whole of 2005. At its peak, in 1987, he trained 180. Bereavement, divorce, drink and depression reduced the ten-times champion trainer to a brooding husk, and Cecil heard insolent whispers that he should retire to spare everyone embarrassment. Yet in 2010, even as his features became drawn and sallow, Cecil won six races at the elite, Group One level, something he had achieved only once in the previous twenty seasons. These included the Dewhurst Stakes, with Frankel: the season's top prize for two-year-olds, the novices who would be eligible for the Classics in 2011.

Frankel has so much speed that it already seems fanciful to hope that his stamina might stretch to either the Derby or the St Leger – both still more venerable than the 2000 Guineas, which was first run in 1809, but both run over much longer distances. For Frankel, then, today is his only chance of winning an English Classic. The one chink in his armour is that he might burn out even at a mile. Everyone is fascinated to see whether Cecil, the old master, has managed to teach Frankel how to conserve his fuel sufficiently to last the course.

The other riders think they know just what to expect from Queally. There is a standard formula for this kind of scenario. The jockey restrains his mount behind his rivals in the early stages, trying to keep him relaxed, and only takes the pin out of the grenade as they reach the closing stages, to explode past the tiring front-runners. Things can still go wrong. If the pace is too slow, Frankel might squander too much energy trying to go faster, fighting his taut reins; if too strong, on the other hand, then the dour, staying types in the field could draw his sting.

Then the stalls clatter open, and the shock is heard around the racing world.

Queally, on an easy rein, allows Frankel to stretch out at will. There is an immediate, mesmerising buoyancy to the horse: after two furlongs, a quarter of the race, he is already three lengths clear of the pack. This was in nobody's script but Cecil's. Yet it is done almost casually. Frankel weighs half a ton but looks as though he would leave no trace of his passage over wet cement. Think of Roger Federer skimming on soundless feet after a lob at Wimbledon. And nor is Queally trying shock tactics, some artful bluff to steal an early lead before slackening the pace in front. Every stride takes Frankel further clear; after three furlongs, the lead is five lengths and you sense that the rest are going as fast as they can. A nervous murmuring spreads across the stands. What is Queally playing at? No horse can keep this up. Approaching the next furlong pole, still only halfway, Frankel has opened up a gap of ten lengths. Now a tide of gasps, oaths and even laughter swells through the crowd. Nobody has seen anything like this in a normal race, never mind a Classic.

Approaching the last two furlongs, the bewildered commentator is exclaiming that Frankel is fifteen lengths clear. A roar acclaims the champion. This is the sort of separation familiar in steeplechases, over three miles of muddy ground. The Guineas is usually settled by the sharpest blade at close quarters, often in a photo finish. It is sixty-four years since Tudor Minstrel hurtled clear by a record eight lengths. As Frankel goes careering away – looking not so much in a different class as in a different species – he seems entirely alone.

The other jockeys are urging their mounts forward in a race for second. Few resort to the whip. They know that their horses are already beaten, that it will be hard enough to restore their egos as it is. In the end, it is Queally himself who has to push his mount most firmly as a couple of the pursuers close the gap to half-a-dozen lengths through the last two furlongs. Perhaps Frankel's attention is wandering; maybe he is simply tiring. His exertions early in the race, after all, can have been within the compass of very few thoroughbreds in history.

That is as much as anyone should claim for him. It is enough. He can never race against Tudor Minstrel, or the many champions in between. Even so, the past ninety-seven seconds are enough for some to pronounce Frankel the best racehorse ever. They are doubtless emboldened by his role in Cecil's story, as though the horse is the agent of some redemptive destiny.

But the debate is as fatuous as it is perennial, whenever a new meteor hurtles across the racing firmament. Already there has since been a rival phenomenon on the turf: American Pharoah, the first winner of the US Triple Crown in thirty-seven years and scion of an altogether different branch of the Darley Arabian line. And the fact is that Cecil campaigned Frankel rather too conservatively – he never once risked a race abroad – to shed enough light on his capacity even against his contemporaries, never mind spectres of the past. But the horse's greatest challenge, regardless, is still to come: and that is to outlive all such contention through his sons and daughters.

The following Valentine's Day, Frankel was introduced to the rewards he had won, as an alpha male, through his feats on the track. An apt date, you might think, for the start of the breeding season. But the mating of a thoroughbred stallion is a profoundly unsentimental ritual that never fails to stupefy witnesses. Screaming and snorting, side-stepping and prancing, he is led into a barn that might, on the more opulent studs, have made a serviceable cathedral. His nostrils flare at the reek of a mare in heat; he rolls his eyes and bares his teeth; his neck and shoulders and crest inflate. His handlers skitter and lurch as they marry the groaning, hollering monster with his hobbled, quivering mate, bracing her on the rubberised flooring. Forelimbs dangling, the stallion tears manically at his partner's neck – he might reduce it to a bloody pulp but for the protective padding – until the final, shuddering convulsion. And is then led away, dazed and vacant. He does not as much as glance at the recent subject of his earth-shaking lust. Yet the libido will renew sufficiently for many stallions to 'cover' three mares daily, during the breeding season.

Frankel was given a relatively small harem, with a total of 133 partners in four months. Each had an eligible pedigree and had either been a highly accomplished runner or produced one or more already. On delivery of a live foal, eleven months later, the owner of each mare paid a fee of £125,000 to the Saudi prince who owns Frankel. It might sound a lot but the first foal to be auctioned, the following summer, fetched £1.15 million.

Though two dozen of Frankel's partners were Prince Khaled Abdulla's own mares, his excellent fertility ensured revenue of around

£13 million from his first season at stud. This, plainly, is the real endgame. The 2000 Guineas carried a first prize of £200,000. That is thought to be as much as Frankel's sire, Galileo, commands for a few seconds with a mare, albeit his fee is simply listed as 'private' by Coolmore Stud. This self-fulfilling quality, in the value of blood-stock, renders prize money in Flat racing almost incidental. The real stakes, in the great races, await in retirement.

But even a racing career as sensational as Frankel's cannot guar-antee that he will breed horses of similar ability. Any number of champions have flopped at stud. Only now, with Frankel's foals starting to race, can we begin to know whether many have inherited his speed. It may yet be that one of several other top-class runners sired by Galileo will found the most potent branch of their dynasty. The story that follows, then, is one without end. All that can be guaranteed is that their ancestors have left us only one beginning.

All thoroughbreds are descended from one of just three stallions, imported to England around three hundred years ago: the Godolphin Arabian, the Byerley Turk and the Darley Arabian. Over the last century or so, however, the first two of these patriarchs have been more or less eradicated from the 'top line' of racehorse pedigrees – the patrilineal chain, that is, of sons begat by fathers. The Darley Arabian has achieved a virtual monopoly. If Frankel represented a new peak in the modern racing landscape, then he shared the same genetic bedrock as nearly all the horses around him. In his entire career Frankel raced against only two horses who did not ultimately trace their 'male tail' ancestry to the Darley Arabian.

The Darley Arabian never raced, and produced only around a score of foals after being exported to the family estate in Yorkshire by a Levant Company merchant. Yet he has become the fount of a eugenic miracle, uniting the lineage of nineteen out of twenty thoroughbreds lining up for any race, anywhere in the world: from Royal Ascot to the Melbourne Cup to the Kentucky Derby. As founding fathers go, Mr Darley's Arabian must be counted the daddy of them all.

This book follows the story of the thoroughbred's genetic Big Bang. It traces each link in the golden chain of twenty-three generations dividing the Darley Arabian and Frankel. At nearly every stage, the racehorse takes an unpredictable turn, constantly challenging expectations. The precious Darley Arabian line is established and maintained against all odds. Consider the very first link in the chain. The Darley Arabian sired one outstanding racehorse, Flying Childers. But it was his useless brother, Bleeding Childers, so named because he burst blood vessels every time he galloped, who laid the foundations of the modern breed. For him to preserve the genes of their sire, when Flying Childers appeared so much better qualified, represents a fitting start for its meandering, haphazard evolution.

Bleeding Childers then depended on a son, Squirt, who arrived at stud crippled by laminitis. Even the great Eclipse, hailed as the template for the modern thoroughbred, was bred from a mare who had finished last in her only race, her pedigree uncertain to this day. It is also said that he was so fiery in his youth that his owner nearly had him castrated – the fate of countless young horses whose intractability makes the possibility of a stud career far too remote a consideration. Then there was the mother of the first great Irish stallion, Birdcatcher, who was offered to breed hunters but found no buyer at £30. The dam of The Baron, Birdcatcher's great son, was rejected by a country priest as inadequate to take him on his rounds. Several times the Darley Arabian line has survived only through a foal conceived just before a stallion disappeared through neglect or exile.

Yet through every twist and turn, the Darley Arabian line has followed a constant arc – as a monument to economic power. However random its biological provenance, for three centuries the thoroughbred has remained a faithful index of a changing world beyond the racecourse.

In 1875, the richest man in the British Empire resolved to upgrade his stud by acquiring a horse named Doncaster, the latest champion of the Darley Arabian line. But the Duke of Westminster could not bring himself to deal directly with Doncaster's owner. James Merry, a Glaswegian ironmaster, was not just an egregious symbol of the social flux engendered by the Industrial Revolution. He had also had the temerity to register, in his own name, the yellow and black silks made famous by countless horses raised and raced by Westminster's ancestors. Merry had pounced when Westminster's father briefly allowed the family stud to fall into neglect, in the brazen hope of assimilating its kudos along with such other props to his new status as a seat in Parliament, a sporting estate in the Highlands and a townhouse in Eaton Square. The duke's solution could not have been more pointed: he waited for Robert Peck, Doncaster's trainer, to buy the horse from Merry for a record 10,000 guineas. Just two weeks later, he gave Peck 14,000 guineas for a horse now cleansed of Merry's social contamination.

Racehorses have always been luxury goods. As such, the Darley Arabian saga unfailingly reflects the changing complexion of global wealth. Through twenty-five generations, the bloodline demarcates four clear shifts in the Turf's economic centre of gravity. The first four stallions, foaled between 1700 and 1750, transferred the Restoration roots of the thoroughbred into Hanoverian soil. Eclipse, born in 1764, then opened an era dominated by the great landowners, until the repeal of the Corn Laws in 1846. The third phase introduced men like Merry, the new capitalist barons of the Industrial Revolution. Finally, after the First World War, a global market economy divided its rewards between professional breeders and the international plutocrats who could afford to buy into their expertise. Each of these four epochs has been united, at every stage, by the Darley Arabian line.

Go back to the Classic won by Frankel. At least thirty of the thirty-seven winners of the 2000 Guineas before the repeal of the Corn Laws were owned by the landowning classes. Since the Second World War, besides a single success for the queen, the peerage has mustered just two winners. And both these lent lustre to new titles, Weinstock and Beaverbrook, created to match industrial cash (not to mention Polish or Canadian initiative) with social cachet. Though many landowning aristocrats have maintained studs into modern times, they have failed to cling on to the family silver.

The unpredictability of racehorses has attracted a particular type from the privileged classes: whether reckless or merely restless, they have tended to be more quixotic than conservative. Even the two prime ministers who preserved the Darley Arabian line took office with a profound air of scepticism, plainly doubting their will or capacity to influence the tide of affairs. If the Turf had taught them anything, it was that destiny is fickle. But the changing face of the British racecourse also reflects the fact that different strata of society have always converged there, as nowhere else. The sport's best axiom, indeed, declares that all men are equal in only two places: on the Turf, and six feet under it. The archives tend to show only glimpses of those who, emerging from the margins of illiteracy and poverty, toiled in the stables of the rich. Even those malnourished lightweights who achieved fame as jockeys often receded into an abyss via bottle, bulimia or even bullet. Yet the exchanges of the rich with ostlers and hustlers, hookers and hucksters, gradually rotate the mirrors in the social kaleidoscope.

Henry Cecil was one of the latest figures stitched into the vast tapestry, from dukes to desperadoes, that unfurls behind Frankel. All human life is here. The thoroughbred has always divided its allure, among men, as both the noblest of animals and a vehicle for corruption. A champion thoroughbred can define a racing epoch, but the fact is that there will always be another Derby winner along next June. For many, the definitive portrait of the Turf is William Powell Frith's Victorian masterpiece *The Derby Day*. Yet the horses about to contest the race are barely perceptible in the background. It is off the track, as much as on it, that the cavalcade takes us ever forward. 'The clock has run, the horse has run,' says Cormac McCarthy. 'And which has measured which?'

PART I

Roots

The Darley Arabian (1700)
Bleeding Childers (1716)
Squirt (1732)
Marske (1750)

the latter end of march or the begining of Aprill near his
colour is Bay & his near foot before with both his hind feet
has white upon them, he has a blare downe his face some
thing of the Largest he is about 15 hands heigh of the
most esteemed race amongst the arrabs both by Syre &
Dam, & the name of Said race is called manneka,
the onely fear I have at present about him is, that I
shall not be able to git him aboard this war time,
tho I have the promise of a very good intimate freind
the Honble & Reverend Henry Bridges Sonn to the
Lord Chandois, who imbarkes on the Ipswich Capt
William Wakelin who presume will not refuse
takeing in ahorse for him since his Brother
is Lord of ye Admiralty, besides I designe to goe for
Scand to assist in getting him of, wch if can accom
plish & yt he arrives in Safety belive he will not be
much disliked for is esteemed here where could have
Sold him at aconsiderable price, if had not designed
him for England; I have desired Mr. Bridges to
deliver him to my Brother John or Cozen Charles
waite, who he can find, & they are to follow
my Fathers order in sending him into ye Country

Excerpt from a letter written in December 1703 by Thomas Darley, a merchant in Aleppo, to his brother Henry in Yorkshire, giving details of the Arabian stallion he is about to send home.

I

'The most esteemed race amongst the Arrabs both by Syre and Dam'

ANYONE WHO HAS ever delighted in a modern racehorse owes a debt to the Darley Arabian. All the hardscrabble professionals: the breeders and trainers and jockeys, the grooms entering stables at daybreak with buckets, brooms and bridles. All the punters: from the high-rollers prising some win-win margin from software, to mechanics and clerks cutting a Grand National sweepstake out of the newspaper. Anyone, ultimately, who has simply driven a country road and glimpsed between the bars of a gate a thoroughbred at pasture – head bowed towards the turf and frame silhouetted against the sky.

Look into the eye of one of these animals. Somewhere within, somewhere beyond, smoulders another world altogether: endless corrugations of desert, the land of his fathers. A habitat less alien, perhaps, even to modern thoroughbreds than it was to two English adventurers over three hundred years ago – neither of whom had the faintest suspicion they were about to transform the course of Turf history.

During the eleven weeks HMS *Ipswich* had been moored at Scanderoon* there were many mornings when the crags of the bay showed only dimly in the vapours exhaled overnight by a notorious swamp. But at first light on 3 January 1704 the wind was fresh, the skies fair, and Captain William Wakelin was able to signal for the whole convoy to weigh anchor. As his crew clambered up and down the rigging, he watched the dilapidated warehouses of the Levant Company depot gradually recede beneath the bluff.

The *Ipswich* was flanked by another man-of-war, the *Pembroke*,

* Today İskenderun, in Turkey, near the Syrian border.

plus a sloop and a fireship. Fifty demi-culverins and 24-pounders bristled from her gundeck; twenty smaller cannon were spread across roundhouse, quarterdeck and forecastle. Nonetheless, anxiety pervaded the flotilla of nine merchant ships Wakelin was escorting back to England. Each was laden with silk and other goods brought along the ancient caravan trail from Basra to Aleppo, ninety miles inland – and ahead of them lay four months of peril.

In more peaceful times Wakelin would have been inclined to shun the most direct route, along the coast of North Africa. The reputation of Barbary corsairs was such that it was generally worth steering a wide course, sometimes taking the chance to restock at Leghorn (Livorno), and then hugging the shores of France and Spain. But the recent death of the childless Spanish king had renewed hostilities with the French, who had destroyed a similar convoy in the Bay of Lagos – 'the richest that ever went for Turkey' – ten years previously. As a result Wakelin had resolved on a brief stay in Cyprus, before an all-out dash to the Straits of Gibraltar. 'I pray God send you safe,' the Levant Company consul George Brandon had written from Aleppo. 'For you have a very rich Convoy under your care.'

The atmosphere of tension had been heightened by the murder, a few days previously, of a sailor from the *Pembroke* while foraging for firewood. With so much already on his plate it is not hard to imagine Wakelin's opinion of the two uninvited guests he had been inveigled into taking aboard. The Hon. Rev. Henry Brydges had not lasted three years as chaplain to the Aleppo merchants, one recording archly that 'the generallity esteem Mr Bridges behaviour too youthfull'. But his return had been commanded by his father, Lord Chandos, alarmed that so many other young expatriates in the city tended to succumb to its sporadic epidemics. Brydges's predecessor had died abruptly of 'small pox and purples' at thirty-five; his successor, in turn, would survive only three years. Wakelin's problem was that Brydges had a brother in a senior position at the Admiralty. Whatever he asked, Wakelin would have to provide. And that was why somewhere below, in the airless, crowded hold, there cowered a beautiful Arabian colt.

He had the elegance of a deer, with small ears, a fine muzzle and bold eye. His bearing was at once mild and alert. When warm, a filigree of veins stood upon his bay coat. Bred and raised by desert tribesmen, he had a congenital dread even of regular stabling. Someone must have been found, among the crew, sufficiently lacking either fear or rank to accept responsibility for a 'blood' horse in a state of stress. It would be nothing like dealing with the rugged, stocky workhorses of England. This was an *asil*, a pure-bred Arabian. Sweetened in physique and temperament by generations of selective breeding, his kind had been purged of all coarseness, all volatility. But the coming ordeal threatened a fatal loss of equanimity: he could shrink into some morbid recess of his placidity, or simply panic and shatter one of those delicate limbs.

A hammock, looped under the torso, suspended the colt so that only his hind feet touched the floor. His head was loosely secured to the beams, above an improvised manger of canvas, and his ankles roped front to back. But little could be done to soothe his claustrophobia, beyond daubing his nostrils in vinegar or adjusting the sling that chafed his shoulders. The voyage would tax the endurance even of a horse accustomed to dehydration and poor grazing. With no scope for exercise, he could not be expected to digest oats or barley. Subsisting instead on hay and water – one impractical in terms of storage, the other precious enough as it was – he became an even less convenient passenger. Horses, moreover, cannot vomit. In heavy seas their nausea instead causes colic, a bad attack of which could be lethal. The colt's brother had been sent to England the previous year, but seems not to have survived the journey. John Evelyn, recording the transit of four Turkish horses, noted that one died even on the relatively short voyage from Hamburg. The odds against this enterprise, though, were balanced by the stakes. This horse was worth £300: the equivalent, in England, of forty good coaching mares.

Wakelin and Brydges were almost certainly breaking Ottoman law – though a prohibition on the export of pure-bred desert horses seems to have been enforced more rigorously at some times than others. In 1667, Charles II's ambassador in Constantinople had apologised for his failure to send a stallion requested 'from Aleppo, where my correspondent cannot even procure any for a king'. In 1715 another English merchant would smuggle out of Aleppo a colt so coveted that the mountain passes and ports were put under watch. 'I have heard of his being got Safe to the place where I ordered him,' he wrote. 'But Shan't be easy till I hear He is got board the Ship.' One way or another, secreting this animal among all those precious bales of silk – purely as a favour to one of Brydges's friends in Aleppo – must have taken Wakelin to the very limit of his deference.

Thomas Darley's career in the Levant had not worked out quite as hoped. After eighteen years, in fact, he had now been ordered home by his father – not the kind of man, as a Puritan squire of uncompromising Yorkshire stock, to be lightly disobliged. In a letter to his brother Henry, giving details of the horse preceding him to England, Darley assures his family that he was 'not soe in love with this place to stay an hour longer than is absolutely necessary'. Unfortunately, he could not quit Aleppo until he had straightened out his affairs. This, though he did not concede as much, was becoming a thoroughly desperate process. In the meantime, this glossy stallion – satisfying a specific request by his father – was evidently intended to keep the heat off at home.

Two unnamed portraits, apparently of brothers who both went to Aleppo, still hang at Aldby, the Darley family seat just east of York. It is not hard to decide which must be Thomas. Certainly one has the look of a seasoned expatriate, the backdrop suggestive of the Tropic of Cancer. Basking in the adoration of a hunting dog, he gazes wryly across the centuries, one eyebrow slightly arched.

Conceivably the painting might have been sent home for the edification of a kinswoman Darley cannot have seen since she was a girl. For his letter discloses an additional spur to hasten back: 'When you see Cozen [cousin] Peirson pray tender him my humble salutes & since his Daughter is ready I shall endeavour with all speed to prepare myself.' Belatedly, as he approached his fortieth birthday, Darley was about to conform to standard Levant Company practice. The merchants posted there – younger sons of the gentry, who might previously have gone into the church, law or army – were invariably bachelors, working on commission for London-based principals who had themselves once learned their trade as 'factors' in Constantinople, Smyrna or Aleppo. Typically, after six to ten years, they returned to become prominent figures in the City of London, aldermen or MPs with handsome young wives. Darley, in contrast, would be returning with his tail between his legs. Aleppo had beaten him. His only hope now was that he might at least gain some kudos, in the East Riding, as the importer of the Arabian colt.

Perhaps he had simply been unlucky. His admission to the Levant Company had coincided with the beginning of its long decline. Since its Elizabethan foundation, the company had exchanged a monopoly on home trade, together with local immunities, for the cost of all diplomatic representation to the sultan. At its height, just a decade before Darley's arrival, there had been 377 'Turkey merchants'. By the 1730s, the roster would dwindle to 80 or 90. In Aleppo, Darley was among a couple of dozen merchants quietly immured in the English compound. The chances are that his fortunes had never recovered from losses incurred in the Bay of Lagos disaster. One colleague, expressing relief that his own business had not been injured too severely, wrote at the time of 'others who have lost not only the labour of ten or twelve years but are deprived also of all future hopes'.

At the best of times, the bartering of English cloth for Persian silk entailed precarious credit arrangements. Now European weavers were turning to silk producers in Italy, Bengal and China; the Persian market had been eroded by expansion of the East India Company; and other staple trades had been undercut by Caribbean cotton and coffee. Then there were the occasional depredations of desert bandits, the cause of alarming fluctuation in prices. In 1702 a Mecca caravan had been destroyed; the following year 3,000 camels from Baghdad were plundered within a day of Aleppo.

At some stage Darley received a bailout of £500 from his father, but that did not prevent him slithering deeper into debt. He had become trapped between the twin cycles of the merchant's year: the arrival and departure of convoys, and the harvest of silk cocoons. Darley could appraise the first samples of the 'racolta' in July, standing outside tiny stores in the labyrinthine bazaar. But the bulk of the crop would not arrive until autumn. In the meantime, the dog days would be passed slackly with Armenian brokers or Ottoman officials seated on thick carpets in shady courtyards, sipping coffee. Between May and September the English merchants slept on flat rooftops, listening to the jackals and nightingales. A westerly breeze offered some respite against the heat; the desert wind, from the east, would only thicken it, leaving even locals drowsy and short of breath. How Darley must have yearned, then, for the cool green banks of the Derwent back home in Aldby.

One of the world's oldest cities, Aleppo was also among its greatest – a population of around 115,000 only surpassed, in the region, by Cairo and Constantinople. Aleppo was the principal hub for regional goods: galls from Mosul, goats' hair from the desert, drugs from Basra. An intricate serration of minarets and cypresses rippled around the ancient citadel, squatting massively on its mound. Cool gardens and orchards seamed the hot white cascade of roof terraces, while narrow, twisting alleys afforded glimpses of secluded courtyards and fountains. In springtime wild flowers and herbs exploded into a heady musk, streaked gold and blue by the flight of bee-eaters.

Contemporary accounts describe a collegiate, cloistered quality to the lives of the English merchants, who shared private chambers above a quadrangle of stabling and stores. In contrast with the East India Company, with its salaried hierarchy, they traded independently and in competition. But they had set times for communal meals, prayer and entertainment, and at night secured themselves behind immense bolted gates. Most were too wary of disease to mix any more than necessary with the locals – during epidemics cats entering the compound were shot and tossed out with tongs – and few merchants bothered to learn Arabic, depending instead on Greek or Italian interpreters. Their approach to dress, however, varied according to period and personality. The Aleppo consul in the 1730s, for instance, was painted in full local habit. Significantly, he is also showing off the spoils of a hunt: from autumn to spring the merchants rode out of the city twice a week to stalk gazelle with greyhounds and falcons.

One visiting cleric described a typical excursion to a green river-bank, 'where a princely tent was pitched; and wee had severall pastimes and sports, as duck-hunting, fishing, shooting, handball, krickett, scrofilo; and then a noble dinner brought thither, with greate plenty of all sorts of wines, punch, and limonads'. Brandon, the consul, claimed that 'there is not a set of more orderly sober young gentlemen who live out of England'. But outbreaks of the plague encouraged the merchants to indulge the convenient misapprehension that immunity could be secured by alcohol. 'It is certain', vouched one, 'they that drank the hardest escaped best.' In such crises, the entire English community would retreat to the mountains. 'We live here under tents after the manner of the old Patriarchs, with our flocks and herds about us,' Brandon wrote. 'And want nothing to make the scene compleat but some Sarahs and Rebeccas to console us in our retirement.'

It was a familiar complaint, the merchants no longer being permitted to marry local Christians. A visiting clergyman – having complained that the 'choyce women never com out into the streets, but they have their peepe-holes' – did record how one sent her servant to tell a young Englishman that 'a person of greate quality did desyre his company; with assurances that he should have courteouse reception'. Our baffled hero consulted the consul, who 'in short told him he must goe, or expect to be stabd the next time he went out'. Escorted to the stately apartments of a beautiful woman, for several nights he was 'entertayned . . . above what was promised' until horrified by the unexpected return of her husband. Her insistence that he could stay regardless was too much, and he fled Aleppo the next morning.

The sultan's authority was devolved to capricious local militia, making it prudent for foreigners – 'Franks' as they were known – always to maintain a low profile. Englishmen in the Ottoman Empire shuddered over its gruesome punishments: impalements and the flaying of heads, the skin then stuffed with cotton and sent back to the court in Constantinople. At the same time, sizeable Greek, Balkan and Jewish minorities could testify to Aleppo's cosmopolitan ambience and religious autonomy. The indigenous populace, in turn, exhibited a robust indifference to conservative disapprovals. Hashish was widely mixed with tobacco, while the coffee houses were enlivened by board games, obscene shadow plays and puppet shows. And when dealing with the more enterprising English merchants, the sultan's subjects had every incentive to flout a particular stricture above all others – and that was the one concerning the export of pure-bred horses.

As early as 1597, John Sanderson, the deputy ambassador to Constantinople, reported to Englishmen his wonder over the 'Babilonian' grey he rode to Aleppo. Despite the horse's lack of substance, Sanderson reckoned his mount 'the best . . . that ever I shalbe master of'. The horse was not only indefatigable, he showed uncommon intelligence and affection. 'He would walke by me, licking my hand; stand still when I backed him; and kneele at my pleasure.' On reaching Aleppo, Sanderson presented the horse to a Levant Company colleague who rode him to win a race against 'the most famouse beast in Alepo, cauled Berthrams mare'.

By 1684, Charles II was assembling his entire court in St James's Park to marvel at three desert horses, captured at the siege of Vienna. John Evelyn was captivated: 'They trotted like Does, as if they did not feele the ground.' Upon mounts so gorgeous, in ermine mantles and crimson silk reins, 'one may estimate how gallantly and magnificently those Infidels appeare in the fild'. They came with a corresponding price tag, 500 guineas being asked for the finest of the three: 'Never did I behold so delicate a Creature . . . such an head, eye, eares, neck, breast, belly, buttock, Gaskins, leggs, pasterns, & feete in all reguards beautifull & proportion'd to admiration, spirituous & prowd, making halt, turning with that sweiftnesse & in so small a compasse as was incomparable, with all this so gentle & tractable.'

Horses were just one index of a pan-European vogue for *Turquerie*. Originally dreaded as barbarian marauders, the Ottomans had become an increasing inspiration to those Western powers prospecting empires of their own. They had settled vast territories as a stable zone for mercantile and cultural exchange, from a court that had become a byword for opulence – while Britain remained a shivering outcrop among the northern seas, insular and backward.

Mr Darley's Arabian arrived in Europe in the same year as the first volume of *The Arabian Nights*. Already the mystique of the Orient had been stimulated in England by translations of pioneering journeys by Jean-Baptiste Tavernier, the jewel trader, and Jean de

Thévenot, in 1677 and 1687 respectively. Sir Henry Blount, in *A Voyage to the Levant*, lauded the military and social organisation of the 'Turkes, who are the only moderne people, great in action'. In 1693 Oxford University bought a priceless hoard of oriental manuscripts from the estate of its first professor of Arabic, Edward Pococke, who had started his collection as chaplain to the Levant Company in Aleppo. By the time Lady Mary Wortley Montagu began her celebrated correspondence from Constantinople, in 1717, she could survey her environment much as a modern traveller, who has previously seen New York or Venice only in films, recognises his first yellow taxi or gondola. 'This, you will say, is but too like the Arabian tales,' she acknowledged. 'These embroidered napkins! and a jewel as large as a turkey's egg! You forget, dear sister, those very tales were written by an author of this country, and (excepting the enchantments) are a real representation of the manners here.'

And now there was an ultimate accessory in imperial chic. Throughout Europe and Asia, horses had long been a currency of diplomatic flattery or exhibitionism – whether it was a sultan sending Turkish pure-breds to the Mughal court, or Henry VIII receiving Barbary horses from the Duke of Mantua. (He sent back Irish hobbies for Palio racing.) In 1599 Gervase Markham's landmark treatise on horsemanship had acclaimed the Arabian as 'paerlesse, for he hath in him the purity and virtue of all other horses'. When Nicholas Morgan listed thirteen breeds by quality in *The Perfection of Horsemanship*, ten years later, he put the Arabian at the top. Lady Mary herself, while exciting much astonishment with her side-saddle, was to contribute to the cult: the local horses were 'very gentle . . . with all their vivacity, and also swift and surefooted. I have a little white favourite, that I would not part with on any terms: he prances under me with so much fire, you would think that I have a great deal of courage to dare mount him; yet, I'll assure you, I never rid a horse so much at my command in my life.'

One of the first Europeans to describe horses domesticated among the Bedouin was Laurent d'Arvieux, French consul in Aleppo during the 1680s. Like Sanderson, he identified an extraordinary equilibrium between their physical capacity and docility:

The Emir Turabeye had a Mare that he would not part with for Five thousand Crowns, because she had travell'd three Days and three Nights without drawing Bit, and by that means got him clear off from those that pursued him. Nothing indeed was handsomer than that Mare, as well for her Size, her Shape, her Coat, and her Marks, as for her Gentleness, her Strength, and her Swiftness. They never tied her up when she was not bridled and saddled: She went into all the Tents with a little Colt of her's, and so visited every body that us'd to kiss her.

Even the Duke of Newcastle, who preferred the great beasts of the riding school, acknowledged their unsuspected capacities: 'I had a Groom, a Heavy English Clown, whom I set Upon them and they made no more of him than if he had been as Leight as a Feather.' Nonetheless he was bewildered by 'strange reports in the world . . . that the price of right Arabians is One thousand, Two thousand, and Three thousand pounds a horse (an Intollerable and Incredible price).'

Englishmen became ever more intrigued by the hardihood and empathy of these animals. Stories were told of a mare returning to the thick of a battle to pick up a wounded master with her teeth and carry him to safety. It was almost as though she understood that some tribes, on the death of her master, would tether her by his grave until her bones lay bleaching in the sun. One Ottoman general, after an expedition against a southern tribe, reported that the 'men had no religion; the women no drawers; and the horses no bridles'. Yet he could not fail to admire the way desert horses had been attuned by centuries of domestication. A foal would wander the camp untethered, lying down to sleep among the children who fed him camel's milk. As soon as he could bear their weight, they would clamber onto his back. In their hands, with no more than a crude halter and reins of woven camel-hair, he proved supple and pliant. But he would also become extremely tough, sheltered only by the lee of tents and often without water for days at a time. One British explorer reported that Bedouin horses, unblanketed through bitter winter nights, resembled 'ragged-looking scarecrows, half starved' – yet in summer their coats became 'as fine as satin'. That was when southern tribes would follow a migratory cycle through the marl and gypsum scrub of the Euphrates basin. Traders who knew where they might be would seek them out and purchase young colts.

The Bedouin who sold one to Thomas Darley would never have let him buy a filly. Females always remained with the tribe, vessels of a sacrosanct genealogy. Tales survive of children, with their dying breaths, gasping the pedigrees of mares so that their captors might cherish them. Even in relatively modern times, one English traveller came across downcast tribesmen lamenting the loss of forty mares to raiders. Among them he was amazed to find an emissary from their conquerors, awaiting instruction in their pedigrees. 'Although there was blood between the tribes, his person was as sacred as that of an ambassador in any civilised community,' he wrote. 'Whenever a horse falls into the hands of an Arab, his first thought is how to ascertain its descent.'

To Darley's compatriots, the whole concept of pure breeding remained outlandish. The Duke of Newcastle remarked in amazement how 'the Arabs are as Careful, and Diligent, in Keeping the Genealogies of their Horses, as any Princes can be in keeping their own Pedigrees'. Henry Blount, visiting Cairo, described a stud book of a local breed held 'in such esteeme, as there is an Officer appointed to see the Fole, when any of that race is Foled, to Register it, with the colour, and to take testimomny of the right brood; one of these at three years old, is ordinarily sold for a thousand peeces of eight, sometimes more: the reason is because they will runne, without eating or drinking one jot, foure days and nights together.'

This Egyptian registry was a legacy of Al-Nasir Muhammad, a Mamluk sultan who built up a stable of 4,800 horses during his long reign, ending in 1341. The prices he paid drew Bedouin traders from far beyond the Euphrates. For a single mare he once gave 290,000 dirhams and, as an equivalent value, a village near Aleppo. He staged racing at a great hippodrome, with fountains and grandstands, favouring above all horses raised by two tribes in the Syrian desert. These, arriving from the steppes of Tajikistan around 300 years earlier, had emulated an ancient migration of Bactrian stockmen – itself the pivotal moment in the spread of the mounted horse. According to folklore, the Bactrians bred horses of great stamina and quality by turning loose their mares into the mountains to mate with wild stallions. Certainly they preceded by millennia any tradition of Arabian horsemanship, their animals and skills spread through the Near East and North Africa by Graeco-Roman imperialism and raiders from the Asian plains. It was only in propagating a new religion, Islam, that Arabs discovered their own excellence as horsemen.

Yet across so many forgotten centuries perhaps there had never been a single transaction over a horse as momentous as the one completed by Thomas Darley. Doubtless he had heeded the enterprise of a colleague in Aleppo, on receiving from a local chieftain 'a couple of fine Horses, one Hawke, a tame Mountaine Catt . . . which . . . runs now loose in my House & is very familliar'. Such horses, his compatriot had urged, were 'extraordinary fit to send to England'.

In 1678, rumours reached the English compound of a ruined city, some six days into the desert. Could it be Palmyra, the lost seat of Zenobia's rebellion against Rome? A party of merchants decided to investigate. After a perilous trek they approached their destination with carbines and pistols drawn. Sent word that the strangers were guaranteed all hospitality, two of the merchants ventured to an emir's tent with gifts and assurances that they were merely curious about the ruins. They were given tobacco, and cheerfully advised that they would be hanged on the spot unless their party handed over all money and chattels. The ransom was promptly paid, and the chastened adventurers fled back to Aleppo.

For the next attempt, in 1691, a promise of security was obtained from a new warlord. Darley, already resident in Aleppo for six years and plainly disposed to adventure, was surely among the thirty armed men who again set out into the wilderness. 'Near dead with thirst' they rode between noisome wells, abandoned villages and derelict monasteries until finally reaching Zenobia's sumptuous metropolis – now sanctuary only to thirty or forty families, huddled in mud huts in the ruins of a vast temple. This was surrounded by the eerie ossuary of a forgotten civilisation: marble pillars, great domes, delicate pilasters and cornices, exquisite carvings and mysterious inscriptions. The boldness of these amateurs should not be underestimated. It would be another sixty years before antiquarians arrived to document their discovery more thoroughly.

Darley did not purchase his Arabian for another eleven years. Perhaps he was made aware of Bedouin horse dealers by Brydges's predecessor as chaplain, who encountered herders of 'about one thousand horse' near the Euphrates in 1699. The fateful sortie was almost certainly the one mentioned by a Levant Company correspondent in April 1702, when he spent four or five days riding with Darley across the plain south of the city. Through the hills on its fringe lay the Palmyra desert, and the timing certainly makes sense. In the letter to his brother, on 21 December 1703, Darley records that he had acquired his horse 'about a Year & a half agoe'.

The colt had been foaled in 1700, in March or April, a bay with a large blaze and three white ankles. 'He is about 15 hands high of the most esteemed race amongst the arrabs both by Syre and Dam, and the name of said race is called Mannicka.' Otherwise the Darley Arabian's canvas remains so blank that later generations, having grasped how precious a seed he had sown, sought to fill it with fanciful streaks of colour. These tend to dignify Darley as a 'consul' and his horse as *Ras-el-Fedowi*, 'The Headstrong One'. One story claimed that Darley secured his colt in exchange for a single flintlock rifle. Another described the purported fury of a Sheikh Mirza, who agreed to sell for 300 gold sovereigns but then reneged on the deal, writing bitterly to Queen Anne about the colt's abduction by British sailors. Yet Darley's own letter details only the mundane practicalities of embarking his horse, his concern limited to the possibility that he might 'not be able to get him aboard this war time'.

However pedestrian the true circumstances, he showed ample nerve even in tracking down a wandering tribe of breeders in such a dangerous outback. Some sense of the transaction survives in a nineteenth-century sporting magazine, which depicts horse-trading in Syria as an enterprise that could hardly have altered since Darley's time. Its author marvels as each new stallion is led into the camp: 'Noble, knightly, heroic, he seems less a brute than an incarnation of high blood and fiery energy; a steed that Saladin might have mounted, and that would have well matched his master.' Nor, despite a new tone of imperial contempt for the desert tribesmen, can he help admiring their horsemanship, 'wheeling and sweeping like a swallow on the wing, as if man and beast were inspired by one will'.

Bedouin salesmanship was artless. Horses were first exhibited in plain halter and saddle. If rejected, the same animals would then be crudely disguised by heavy tassels one day, a braided saddle the next. Things became no easier once a horse had been chosen. 'If the owner condescends to put a price upon him, it is about three times what he means to take; frequently he refuses to do it at all, but tells you to make an offer. You do so: he receives it with contempt, and the word "Béid" – "Far off" – pronounced with a lengthened emphasis, "Bé-i . . . d", that sets strongly before you the inadequacy of your proposal. You raise your price, and a contention of bargaining ensues, which is terminated by the owner riding off with his horse as if he never meant to come back.' After an hour or two, or a day or two, he returns – only for the whole pantomime to be repeated. When a price is at last agreed, the vendor is 'attended by one or two friends and counsellors, sages supposed to be learned in Frank coins, and wide awake to the ring of a bad piece. All solemnly squat on the ground, and you proceed to count out the gold.'

In other accounts the sale concludes with a pathetic ritual. The vendor hands over the horse's halter, along with bread and salt; he then walks away, pointedly refraining from one last look and so conveying to the horse the transfer of his fidelity. The horse, naturally, has been fully aware of the matter under negotiation, furiously baring his teeth and kicking at his prospective purchaser. On observing the conclusion of the deal, however, he meekly bows his head and follows his new master out of the camp.

The road from Aleppo to Scanderoon lay through mountains notorious to one consul for 'robberies, rapes and murders and every species of villainy which perfidy can contrive and desperation execute'. To avoid both brigands and the midday heat, the Levant Company tended to transport goods to its marine depot by moonlight, its caravans mounting up at 2 a.m. Slower caravans could take a full week. Few merchants, porters or guards were ever reluctant to break up a restless, vermin-infested camp, the Englishmen passing brandy round the fire to steel themselves against the rumour of

24

mountain lions. One who came this way saw a 'serpent, as thick as the middle of an ordinary man . . . at least 4 yards longe'.

The trek did not lack its consolations. At Martavan, an elder offered travellers their choice of the village's wives and daughters at a trifling rate. (One Frenchman recommended the women as 'in general pretty'; another visitor claimed to find them 'disgusting . . . long abstinence at sea, and the vanity of intrigue, constitute all their merit'.) Then there was Balian, clinging to a high gorge, its delicious air booming with the roar of meltwater torrents. Scanderoon itself, however, was infamous for its rank mists and distempers. The expatriates here had 'a languid air, yellow complexion, livid eyes and dropsical bellies'. A typical tombstone lamented an Englishman 'carried off in the flower of his age, by the fatal effects of a contagious air'. To the Levant Company officials posted here, fleeting conviviality both relieved and reiterated their isolation. Doubtless they entertained Darley, Brydges and Wakelin much as they had the chaplain on another man-of-war, a few years earlier: 'Every health that wee dranke, every man broake the glasse he dranke in; so that before night wee had destroyd a whole chest of pure Venice glasses.' But no visitor ever seemed sorry to leave. As one concluded: 'They must be men who love money at a strange rate, who accept of these employments.'

Having bade farewell to his 'very good and intimate friend' Brydges, not to mention the precious colt, Darley determined to follow them home as soon as possible. Barely two months later, he was dead. As with his horse, some robust fictions survive about Darley's fate: for instance, that he was poisoned or drowned. (Perhaps some such fate instead claimed the brother whose portrait hangs at Aldby.) The reality is apt enough. For the tribesmen who sold him the Arabian might also have passed on one of their proverbs: *qabr al-khâyâl maftûh* – 'The rider's grave is always open.' Thomas Darley suffered chest injuries in a fall from a horse, quite possibly on the way back to Aleppo. After 'a long and lingering fit of sickness', he died on 9 March 1704.

As his condition deteriorated, Darley had made a will, leaving settlement of his outstanding accounts to his partner in Aleppo, Robert Marriott. The upshot was a failure of Marriott's credit so dramatic that he was briefly locked up by the consul. After interviewing him, however, Brandon commended the integrity of a man ruined 'by the Knavery of his deceased partner'. Brandon explained to Marriott's creditors that Darley had disguised his liabilities 'by forging a false pair of Books' as security for their partnership.

Marriott himself died a few months later – also, curiously, through a riding accident. Thrown violently against the pommel of his saddle, his wounds festered 'so very ill that the very Physicians could hardly endure the room'. An equivalent stench issued from the financial mess bequeathed to the Marriott and Darley families. One Aleppo merchant, approached by the Darleys for help in pursuing debts through Marriott's estate, replied that it was 'an affair of so great trouble and intreague that I don't think anyone here would accept of it; nothing can be recovered but by force'. As late as 1715 the administrators of both wills were pursuing claims against each other in Chancery – in the Marriott cause 'particularly for an Arabian Horse worth three hundred pounds and for wine and for other merchandizes'.

Darley died a reluctant exile, stranded by his failed business. The allegations against him suggest a desperate man. And his final decline can only have been horrible: sweating and choking, the chant of the muezzin threading intervals of clarity and delirium, its timeless lilt as indifferent to his passage as the waves that bore him there. Did he gaze into some glaring angle of sunlight on a whitewashed wall, and see the green dales of home, shady glades, cool rivers? Faces of the disappointed, the betrayed . . . Marriott, Miss Peirson, his father. Perhaps the stallion would console the old man somewhat. But could Darley really expect his name to be redeemed, by the same brute species that had killed him?

2

'The cross strains now in being are without end'

ENGLAND WAS SUPPOSED to be the kingdom of the horse. Shakespeare went so far as to have Richard III offer one for the other. Every English child was once taught how 'the want of a nail' to shoe a horse might ultimately lead to loss of a kingdom, and this ancestral connection remains strewn across modern discourse: 'Shanks's pony', for instance, describes the pedestrian forced to rely on his own legs or 'shanks'; 'looking a gift horse in the mouth' refers to the practice, continued today, of establishing a horse's age from the growth of its teeth; 'a shakedown for the night' relates to the spreading of a straw litter in a stable; while a 'knock-down price' is that paid by a knacker.

By the time Mr Darley received his son's Arabian, three in every five households in a typical English parish owned horses – compared with one in five a century previously. A French visitor in 1699 remarked that 'travelling on horseback is so common a thing in England that the meanest sort of people use it as well as the rest'. As English roads began to reach continental standards, indeed, the wealthy increasingly kept themselves out of the rain in coaches, and mounted up primarily in the name of sport. It was the lower classes who exploited the economic value of horses, in haulage and mobility, to the extent that horses and their tack would typically comprise 15 per cent of the value of estates left by smallholders and tradesmen. Moreover, to keep horses on the road, or pulling the plough, required farriers and saddlers, copers and breakers, not to mention cartwrights, wheelwrights or the farmers who supplied bedding and fodder.

Yet it was not just the animals themselves that needed an Ottoman upgrade. English equitation manuals were still suggesting that 'a shrewed catte' be tied to a pole to scratch and bite the thighs, rump

27

and testicles of a reluctant horse. The aspiration was always to subdue, to govern. Over the coming century it would be acknowledged that the eastern horse – spirited, sinewy and intelligent – not only deserved very different handling, but also reflected generations of superior horsemanship.

When viewing the Ottoman horses in St James's Park, John Evelyn had been reminded of a rebuke to European grooms by Ogier Ghiselin de Busbecq, a Hapsburg ambassador to Constantinople in the sixteenth century. De Busbecq had observed a connection between the tenderness of the Bedouin to their horses, and a reciprocal anxiety to please:

> I my self saw . . . how indulgent the Country-men were to young Colts . . . They would stroke them, bring them into their Parlors, and almost to their Tables, and use them even like Children . . . This makes their Horses great lovers of Mankind, and they are so far from kicking, wincing or growing untractable by this gentle usage, that you shall hardly find such a masterless Horse among them . . . Alas! Our Christian-grooms treat Horses at quite another rate; they never think them rightly curried, till they thunder at them with their Voice, and let their Club or Horse-whip dwell, as it were, on their Sides. This makes some horses even to tremble when their Keepers come into the Stable, so that they hate and fear them.

By 1729, an English husbandry manual had begun to absorb these lessons, suggesting that horses should 'be used with Tenderness, rather than Roughness, and no passionate Person ought to be concerned in their Breaking or Management'. With time, the proliferation of oriental blood in English horses would also promote a more genial style of equitation, assisted by a shorter stirrup and lighter bridle. Instead of clamping their shanks despotically around a horse's torso, and manacling its head in a severe bit, English sportsmen began to perch higher and keep the reins looser, permitting their mounts uninhibited momentum. Attempts have even been made to link evolving English principles of liberty and the development of a less coercive riding seat.

The Romans had raced Arabian horses in Thomas Darley's home county as early as 210 AD, when the Emperor Severus Alexander

made provision for their cold-weather stabling and training at
Netherby, near Harrogate, while Bede records how noble Anglo-
Saxon youths would measure the fleetness of their mounts over open
ground – including one 'animated horse, attempting to clear a cavity
in the way, by a violent leap, [throwing his rider] senseless against
a stone, and with difficulty brought to life'. In the reign of Henry
II some motley form of racing seems to have been staged at
Smithfield, probably as a means of exhibiting lots for auction, and
the future Richard II – whose infatuation with a 'Roan Barbury'
was preserved by Shakespeare – rode a match race against the Earl
of Arundel in 1377. But it was only under Henry VIII that the Turf
began to emerge from its dark ages, as both a court and public
entertainment.

The king's first priority was to upgrade the size and quality of
his cavalry, requiring the knightly classes to breed from stallions
standing 14 hands or more. Many of the horses he imported from
Italy or Spain contained Turkoman or Arabian strains. Andalusian
jennets, for instance, had been exposed to North African Barbs.
Smaller, brisker nags from the Celtic fringes – Galloways and Irish
hobbies – meanwhile serviced the evolving sport of horse racing.

Town corporations began to promote race meetings on their own
land, furnishing some plate or other trophy, a token of the benefits
to local commerce. The oldest extant prize on the Turf is the Carlisle
Bell, donated by a prominent local family in 1599. The original
silver bell, now displayed in a museum in the town, is engraved in
honour of 'my lady Dacre', wife of the town's governor: 'The sweftes
horse thes bel to tak for mi lade Daker sake.'

Though a conservative cadre of knights and courtiers grieved the
obsolescence, since the advent of gunpowder, of the destrier – an
elephantine, medieval charger, bred to bear 30 stone of knight and
armour – the sporting gentry were gradually learning that the modern
cavalry horse required the same assets as their 'running horses': speed,
mobility, soundness, tractability and courage. And that, in turn,
meant that military stock could benefit from the sort of oriental
blood hitherto reserved for sport. Even hunters, while cross-bred
for size and scope, profited from a dash of oriental blood. It was
just a question of getting the right balance – and the desert horses

were creating a far more reliable genetic footprint than those other ill-sorted animals long cross-bred in England.

On Yorkshire studs, in particular, the merits of more selective breeding – first explored there by Cistercian monks – were becoming abundantly clear on the racecourse. In 1686, even as Ottoman horses seemed at their most seductive, one English authority was able to pronounce: 'Our Running-Horses, Hunters and Pads, and our horses for all manner of fatigue of what nature soever, are not matched in Europe: nor is any horse better for an officer in war, than one of our Twelve-stone horses (such as usually run for plates).' The trend squared obligingly with Restoration doctrine. It appeared that horses, no less than monarchs, owed their potency to blood succession.

Though his Arabian had a start of two months, news of Thomas Darley's death reached Aldby first. In fact, the horse was not introduced to his first mares there until the spring of 1706, nearly two years after Captain Wakelin offloaded his exotic stowaway at Kinsale in Co. Cork. How long the horse spent in Ireland is not clear, though it was probably only a few days; nor did he reach his final destination to any great fanfare. Mr Darley's Arabian was just one of around two hundred stallions imported from North Africa, the Levant or Turkey in the century following the regicide of 1649, many congregating in North Yorkshire. As such, he was mated with only a handful of mares each spring, mostly owned by the Darleys or their kinsmen.

Whereas the county's horsebreeding set had mostly remained loyal to the Crown during the Civil War, Aldby had been a Parliamentarian outpost. One of Thomas Darley's grandfathers had been a signatory to the king's death warrant; the other was repeatedly imprisoned, both before and after the Protectorate, for intrigues against the Crown. His status can be judged from a celebrated propaganda coup at the height of the Civil War, when fifty Royalists galloped through the night to haul him from his bedroom at Aldby and kept him hostage at their besieged garrison at Scarborough. Yet it was the Civil War that also laid the foundations for the success of Mr Darley's Arabian.

Having been isolated from the Thirty Years' War, the English military classes had not yet awoken to the need for a quick, agile cavalry. When the Civil War began, breeders tried dredging the genetic depths of their horses for a new destrier. Thomas Fairfax, Cromwell's general, lambasted the 'over-valued pigmy baubles' bred for hunting and racing under Charles I. Once in power, however, Cromwell soon recognised the need for faster, lighter horses. He not only maintained a rump of the royal stud at Hampton Court but even requested that the Levant Company procure Arabian stallions. In the event, he had to settle for a grey 'Turk', or Turkoman, sent as a present by the sultan.* On Cromwell's death, his stud master Rowland Place spirited this stallion to his own estate, on the north bank of the Tees, where he was conveniently sited for the Yorkshire stud farms.

These had benefited from the break-up of the royal stud at Tutbury, now able to disseminate exotic stock previously monopolised by the monarch. James D'Arcy, for instance, salvaged several 'royal mares' for his stud at Sedbury, near Richmond. And while the Buckinghams' estate at Helmsley had been awarded to General Fairfax – compensation for a musket ball in his shoulder while besieging the castle there – he proved a fastidious steward of their stud. By the time he helped to bring about a bloodless Restoration, Fairfax had already returned Helmsley to the young Duke of Buckingham, rewarding an impudent suit for the hand of his daughter. Symbolically, Fairfax presented Charles II with a chestnut mare bred at Helmsley to ride at his coronation, herself a daughter of his own mount at the Battle of Naseby.

In a treatise on breeding, Fairfax commended the combination of native stock with eastern horses 'because naturally ours be more phlegmatic than those which are bred nearer the sun'. That way England could produce 'the most useful Horses in the world, for then will Spirit, Beauty and Strength be met'. Even as it was, after all, 'we have scarce a Horse that we may properly say is wholly

---

* This breed, from rugged country between the Caspian and Black Seas, was a standard diplomatic gift. But labelling as Turk, Arabian or Barb was notoriously inexact, likely to reflect a point of embarkation or a commercial vogue. A 'Turk' was liable to emerge from any steppe from the Balkans to Mesopotamia; and the 'Barb', in principle from North Africa, sometimes denoted any swift racer.

descended from the English, but hath had some mixture with the Strangers'.

For a long time, the thoroughbred nonetheless remained idealised as 'the true son of Arabia Deserta, without a drop of English blood in his veins'. Even into the twentieth century, purists were still insisting that the breed owed its genesis exclusively to desert blood, funnelled through a tiny immigrant band in Yorkshire. If not quite embracing Bedouin fables that formed the first horse from condensation of the south wind, they recycled family trees that extended all the way back to the Ark. But while many Yorkshire mares had eastern blood flowing in their veins, even those that had concentrated foreign strains for three or four generations retained a bedrock of chromosomes sown by native stock. DNA analysis has now definitively established British and Irish roots in many of these foundation mares. One expert stockman, assessing the English racehorse in 1729, would have been mystified by later dogmatism: 'The cross Strains which are now in Being are without End.'

The first attempt to catalogue pedigrees, in a *General Stud Book*, was not made until 1791. This register of seventy-eight mares, nearly all based in Yorkshire, eventually became viewed as a source of certification. In order to be designated 'thorough-bred', a horse would have to extend those bloodlines arbitrarily collected in the *Stud Book*. But the very concept was improvised. The earliest pedigrees contain horses with several different names, or none – none more specific, at any rate, than Royal Mare, Barb Mare, and the like. And these mares might have been trafficked across seas and mountains, or cross-bred in the next paddock. By 1761 a Yorkshire farrier was able to write tentatively of animals 'originally bred from Arabian horses, and mares, or the descendants of such, which I suppose is all that is understood by the word "thoroughbred"'. A typical Yorkshire mare, mated with an imported Ottoman stallion, might have been bred by an Andalusian cavalry sire and a Hobby dam. Certainly it was a potent synthesis of Sedbury and Helmsley blood, of imported and indigenous genes, that ultimately produced a mare named Betty Leedes in 1700. And it was this cocktail that would be shaken up, to epoch-making effect, by her trysts with the Darley Arabian.

★

The Turf retained an antediluvian look for more than a century after the Restoration, with races still staged over prodigious distances. Today two miles is considered an arduous test. Yet it was not uncommon for horses to contest three heats of four miles in one afternoon – and sometimes to do it all again the next day. This premium on strength and maturity meant that they tended not to be raced until six years old.

Cromwell had banned racing to discourage public assembly rather than through Puritan distaste. But the hedonistic Restoration court, suddenly relieved from the poverty and tedium of exile, quickly renewed the racetrack as an environment of glamour, spectacle and risk. The magnetism of racehorses has always been weighed against a moral cost, whether in public disorder or private ruin. In 1615, for instance, the Doncaster Corporation had briefly resolved to discontinue racing 'for the prevention of sutes, quarrels, murders, and bloodsheds'. Six years later Robert Burton's *The Anatomy of Melancholy* cautioned against the Turf as 'many gentlemen by that means gallop quite out of their fortunes'.

These contrasting forms of perdition reflected the different character of racing at Newmarket, maintained as a year-round training and racing centre by a clique of court adventurers; and every other track, where crowds of all classes convened for holiday jamborees. Without a resident population of racehorses, these venues depended on runners that had been walked long distances. As numbers were limited, it became necessary to drag out the races through a series of heats. Conversely there was no shortage of spectators, largely on foot, of both sexes and all classes. While rickety viewing platforms were prone to collapse – as when fifty spectators broke limbs at Preston in 1787 – the carnival atmosphere and social dynamics of these meetings gave them sturdy civic foundations.

Things were very different at the racecourse that became the hub of Restoration Turf: Newmarket meetings were virtually private court events. In contrast with annual race weeks held elsewhere, so many of the nobility stabled their horses locally that Newmarket could support a programme of regular fixtures. These were dominated by 'match' races, typically proposed over a bottle after dinner and watched only by a small number of gentlemen on horseback.

Its intimacy and isolation rendered this straggling little town, on a bleak East Anglian plain, the Merry Monarch's favourite resort in and out of the saddle. His grandfather, James I, had first built a lodge here for coursing and hawking, and ever since Stuart monarchs and ministers had neglected duty in the capital to indulge themselves at Newmarket. Though the Parliamentarians ploughed over the Heath, and largely demolished the royal residence in the town, new tracks were quickly sown in the 1660s and Charles II built a mansion just over the lane from Nell Gwyn's cottage – apocryphally linked by an underground tunnel. Every spring and autumn he moved his court here for a marathon of cockfights, theatricals and fornication. The king loved the informality of Newmarket, where he 'let himself down from majesty to the very degree of a country gentleman . . . mixed himself amongst the crowd, allowed every man to speak to him that pleased'.

Charles rode several winners here himself – and not, by all accounts, merely through the deference of his rivals. 'Yesterday his majestie Rode himself three heats and a course and won the Plate, all fower were hard and nere run,' a courtier reported to Whitehall in 1675. 'And I doe assure you the King wonn by good Horseman Ship.' On another occasion he beat his illegitimate son, the Duke of Monmouth, to win a Royal Plate – one in a series of such races he endowed, with heats over four miles. Even as a spectator, the king often led a parallel stampede of mounted bloods yelling encouragement to the jockeys. His favourite hack, Old Rowley, has been honoured ever since by the Rowley Mile, the course over which Frankel won the 2000 Guineas in 2011. And though Charles II did not renew a royal stud, he appointed James D'Arcy as Master of the Horse and paid him to supply racers from Sedbury.

But the sport at Newmarket was never confined to the track. Visiting in 1671, John Evelyn was dismayed to find 'the jolly blades raceing, dauncing, feasting, and revelling, more resembling a luxurious and abandon'd rout, than a Christian Court'. The king's favourites, Rochester and Buckingham, reserved some of their most flagrant escapades for Newmarket, setting themselves up incognito as landlords of the Green Man in Six Mile Bottom in an elaborate scheme to seduce the wife of one of its regulars. By the time they tired of her, her husband had hanged himself and she was left to tout her ruined reputation on the streets of London. Even the more harmless antics of the king's entourage had a wanton edge. In 1670, the court boisterously followed a young Irish baron's attempt to win £50 by walking five miles in an hour. There were only two conditions: he would be disqualified if running a single step, and had to perform the task 'stark naked and barefoot'. (He failed to meet his target by half a minute.) As Alexander Pope dismally observed: 'Newmarket's glory rose, as Britain's fell.'

The king's brother and successor, James II, was another devotee of Newmarket, and William of Orange then identified the royal stable as a useful symbol of continuity after deposing his Catholic uncle in 1688. Queen Anne, genuinely passionate about horses, further cemented the new regime by becoming the first monarch to race at York. The Parliamentarian Darleys witnessed this, and took note: the Turf, it seemed, remained a medium of conciliation.

One of the first breeders to send a mare to the new Arabian at Aldby, in 1708, was William Metcalfe – scion of a fiercely Royalist clan, and related to a number of other old breeding families. Metcalfe, offering exactly the kind of rehabilitation the Darleys had sought through their stallion, proceeded to marry a daughter of Thomas Darley's cousin.*

Thomas's brother Henry had inherited the Aldby estate on their father's death in 1706. Whether he cherished the Arabian stallion as a status symbol, or as the last bequest of his tragic sibling, he commissioned a life-size portrait in 1709. It hangs at Aldby to this day. The subsequent fame of the Darley Arabian would later cause some to reject the authenticity of his depiction, in one agonised verdict, as 'a very inferior common-bred hunter'; and John Wootton to oblige purists with a posthumous, stylised fantasy that furnished the horse with all the Arabian flamboyance they could desire. But

---

* Metcalfe's father owned the first winner recorded in an English racing calendar: Wart, winner of a gold cup at York in 1709. Moreover, the foal delivered by Metcalfe's mare that spring, Bully Rock, would be identified as the first North American thoroughbred after his export to a Virginia tobacco merchant.

in his letter home Thomas himself attested that the horse belonged to the 'Mannicka' blood – and the *mu'niqi* are today characterised as long-necked and angular, fleet of foot 'but lacking the beauty and rounded outlines of the classic-type Arabians'.

There is reliable evidence for no more than around twenty foals by the Darley Arabian, though he doubtless produced other stock too mediocre to be preserved by the *General Stud Book*, which did not appear until long after his death. (He may even have bred hunters.) Few other breeders followed Metcalfe's example, while the Darleys themselves owned just a handful of mares. Fittingly, the only one of these with any real pedigree had been acquired from the Peirsons: compensation, perhaps, for the dowry lost when Thomas failed to return. This mare's colts by the Arabian, named Aleppo and Almanzor, both had respectable careers on the track and then at stud. But it was his very first winner, a colt named Whistlejacket, who put Mr Darley's Arabian on the road to immortality.

Whistlejacket – nothing to do with the one later painted by Stubbs – won a race down the road at York, in 1712, and was then sold to Leonard Childers for £129. Childers was a feisty character. A couple of years later he was to fight a duel with one of the Peirsons over rough riding by their respective jockeys at York. At the end of the race, the riders still 'cut away at one another amidst the cheers of the bystanders, till blood was streaming down their faces'. The irate owners initially allowed friends to persuade them that the heat should be run again, but the rematch only resulted in further violence between the jockeys, a lawsuit and eventually a shoot-out between the owners. Peirson, hit in the thigh, was maimed for life. Anyhow, Childers was so taken by Whistlejacket that he decided to send one of his mares to the horse's sire, in the hope of rearing a similar animal. In the event, he found himself with something immeasurably superior: 'the fleetest horse that ever ran at Newmarket, or, as generally believed, was ever bred in the world'.

There is no doubt that the legend of Flying Childers owes much to embroidery: employment in his youth, for instance, as a hack to take the mailbag to Doncaster Post Office; or prowess in the hunting field that persuaded Childers to send him into training. Modern experts doubt that any horse of that era could have covered a distance of more than three and three-quarter miles in 6 minutes and 40 seconds, as was claimed by his purchaser, the Duke of Devonshire. The bottom line is that Flying Childers, aside from various informal but spectacular trials, is known to have won only two matches: one against a decrepit twelve-year-old, over six miles; the other against a Galloway of such leisurely locomotion that he had previously contested a match in *heats of twelve miles*. Without the breed's first great champion, however, nobody would ever have grasped the potency of the genes he had inherited from the Darley Arabian. James Seymour's portrait shows his jockey tilted against the stirrups, reins taut, a wild-eyed, virile animal, full of Arabian quality, uncoiling his shoulders into an immense bound. Breeders could be in no doubt that the thoroughbred had made a giant leap forward.

3

A Groom with a View

FLYING CHILDERS, RETIRING to the Chatsworth stud, proved the first of many champions unable to extend a dominating vitality on the track into his career as a stallion. By this time the Darley Arabian was long dead, disappearing from the record soon after a second mating with Betty Leedes in 1715. And the resulting colt had quickly revealed himself a dud: every time he was worked, he bled from the nose. Childers gave up and sold him to John Bartlett, a Richmond wool dyer.

Bartlett's little stable, outside Masham, still stands today: a pastoral idyll by the River Ure, curling lazily between meadows and woodland, heath and hills. Nutwith Cote was only a modest farmstead, a former grange of Fountains Abbey, but Bartlett was obviously prospering, and appointed its three stalls with paving, plastering and masonry better suited to a mansion than a stable. There was a practical purpose to this luxury. It had long been customary to leave a stallion out with his herd, to inseminate mares as in the wild. But increasingly stallions imported from hotter climates were being kept warm in stables, and led out by hand for each tryst.

To distance the lordly Chatsworth stallion from the black sheep of the family, the brothers had been given the names 'Flying' and 'Bleeding' Childers. But Flying Childers was largely confined to the Duke of Devonshire's own mares, and Bartlett was offering breeders a commercial alternative with exactly the same genes. These included William Metcalfe, who in 1731 sent a mare to Bleeding Childers. She was known, splendidly, only as 'Sister to Old Country Wench'.

The mare represented a typical blend of those indigenous and imported strains now being combined to develop an elite breed of racehorse. Her maternal pedigree was saturated with Sedbury blood;

while her grandsire had been captured from the Ottomans at the siege of Buda. Yorkshire breeders had observed that the infusion of Arabian, Turk or Barb genes was far more successful than any previous experiments in cross-breeding. Early signs of the particular potency of the Darley Arabian can be gleaned from the annals of the Hambledon Gold Cup, then one of the county's most coveted prizes. In 1727 it was won by a daughter of his early son, Manica; and in 1731 by a daughter of Almanzor. Between 1734 and 1741, three winners were sired by 'Mr Bartlett's Childers' and another 'by a son of Almanzor'.

All the evidence is that any pure-bred Arabian, strictly as a runner, was hopelessly outmatched. The previous century, a black hobby was recorded as beating choice Barbs at Salisbury; he in turn could not match the unbeaten Valentine, 'a plaine bredde English Horse both his Syre and Dame'. An Arabian bought by James I around the same time could not live with native runners: 'being Trained up for a course, when he came to Run, every Horse beat him'. Daniel Defoe, making his 1724 tour of Britain, contended that Yorkshire horses would

> outdo for speed and strength the swiftest horse that was ever bred in Turkey or Barbary . . . The Barb or jennet is a fine delicate creature, of a beautiful shape, clean limbs, and a soft coat, but then he is long-jointed, weak-pasterned, and under-limbed; whereas [the] Yorkshire has as light a body and stronger limbs, short joints, and well-boned. This gives him not speed only, but strength to hold it; and I believe I do not boast it in their behalf without good vouchers, when I say that English horses, take them one with the other, will beat all the world.

Defoe still considered it worthy of comment that local breeders were keeping even the most rudimentary records: 'Though they do not preserve the pedigree of their horses for a succession of ages, as they say they do in Arabia and Barbary, they christen their stallions here, and know them, and will advance the price of a horse according to the reputation of the horse he came from.' Yet English breeders would eventually claim not merely to have adopted the desert horse, but to have rescued its defining assets – purity of blood and elegance of form – from the degeneration of the Ottoman Empire. It can hardly be a coincidence, of course, that the English thoroughbred had begun to obtain a cogent identity even as the nation asserted its new, imperial confidence. (Flying Childers was born two years after the Treaty of Utrecht.)

Not that anyone could have identified the chestnut colt delivered by Sister to Old Country Wench as a milestone in the evolution of the thoroughbred. Even so, he was striking and Metcalfe decided to reserve him for an extravagant new client.

'Beau' Colyear had unexpectedly inherited the earldom of Portmore in 1730, after losing both his elder brother and his father. His grandfather, Sir Charles Sedley, had been one of the great Restoration provocateurs. On one occasion Sedley caused a riot with a parody of a Puritan sermon from a tavern balcony, upon which he then perched naked to excrete upon his enraged 'congregation'. Sedley's daughter Catharine had been a mistress of James II but then coolly secured herself in the new regime by marrying one of William of Orange's officers, soon created Earl of Portmore. Their son owed his nickname to his wardrobe rather than his countenance: 'Beau' was a ludicrous, Francophile fop, complete with cane, feathered chapeau and outsized muff. But nothing appealed more to his sensibilities than these elegant, new model racehorses. And here was Metcalfe, offering him a grandson of the same sire that had produced the most electrifying example yet.

Unfortunately young Portmore got it into his head to christen his new acquisition Squirt – a name then even less flattering than now. In slang 'the squirt' retained a purely scatological usage, since pluralised as 'the squits'; it did not acquire the modern sense of 'runt' until Victorian times. To be fair, this indignity was entirely consistent with the practice of owners then and afterwards. Even in the nineteenth century owners were still burdening their horses with such names as To Bed, To Bed, Says Sleepy-Head or Put On The Pot Says Greedy Gut. King William III's favourite racehorse had gloried in the name of Stiff Dick; others in Portmore's era showed a more wistful levity in naming Peggy Grieves Me, Sweeter When Clothed, Jack Come Tickle Me and even I Am Little, Pity My

Condition. Some, lurid to the modern ear, referred only to coat markings, as in Bloody Buttocks or Old Bald Peg.

In April 1737, Squirt became the first horse in the core Darley Arabian line to set foot on a racecourse. In doing so, however, he seemed only to enter a dead end. For compared with its heyday, in the youth of Portmore's mother, Newmarket had become a ghost town. George I, perplexed by the sporting enthusiasms of the late Queen Anne and her court, had even rented out the royal palace – excepting its forge and coach house, where old Tregonwell Frampton hunched morbidly over the embers of his career as Keeper of the Running Horses.

Frampton, son of a Dorset squire, had been one of the first commoners to run horses on the Heath and the first 'jockey' – a term then denoting anyone earnestly engaged on the Turf, as likely to apply to a breeder or owner as a rider – to achieve genuine celebrity as a racing professional. In one of his early matches it was recorded that 'Mr Frampton, a gentleman of some £120 rent, is engaged £900 deep'. But the advent of specialist skill, as ever, introduced serpents under the tree of knowledge. Defoe was shocked to see horses disguised 'to look as clumsy, and as dirty, and as much like a cart-horse as all the cunning of his master and the grooms could make him'. And he credited Frampton 'the oldest, and, as they say, the cunningest jockey in England . . . perfectly calm, cheerful, and unconcerned when he had lost a thousand pounds as when he had won it'. Defoe's denunciation, reprised by so many generations since, echoes across the centuries:

> I had the opportunity to see the horse races and a great concourse of the nobility and gentry, as well from London as from all parts of England, but they were all so intent, so eager, so busy upon the sharping part of the sport – their wagers and bets – that to me they seemed just as so many horse-coursers in Smithfield, descending (the greatest of them) from their high dignity and quality to picking one another's pockets, and biting one another as much as possible, and that with such eagerness as that it might be said they acted without respect to faith, honour, or good manners.

Another contemporary visitor cautioned against gambling in the Newmarket coffee houses: 'There is no safe Play without knowing one's Company very well. For you will see Fellows in the Habits of Grooms, that play for as much Money as a Lord, and perhaps know more of the Matter. In short, *Sharp* is the word here; and it's a common Proverb all over England, *A New-Market Bite*.'

On the track riders were so mistrusted that honest ones sometimes felt obliged to maltreat their horses. 'Make him win,' one was told before mounting. 'Or cut his bloody entrails out.' This was not an age for the squeamish, albeit a notorious story about Frampton is almost certainly apocryphal. It is said that an opponent, vexed to lose a 1,000-guinea match against Frampton's Dragon, offered to run his horse again the next day for 2,000 guineas, against any mare or gelding; and that Frampton castrated Dragon overnight, to qualify him as a gelding. The poor animal, still bleeding from the surgery, dropped dead after duly winning the race. Whatever the truth, Frampton was soon charging William III an annual training fee of around £100 per animal, to include maintenance of its groom.

An enormously long nose and narrow mouth gave Frampton the look of a particularly surly horse himself. He liked to roll up at court in his country clothing and call for the monarch as though for a farrier. Queen Anne nonetheless tolerated his shortcomings to the extent that she asked him to arbitrate local racing disputes on her behalf. He may also have assisted her in setting up a new 'court' racecourse on Ascot Heath in 1711.

Increasing obesity and ill-health, following eighteen pregnancies, required the queen to follow the buckhounds in a specially constructed chaise, which she drove at a furious rate. The 'almost square' coffin in which she was interred three years later left only Frampton above ground to preserve the Turf against the apathy of her German kin. His own death, in 1728, unmistakably marked the end of an era at Newmarket. Its race programme was decimated, dwindling from thirty-four races in 1731 to just five in 1742. Curious, then, that the race contested by Squirt on his debut – right in the middle of this slump – should not only have anticipated the look of the sport that flourished in the next century, but also showcased two of the three bloodlines that would best fulfil its needs.

★

By the time the *General Stud Book* was adopted as a formal register of 'thoroughbred' eligibility, all elite racehorses could trace their male ancestry to one of three sires. Though several other early stallions had helped to seed the root families, only three founding fathers now remained: the Darley Arabian, the Byerley Turk and the Godolphin Arabian. The latter two lines have nearly disappeared from twenty-first-century pedigrees – in 'patrilineal' terms, at any rate: via the chain of sons, that is, who begat sons – but the Godolphin Arabian in particular played a pivotal role in shaping the eighteenth-century racehorse. And it so happens that his first ever foal, Lath, made his debut in the same race as Squirt.

Moreover, they squared up in a fashion that foreshadowed a new type of race, tailored to the speed and precocity of these emerging, East-West hybrids. Albeit still stretching four miles, the Great Stakes was settled by a one-off stampede of ten horses whose owners had subscribed 100 guineas apiece. Here was an early intimation of the eventual extinction of both matches and heats. The former had been the speciality of court rivalries at Newmarket; the latter, the mainstay of provincial holiday meetings. During the nineteenth century, both would be supplanted by races contested in a single dash, like this one, by bigger fields – eventually comprising much younger horses, and staged over much shorter distances.

The laconic racing calendars of the time tell us only that Lath was first past the judge's box, although Squirt evidently ran him close enough for Portmore to seek a rematch the following year. The result was no different, however, leaving posterity to allocate Lath a key role in the usual posthumous legends about his sire.*

Squirt, for his part, persevered as a modestly successful racehorse

---

* The Godolphin Arabian, a gift from the Bey of Tunis to the King of France, was said to have been discovered by an English aristocrat towing a water cart through Paris; and the Byerley Turk to have been captured from the Ottomans in battle. Though he did serve as a charger at the Battle of the Boyne, the latter may actually have been only the son of an imported north country stallion. Both the Godolphin Arabian and Byerley Turk probably introduced Turkoman strains, accounting, along with the plain *mu'niqi* blood of the Darley Arabian, for the modern thoroughbred's closer resemblance to horses bred in the central steppes than to the pure-bred Arabian.

until sold to Sir Henry Harpur for his stud at Calke Abbey in Derbyshire. Portmore probably needed the cash: addicted to luxury, he was perennially short of funds. Contemporary likenesses do not flatter him. John Wootton depicts a waspish figure, presiding over the exercise of his horses on Warren Hill, swivelling in his saddle to rebuke some apparent insolence by one of his riders; Hogarth shows him alongside a robed monkey in effeminate raptures over a porcelain cup and saucer.

Portmore evidently still maintained a stable at Hamm Court, his Surrey estate, as an old tale claims that a highwayman who terrorised the district was ultimately unmasked as his chief groom there. (The robber's mount was recognised as his employer's favourite hunter.) But eventually Portmore reached the bottom of the barrel. 'Lord Portmore's goods are all seized,' George Selwyn recorded in 1781. 'And a great deal of fine china and other things belonging to [his mother] will be sold next week at his house in Upper Grosvenor Street. I was in hopes that the old jockey had contrived more comfort for the remainder of his days.'

The bloodline that would eventually inundate the Turf could hardly have trickled into being less auspiciously. Of the first two sires to establish the Darley Arabian line, 'Bleeding' Childers could not even raise a gallop without bursting blood vessels; and Squirt, on retiring to Derbyshire, was so crippled by laminitis – a disease of the hoof, sometimes still deadly even today – that Sir Henry Harpur ordered an employee named Thistlethwaite to have him butchered for the hunt kennels. Happily one of the stable grooms had seen enough of his master's temper to delay until Sir Henry had calmed down, before talking him into a stay of execution.

Who was the anonymous saviour of the Darley Arabian line? He may have been just a boy, quartered somewhere above an arcade of wooden stalls round the magnificent brick quadrangle of the new stableyard. Grooms tended to start very young. The survival of the word 'lad', in modern usage, reflects factors that have changed little: wages that would hardly keep a family, and a need for riders of slight build. In fact, horses allotted 'a feather' in a race were often ridden by boys weighing four stone or even less. (A 'feather' denoted

44

receipt of the maximum possible weight concession in a race. It is claimed – not very credibly – that one boy rode at Ascot, fully a century later, with a bodyweight of 2st 1lb.) At the same time, the division of labour between groom, trainer and jockey still remained extremely blurred. Horses were as likely to be ridden in matches by their aristocratic owners, as by the lads who mucked them out daily. By the second half of the eighteenth century, as the weights carried and distances covered in races both diminished, specialist jockeys were beginning to emerge; and sometimes these would also be responsible for the training schedule.*

The opportunities available to a stableboy were measured by the adolescent Joseph Andrews, as introduced by Henry Fielding in 1742:

> He soon gave Proofs of Strength and Agility, beyond his Years, and constantly rode the most spirited and vicious Horses to water with an Intrepidity that surprized everyone. While he was in this Station, he rode several races for Sir Thomas, and this with such Expertness and Success, that the neighbouring Gentlemen frequently solicited the Knight, to permit little Joey (for so he was called) to ride their Matches. The best Gamesters, before they laid their Money, always enquired which Horse little Joey was to ride, and the Betts were rather proportioned by the Rider than by the Horse himself; especially after he had scornfully refused a considerable Bribe to play booty on such an Occasion.

But even the lad who never won promotion from menial duties could bask in a degree of glamour. Thomas Holcroft, the radical writer, entered a Newmarket stable in the 1750s as a thirteen-year-old apprentice at four guineas per annum, plus a 'gorgeous' livery. During a visit to Nottingham races, he had noted enviously how the grooms were 'healthy, clean, well fed, well clothed, and remarkable rather for their impudence, than seeming to live under any fear or hardship'. Nor, after the hardships of his boyhood, was he disappointed. Though his working day might end eighteen hours after it began, it contained long hours of liberty between the dawn and afternoon

---

* The first public trainers of the next century evolved from the kind of 'training-groom' depicted by Stubbs, their status attested by frockcoat, cravat and hat. The lad, in contrast, remains virtually unchanged through the 250 years dividing Stubbs and Munnings, in waistcoat, calf-length breeches and stockings.

shifts; and these would be sustained by a breakfast of porridge, cold meat and Gloucester cheese, fine white bread and beer, followed by a nap. 'I fed voluptuously, not a prince on earth perhaps with half the appetite,' he recalled. 'And instead of being obliged to drag through the dirt after the most sluggish, obstinate and despised among our animals, I was mounted on the noblest that the earth contains, had him under my care, and was borne by him over hill and dale, far outstripping the wings of the wind.'

But if the lot of the modern groom is little changed, his days long and his duties Sisyphean, his employment only remains sustainable because of a transformation in training methods since the eighteenth century. The old manuals place a horrifying emphasis on sweat, as opposed to exercise. When Defoe visited Newmarket, he found the runners pressed 'to such an extremity that one or two of them died in the stable when they came to be rubbed after the first heat'. One standard handbook urged the trainer of a horse 'to purge his body . . . and make him the more apt to sweat and evacuate humours' with a sequence of two woollen cloths, divided by a sheet, followed by 'a canvase cloath or two above it, and before his breast a woollen cloath of at least two double'. Yet the only sympathy prompted by this regime, at the time, was reserved for the grooms. It entailed a prodigious amount of work.

It was still dark when the groom first entered his horse's stall – according to Holcroft, between 4 a.m. and 5 a.m. in midwinter, but as early as 2.30 a.m. in summer. (This could simply involve descending a ladder from a bed of hay in the loft.) Some old manuals begin the day with ale: a little to wash the bridle, and then a few spoons into the horse's mouth. Presumably few grooms resisted the opportunity to share this ration. On the two mornings a week when the horse was to be worked, his nostrils and tongue would be washed in vinegar – or an outlandish alternative: 'to piss in his mouth ere you take his back, is very wholsome'. After exercise, itself often undertaken in rugs, the horse was cooled off wading into a river or spring. Back in the stall, on fresh straw, his bridle would be tied to the hayrack as his groom began a gruelling rubdown: first the limbs, with handfuls of straw; then the head and neck, with a dry cloth; and then the torso. The horse was next trussed in his asphyxiating cocoon of blankets, and fed first hay and then 'good sweet oats well dryed, sunned and beaten' or a special bread made with eggs and ale. The groom's chance for rest and recreation came on leaving his charge for a long siesta in a darkened stall, sometimes perfumed in juniper. The whole ritual would be repeated as night approached, and the last of four daily rounds of feeding might take place as late as 10 p.m.

It was considered a merit of the 'greasing' regime that it could be maintained, in some form, when weather or lameness prevented exercise. A horse could then be swathed in blankets heated next to a fire, and then poked and pushed around the stall. The rubdown, after this kind of torment, was a frenzied business – cloth after cloth drenching up the sweat until the poor creature at last stood cool and dry. His reward then, as after galloping, would be a purgative concocted from an alphabet soup of ingredients: aniseed, brimstone, candy, cardamom, cumin, and so on.

Such being the regular ministrations to a healthy racehorse, you would be right to fear for one with problems. Husbandry tracts offered hair-raising cures for every conceivable crisis. *To cure the Mad Staggers in a Horse*: 'Bleed him in both his neck veins, within one or two days after he complains: on the third, furrow in the palate of his mouth with the point of your cornet horn; you may likewise run an awl into the gristles of his nose.' *To provoke Lust* in your mare, should she refuse a stallion, she need only be fed clarified honey mixed in new milk; thereafter 'with a bush of nettles pat her hinder parts, and immediately after offer her the horse, which she will receive'. But the manuals pretended no cure for Squirt's condition. 'The dry foundring', one pronounced baldly, 'is incurable'.

Nonetheless, there was a generic recipe for hoof problems that could still be tried. The toes must first be bled, and the wound filled with frankincense melted by a hot iron. 'Then take half a pound of hog's grease, and melt it; mix it with wheat-bran till it be thick as a poultice; then stop up the horse's foot with it as hot as possible.' As with most such quack treatments, it was kill-or-cure. Perhaps someone at Calke knew a less perilous alternative. All we know is that Squirt, against all odds, made a full recovery and was still receiving mares in 1749, at the age of seventeen. One of these was sent over the Pennines by a Yorkshireman named John Hutton.

A Day at the Races

Outwood Racecourse, Wakefield, 4 September 1745

Wakefield's grand annual holiday, for the Decollation of St John the Baptist, had included horse racing since 1678. And the meeting, this year, promised to be an especially festive one – the first staged on the new track at Outwood. The hotels were full of county gentry, percolating from public breakfasts to the splendid new grandstand, and afterwards to the assembly rooms at the White Hart. Gentlemen with runners took friends down to the stable yard at the Black Swan, and had their grooms remove the blankets to show off the glistening hard flanks of their horses. 'The Races,' recalled a local historian, 'made the town exceedingly merry, and brought in the crowds of carriage folks.'

Even as Newmarket foundered on the apathy of the Hanoverian court, horse racing elsewhere was thriving to the extent that it could now be described as the closest thing Britain had to a national sport. 'There is scarce a village so mean,' attested one Yorkshireman in 1736, 'that has not a bit of plate raised once a year.' Wakefield was typical of those towns that had grafted racing onto some existing institution of the county calendar: the Assizes, a hiring fair or harvest festival. The Knavesmire at York, for instance, had been the site of the city gallows for nearly four hundred years and those who convened for the opening of a Palladian grandstand there in 1754 would first be entertained by a couple of executions. And though destined to disappear from the Victorian Turf, for now it was Wakefield that showed the way to its northern citadels at York and Doncaster.

Patrons of the new stand strolled out of a great, glazed salon onto a stone balcony, or up onto the rooftop gallery, and surveyed the recreations of the men and women who normally toiled in their service. Pedlars' stalls tempted milkmaids with lace and ribbons, bracelets and combs, scissors and thimbles. Then there were the booths and freak shows, common to all such fetes, typically exhibiting 'Drolls, Puppet Shows, Legerdemain, Mountebanks, Wild Beasts, Monsters, Giants, Rope Dancers, etc.' The taverns and coffee houses of the town were packed; on the raceground itself, luncheon tents served hot and cold goose or pork. Other appetites were less innocent. Prostitutes and pickpockets insinuated themselves among the gullible countrymen pressing round the 'EO' men and thimbleriggers. The former bet Even or Odd in a crude form of roulette; the latter practised a variation on the three-card trick, with three large thimbles and a pea. Sometimes it was only as a yeoman left the beer tent, wits bleared by the sweet fug of hops and trampled grass, that he missed his purse or watch.

Wagering remained informal – bookmaking would not develop until the end of the century – but fervent. For days beforehand the rumoured flaws or capacities of particular horses had grown from one alehouse to the next. Thomas Holcroft remembered a match, in his Nottingham boyhood, between two horses each acclaimed 'undoubtedly the best in England, and perhaps equal to any that had ever been known, Childers alone excepted'.

Nor was betting any less avid on the various ancillary entertainments available on raceday: singlesticks, for instance, where duellists were required 'to break a head' with rods or batons. (A newspaper advertisement of 1753 specified: 'No Head to be deemed broke unless the Blood runs an Inch.') Or a couple of brawny ploughmen stripped to the waist to settle some grievance, encircled by spectators calling odds. Or the baiting of bulls and bears, and of course the various ghastly torments devised for cockerels. Cockfighting would remain an adjunct to horse racing well into the next century, the official Racing Calendar still cheerfully reporting 'mains' as late as 1840. Like the racecourse, the cockpit brought different strata of society into unusual intimacy. Zacharias Von Uffenbach, a German tourist in the early eighteenth century, was amazed to see how 'gentle and simple (they sit with no distinction of place) act like madmen, and go on raising the odds . . . An hostler in his apron often wins several guineas from a Lord. If a man has made a bet and is unable to pay, for a punishment he is made to sit in a basket fastened to a ceiling, and is drawn up in it amidst peals of laughter.'

A curious Act of Parliament 'to restrain and prevent the excessive Increase of Horse Races' had, in 1740, prohibited purses of less than £50, on the basis that 'small plates, prizes, or sums of money have contributed very much to the encouragement of idleness, to the impoverishment of many of the meaner sort of the subjects of this kingdom, and the breed of strong and useful horses hath been much prejudiced thereby'. Recorded fixtures fell by two-thirds over the next decade and those that survived tended to rely for funding either on the town corporation or a subscription by tradesmen. At a time when horses had to be walked between meetings, inns and shops could profit from extra business for days in advance. Holcroft remembered the excitement as Nottingham race week approached: 'Ten days or a fortnight before the time, straggling horses for the different plates began to drop in and . . . take their morning and evening exercise on the course.'

In contrast with Newmarket, where Defoe grieved the absence of ladies, Von Uffenbach found a more typical meeting congested by 'vast crowds on horseback, both men and females; many of the latter wore men's clothes and feathered hats, which is quite usual in England – they may, indeed, be seen in companies of ten or a dozen riding through the streets at prodigious speed.' The chaos of the raceground left him thoroughly dazed. One of his party became entangled, stirrup to spur, with another spectator; while 'great unpleasantness can also arise if one crosses the path of anyone racing and hinders him; for then all his backers fall on one'.

With the course staked out only by rudimentary markers, collisions were frequent and sometimes fatal. The more organised venues would at least rope off the closing stages, and have the judge remove a flag from the final post to strike the ground as the winner passed. The horses were then led away to a 'rubbing' hut, where they would be given 'a large glass of sack' and brushed down with handfuls of straw. For all the informality, the jockeys in their silk and taffeta doublets were weighed in scrupulously after each heat. Von Uffenbach was told of an occasion when a rider, feeling sick, took care to vomit into his cap 'and brought it with him, so that he should not be any lighter' when returning to the scales. But the racing surface tended to be undulating and rough, especially after a dry summer – and the new course at Wakefield received a shocking baptism when a grey mare, Polly Peachum, shattered a leg in the first heat of the £50 Plate.

Many who witnessed this sickening spectacle would soon recognise a disquieting portent for all Yorkshire. That same evening the Lord Lieutenant of the East Riding, Viscount Irwin, was seen touring the assembly rooms at the White Hart, buttonholing one after another of the various sporting squires gathered there. The gentlemen turned pale as Irwin whispered his news. All the gaiety of Wakefield race week had suddenly come to represent a disastrous complacency in people and government alike.

4

'He won as many hearts in Newmarket as he lost in Scotland'

Fᴿᴏᴍ ᴛʜᴇ ʀᴇᴍᴏᴛᴇ vantage of London, reports that Charles Edward Stuart was now ready to march out of the glens were easy to dismiss. Since his audacious appearance on the Moidart peninsula in May, the Young Pretender had mustered only a rabble of reivers. Here, in the north country, however, the kingdom seemed dangerously unprepared.

William Augustus, Duke of Cumberland, the younger son in whom George II had vested so much authority while he kept disappearing to his beloved Hanover, was tied down with 16,000 troops in Flanders. That left only a scratch force in the north, under Sir John Cope, while the county militia had been allowed to wither away since the last major Jacobite rising, a generation ago in 1715. To Lord Irwin, then, the fact that all the leading Whigs in the county were to be found in the same place was a godsend. 'I have been this week at this place where under ye Pretence of a race I have had an opportunity of meeting many of our Principal Gentleman,' he wrote from his Wakefield lodgings on 6 September 1745. 'Many have entered into an engagement to forward an association, to find arms and to raise men if we are allowed.'

As it happens, the seeds of the rising had actually been sown on the Turf. Two years previously, Louis XV had dispatched his Master of the Horse to Britain, ostensibly to purchase bloodstock for the French royal stables. Under this cover, the Jacobite envoy had met eminent sympathisers at Lichfield races to gauge the extent of any fifth column that might support an invasion. More typical, however, were the men rallied by Irwin at Wakefield – none more fervent than John Hutton, whose stud at Marske, above the River Swale, was one of the principal nurseries of the Yorkshire thoroughbred. Though his brother was a bishop, Hutton belonged to a hard-drinking, hard-swearing, hard-riding bevy of huntsmen. One friend liked to lock guests in his dining room until each had consumed his sixth bottle of wine, before having their horses brought in to be ridden upstairs to bed. A letter survives from Hutton's youth, recounting a typical family jaunt 'to see eight women ride three heats once round Ripon Common for a £12 Plate and [be] well entertain'd. They rid all astride in Jockey dresses, two or three of 'em fell every heat but they got up again and were no worse.'

Like most of Yorkshire's other horse breeders, the Huttons had been ardent Royalists during the Civil War. Now, at fifty-three, Hutton found that loyalty to the Crown obliged him to defend an Elector of Hanover against the great-grandson of Charles I. Hutton was among 813 landowners and clergymen summoned to a great assembly in the castle yard at York on 24 September. The atmosphere was feverish. Three days previously, at Prestonpans, the Highlanders had routed Cope's professional army in ten bloodcurdling minutes. With no artillery and little cavalry, their broadswords had left limbs and heads strewn across a field of reddened stubble.

The principal speaker was Hutton's friend Archbishop Herring, who now told his flock to galvanise the nation: 'This county, as it exceeds every other for its extent and riches . . . very naturally takes the lead of the inferior ones.' Within days, his audience had mustered forty-one volunteer companies. Hutton's Company of Foot had probably been filled from his own workforce: as well as the stud, his estate encompassed several farmsteads and a small lead mine.

The ministry had finally summoned the Duke of Cumberland from Flanders, together with thousands of battle-hardened redcoats and mercenaries. But the insurgents seized Carlisle within a week of crossing the border, leaving Hutton and the other North Riding volunteers nervously mounting roadblocks in the Westmoreland passes. They comprised just 350 men, knew little about their new weapons and less about military discipline. Even Archbishop Herring admitted to Hutton that he was now contemplating flight. It was with enormous relief, then, that they learned the rebels were heading towards Derby instead.

The legend of the 'Bonnie Prince' would survive both his subsequent retreat and the eventual rout at Culloden. All those Hebridean bothies, clefts and creeks provided a perfect counterpoint to the oak tree of his great-uncle. In turn, perhaps, Cumberland's infamy as the 'Butcher of Culloden' owes something to idealisation of his adversary. It was said that he personally orchestrated a campaign of depraved retribution, his prisoners pulped in cold blood by rifle butts or bayoneted into burning barns, in a scorched-earth campaign to burn out the roots of rebellion. Yet whatever the substance of his crimes – and however sheepishly, in consequence – at least one community counts itself eternally in his debt.

After Culloden, Cumberland entertained his men in the ruins of Fort Augustus by offering plates to be contested by Galloways seized from the rebels. These were ridden bareback – some even by 'ladies who are commonly half drunk to raise their spirits', with predictably comic results. Cumberland matched one of his own horses against one owned by Captain Boscawen, subsequently his racing manager. Boscawen won the first heat; Cumberland, the other two – 'to the great joy of the soldiers, who upon winning huzza'd as if they had gained a victory'.

Racehorses were Cumberland's governing passion. Boyhood thrills with the Windsor Forest buckhounds had nourished a mania for racing, and then betting. As he returned south, he made a fleeting visit to York to be presented with the freedom of the city. (Herring, in his address, congratulated the young general on his clemency and restraint in victory.) This was almost certainly the night where he made the acquaintance of John Hutton – a welcome relief from the suffocating attention of so many worthies and sycophants. Though yet to get his own stud up and running, Cumberland could not fail to recognise the name. A series of Hutton sires had peppered Yorkshire pedigrees since the turn of the century: Hutton's Bay Turk, Hutton's Grey Barb, Hutton's Blacklegs. For his own part, Hutton had been advised by Herring at the height of the crisis that Cumberland had 'behav'd in all points as became him, & beyond his years'. Each could only find the other a man after his own heart. The ultimate result, four years later, would be a transfusion of Dales blood into the royal stud – and a paradigm for the modern racehorse.

Still only twenty-five, Cumberland must have felt himself set up for life as a soldier and statesman. On his return to London, he was greeted with gun salutes, church bells and a premiere of Handel's *Judas Maccabaeus*, and awarded a lifetime annuity of £25,000 by Parliament. He then returned to the Low Countries to take command of the Hungarians, Hessians and Hanoverians lining up alongside the Dutch against the French under General Saxe, who had humbled him in his first command at Fontenoy. Cumberland hit it off at once with the Hungarian general, Batthyány, who arranged for six horses to be sent from his own stud to Windsor. But Saxe again proved his nemesis, and the Cumberland who returned to civil life found himself increasingly distrusted, notably during the Regency crisis that followed the death of his elder brother.

On the Turf, however, he remained adored for ending a generation of royal neglect. He began a stud at Windsor around 1750, while his membership gave kudos and momentum to a Jockey Club still confined to a cocoon of mere conviviality. The Star and Garter in Pall Mall, venue for many of its early meetings, had a reputation for fine cuisine and made no contribution to the regulation of sport until the laws of cricket were revised there in 1774.

In 1752 the Jockey Club leased a plot at Newmarket for the construction of a coffee room. Two years later, Cumberland won a race there restricted to its members, with a four-year-old son of Squirt. His name was Marske, and he had been presented to Cumberland's stable as a yearling, in 1751, by John Hutton. (In return, the stalwart of 'The '45' had received a chestnut Arabian.)

Marske is likely to have been trained up Gore Hill, at East Ilsley in Berkshire, where Cumberland had a stable. In four subsequent races he only beat one other horse; yet there was no disgrace in twice yielding to Snap, who would become a champion stallion. Marske's own prospects at stud seemed limited when quietly retired to Cranbourne Lodge in Windsor Forest, under the supervision of Studholme Hodgson – who had once served his owner as aide-de-camp at Culloden. But the horse had certainly helped Cumberland to view the Turf as a sanctuary from his travails at court, his military reputation having suffered a terminal blow during renewed hostilities on the continent. In fairness, he had been left in an impossible position by his father's desperation to preserve Hanover from the French. Not that the king recognised as much on Cumberland's return to court. Looking up from a card table, he declared: 'Here is my son who has ruined me and disgraced himself.' Cumberland promptly resigned all his commissions.

Disillusion and dishonour were compounded by deteriorating health. In his first battle, at Dettingen, he had been fortunate to avoid an amputation after sustaining severe grapeshot wounds below his knee. He had never really recovered and now an increasing lack of mobility made him so obese that only a mount with limbs of teak could support him. One wag observed that Cumberland, seated behind a pile of gold coins at the hazard table, resembled 'the prodigal son and the fatted calf both'. A series of mild strokes, after 1760, left him with a disconcerting leer. But there was one place that always seemed to put an authentic spring in his step.

'His Royal Highness has won as many hearts at Newmarket as he lost in Scotland,' Walpole wrote of his first visit, in 1753. 'He played deep and handsomely; received everybody at his table with the greatest good humour, and permitted the familiarities of the place with ease and sense.' On one occasion he told the half-pay officer who had found his wallet to keep it, though it contained several hundred pounds. The money had at least fallen into good hands, he remarked, and would otherwise only have been 'scattered among the blacklegs of Newmarket'. The marginal nature of such a loss can be judged from Walpole's remark that Cumberland was at Newmarket 'making a campaign with half the nobility and half the money in England attending him – they really say that not less than £100,000 has been carried thither for the hazard of this single week'.

Brief as it was, Cumberland's career on the Turf had eternal dividends. He bred two champions, Eclipse and Herod, whose genetic combination would seal the emergence of the thoroughbred as a coherent entity. Yet much credit for this alchemy is due to the forgotten John Hutton. Eclipse, after all, was bred from the basest metal.

Early in 1760, as Cumberland's nephew was crowned George III, Marske was paired with one of the Cranbourne mares, Spilletta.

Her pedigree was obscure, and she had finished last in her one and only race. Nor did she seem any more productive as a broodmare. That first mating with Marske proved barren, and Spilletta must have been very close to being culled from the stud. Fortunately she was given another chance with Marske, three years later, and they succeeded in producing a gawky chestnut colt with a white blaze and hindleg – though there is a suspiciously messianic whiff to the tradition that he acquired his name by his delivery during the solar eclipse of 1 April 1764.

That autumn Cumberland ignored the orders of his physicians to witness Herod's momentous duel with Antinous at Newmarket. It was said that £100,000 was wagered on the match, which Herod won by a neck. Cumberland was evidently impressed by the conduct in defeat of the young Duke of Grafton, who owned Antinous. A few months later Grafton, only twenty-nine, was given his first taste of junior office in a ministry transparently dependent, since the accession of George III, on the seasoned judgement of the new king's uncle. Its leader, Rockingham, was himself a man of the Turf who had come to Cumberland's attention as another star of Yorkshire's stand in 'The '45'.

Rockingham's regard for his old general now meant that affairs of state were once again as likely to be settled in Newmarket as London. The ousted factions railed against 'persons called from the Stud to the State and transformed miraculously out of jockeys into Ministers'. Yet even as Cumberland's political authority grew, his health continued to decline. He did manage to attend both autumn meetings at Newmarket the following year, one night lasting at the baize until 4 a.m. But the young ministers attending a Cabinet back at his townhouse, on 31 October, were aghast to witness a sudden and final seizure. He was dead within the hour, at just forty-four.

A few weeks later, the Cumberland stud was dispersed in one of the most remarkable sales in Turf history. As the outstanding lot in the catalogue, Herod fetched 500 guineas. Marske, however, was sold for just 26 guineas and reduced to covering New Forest mares on a farm in Dorset; while Lot 29, his yearling colt out of Spilletta, raised no more than 45 guineas. And so it was that the greatest thoroughbred of the century passed from one butcher to another:

from the hands bloodied in the abattoir of Culloden, to those of a Smithfield wholesaler. But William Wildman, prudent and respectable as he was, would in turn sell Eclipse to a man who might have borne his surname far more eligibly.

PART II

Rakes

Eclipse (1764)
Pot8os (1773)
Waxy (1790)
Whalebone (1807)

5

'Eclipse first, the rest nowhere'

Dennis O'Kelly arrived in London from Ireland in the 1740s as a prototype of Thackeray's Barry Lyndon, only less believable. Adamant he was born for better things, O'Kelly had been reduced to two last assets: fast talk and, with a deck of cards in his hand, faster fingers. Yet he would end up with dukes and princes dining at his table, enviously asking how it felt to own the greatest racehorse anyone had ever seen.

It was almost certainly O'Kelly who prompted a celebrated remark by Samuel Foote, the actor and playwright he befriended in the coffee houses of Covent Garden: 'Throw an Irishman into the Thames, naked at low water, and he will come up with the tide at Westminster Bridge, with a laced coat and sword.' On the other hand, it may also have been O'Kelly who so bored the company with his noble antecedents that Foote exclaimed: 'Very likely you have a coat of arms – but I see you have hardly got arms to your coat!'

O'Kelly is said to have started out as a sedan chairman, whose bulging forearms caused a beautiful peeress to extend his hire to her bedroom. With an accomplice, he then entrapped two sisters in a sham wedding, only to disappear with the dowries of both. He gambled at hazard, billiards and tennis until finally an army officer, suspecting himself defrauded, reported O'Kelly to the magistrate: Sir John Fielding, Henry's half-brother, known as 'the Blind Beak of Bow Street' and reputed to recognise 3,000 thieves by the sound of their voices alone. Only Foote's eloquent intercession diverted our hero from Tyburn to the Fleet Prison, where he would spend the next five years.

The debtors' jail condensed the inequalities of the world outside. One wing was reserved for inmates of sufficient means to buy a range of privileges. Their cells were commodious apartments, and some were even granted day release. The Fleet was more a safe haven than a place of punishment, its coffee parlour and alehouse so convivial that Smithfield butchers would pop in for a game of billiards or ninepins. In the other wing, however, a dead prisoner would sometimes be left to rot in his dormitory until a sufficient fee was paid for his removal.

It was here, in the late 1750s, that O'Kelly met Charlotte Hayes. She too was in her early thirties. Her mother had run a brothel behind the chaste facade of a millinery, and raised her to neglect no opportunity in the exploitation of naive girls or wicked men. (If the latter were prepared to pay 50 guineas to deflower a virgin, the least they deserved was to be deceived with a sac of animal blood. 'A maidenhead,' Hayes would say, 'is as easily made as a pudding.') Her own career as a kept woman had backfired – she discovered her patron's bankruptcy only on his death – but Hayes now perceived fresh possibilities in the brawn, wit and plausibility of an Irishman whose gentlemanly bearing prompted fellow inmates to label him 'Count' O'Kelly.

They seem never to have married. Perhaps O'Kelly's earlier wedding had not been bogus, after all; or maybe he simply heeded Foote's counsel against betrothal as the equivalent of 'bobbing for a single eel in a barrel of snakes'. And there would be an occasion when O'Kelly, stumbling into the wrong bedroom during York races, had his opportunism exposed by a maiden whose screams advertised the outrage through every corridor of the inn. He was obliged to publish a statement of contrition in the newspaper, confirming that his advances had been successfully quelled, and to donate £500 to charity. Otherwise, however, the longevity of their partnership suggests a greater capacity for tenderness and fidelity, in both O'Kelly and Hayes, than can be inferred from their perfidy to everyone else.

She soon redeemed him from the have-nots' wing; clothed him, fed him and secured the indulgence of the guards when he broke curfew to gamble in Covent Garden taverns. By the time they were both released in 1761, through an amnesty to celebrate the accession of George III, she had dovetailed their respective skills in an ingenious plan.

First O'Kelly was sent out to generate funds. He appeared in fashionable coffee houses in the guise of a highborn sportsman, sword at his hip, laughing off losses with a confidence that seldom proved misplaced when the stakes were raised. But it was on the racecourse that his real work was done. O'Kelly was one of the first 'legs' – 'blacklegs', that is, apparently named after the black boots typically worn by the new breed of professional gamblers. Forerunners of the modern bookmaker, they sought to lay bets from all-comers. Previously, wagers had typically been made between the owners of matched horses or their peers at White's or Brook's. Now a shouting throng gathered round a betting post at every track, offering or taking odds as their mounts jostled together.

But Hayes had another use for the patricians who did business with O'Kelly. The higher he rose, as a force on the Turf, the richer the clients he was able to introduce to her new, boutique 'nunnery'. The idea had been imported from Paris: a sanctuary from the disease, thievery and shame that lurked in the squalid bagnios of Covent Garden. Hayes recruited girls who could be taught to talk, walk and dance like a lady, and installed them in boudoirs a world apart from the verminous garrets elsewhere.

Needless to say the difference was fully reflected in the fees she charged. Hayes soon emerged as the most celebrated madam in London, eventually able to lease premises adjacent to St James's Palace. She emanated a genteel decorum that seemed to sanitise every perversion perpetrated under her roof. Yet the procurement of her girls was a vile business. Street prostitution was often the only resort of young women otherwise facing vagrancy, but Hayes greatly preferred middle-class girls: they needed less instruction in diction and deportment. They also took more finding. Innocents from the shires were accosted as they descended nervously from a coach, like Hogarth's Moll Hackabout in *The Harlot's Progress*, or as they registered at employment agencies. Hayes would give her victim a meal and a bed, to sleep off her spiked drinks. An incubus would then emerge from the shadows: a client with an expensive taste for the rape of virgins.

Once relieved of her virtue, the fallen daughter of a parson or doctor could be fast-tracked through a finishing school in music, manners and elocution, and urged to take comfort from such predecessors as Harriet Powell, an apothecary's daughter who had married the Earl of Seaforth. But most would soon discover how their charms and earnings would be confined.

Increasing corpulence did little to diminish the physical menace of Hayes's enforcer. Even his most sympathetic biographer was able to perceive in the 'bulldog jowl and retreating brow' of O'Kelly only 'great strength of purpose combined with lack of imagination'. But his own career, if less consistent in its yield, was progressing in tandem with that of his partner. As Hayes paraded her 'nuns' in opera boxes or lacquered coaches through the park, O'Kelly was mixing ever more comfortably at the races with a circle of aristocratic hedonists. All he needed was a couple of accessories to corroborate his status. First he bought himself a commission in the Middlesex Militia: if palpably no 'count', he could at least start calling himself 'captain', and eventually 'colonel'. Next he set about starting a small racing stable and, ideally, finding a champion to lead it.

In the spring of 1769, eight years after leaving the Fleet Prison, O'Kelly lent one of his racehorses to William Wildman so that he could give a trial gallop at Epsom to a son of Marske. O'Kelly had already sent his own training groom over to Wildman's stable, to assist in the taming of this horse 'of incomparable mettle and abominable temper'. He had been so difficult that Wildman had even asked a 'rough rider' to tame him in nocturnal poaching excursions. The time had now come to establish whether Eclipse, at five years old, had learned to channel his energies more productively.

As ever, when word got out that an unraced horse was to be tried, a posse of spies and touts made their way onto the Downs. For once, though, they had been outwitted. The horses had already finished their trial. They asked an old woman if she had seen anything. She replied that all she had noticed was a horse with a white leg 'running away at a monstrous rate' under its rider; and that in due course another had appeared in its wake, but would never catch the first one if they 'ran to the world's end'.

The only other witnesses to this extraordinary exhibition had a rather keener understanding of their privilege. Wildman immediately tracked down Marske to a farm in Dorset, where he was covering New Forest mares for a fee of 5 shillings, and bought him for just 20 guineas. John Hutton's memorial to 'The '45' was now nearly twenty years old, but Wildman had a hunch that Eclipse had the potential to renew interest in his sire's forgotten prowess.

O'Kelly, meanwhile, prepared to stake the bet of his life when Eclipse made his debut. Unfortunately the old woman had told the touts as much as they needed to know. For the first heat of the Epsom Noblemen and Gentlemen's Plate, contested by four other horses, the odds against the newcomer were hopelessly short: 1–4. These were not the kind of terms on which O'Kelly liked to do business, and he watched glumly as Eclipse introduced the wider world to his long, low-slung way of galloping, hindlegs oddly splayed, bounding clear at his leisure through the last of the four miles. As he did so, O'Kelly was suddenly struck by a new possibility.

Though his sons would one day prove the potency of his blood for a shorter, faster format of racing, Eclipse had to stretch his brilliance through the old, arduous regime of serial heats over four miles. True, the limits of his endurance would never be explored: whenever the same horse won both the first two heats, there was no need to stage a third. But if it was already obvious that Eclipse would wrap things up in the second heat, O'Kelly now asked for odds against him naming the full finishing order. Offered 6–4, he did not hesitate. 'Eclipse first,' he said, 'the rest nowhere.'

This was typically devious. The rules eliminated from the next heat any horse still beyond the 'distance' marker, 240 yards behind, when the winner reached the finish. An 'outdistanced' runner was given no formal finishing position. Sure enough, in the second heat Eclipse left his exhausted pursuers strung out towards the horizon. O'Kelly had won his bet, in a formula so audacious that it is preserved in the modern sporting lexicon – 'the rest nowhere' – for any performer who completely outclasses his field.

He now became thoroughly infatuated with Eclipse, first persuading Wildman to take 650 guineas just for a share in his ownership and eventually another 1,100 to buy him out. Wildman appears to have been unnerved by the horse's growing celebrity, having received anonymous threats after Eclipse proceeded to win five King's Plates that first season. Unsurprisingly it has been suggested that O'Kelly himself was behind these letters. Either way, the transfer of ownership took place around the time Eclipse proved equal to the most searching task of his career.

Bucephalus, likewise unbeaten, was the pride of the north. In April 1770 the two horses were walked from their respective bases in Epsom and Yorkshire for a match at Newmarket. For the only time in his life, Eclipse met a rival reckless enough to lay down a challenge within sight of the finish; but the outcome was inevitable. Eclipse opened up again, and poor Bucephalus was so broken in body and spirit that he was never the same again. Like Frankel, burning up the same Heath 241 years later, Eclipse seemed to set off far too fast – yet just kept going.

O'Kelly was ecstatic. Perhaps the horse that had sealed his reputation as a gambler could now do something similar for his status as a gentleman – albeit that status, on the Turf, for now depended on the most tenuous standards.

Since taking one step forward with its first Hanoverian patron, the Duke of Cumberland, Newmarket was in the process of taking two steps back with a new set of louche, braying young aristocrats. Their sottish mascot was the deplorable Frederick St John, 2nd Viscount Bolingbroke. 'Bully' had inherited his title and estates from his uncle, a Tory colossus who extolled an incorruptible, educated gentry, impervious to commercial interests and Crown patronage, to supervise the nation. As soon as the old man died, Bully wasted no time in exposing the flaws in that vision. His extravagances extended to a racing stable that would briefly include two great champions: Gimcrack, a silver nugget purchased from William Wildman, peevishly offloaded to a French count after a first defeat; and Highflyer, seized at the height of his fame as restitution for his owner's debts.

One of Charlotte Hayes's most depraved clients, Bully had got himself engaged to Lady Diana Spencer as impulsively as he did everything else: by a flippant, throwaway exchange one evening at the Vauxhall Gardens. It did not take long for his wife to realise that she had made a disastrous mistake. Bully's ongoing affair with

Lady Coventry ended only with her death – probably from consumption, though most found a sententious satisfaction in blaming the white lead and mercury water that had maintained her genteel pallor – and he responded by lavishing ever more money on his stud and courtesans. Diana, an accomplished artist, was left to sketch the mares and foals grazing the paddocks at his Wiltshire seat, contrasting their innate nobility with the degeneration they represented in her husband.

Not that the older, more sophisticated members of Bully's clique did any more for the reputation of the Turf. Drowsy, languid George Selwyn preserved some appeal, perhaps, as an avuncular refuge for rakes in difficulty, albeit his morbid obsessions were such that he once went all the way to Paris to see a traitor torn asunder by horses. A friend on his deathbed asked for Selwyn to be admitted, if happening to call. 'If I am alive I shall be delighted to see him,' he said. 'And if I am dead he will be delighted to see me.'

More sinister, at root, was that hook-beaked vulture, the Earl of March – later Duke of Queensberry, the notorious 'Old Q' – whose leering abuses transfixed moralists of the next century. Thackeray gave him 'not one, but several devils . . . He loves horse-racing, he loves betting, he loves drinking, he loves eating, he loves money, he loves women . . . He will play you for every acre you have.' Few, among the great sensualists of that heady age, were so brutally devoid of feeling; and few, equally, brought such glacial calculation to an era of heedless betting. Once March cleaned out the members at White's by wagering that he could send a message 50 miles in one hour. He simply placed the letter inside a cricket ball, and assembled twenty expert fielders to fling it round a large circle. On another occasion he wagered 1,000 guineas that four horses could haul a four-wheeled carriage the outlandish distance of 19 miles in the same period. He commissioned a surreal contraption that suspended a miniature velvet seat on leather straps between a skeletal frame, which duly covered the distance over Newmarket Heath in 53 minutes and 27 seconds.

His stratagems were not always so artistic, as when he was observed brazenly removing the lead ballast supposed to bring his jockey's saddle up to the stipulated weight. His Irish opponent, a crack shot, promptly challenged March to a duel. As well as his second and a surgeon, the Irishman arrived at the appointed venue with a third man, hauling an oak coffin with a brass plate, bearing March's arms and the date. Never one to permit vagaries of honour to skew the odds against him, March swiftly apologised.

Among nobles such as these, what was to stop even Dennis O'Kelly calling himself a gentleman?

Eclipse had little of the physical refinement associated with Arabian blood. There was even a hint of coarseness to a physique all about power: his joints, thighs and haunches were enormous, his back long and sloping. But if Eclipse was no oil painting, that did not prevent his immortalisation on canvas.

Sporting art had long depicted galloping horses clumsily outspread, as though falling from a great height. George Stubbs, recently settled in London, was now matching an unprecedented technical accuracy with a deeper veracity. At the same time, he was prepared to exalt rowdy, urban profligates like Bully through not just their thorough-breds, as obvious status symbols, but also the pastoral idylls surrounding their sumptuous new country houses. This new iconography of sophistication and wealth was typified by Stubbs in *Viscount Bolingbroke's Favourite Hunter*, with the horse framed against manor house and church. Of course, everybody knew what men such as Bully and Dennis O'Kelly were really like. By vesting such placidity and dignity in their humble stableboys, grooms and riders, Stubbs presumably intended a pointed contrast.

Both Wildman and O'Kelly commissioned Stubbs to paint Eclipse. Wildman and his two sons were depicted alongside the horse beneath a great oak, a charming scene to certify the accession of a tradesman and his family as minor gentry. But the scene of Eclipse before his showdown with Bucephalus commemorates the grace of the horse himself. All tension is diffused in his tranquillity and the veneration of his groom and jockey; the rubbing house beyond, with its tri-angular pitched roof, might as well be a chapel.

This notion of Eclipse as *the* consummate thoroughbred has proved strangely durable. It was at stud that he would achieve true greatness, his genes proving ideal for the growing emphasis on speed and precocity. In his own time, however, Eclipse predated any definitive sense of what a thoroughbred actually was. In his entire career, Eclipse met just twenty-one horses in eighteen engagements. After beating Bucephalus, he was reduced to a perfunctory series of mismatches. In his last seven 'races' he expended more effort crossing the country on foot than in galloping: five were walkovers, and in the others he faced two rivals and one respectively, at odds of 1–20 and 1–70. Yet the baloney surrounding his name extended to a medieval proliferation of reliquary after his death. One biographer counted six authentic skeletons as well as nine separate feet, mounted as inkstands and so forth. As he wryly observed, the speed of Eclipse could perhaps be explained by 'the abnormal quantity of legs in which he apparently rejoiced'.

If nothing else, Eclipse broke new ground as a commercial stallion. He was soon covering sixty mares a season, his fee settling at 30 guineas, and O'Kelly ultimately claimed to have made £25,000 as a result – an unheard-of sum. In the process, O'Kelly achieved a unique, if ambiguous, status on the Turf. Only at Clay Hill, the stud he bought himself at Epsom, could a typical house party bring together 'the Peer and the Black Leg at the same table . . . the Duke of Cumberland* and Dick England; the Prince of Wales and Jack Tetherington; Lord Egremont and Ned Bishop; Lord Grosvenor and Monsieur Champreaux; the Duke of Orléans and Jack Stacie . . . circulating the same bottle with equal familiarity and merriment.'

What a gallery of gargoyles! The monstrous Dick England, for instance, was as perilous to life and limb as to the patrimonies of feckless young peers. One victim, hustled of his fortune, had been too familiar with England's homicidal reputation to seek any kind of redress. Instead he had half-a-dozen whores and a blind fiddler brought to his room in Stacie's hotel, which exotic ensemble preceded only a bullet from his own gun in his final impressions of this life.

O'Kelly was astute enough, therefore, to prohibit gambling at his table. Instead, while Eclipse mounted their mares, his guests could take their pick from the delectable girls shuttled out from London by

* The king's brother, reviving a title left vacant by the death of their uncle, the breeder of Eclipse.

Charlotte Hayes. Unfortunately, the lascivious habits of men like Lord Grosvenor and the new Duke of Cumberland tended to cause far more embarrassment than any gambling dispute. Not even O'Kelly could keep these two round the same table, once Grosvenor had sued the duke for the seduction of his wife. This was one of three consecutive scandals, between 1768 and 1770, that gave Grosvenor, Bolingbroke and the Duke of Grafton as significant a role in the evolution of divorce as they would take in that of the thoroughbred.

6

Breeding Discontent

A NY OF THE three – Bully, Grafton or Grosvenor – might equally have prompted Ben Marshall's discovery 'that many a man will pay me fifty guineas for painting a horse who thinks ten guineas too much for painting his wife'. Certainly they all exploited the odious legal bias of the times, shamelessly parading the infidelities of wives driven into other arms by their own vile conduct. In fact, each modelled his domestic arrangements on those made for his stallions: the male to share his pleasure among many different mates, while granting the female no reciprocal freedom.

These were men of their time. The excesses of Newmarket, no doubt, were little different from those of Haymarket. Lord Egremont, another who would eventually succeed his host at Clay Hill as a preserver of the Darley Arabian line, in later years recalled the pandemic of betrayal in his youth. 'There was hardly a young lady of fashion who did not think it almost a stain on her reputation if she was not known to have cuckolded her husband,' he wrote. But a divorce, ultimately contingent on an Act of Parliament, still remained the drastic recourse of only the very wealthy.

When his wife, Lady Diana, first embarked on affairs of her own, Bully deliberately sought out a dose of the pox in Covent Garden, in order to infect whoever was sharing her favours. Nonetheless, she proceeded to deliver a daughter to Topham Beauclerk, a great-grandson of Charles II and Nell Gwyn and the last word in style before the macaronies succumbed to spy-glasses and towering seracs of curls. Violent, boorish Bully presented the outrage to a packed sitting of the Lords. It was obvious what he was up to. His losses were spiralling, at the tables and on the Turf, and his only hope was to free himself 'to marry a rich monster and retrieve his affairs'.

73

Grafton, likewise, triumphantly secured a divorce after his wife had a baby by her new lover – even though many of them had seen him at Ascot races fawning over Nancy Parsons. In her youth, his mistress had made 100 guineas from a single week's prostitution at a guinea a time. Even to a society inured to the promiscuity of the elite, this was an unpardonable provocation in one of the youngest prime ministers in history.*

At thirty-three, in the memorable verdict of Walpole, Grafton felt 'the world should be postponed to a whore and a horse race'. But the fact was that he had only ever been an accidental prime minister, hopelessly exposed when Pitt – who had installed him as a loyal and unambitious figurehead – suffered a nervous breakdown. Too pliant to resist the hardliners in a cabinet of misfits and malcontents, Grafton managed no more lasting legacy from his brief ministry than the scathing *Letters of Junius*. These lampooned him as a vapid voluptuary, presiding over cynical abuse of civil liberties at home and in the American colonies.

Grafton was so timorous of cabinet meetings that he sometimes simply sidled off to Newmarket instead. Much like his mentor, forever tainted by Culloden, he would depend on the Turf for posterity to mitigate the offences of his public career. Once ousted, Grafton slid into the bucolic balm of his mansion, hunt kennels and stud at Euston, near Newmarket. His retirement from politics would have immense consequences for the thoroughbred.

The last of these three barefaced hypocrites, Lord Grosvenor, was notorious for a concupiscence eclectic even by the standards of the time. But he did have one other fixation. In 1761 Walpole had recorded his creation as 'a Viscount or a Baron, I don't know which, nor does he, for yesterday when he should have kissed hands, he was gone to Newmarket to see the trial of a race-horse'. According to his wife, Henrietta, even his own brother considered Grosvenor so obsessed by racing that 'he could never have any Discourse with him, and that he would lose all Acquaintance but Jockies'.

---

* That status was implied, rather than formal, until the next century. Strictly, he led the ministry as First Lord of the Treasury.

Not that Henrietta showed any better judgement in choosing a lover than she had a husband. The king's brother presented an effete contrast with the previous Duke of Cumberland, his martial late uncle. Walpole dismissed the prince as weak and debauched, 'familiarizing with bad company, and yet presuming on a rank which he degraded'. If his looks were fair, they amounted to no more than a froth of cream to his curdled intelligence. Typically the dashing scar on his face traced only to the day, at Ascot races, when he had been thrown from his horse as a mere spectator. Grosvenor went for broke, demanding the astonishing sum of £100,000 as damages for a royal cuckolding. It was a dangerous stunt. The lawsuit was bound to be mercilessly amplified in print, and Grosvenor must have known that his panicked wife could fight fire with fire.

The hearing was dominated by the evidence of sundry chambermaids, footmen and ostlers concerning the prince's trysts with Henrietta at inns up and down the country. The prince would arrive one night as a cattle dealer, the next as a Welsh farmer, another as an aristocratic halfwit. It is not hard to imagine which of these roles he rendered with most conviction. On one occasion he could not resist presenting himself at Grosvenor's stud in Flintshire, hamming atrociously, as an envoy from the King of France with a commission to buy 200 horses.

Eventually a butler loyal to Henrietta's husband laid a trap. As she dined at the White Hart in St Albans, he bored two spyholes in her door. When it turned out that these did not afford a view of the bed, the appointed witnesses agreed to break down the door. As pokers forced the jambs, the lovers hastened to repair their dishevelment. Enough buttons on Lady Grosvenor's dress remained open for a groom to testify that he 'saw part of her breast naked'. The jury awarded Grosvenor damages of £10,000.

A series of pitiful young harlots, including one working for Charlotte Hayes, now lined up to attest to his ineligibility to seek a divorce. Henrietta was granted the right to live separately and awarded an annual allowance of £1,200. But if all the world now knew that Grosvenor had been infested with lice when pursuing ragged girls down filthy alleys, then it was also clear that he would stop at nothing to achieve gratification. And the thing he wanted most, now, was to breed a new Eclipse.

Grosvenor, Bully and Grafton would all help to establish a dynasty round Dennis O'Kelly's stallion. It was almost as though the dysfunctions in their own choice of mates was offset by the felicity of the matches they arranged for their mares. But the moral ambivalence of the Turf would find very different expression in the man who now bred the principal heir of Eclipse. Willoughby Bertie, 4th Earl of Abingdon, sometimes stood out among even the great men of his day as one ahead of his time, principled and bold; but he was just as capable of seeming petty, arrogant and cussed. His addiction to the Turf, now that he was well into his thirties, he resented as a curse – not just because his gambling and stud plunged him so steeply into debt, but because they threw him together with men like O'Kelly. Even those who deigned to accept his hospitality at Clay Hill had never viewed the owner of Eclipse as more than a glorified hustler, pimping his stallion and Charlotte's wenches with the same insolence. O'Kelly knew their hidden weaknesses, and that made him as unforgivable as he was indispensable. In condescending to deal with him, his clients suffered a moral schizophrenia that would continue to torment the sport until Victorian times.

Abingdon's relationship with O'Kelly reached a nadir over dinner at Burford races in 1775, when some mischievous person appealed to 'Captain' O'Kelly to share the stake for a match against Abingdon the following year. 'I, and the gentlemen on my side of the table, race for honour,' Abingdon retorted archly. 'The Captain and his friends, for profit.' O'Kelly was livid. True, he set flesh at too high a price to risk a duel. But the proposed match, he shouted, should have been 'cross and jostle' – that is, on terms that permitted rough riding in the closing stages. Then he would 'have brought a spalpeen* from Newmarket, no higher than a two-penny loaf, that should (by Jasus!) have driven his lordship's horse and jockey into the furzes, and have kept him there for three weeks.'

So surefooted among the foibles that fissured the highest society, O'Kelly could never get any purchase on the unpredictable Abingdon.

* A low, mean fellow: a rogue or rascal.

It was very different with Grosvenor. Both earls were infatuated with the champion who had come into O'Kelly's ill-bred hands. But while Grosvenor went so far as to offer the fabulous sum of 11,000 guineas for Eclipse – O'Kelly preposterously replied that he would accept nothing less than 20,000 guineas, along with an annuity of £500 and three broodmares – Abingdon had no intention of being taken for a fool. Instead he sought out William Wildman and offered him 1,000 guineas for Marske. Having been salvaged from obscurity, the ageing sire of Eclipse was now being hired out at 30 guineas per mare. As when dealing with O'Kelly over Eclipse, Wildman had the worst of the bargain. The stallion would live another five years, his progeny topping the prize-money table in both 1775 and 1776, and Abingdon was able to raise his fee to a staggering 100 guineas.

It is typical of Abingdon's chaotic sense of 'honour' that he would subsequently absolve himself from several years of forfeits accumulated at Newmarket. Eventually the Jockey Club secretariat sent him an account for £475 2s 6d – payable to Colonel O'Kelly. By that stage, having formally renounced the Turf, Abingdon doubtless felt entitled to disown his debts as well. In the meantime, unfortunately, he also permitted Grosvenor to obtain stewardship of Eclipse's legacy, after all.

Where O'Kelly resented Abingdon as lordly and supercilious, Grosvenor despised him as a traitor to their class. It was widely known that Abingdon, at Geneva on the Grand Tour, had once paid homage to Voltaire with the exiled radical, John Wilkes. But matters came to a head in 1777 when he volunteered himself as an unexpected champion of American liberty.

Abingdon had become disgusted not only by Grafton's successor, Lord North, whose ministry was proving highly biddable to a meddlesome new monarch, but also by an opposition confining itself to a policy of sullen abstention. His was the only vote cast in the House of Lords even against suspension of habeas corpus. When Edmund Burke defended this passivity in a letter to his Bristol constituents, Abingdon published a response so exuberant that the American rebels found fresh heart even as famine and frostbite brought them to the brink at Valley Forge.

Here out of nowhere, was an English earl prescribing a laxative to the constipated forces of liberalism of the mother country. 'What!' Abingdon roared. 'Are the rights of Englishmen to be held at the *discretion* of Ministers? . . . Wherein does *civil discretion* differ from *will*, the law of tyrants? . . . Parliaments have ever been the works of men's hands, as, thank God, we now know that our Kings are.' A parliament that subverted these rights was owed no obedience. Nor should any Englishman be deceived that he might preserve his own rights, if his fellow subjects over the ocean were to forfeit theirs: 'The dagger uplifted against the breast of America is meant for the heart of Old England.'

'Are you not glad he has so well puffed away Burke's sophistries?' William Mason, the poet, asked Walpole. 'Who would have thought of this little David?' Walpole agreed: Abingdon's 'plain dealing and severe truths were far more detrimental to the Court than the laboured subterfuges and inconsistent Jesuitism of Burke'. Abingdon was exhilarated. Even if he would never again get others to do the same, he decided it was high time he took himself more seriously. He sat down and, assessing the appalling cost of his racing career, accepted that things had to change.

That May, Abingdon had been optimistic of winning the richest prize ever contested on British Turf, at Newmarket, with a four-year-old son of the great Eclipse. Pot8os had acquired his name in picturesque circumstances. He had started out as plain old Potatoes, until a groom was asked to label his corn bin with a piece of chalk. Abingdon was so amused by the result – 'Potooooooooo' – that he registered the name accordingly, ultimately condensed as Pot-8-o's or Pot8os. A chestnut with a white blaze, just like his sire, he had shown such promise in his first couple of races that only one of his nineteen rivals started at shorter odds for this unprecedented stake of 5,600 guineas.*

It is fitting, given the eventual impact of his bloodline, that Pot8os should have contested a race that so anticipated the future direction of the sport. Only the previous September, the first running of the

---

* Fifty-six gentlemen had subscribed 100 guineas apiece to enter. Twenty-five years later, there had still only been three other races worth even 3,000 guineas.

St Leger at Doncaster had set a template for five races, confined to three-year-olds, eventually identified as 'Classics'. The St Leger, and soon the Derby at Epsom, would nourish interest in a new type of racing, for younger horses over much shorter distances in bigger fields. Even at four miles, however, the jockey of Pot8os proved unable to adapt the cat-and-mouse tactics of heat racing and was caught out by this single, hectic stampede. Permitting a clear lead to Grosvenor's unfancied Grey Robin, he left himself just too much ground to make up.

Grosvenor was not deceived by the result. The following spring, the two horses lined up for a rematch at Newmarket. This time, there was just one other runner and little prospect of the jockey repeating his mistake. Grosvenor knew that Abingdon had resolved to cut his losses on the Turf. Even as the race started, he pulled up his hack to watch alongside his rival. Abingdon turned and saw the familiar features: cold, dark eyes; residual ravages of smallpox; nose and chin plunging sharply around mean lips. He must have had a nauseous certainty what was coming next. Sure enough, Grosvenor baldly asked the price at which Abingdon might be prepared to sell Pot8os. A straight question was answered in kind. The horse could be had for 1,500 guineas – and his purchaser should have 'the chance of the race' into the bargain. In other words, he could have any prize money won in the race already underway. Grosvenor immediately extended a hand, and the deal was struck.

Within minutes Pot8os had started to repay his new owner with a win that signalled his bloom as one of the outstanding racehorses of the century, and certainly one of the toughest. Though still racing over extreme distances, he kept going for seven seasons and was counted a winner at least twenty-eight times.*

Abingdon must have been appalled by the unfolding cost of his pact with the devil. Immediately after the sale, he wrote 'An Adieu

---

* His longevity may reflect the fact that Grosvenor had a stud groom, William Griffiths, so respected that a compendium of his herbal remedies was published by public subscription. These ranged from 'the Genuine Pissing Ball' to 'a drink for a tired Hunter' – the effects of which seem unsurprising, given that it was essentially a quart of warm port wine mixed with opium.

to the Turf' – a rollicking renunciation of the low company he had
now forsworn. 'Kelly', as owner of Eclipse, is still unable

> *To cleanse the foul Augaean stable,*
> *For which his Wife maintains him.*

As for the new owner of Pot8os:

> *I saw three Sweepstakes and a Plate*
> *By Grosvenor carried home.*
> *What finds he there? A strumpet Wife*
> *Blasting the sweets of wedded life*
> *And Children not his own.*

How their fellow Jockey Club members must have sniggered. Since
Grosvenor's infamous divorce suit none of the three parties had relieved
their opprobrium. Cumberland had quickly abandoned Henrietta,
instead stunning the king with his clandestine marriage to a commoner
accounted by Walpole 'artful as Cleopatra' in deployment of 'eyelashes
a yard long'. Henrietta's immersion in the demi-monde, meanwhile,
can be measured by a story that she appeared at an orgiastic masked
ball 'dressed' as Mother Eve. She wore only fig leaves – and these
only about her face – and was then ravished, incognita, by her own
estranged husband.

No more authentic, perhaps, is a suggestion that a groom once cut
down Grosvenor from the beam of a stable in York. If he really did
attempt suicide, his immunity to shame and loneliness would appear
to have been exaggerated. Laurence Sterne, after all, once wrote from
Montpellier to thank him for relieving his financial embarrassment,
declaring: 'Nobody but Lord Grosvenor would have thought of such
a thing.' On the other hand, a magazine had published a letter purport-
edly written by Grosvenor to Charlotte Hayes: 'The last Piece you
recommended was not the Thing; but I should not have minded that
so much, if I had not detected her with my Valet de Chambre.'

As for Abingdon, he was only ever consistent in being erratic.
Walpole remembered him as 'rough, wrongheaded, extremely under-
bred, but warmly honest . . . eager in every pursuit without any

knowledge of the world'. Certainly he did not take long to squander his claims as a prophet of liberalism, opposing limitations on slavery and concessions of autonomy to the Irish. Describing Abingdon as 'a man of genius, but eccentric, and irregular almost to the point of madness', Lord Charlemont reassured the Irish that nobody would be paying Abingdon the slightest attention. Nor did Abingdon prove any more far-sighted as a capitalist, selling off his wife's estates on Manhattan Island as soon as possible after the American War of Independence. Future generations would know the site as Greenwich Village.*

Yet Abingdon reflected more enlightened times in England. After a long era of bloodshed and bigotry, from Marston Moor to the Boyne to Culloden, he was inspired by Voltaire rather than Robespierre. Those classes first granted free rein with the rights of the individual, often remained capricious – or, like Grosvenor, vicious – in their experiments: Lord Orford, for instance, driving his phaeton to Newmarket with a team of four red stags. (And pursued into the stable yard of the Ram Inn, at full pelt, by an excited pack of hounds.) But at least superstition and oppression were being dismantled in temperate increments. Thanks to a radical modernisation in the type of tasks it could be set, moreover, this process of refinement was now extending to the English thoroughbred itself.

* He did find some serenity in music. Over a hundred of his compositions survive, including a series of glees to which Haydn provided harp or pianoforte accompaniments.

7

The Way Ahead

THE TURF WAS now being weeded and mown by its first proper superintendent. Sir Charles Bunbury was appointed steward of the Jockey Club as early as 1768, when still only twenty-eight, albeit old enough to have been abandoned by one of the most beautiful brides of the Hanoverian era. Walpole drooled that 'no Magdalene by Correggio was half so lovely and expressive' as Lady Sarah Lennox; but nor was any Magdalene ever half so bored. 'Mr B has been coursing, hunting and doing every pleasant thing upon earth,' she complained to a friend. 'And poor me sat fretting and fuming at home.' Lady Sarah soon found more stimulating companions, and was pregnant by the latest of them when finally absconding. Bunbury promptly joined Bully, Grosvenor and Grafton in the queue from racecourse to divorce court. In this instance, happily, both parties would find fulfilment in remarriage, she raising three generals and he racing three Derby winners.

For the next half-century Bunbury was de facto 'perpetual president' of the Jockey Club. Its powers were already widening: in 1758, for instance, it had ordered disqualification from Newmarket of any jockey who failed to pass the scales after a race, and Bunbury now developed a regulatory service that would gradually be adopted throughout the country. He would also make no less a contribution to the evolution of the racehorse itself: his stud cultivated speed rather than stamina, while his trainers favoured a far less punishing regime than the norm.

It would perhaps have been more fitting, then, had Bunbury won the famous toss of a coin with the 12th Earl of Derby, over the naming of a race run for the first time at Epsom in 1780. Its countless imitations, all round the world, would then have been known as the Kentucky Bunbury, and so on. As it was, the new sweepstakes for three-year-olds became the Derby Stakes, a variation on one inaugurated for fillies over the same track the previous year. Though of limited importance in their early years, the Derby and the Oaks would eventually be linked with the St Leger and two other Classics – the 1000 and 2000 Guineas – introduced by Newmarket early in the next century. Their emergence was organic, reflecting a trend that favoured horses, owners and spectators alike. Shorter races reduced the premium on brute physical resources, bringing into play horses not only less mature but more finely assembled. Meanwhile, bigger fields ensured that a meaningful purse could be subscribed more affordably than in staking a match race. And the two combined, of course, produced a far more exciting spectacle.

The Jockey Club had abolished heats in its own Plate races by 1756; in the same year, a first race was staged at Newmarket for horses as young as three. Even at the start of the century, racehorses had seldom been raced before they were six, the age stipulated for King's Plates. But it was now only a matter of time before two-year-olds would venture onto the racetrack, a prospect that would have been considered an abomination only a generation before. Some of the early experiments still seem horrible. It is easy to conceive the distress of a half-grown two-year-old forced to contest two matches over four miles on the same day in 1773. (Not that things can have been much easier for his four-year-old opponent, who was required to carry an extra 98lbs in his saddle.) For a while there were even attempts to race yearlings.

The Derby took its place among all these improvisations – initially contested, in fact, over a bare mile.* And if the fall of a coin had not favoured Bunbury, his name was nonetheless preserved as owner of the first winner, Diomed. Dennis O'Kelly owned the runner-up and would win the second and fifth runnings with sons of Eclipse, whose stock were showing a gusto suited to the changing demands of the sport.

In 1787, O'Kelly bought a villa and deer park at Cannons near

---

* It gained its four extra furlongs in 1784; the St Leger, conversely, gradually shed 308 yards from an initial distance of two miles.

Edgware. Eclipse, by now twenty-three years old and suffering from sore feet, was conveyed there from Clay Hill on a specially constructed carriage. O'Kelly was now in his sixties, obese and tormented by gout. He had never been able to fumigate a reputation stained equally by the prejudice of others and his own venality. On one occasion he was nearly lynched by a racecourse mob after withdrawing a favourite, to his presumed financial advantage, at the eleventh hour. Anyone else who owned a horse as good as Eclipse could have expected automatic membership of the Jockey Club, but O'Kelly had to affect a growling indifference to his exclusion from the 'humbug societies' where his enemies could 'meet and rob one another without fear of detection'. On his death that Christmas, however, his heir was almost immediately elected to the Jockey Club. Schooled as sedulously as Charlotte's 'nuns', Andrew O'Kelly had so thoroughly shed the coarse brogue and bearing of his uncle that he was soon racing horses in partnership with the Prince of Wales.

Charlotte Hayes, comforted by a parrot whose repertoire extended to the 104th Psalm, lived well into her eighties. But Eclipse survived O'Kelly by just fourteen months, succumbing to colic at 7 p.m. on 27 February 1789. No meteor shower or earthquake was reported, though the French veterinarian who conducted the autopsy did discover a heart of freakish proportions. At 14lbs, it weighed around 5lbs more than average.

'If anything can make a democracy in England,' sighed Lord Minto in 1792, 'it will be the Royal Family.' And it was on the racecourse that the sons of George III, heedless of the chaos in France, were reaching the height of their infamy. At Newmarket the Duke of York had lost so heavily that rumours even reached town that he had shot himself. The Prince of Wales himself, meanwhile, had just broken up his hugely expensive stable of racehorses for the second time in six years. In 1786, when reputed to be spending £30,000 a year on bloodstock, he had been forced into a fire-sale to repair his debts. After a parliamentary bailout he had resumed his Turf career with incorrigible extravagance. He won the 1788 Derby with Sir Thomas, a half-brother to Pot8os he had bought for 2,000 guineas, and had soon built his stable back up to forty horses. But then came the infamous affair that would cause him to turn his back on Newmarket for good.

In the autumn of 1791 Samuel Chifney, wearing the royal silks on a horse named Escape, finished last of four in a race for which he had started the odds-on favourite. The very next day, he won at 5-1 against two rivals who had finished in front of him the previous afternoon. Whispers immediately began that Chifney had stopped Escape on the first day, and backed him on the second.

Chifney's status, as the first jockey to achieve fame and prosperity, had recently been sealed by a stupendous contract of 200 guineas to ride for the prince. (Retainers exceeding £50 were still rare half a century later.) His success itself reflected the evolution of a speedier, more highly bred racehorse. It was all very well for gentlemen to ride big, mature stayers over four miles, but the weights carried by younger horses over lesser distances required specialist, lightweight partners. The 'Chifney rush' was tailored to the new racing environment – his mounts typically held back during the early stages of races run at a stronger pace before being urged to pick off the tiring front-runners. But this could only be done so long as you kept your mount properly relaxed. Chifney, who liked to ride with a slack rein, viewed control of a feisty thoroughbred as a matter of extreme delicacy. It should, he wrote, 'be done as if you had a silken rein as fine as a hair, and you were afraid of breaking it'. At 5ft 5in and 7st 12lbs, he could subdue horses that would buck off the sturdiest Master of Hounds.

But the little man had a mighty ego. In his autobiography, *Genius Genuine*, he announced that he 'could ride horses in a better manner in a race than any other person ever known in my time, and . . . train horses for running better than any person I ever yet saw.' With dark hair tumbling romantically over his collar, he preened himself at the races with ruffles, frills and lovelocks. Such an upstart, it was suspected, might not just take horses for a ride. To be fair, jockeys had not yet been prohibited from betting. But nor could Chifney measure up to his rival, Frank Buckle, who once struck an aristocratic patron across the face with his whip when quietly invited to 'throw' a match. Nowadays, the fact that Escape's first race was half the distance of the second – two miles, as opposed to four – would be considered ample to exculpate Chifney. But Bunbury, after inter-viewing the jockey, coolly advised the flabbergasted heir to the throne that 'no gentleman would start [a horse] against him' if he persevered in employing Chifney.

It is impossible to know whether Bunbury's principal target was the owner or rider of Escape. Chifney's integrity had long been in question, and Bunbury's view of a jockey's proper place can be judged from the way he gave Dick Goodison just £10 for winning him a Derby – drily remarking that there might have been more, but for the fact that the gentleman who laid his bets had not only defaulted but also killed himself. Equally it has been speculated that the king himself might have solicited Bunbury to create a scandal of this kind, in the hope of prompting his son to abandon his expensive addiction to racing. Either way, the Jockey Club had proved itself capable of asserting its jurisdiction over both a 'Genius Genuine' and a future king.

Whether through principle or pique, the Prince of Wales stood by his man. He promised that he would renounce the royal stable before he did Chifney's good name, and extended the 200-guinea retainer for the rest of his life. It may have been debt, rather than honour, that caused the prince to sell off his stable in 1792. Either way, he could not save Chifney's career. The jockey seems to have persevered after a fashion for several years. But he then sold the prince's annuity and, though patenting a bridle still in wide use, died in the Fleet Prison at just fifty-two.

The mare who would seal the place of Pot8os as the principal heir to Eclipse was bred by Bully even as he entered a final freefall. His fortune exhausted by his stud, mistresses and gambling, he was helpless as Richard Tattersall, the bloodstock auctioneer, seized Highflyer in a nocturnal raid. After the divorce, his misogyny obtained a chillingly punitive quality. Even the plainest heiresses fled a known rapist. A reckoning loomed. 'Poor Bolingbroke's illness took a sudden turn,' recorded a friend. 'He became raving mad and is confined.' He may well have been suffering the effects of syphilis – which, by a horrible coincidence, was probably responsible for an equivalent disintegration in Lady Diana's second husband. Topham Beauclerk, the livewire and flâneur adored by Dr Johnson, had become slovenly, cantankerous and hooked on laudanum. He was still only forty when he died in 1780. The same day, some of Bully's last valuables were auctioned to reduce his debts. Two canvases by Stubbs were bought back by his heir for 27 guineas apiece.* Meanwhile, Highflyer went on to be the leading stallion every year from 1785 to 1796; Tattersall built himself a mansion with the proceeds and named it Highflyer Hall.

Before entering the asylum, Bully had already been forced to sell a mare named Maria. In due course, she found herself at Ferdinando Poole's stud, The Friary at Lewes in Sussex. Sir Ferdinando would host lavish parties during the town's race meetings, the Prince of Wales among the guests admiring the mares and foals grazing the paddocks beyond the dining-room windows. His hospitality also extended to the poor of the town, who would be ferried up to the racetrack in his elegant family carriage – affectionately known, by its grateful passengers, as 'the tub'. Though Sir Ferdinando had no surviving children, life at The Friary had retained a zest of youth through his pretty niece, Bessy Pilfold, taken into the household after the death of her mother. In 1791 she married Tim Shelley, nephew of one of Sir Ferdinando's boon companions and a future baronet.

Perhaps this development pained another Lewes regular, the 39-year-old George O'Brien Wyndham, 3rd Earl of Egremont. The twin proclivities of the county's premier magnate were so well known, after all, that the contemporary author of *Modern Characters by Shakespeare* allocated him these lines from Henry VI, Part I:

> *Between two horses, which doth bear him best,*
> *Between two girls, which hath the merriest eye,*
> *I have, perhaps, some shallow spirit of judgement.*

But Egremont had none of the sleaziness of Bully or Grosvenor. His longest-serving mistress was an inventor and painter, a patroness

---

* These would remain in the family until 1943, when *Gimcrack on Newmarket Heath* raised 4,200 guineas; at Christie's in 2011 it fetched £22.4 million.

of William Blake, her status as unofficial chatelaine of Petworth underlined by the family they raised there together. Egremont was also said to have fathered at least two children with Viscountess Melbourne: William, who eventually succeeded as Lord Melbourne; and Emily, who grew up to marry Lord Palmerston. As such, Egremont is credited with the paternity of one prime minister and the wife of another. It is no small compliment, then, to hail him as an equally significant breeder of thoroughbreds.

One of his very first horses, Assassin, won the third running of the Derby and later beat Pot8os at Newmarket. In the meantime Egremont paid Dennis O'Kelly the terrific sum of 2,500 guineas for a yearling by Eclipse. Mercury, as he was named, beat one of Sir Ferdinando's horses for a King's Plate at Lewes before being retired to the stud at Petworth. His 1790 crop included a colt eventually named Gohanna, who quickly matured into a very powerful specimen.

In the same breeding season, Maria had produced a sensational colt by Pot8os. Imposing but perfectly proportioned, the colt had a mahogany coat and a concave, chiselled profile. As a tribute to his sire he was named Waxy, after a variety of potato. Sir Ferdinando, who had lost his wife in 1786, had a heartening sense that new life was returning to his world. Bessy safely delivered a baby son within a year of her marriage – and there was also a fresh start at The Friary stables, where Sir Ferdinando had hired Robert Robson, a young man full of ideas, as his new training groom.

Though his father had trained Highflyer for Bully, Robson distrusted the methods of the old school. He perceived that the new emphasis on speed and precocity, exemplified by the Classic races, demanded innovation from trainers as much as breeders. Most trainers presumed that young horses would simply have to be pushed harder, earlier, to be ready for these prestigious new races for three-year-olds. But Robson saw that they would require more indulgent handling than had been traditional with mature, dour sloggers. If they were to blossom in time, they needed to be nurtured delicately. Most trainers viewed the new programme for two-year-olds as a vital opportunity to season potential Classic horses. But Robson declined to race two-year-olds at all and, critically, also abjured the more murderous excesses of the old 'sweats' regime. The results would be so spectacular that he would secure a new professional dignity for a role hitherto as anonymous as that of any other agricultural foreman. And it was Waxy who set the template.

Waxy had been given his one and only race at Newmarket the previous month – in contrast with Egremont's Gohanna, who had contested five races already that spring. He had won the last four impressively, and went to Epsom as hot favourite. The great crowd was quite right to suspect that the Derby, in its fourteenth running, was about to seal the thoroughbred's coming of age. They were just looking at the wrong horse.

A Day at the Races

Epsom, 16 May 1793

Waxy's brilliance vindicated bold experiments in both training and breeding. His trainer had grasped that the traditional, sweat-and-swaddle regime was no way to sharpen younger, faster horses for the new, shorter races. His breeder, meanwhile, had heeded the impact of Eclipse blood in what would become known as the Classics. On Derby day, Waxy was just one of seven sons of Pot8os lining up in a field of thirteen; once retired to stud he would sire four Derby winners of his own.

His success was applauded 'as numerous a company as ever appeared upon a course' – as numerous, and as diverse. The throng included the first recognisable bookmaker, Harry Ogden, and the Prince of Wales, still smarting from the discovery that there was one corner of his future dominion – the Jockey Club demesne of Newmarket Heath – where he would be treated the same as his subjects.

In fact, the Derby had discovered that its greatest asset – an equal ability to lure both prince and pauper from the adjacent capital – was also its greatest problem. Over thirty carriages were held up and robbed returning to town after a typical Derby of the 1790s, and things were scarcely less dangerous at the track. 'Several carriages were broken to pieces, one Lady had her arm broken', and many watches and purses disappeared. The racecourse, where the crush of bodies made exposure less likely, offered exceptionally attractive odds to the light-fingered. Three years previously Lord Egremont had been relieved of a wallet at Lewes races. Its new owner must have been speechless to discover that it contained £500.

Ogden's emergence as the father of bookmaking was a response to the larger fields drawn by the new style of racing. As match racing and heats were gradually phased out, in favour of the all-action sweepstake, the old practice of private side-bets was dying out. Blacklegs like Dennis O'Kelly had responded by seeking to 'hedge' wagers about different runners, in the hope of guaranteeing a profit. Besides the institution of a betting post at tracks, this would also give an extra role to Tattersall's auction house on Hyde Park Corner, where subscribers and professional layers could convene weekly. But it was Ogden who anticipated the future. Though not yet offering odds against each individual runner, he would lay 'the field' against a single horse – making him the first layer prepared to take bets on all runners.

From a viewing platform on a two-storey, crenellated royal box, the Prince of Wales surveyed the scene with satisfaction. He was determined that Bunbury's effrontery, and the latest dispersal of his stable, would not divide him from the pleasures of the racecourse. After all, his circle was badly in need of cheer. That very day their madcap mascot, the twenty-three-year-old Earl of Barrymore, was being buried in secrecy to avoid the seizure of his remains by creditors. Thespian, prankster and skilled jockey, Barrymore had contrived a suitably antic exit a couple of weeks previously when inadvertently discharging his shotgun as he escorted French prisoners at Folkestone.

It fell to Sir John Lade to rally spirits at Epsom. The prince's racing manager stood out from the crowd more than ever, one magazine observing that his 'loose undress of blue and white striped trowsers . . . puzzled the crowd to tell whether he was the Captain of a Privateer, or an Ambassador from the Great Mogul.' Lade was a svelte Falstaff to the prince's fattening Hal. As a master of the new art of carriage-driving, he liked to take charge of the royal barouche while adopting the dress and language of a common groom. A time would come, after his patron became regent, when Lade would find himself imprisoned for debt – 'reduced to beggary', as the diarist Thomas Creevey remarked, 'by having kept such good company'. For now, though, he continued to set a raucous tone at Brighton and Carlton House.

He lost 1,000 guineas to Lord March, for instance, in a wager that either could nominate a gourmand to outlast the other in one sitting. March's man 'beat his antagonist by a pig and an apple-pie'. His wife, Letty, also kept things interesting: she had been mistress to Sixteen String Jack until his dashing career as a highwayman came to an end at Tyburn. Sadly, while her driving skills were nearly a match for her husband, there is no record of the outcome when Letty challenged a Mrs Hodges to a five-mile curricle race at Newmarket.

Little detail survives of the first Derbys. Winning distances would not be regularly recorded before 1805, nor the full list of jockeys until 1830.

Gohanna himself had not even been named as yet, still known only as 'Brother to Precipitate' despite starting as odds-on favourite. But such tantalising glimpses that do survive suggest the race must have been an exceptionally exciting one. Gohanna's jockey set out to make the running, but William Clift on Waxy seized control by barging his way past on the first turn. This was perfectly in character. Clift, a former shepherd, had never acquired any frills and was appallingly severe on his mounts in a finish. This time he found himself being harried by Gohanna's rider all the way – even though there was barely room for the pair to race side by side. The course ran straight through the middle of the crowd, only the very last portion railed off where the gentry had lined up their carriages three or four deep. It took tremendous nerve to ride flat out into this shouting, swaying tunnel of spectators, their instincts of self-preservation dulled by drink or bets. As late as 1821 the course markers were still so primitive that the two jockeys fighting out the finish were hardly able to force a passage. 'We wound in and out,' recalled the winner that day, 'for all the world like a dog at a fair.'

Matters were made still worse by the mounted spectators following the closing stages at a gallop. This habit, acquired over the open spaces of Newmarket Heath, was not so practicable elsewhere. On one occasion a judge complained that he 'ought by rights to have placed a tall gentleman in a white mackintosh first'. Charles James Fox, the great Whig orator and incorrigible gambler, was often found at the head of these cavaliers. 'He eyed the horses advancing with the most immovable look,' Walpole recalled. 'He breathed quicker as they accelerated their pace; and when they came opposite to him he rode in with them at full speed, whipping, spurring, and blowing, as if he would have infused his whole soul into the courage, speed, and perseverance of his favourite racer.'

On the rough, untended downland, the finish was shrouded in swirls of dust. Even after they had pulled up, it was impossible to know who had won. Only the surge of waving hats around Clift finally told that Waxy had held out, by half a length. A French visitor to one Epsom raceday was amazed to record how 'the victor, when he has arrived at the goal, finds it a difficult matter to disengage himself from the crowd, who congratulate, caress and embrace him with an effusion of heart, which it is not easy to form an idea of, without having seen it.' The throng doubtless parted, however, for Egremont and Sir Ferdinando to exchange a warm handshake. One way or another, it was Sussex's race.

8

The Regeneration Gap

SIR JOHN LADE drove the royal barouche as usual, the prince seated alongside, followed by Henry Mellish driving the ladies. Strange, smiling, shimmering Mellish, all in white, stockings to hat, a pale spectre of his lurid times. Did he sense, deep down, that the meteor was almost burned out? Thirty thousand on the table, today, in dear old Sancho's match at Lewes; and still nearly two months to the St Leger, a market he had so inflamed that 1 million guineas was already riding on the outcome. Though not yet twenty-five, Mellish had led in the last two St Leger winners – and celebrated one of them by losing £40,000 on a single throw of the dice. Who was counting? If he ever did, the young cavalry officer could tot up 38 thoroughbreds, 17 carriage horses, 12 hunters in Leicestershire, and 4 chargers here at the Brighton garrison.

Sancho was the first of his St Leger winners, in 1804. Yet here he was, two summers later, squaring up for a match over fully four miles. Thirteen years after Waxy's Derby, even Classic winners were still obliged to share the sporting attrition of their forefathers. Sancho's match with Pavilion at Lewes preserves a snapshot of the Turf as it continued to look to most of its patrons.

The Prince of Wales, having refused an olive branch from the Jockey Club, was maintaining his boycott of Newmarket. And, by making 'Brighton and Lewes Races the gayest scene of the year in England' he was doing his utmost to ensure that few in his circle hankered for the dreary Suffolk plain. Once the royal party had swept onto the racecourse, thousands craned their necks to see the two horses parading by: the betting had been turned on its head by rumours that Sancho had been lame in recent days. Lord Darlington, owner of Pavilion, peered intently at his adversary's horse from the prince's carriage. Mellish, pulling up his gig in front of the stand, raised his white hat to friends above. A wan smile: 'If Sancho's beat, I hope some of you may take me for a coachman.'

But he could not disguise his nerves, as he helped to move the crowd behind a rudimentary rope boundary. It remained common for spectators to risk crossing the course even after the bell had been sounded for the start of the race, or to spill onto the track in seeking a better view. A last conference with Frank Buckle, in his white silks with crimson sleeves. Then Mellish led his champion up to the start, and watched helplessly as the two horses launched into a swinging canter. Buckle allowed Sam Chifney Jr. to set the early pace on Pavilion, biding his time for the first two miles. From halfway he began to nudge Sancho closer, so that as they bore down towards the crowd they were neck and neck. Those who had been calling odds against Sancho now began to reverse their position. With 300 yards to go Buckle was looking so confident that someone called 5–1 against Pavilion.

And then – disaster. The roars of the crowd suddenly changed pitch: shrieks of horror, a few callous cheers. Sancho's inexorable rhythm had suddenly given way to a hideous, crab-like lurch. One of his forelegs had given way. Buckle clung to his neck and hoped that the poor creature would hold out until he could jump off. Meanwhile Chifney Jr., looking over his shoulder, eased Pavilion down to walk past the winning post. Sancho's owner was aghast. In contrast with so many in the prince's coterie, Mellish was remembered as having 'never wronged anyone but himself . . . As an owner of racehorses, and a bettor, his character as without spot.' For once, however, he must have felt rather a cad. He had sent Sancho across a highwire, following his lameness, and now it had snapped.

Sancho, in fairness, had very nearly made it home and was ultimately patched together to go to stud. Mellish, heartened by the prognosis, repaired with Lord Darlington and the prince to the Star Inn. Though he had taken a massive hit, he looked 'as if he had been only losing threepenny points at whist'. Then, no doubt, it was back to the Pavilion, gaudily lit up, to take his place among his brother Hussars: 'very ornamental monkeys', according to Creevey, 'in their red breeches with gold fringe and yellow boots'. Here poor

Sancho could be forgotten, perhaps as the ladies tried their hand with an air gun in the map room – as when 'Lady Downshire hit a fiddler in the dining-room, Miss Johnstone a door and Bloomfield the ceiling'.

A less frivolous challenge in marksmanship was still to detain Mellish at first light, as second to Lord Barrymore in a duel with Humphrey Howorth over a dispute at cards. Prior to investing an opium fortune in his Newmarket stable, Howorth had been a surgeon in India and, attesting that gunshot wounds were more serious when tangled with clothing, he duly stripped naked for the duel. Whether on account of this distraction, or their bleary condition, both gentlemen missed and Mellish persuaded them to consider the matter closed.

The next afternoon Mellish went up to Brighton's own racecourse and won the first running of the Pavilion Stakes with Trafalgar, a colt he had just purchased from Lord Egremont. Confined to three-year-olds, over a bare mile, the new race was following the trend that had given rise to the first Classics. Even so, this particular experiment would never really get off the ground – soon supplanted by the prince's enemies at Newmarket, who inaugurated their own version, the 2000 Guineas, three years later. Nor could Trafalgar stop the unravelling of his new owner. A catastrophic St Leger, just two months later, obliged Mellish to sell off his estate and remove himself to the Peninsular War in Spain. There he was reduced to riding a hack so wretched that another officer scoffed that it would not fetch £5. Mellish promptly wagered that he could secure nine times as much – and spurred the hapless animal at speed towards the French lines, until it was shot dead beneath him. Mellish 'then went back on foot under a hail of shot, but the winner of the wager, since the government allowed £45 for every horse shot by the enemy'.

Trafalgar was a son of Gohanna, now the most expensive stallion in the land with a fee of 50 guineas per mare. Gohanna's Derby defeat by Waxy had initiated one of the great rivalries of the age, climaxing in a gladiatorial dogfight at Guildford in 1796. It was straight out of the heyday of Eclipse: a series of four-mile heats in one afternoon. Three times they slugged it out; three times they finished all out, neck and neck. First it was Waxy, by a nose; then a dead-heat; and at last Waxy again, by half a length. That settled it: even in so extreme a test, his speed could cut across the sheer guts of Gohanna.

Waxy was retired to The Friary stud, where Sir Ferdinando's former ward Bessy could bring her growing son to see the famous stallion. Percy Bysshe Shelley had inherited Bessy's love of riding and would one day, as icon of a new, romantic age, describe horses as 'shapes of some diviner element'. But it would be at Petworth, home of his old rival Gohanna, that Waxy would himself create a bridge into the new century – and a new era on the Turf – thanks to a colt named Whalebone born, in the spring of 1807, on the Duke of Grafton's stud near Newmarket.

In their youth, both Egremont and Grafton had been suffused with the sensuality and egotism common to so many rakes of their era. As they aged, however, they presented much altered faces to the new century: Egremont, a model of mellow paternalism; Grafton, a desiccated theologian. It was almost as though their chaotic moral compass, in the heyday of Charlotte Hayes, had finally settled on some distant, Victorian horizon of social responsibility. Grafton, the prime minister who took a whore to the opera, had since joined London's first Unitarian congregation, at Essex Street, and even published *Hints, & c. Submitted to the Serious Attention of the Clergy, Nobility and Gentry*, 'by a Layman'. Bird-like, his hair lank and cheeks hollowed, Grafton rocked on his heels, making captious, unpredictable pronouncements to the few whose society he tolerated. The masses, he declared, would never achieve spiritual improvement unless shown how. 'Rank and character seldom now meet with a suitable distinction,' he complained. 'In no country, at no time, [has] the bad example of superiors . . . operated so stupidly, and so generally, through every class of the people.'

Learning that Grafton was trying to balance the ledger against his moral debits, Walpole was beside himself. 'What a compound,' he exclaimed. 'A Prime Minister, a jockey, a missionary! So he is hedging off upon religion.' Himself aware of the incongruities, Grafton professed a daily regret that he 'had lost so many of the best days of my life in . . . indulgence of the fashionable vices of the age'. Significantly, however, a continued interest in the Turf remained perfectly consistent with his reformation. Bunbury's work at the Jockey Club was plainly beginning to pay off.

In 1802, Grafton won his first Derby with a son of Pot8os named Tyrant. Here was a first sign that his stud at Euston was perfecting a new genetic formula for the changing demands of the sport. It was based on the two champions bred by Grafton's political mentor, the Duke of Cumberland: Herod and Eclipse. Waxy's pedigree was ideal: he was by Eclipse's son, Pot8os, out of a daughter of Herod. Grafton had meanwhile bred a daughter of Herod's son, Highflyer, named Prunella. His combination of Prunella and her daughters with Pot8os and Waxy would create the combustion engine of the modern race-horse. (Pivotal to this process was the blood of the Darley Arabian: Prunella's pedigree contained no fewer than five separate strains, none through Eclipse.)

Grafton quickly identified Waxy as the obvious successor to Pot8os, and persuaded Sir Ferdinando's heir to sell him for just 300 guineas. By this stage the stallion had lost one eye, and he would eventually go blind in the other. But he retained the docile, companionable outlook that complemented his Arabian intelligence, forming a celebrated attachment to a particular rabbit, which ate from his manger and curled up against him when he lay down. Waxy's impact with the Euston mares proved explosive. Pope, his 1809 Derby winner, was a son of Prunella; and a year later came Whalebone, out of Prunella's daughter, Penelope.

Admittedly Whalebone lacked the elegance of his sire: one of his grooms remembered him as 'the lowest and longest and most double-jointed horse, with the best legs and the worst feet I ever saw'. When out training he would rear up 'and knock his feet together like a pair of castanets', on one occasion causing him to fall over three times in a single morning. But he could run, all right. His debut at Newmarket, just a month before the 1810 Derby, was so impressive he started 2–1 favourite at Epsom. Just like his sire, he was ridden by William Clift. Sent straight into the lead, he was in command a long way out and held off a colt named The Dandy with ease. It must have tickled Clift that the runner-up was a son of Waxy's old rival, Gohanna.

But a more important connection to 1793 was Robert Robson. Not yet thirty when he trained Waxy, Robson left Lewes soon afterwards to take over his late father's stable in Newmarket. Here he discovered an optimal combination between the horses bred at Euston, his trailblazing methods and the need for speed and precocity in Classic races. Some of the more progressive trainers, observing his success, began to adapt. Instead of tormenting horses with two long, hamster-wheel workouts, at 4 a.m. and 4 p.m., they began to send them out for a single, sharper spin at 8 a.m. Yet not even thirty-three Classic successes would be enough for Robson to win over the diehards.

Sam Chifney Sr., in his autobiography, had reprimanded Newmarket trainers for still flogging horses six miles under rugs and then trussing them in extra layers as soon as they returned to the stable. 'Nature cannot bear this,' he wrote. 'The horses must dwindle . . . The clothing and stoving him forces his juices from him in such quantities, must destroy their spirits, strength and speed; and much clothing jades horses.' Yet Chifney's own son, Will, would persevere in the old ways even when setting himself up as one of Robson's biggest rivals at Newmarket. As late as 1823, when Robson won his *seventh* Derby with Emilius, the Chifney brothers, Will and Sam Jr., were said to be 'persistently inflicting upon their Derby horses eight-mile sweats two or three times a week'. Will Chifney's 1820 Derby winner, Sailor, would even be joined by fresh horses, in stages, throughout his 'sweats'. One morning Sailor keeled over dead on the gallops. No wonder the Chifneys' horses were typically brought to post 'as fine as wax-work, but very light'. Aside from their punishing work regime, they were deliberately dehydrated: bled half a gallon weekly, and their water rationed.

Though Grafton himself died just ten months after Whalebone's Derby, the Euston pedigrees continued to blossom for his son, George, as the 4th Duke – above all in the new Classics over a bare mile. Robson achieved a virtual monopoly in the 1000 Guineas, with eight wins out of nine between 1819 and 1827. Fittingly, his last Classic winner, in the 1828 Oaks, was a granddaughter of Prunella.

Grafton horses were more consistent in character than Grafton dukes. On one occasion, having taken a fall in the hunting field,

George was crawling out of a ditch when a curate came thundering towards him. 'Lie still, your Grace!' he bellowed, before clearing hedge, ditch and duke, and careering away after the hounds without a glance over his shoulder. George got to his feet and announced: 'That young man shall have the first good living at my disposal.'

The year after Waxy beat Gohanna at Epsom, Egremont had sold his Piccadilly townhouse and retreated to Petworth. Not that the fourteen miles of his park wall ever sealed his estate from the world beyond. An American traveller was astonished by Egremont's indulgence of the agricultural proletariat. On summer nights, they poured in for fireworks and feasting, 'plum puddings and loaves piled like cannon-balls'. It is telling that during the Swing Riots, when hayricks were burned and threshing machines sabotaged throughout the south of England, one corner of Sussex was left virtually untouched.

In all, Egremont is reckoned to have devoted over £1 million to philanthropy. A typical story is told of a subscription at White's for a member in distress: Egremont gave £10,000 on condition that his donation was listed as £500. He provided Petworth with schools, doctors, running water and smallpox vaccinations. Tenant farmers were given free use of the Petworth stallions for their mares. Even William Cobbett confessed that 'every thing that I have ever heard of him makes me believe that he is worthy of this princely estate'. Above all, however, Egremont opened his doors to artists.

At a time when other stately homes were importing Old Masters and Italian neoclassicism, he felt a rare obligation to native talent. C. R. Leslie saluted 'the most munificent and . . . least ostentatious nobleman in England'. Benjamin Haydon, recently reprieved from a debtors' jail, was overwhelmed by his reception at Petworth. 'What a destiny is mine!' he wrote. 'One year in the Bench . . . on a flock bed, low & filthy, with black worms crawling over my hands – another, reposing in down & velvet, in a splendid apartment, in a splendid House, the guest of Rank & fashion & beauty!' Painters and sculptors found Egremont's patronage as relaxed as it was lavish. Turner and Francis Chantrey were as likely to be found fishing together on the lake as working in a studio. Charles Greville, in his diaries, compared Petworth to 'a great inn . . . Everybody came and went as they saw fit, and departed without notice or leave-taking.' Though one or two were evicted for pushing their luck, broadly speaking the sole condition of Egremont's hospitality was a reciprocal privacy.

He was forever disappearing down corridors, impossible to pin down in conversation. 'Plain spoken, almost to a degree of bluntness, he never wasted words, nor let others waste words on him,' Leslie wrote. 'After conferring the greatest favours, he was out of the room before there was time to thank him.' With age Egremont increasingly resembled a sort of Lord Emsworth-with-brains: diffident, benign and whimsical, impatient with formality and affectation. There was even an opulent piggery at Petworth, and it was not unknown for guests to be startled by a sow galloping through the house.

Creevey left a vivid account of the household when invited to stay during Goodwood races. Abandoned by a footman, his party was eventually discovered by a pretty young niece, who attempted a hazy tour of the masterpieces. Finally Egremont appeared, 'as extraordinary a person perhaps as any in England, certainly the most so of his own caste or order'. Though then approaching eighty, he could not disguise the vigour of his intellect even in bearing himself with such determined informality, keeping his hands in his pockets, and his remarks 'rambling and desultory'.

A staid visitor could complain of a 'want of comforts, of regularity, and still more the total absence of cleanliness'. The ancient, inbred staff were 'rustic and uncouth'. And guests could but wonder, as they admired a sculpture of Venus, which of their host's mistresses had been exposed for their inspection. Creevey was amused to see two of his party shown portraits of their mother and grandmother, respectively, all present having a pretty shrewd idea why their host should have wished to preserve them in their prime. One outlandish estimate credited Egremont with forty-three children swarming round the house, their mothers discreetly sequestered from view: 'But when any quarrels arise, which few days pass without, each Mother takes part with her Progeny, bursts into the room, fights with each other, Lord E., his children, and, I believe, the Company, and makes scenes worthy of Billingsgate or a Madhouse.' Whatever the true tally, Creevey was plainly indulging in gleeful innuendo when he remarked that Egremont had 'a very numerous stud'.

As many as three hundred horses were sometimes resident at Petworth, including sixty broodmares. In four runnings of the Derby, between 1804 and 1807, Egremont bred three winners and one short-head runner-up. True, the stud manager apparently confessed on his deathbed that two of its Epsom winners had been four-year-olds. (It will be recalled that the Classics are confined to three-year-olds.) But if sheer numbers and casual bookkeeping abetted any such deceit, Egremont himself was assuredly innocent of complicity.

Yet his greatest bequest to the Turf was an adventitious one. Whalebone only arrived at Petworth after being discarded first by the new Duke of Grafton, who deemed him too small to succeed as a stallion, and then by the heirs of his purchaser, who died soon afterwards. Perhaps Egremont liked the similarities between Whalebone and his sire, Waxy: both had exhibited modern speed in the Derby before spending their maturity robustly grinding through four-mile heats – an indignity that had almost entirely disappeared from Newmarket by 1772.

Whalebone started at stud with a fee of just 10 guineas, and was largely confined to resident mares. By the time Thomas Phillips made a last portrait of Egremont, however, a statuette of the stallion would be stationed proudly at his subject's elbow. Whalebone produced an Oaks winner from his second crop and in 1826 his son, Lapdog, gave Egremont a record fifth Derby, forty-four years after Assassin.*

Whalebone would provide the great genetic bridge between the sloggers of the eighteenth century and the sleek racehorses of the Victorian era. In the process, he complemented a rebirth in the owners of the estates where he began and ended his days: the reformation of Grafton, the rustication of Egremont. But Grafton, a contemporary of Grosvenor and Bully, had made a sullen and disjointed journey into the new century; Egremont, born sixteen years later than Grafton in 1751, maintained a far greater congruity. Like everyone else he had been obliged by revolution and war to disown the Francophilia of his youth. Looking back, Egremont

---

* Five years later Lapdog's brother, Spaniel, also won the race – but only after being sold off as a yearling.

credited a parallel renunciation in Charles James Fox to 'his supremacy in oratory and his love of horse racing, both anti-gallican amusements'. For Egremont, the Turf also helped to correct his macaroni excesses, to the extent that he even accepted the hospitality of Dennis O'Kelly at Clay Hill. But he never shared the panting, sordid frenzy of Grafton and his contemporaries, Bully and Grosvenor.

Egremont died after paying court to the young Queen Victoria at Brighton, where he caught a chill. Perhaps he cast his mind back, hobbling along the esplanade, to the old days there: to that faded moonbeam, Mellish; to Sir Ferdinando and the Prince of Wales. What would the demure young monarch have made of her late uncle's antics? The world seemed very different now. On the racecourse, however, it could not be described as a more innocent one.

PART III

Ringers and Wrong 'Uns

Sir Hercules (1826)
Birdcatcher (1833)
The Baron (1842)

9

Nobblers, Broken Heads and the 'artful dodger of the corps'

WHILE A DEGREE of temerity can seem nearly universal in those who depend on racehorses for a living, Thomas H. Masterman surely stands in a class of his own. A trainer in Middleham during the nineteenth century, Masterman sued a young jockey named James Cameron not for 'pulling' his horse, but for failing to do so. Cameron, he complained, was perfectly aware that he had backed another runner, on their mutual behalf, in a race at Newcastle. Yet he failed to prevent Masterman's horse – whose name, of all things, was Honesty – from winning. 'He could have pulled Honesty if he pleased,' Masterman told the judge. 'He won that race, however, against his own interest as well as mine, because he was drunk or tipsy. He said he could not help it. If he had been in his sober senses, he and Honesty would have been in the background.'

If the suit seems breathtaking, then what can be said of the verdict? The judge, sharing the indignation of Masterman, ordered Cameron to pay £82 6s to the injured party. Still more remarkably, this case was heard as late as 1872. Thirty-five years into a reign considered synonymous with a new morality, it is plain that some Turf incorrigibles were still clinging to the pernicious habits of old.

The Jockey Club, to be fair, had already banned Masterman from Newmarket; and, as will be seen, did so in the knowledge that racing was achieving a new respectability. Nonetheless, it is important to recognise that the whole painful process had been deliberately retarded, at the beginning of the century, by many of the Jockey Club's own members.

At that time the racing elite had found the perfect bogeyman in Daniel Dawson. He was poor, scraping a living as a tout in Newmarket; and he was almost certainly in the pay of the sinister

Bland brothers, whose low cunning and uncouth bearing appeared so typical of the new profession of bookmaking. Dawson had dissolved arsenic in a water trough on Newmarket Heath before the first meeting of 1811. Four racehorses died in agony, including The Dandy, second to Whalebone in the previous year's Derby. The Jockey Club offered a 500-guinea reward for information leading to an arrest. Once sentenced to be hanged, however, Dawson derided its members for a hollow stunt, declaring that 'there were not three fair, upright bettors amongst them'. And it is certainly true that many within the racing establishment would persevere, for many years yet, in policing the Turf only to protect their own interests.

On the one hand, a series of exemplary sportsmen seemed to be exorcising the salacious ghosts of Grosvenor and Bully. Grafton's heir George, for one; or the Earl of Jersey, who bought Whalebone's sister from Euston to start a stud in Oxfordshire. Tall and stately, and one of the most dashing huntsmen in the annals of the Quorn, Jersey invested £400,000 in the breeding of thoroughbreds but had little interest in betting. 'He raced for the love of the sport,' stressed one historian. 'There was no mercenary taint about his patronage.'

At the same time, the changing face of the sport was creating new opportunities for the unscrupulous. With bigger fields running over shorter distances, it was easier for a jockey to inflate the odds for a future race by keeping his mount blocked off at the rear. But while nobody knew the true merit of horses better than the professionals hired to train or ride them, it was their wealthy patrons who regarded inside information as a sacred privilege. Since most of them were members of the Jockey Club, the rules against corruption were almost invariably applied in defence of their own prerogatives – against jockeys and trainers, touts and bookmakers – even as they absolved themselves of all kinds of grubby chicanery. One writer, in the year of the queen's accession, became so disgusted he even invoked the memory of Grosvenor as 'a great ornament to the English Turf' for the simple reason that 'he ran his horses honestly and truly'.

In the circumstances, who could blame a jockey for helping himself to a piece of the action? It was rare to receive even a token cut of the fortunes routinely staked by his masters. He was expected to starve himself, in order to keep his weight down; and then to risk his neck for a standard fee of 3 guineas, or 5 for a winner. It was only fear of bribery, rather than shame over their own parsimony, that eventually caused owners to start giving handsome presents to jockeys after big wins. Entering this industrial, urban age, after all, nothing did more to encourage the nervous conflation of poverty and moral delinquency by the ruling classes than the melodramas of the Turf.

By 1829, the St Leger meeting had lost its boisterous, country inno-cence. Year by year, the Ridings gentry found the crowded pavements of Doncaster ever more claustrophobic. This was the last time they would see their ancient talisman, Jemmy Hirst, driving his home-made wickerwork carriage to the races, a pet fox trotting alongside; the last time they admired his waistcoat of drake feathers, his lambskin hat with a circumference of nine feet. Hirst used to go shooting from the back of a bull, employing trained pigs as pointers, and once even crashed a flying machine into the Humber. A month after this meeting, Hirst would finally convert his drinks cabinet to its intended use as a coffin. He must have felt as though he had seen enough at last.

Thieves had always been drawn to racetracks. It was after stealing a gold watch at one that George Barrington, the eighteenth-century prince of pickpockets, was sent to Botany Bay. Itinerant fraternities of petty criminals now toured the circuit, combining to resist any intervention by officers. An arrest at Brighton races in 1822, for instance, resulted in a riot and the stoning of a magistrate. But never had this underworld circus assembled in such numbers as for this St Leger meeting. On its eve, hearing rumours that the dragoons were on their way, they mounted an extraordinary show of strength. As many as seven hundred assorted thimbleriggers, felons and bruisers paraded through the town, brandishing the oak legs of their gaming tables, before setting up camp by the racecourse. The squires of Yorkshire, invoking the spirit of John Hutton, decided to take matters into their own hands. Next morning a miscellany of bloodthirsty huntsmen and their servants launched an amateur cavalry charge across Town Moor. One by one, to horns and cries of 'Tally-Ho', the enemy were flushed from their barricades and chased down in open country. 'Many heads were broken' and 150 sentenced to hard labour at Wakefield Gaol.

This triumph lent extra gusto to the usual St Leger revels: plays and banquets, cocking and prizefights, balls at the Mansion House. Even here, though, they had to beware of the new urban predators. A young Polish countess, for example, had a few months earlier excited frenzied competition among local hostesses with her charming, broken English, mourning a husband whose death fighting the Turks had so grieved his great friend the Tsar. She had run up considerable accounts by the time she was cheerfully accosted at a public breakfast by a passing redcoat: 'What! Rose? Can I believe my eyes? What wind has blown you here? Your old friends in Weedon barracks are quite *au désespoir* at your departure.'

But the most insidious trickery of all was suspected in the big race itself. For days it had been whispered that at least one St Leger fancy had, in the sardonic vernacular, been 'made safe'. His name was Sir Hercules. In due course, as a stallion, Sir Hercules would emerge as the principal heir of Whalebone. Though his pedigree united the precious bloodlines of Euston and Petworth, Egremont had discarded his mother, while pregnant, to a horse dealer in Ulster; and the resulting foal had in turn been sold to (and named after) Hercules Rowley, Baron Langford, at his estate in Co. Meath. For now, Sir Hercules remained a relatively unknown quantity: he had begun his career in Ireland, and his owner seemed prey to provincial delusions in sending him across to Billy Pierse at Richmond to be trained for the St Leger. All Sir Hercules had ever done, it seemed, was outclass a rabble of ill-bred, ill-trained bogtrotters. But then he had won his first race in England and somebody, somewhere in the shadows of the betting market, had decided not to take any unnecessary chances.

The malign influence of early bookmakers was probably exaggerated. Since Harry Ogden had first posted odds against the field, a 'ring' of low-born entrepreneurs, illiterate but highly numerate, had begun offering prices against each individual runner. But these professional layers could only stay in business by paying promptly and uncomplainingly. If anything, their advent had magnified the ethical shortcomings of their highborn customers. Certainly book-makers could not be said to have introduced the practice of 'nobbling'. Back in 1778, for instance, 'one of the best Mares in the kingdom' died shortly before a race at Boroughbridge; the post-mortem disclosed two pounds of duck-shot in her stomach. To some extent the disparagement of bookmakers was probably a reflection of social prejudice. It is true that 'Facetious' Jemmy Bland was connected not only with Daniel Dawson but also the corruption of cricketers. But his greatest offence, having started out as a postilion, was to buy himself a Piccadilly mansion when his character was etched so coarsely upon his features 'that if you had met him eating birds' nests in Pekin with chopsticks you would have known he was a [black] leg'.

Whoever had contrived the lameness of Sir Hercules, it would take all of Billy Pierse's skill to patch him up for the St Leger. Pierse, whose father had fought under Cumberland at Culloden, had come recommended as a cherished veteran of the northern circuit. He had started out with a strolling theatre before riding a first match, at Brass-Side Moor near Durham, weighing 3st 7lbs. One of the most belligerent practitioners of the 'cross-and-jostle' era, he always held his position even if it meant forcing his rivals through a hedge. But his character showed best when he ended an incipient brawl between the two jockeys who had finished in front of him by trot-ting back to the judge and asking: 'How far did I win, Mr Tomline?' 'You, Mr Pierse? Why, you were beaten three lengths.' 'Thank you, sir. That alters the case materially.' By the time the laughter subsided, all differences had been forgotten.

Those had been halcyon days in Yorkshire: the era of John Shaw, of Alicia Thornton. Shaw had ridden the last of his novelty matches in 1800, when challenged to travel 174 miles to the Vine Inn, Bishopsgate, in twelve hours, any conveyance permissible 'with the exception of a balloon'. He needed just over eight hours in the saddle, then 'walked on crutches for four months, and his beard never grew after'. Mrs Thornton, for her part, rode a famous match against her brother-in-law, Captain Flint, in front of 100,000 spec-tators at York in 1804. Though decorously riding side-saddle, her figure-hugging leopard-print jacket caused much excitement. There was universal disappointment when her saddle slipped after leading for three of the four miles. Flint horsewhipped her husband for defaulting on a side-bet, and refused a rematch — wisely enough, given that Mrs Thornton returned to York the following year to win a match against Frank Buckle himself.

But such capers, full-blooded and innocent, seemed a long time ago now. A new, urban underclass was silting up on the racetrack, desperate characters who derided the simple faiths of men like Pierse. Known across the Yorkshire Turf as 'T'auld 'un', he had never had a bet in his life and confined his reading entirely to the Bible and Adam Smith's *The Wealth of Nations*, each of which he was said to have read thirty times. You can see him shaking his head as Sir Hercules was trotted up and down the yard. The colt had always been so light over the ground. How had it happened? How could anyone deliberately harm this charming creature? Sir Hercules was very compact and his coat, curiously, was one of many colours: black in winter, brown in autumn, flecked white in summer. Most depressing of all was the likelihood of some connivance by one of his own grooms. Pierse vowed that he would do everything in his power to get Sir Hercules back on track in time for the big race.

The Classics were slowly maturing into the apogee of the new style of racing. Nonetheless, the St Leger retained a distinctive local quality, and would do so as long as southern runners were obliged to trek the Great North Road on foot. In 1800 a son of Pot8os had become the first Derby winner to follow up in the St Leger. But that feat would not be emulated until 1848 and the coming of the railways. Neither the 3rd nor the 4th Duke of Grafton, for instance, sent any of the horses they ran in other Classics up for a St Leger. Perhaps they were wary of 'the Northern jockeys, who were dreadfully jealous in those days of having their great prize snatched from them by a Southern Derby winner, and still worse by a Newmarket jockey'. When eight false starts had scuppered the Derby winner, in 1827, many presumed the starter to have been bribed. But it may simply have been that the Yorkshire riders had ganged up on Sam Chifney Jr.

Now, two years on, Chifney was back with a big chance on a colt named Voltaire. He had taken his father's trademark 'rush', cutting down the leaders in the last strides, to a new level: the faster pace of modern racing was proving tailor-made to his exceptional judgement of pace. 'The present Samuel Chifney presents the beau ideal of a jockey,' pronounced one contemporary writer. 'Elegance of seat, perfection of hand, judgment of pace all united, and power in the saddle beyond any man of his weight that ever yet sat in one.'

At the same time, his aversion to racing near the lead made even admirers nervous: 'Let whatever number of horses start, Chifney is almost certain to be amongst the last until towards the end of the race, when he creeps up to his brother jockeys in a manner peculiarly his own.' Of course, it looked marvellous when it came off: coolly biding his time until the excessive pace told, often stealing a prize at the post from superior horses by dint of his daring and timing – not to mention 'a cut with his whip that would have . . . made the Bronze Horse at Venice spring from its pedestal'. But it was not just his stealth that prompted Chifney's reputation as 'the artful dodger of the corps'. He had also renewed the aspersions once raised against his father, allegedly pulling a filly named Manuella when second favourite for the 1812 Derby. She won the Oaks the next day, landing him a bet of £2,000 to £100.

His brother, William, had also restored the Chifney name in Newmarket – in his case, as a trainer, albeit one who persisted in the methods exposed by his great rival, Robson. He had married a bookmaker's daughter and was constantly engineering betting coups. One way or another, backers of Voltaire were nervous of the Chifney connection. Tactics on the colt would be closely monitored; it would not be difficult, after all, to find traffic problems among eighteen rivals.

By now this was a typical St Leger field: in 1825 as many as thirty horses had lined up. As a result the start had become a new focus for suspicion and corruption. False starts could be contrived by jockeys, the starter himself, and even owners who entered 'half-trained and half-broken brutes' solely to upset a fancied but temperamental rival. The whole procedure was hopelessly vague, the starter simply shouting 'Go!' and waving his hat the moment he reckoned the field roughly in line. Whether by accident or design, the starter's orders were often anticipated – requiring the field to be summoned back by a bugler. It sometimes took an hour to get the field away.

This was the fourth running of the St Leger since it had been reduced to its present distance of 1 mile 6 furlongs 132 yards: a severe test of a three-year-old today, but then still perceived as something of a sprint. Jockeys found themselves making knife-edge, split-second calls on pace and position – and seldom had their judgement been tested as transparently as in this race.

For the two most famous riders in the field, Sam Chifney Jr. and Bill Scott, could not have played their cards more diversely. Yorkshire's darling, Scott, was setting 'a very tremendous and severe pace' on Rowton. Chifney, as usual, was restraining Voltaire right at the back. The crowd here had never felt much affection for Chifney: they thought him lazy and arrogant. He seldom dignified the great northern meetings with his presence; in fact, he had only won twice at York and once at Doncaster. So what was he up to now? Did he think Scott had gone too hard? Or was he making some less honourable calculation?

Pat Conolly was keeping Sir Hercules much closer to the pace. Turning for home, he wondered whether the work his mount had missed, while Pierse nursed him through his lameness, would now begin to tell. But the little fellow was not just hanging in there: he was closing, from fourth to third, and now from third to second. Just a length down, with a couple of furlongs to go: and Scott's horse would surely begin to tire soon. Certainly Chifney seemed to be banking on that. Voltaire was cutting through the pack at his leisure, eventually arriving on the heels of the leading group. As the crowd bayed impatiently, Chifney finally started pushing. One by one, Voltaire picked off his rivals until only Sir Hercules and Rowton were still holding out. At last, deep into the straight, Sir Hercules began to tread water. But Scott was in a manic overdrive, and only now did Chifney reach for his whip.

In the new stand, subscribed by sixty shareholders at 30 guineas apiece, even the Iron Duke was gripped.* Surely Rowton could not

---

* Although Wellington was no great man of the Turf, his charger at Waterloo had been a grandson of Eclipse – a distinction that qualified its dam as the only 'half-bred' mare in the *Stud Book*.

hold out: his owner, Edward Petre, had won the race for the last two years – not to mention the 1822 running, when Jemmy Bland laid £100 to a walking stick round the corner at the Salutation Inn against Petre's notorious cripple, Theodore. Petre had surely used up his full allowance of good fortune. And yes, look, Rowton was swaying now, all but legless, as Voltaire came bounding alongside. Just half a length to find, and Sir Hercules gamely hanging in there too. As the post loomed, that little dervish Scott conjured one last paroxysm of effort from Rowton – and suddenly both horse and rider sloughed into a lurching, heaving walk, like a poisoned old centaur; and Voltaire rolled on by, full of vim. Too late. At the line, there was still a neck in it.

The chances are that this was a highly artistic ride by Chifney. Had he squared up to the dour Rowton earlier, Voltaire might well have tired and dropped away. But not everyone was convinced. 'Surely Chifney could not think it policy to lay so far out of his ground as he did,' mused the *Sporting Magazine*'s correspondent. 'And why he did so is for him to say, not I.' Voltaire's trainer evidently had his suspicions, as well, proposing a rematch against Rowton with different jockeys. But another reporter rebuked Chifney's critics: Voltaire, asked to challenge sooner, would only have folded sooner. In the idiom of the time, Rowton was 'a horse of infinitely greater bottom' – stamina, that is, and guts.

Perhaps both colts should have been beaten. Sir Hercules went under by less than a length, despite his interrupted preparation. He had, attested the *Sporting Magazine*, shown himself to be 'an uncommon good horse, and, had he not . . . been amiss a short time before the race, would have run very near winning'. It would have been a momentous breakthrough for the Irish. On the other hand, Sir Hercules had been conceived in England and returned there too soon for the Irish to claim a transfer of the Darley Arabian's legacy. This distinction would be reserved for his son, Birdcatcher.

10

The West Awake

L IKE A SHIFTED weathervane catching the sun, Birdcatcher sparkled as a wind of change blew across his homeland. Foaled four years after the Catholic Emancipation Act of 1829, he was a bona fide Irish thoroughbred. True, he raced under the aegis of Anglo-Irish landlords who supervised the Turf of Ireland as ruthlessly as the rest of her soil, but the fact remains that both his parents had been born and raced here, and he would in turn sire a son to propagate the genius of Irish horsemanship.

Horses pervade Ireland's history and culture. Young Cúchulainn had tamed two, risen from a magic lake, by clinging to their manes as they galloped madly round the island. Racing on the Curragh dates back to pagan times. The medieval Brehon Laws stipulated that such open greens, used for *aonach* or sporting fairs, should be left free of obstruction so that racing would be unimpeded. Art MacMurrough-Kavanagh, King of Leinster, rode to meet Richard II upon a white horse 'said to have cost him 400 cows'. Other Irish noblemen imported fleet, nimble mounts from Asturias: these evolved into the Irish hobby, itself a key seeder of the English thoroughbred. By 1498 the Duke of Ferrara was sending an agent to Henry VII seeking hobbies from Ireland. A century later, the first page of John Dymmok's *Treatise of Ireland* extolled 'excellent horses of a fine feature and wonderfull swyftnes . . . thought to be a kinde of the race of the Spanish Genetts'. In time, Barbs and Arabians were also imported, several via Yorkshire – a typical, concentric eddy of the equine gene pool. The first formally recorded race over the Curragh, in 1741, was won by a daughter of Almanzor, a stallion bred by the Darleys from their Arabian.

Irish horsemanship, meanwhile, found pioneering expression in

1752 with the famous, improvised 'steeplechase' between the spires of Buttevant and Doneraile in Co. Cork. 'Certainly it is only in Ireland that one sees all that horses are capable of,' concluded the German Prince Pückler-Muskau, after hunting in Co. Tipperary in the 1820s. 'The English are far behind them in this respect . . . Only very early and perfect training, joined to the excellence of the breed, can produce such [horses].' But he also described a stee-plechase meeting at Athenry as 'exactly suited to a half-savage nation', the horses staggering through a merciless series of heats over a course of stone walls. The prince watched aghast as 'a hand-some young man of good family' mounted on the finest horse at the meeting, was flung to his death. 'His old father . . . fell senseless on the ground, and his sister threw herself with heart-rending cries on the yet palpitating but unconscious body. But the general sympathy was very slight. After the poor young man had been repeatedly bled, so that he lay on the turf weltering in his own blood, he was taken away, and the race began again at the appointed time as if nothing had happened.'

Nor could the Irish horse fail to register generations of feudal conquest and confiscation. In 1695, for instance, Catholics were prohibited ownership of any horse worth £5. The dispossessed majority only ever had one champion: Irish Lass, winner of a famous grudge match against Black and All Black in 1749. Her rival had been imported from England by a local baronet, Sir Ralph Gore, to avenge wounds suffered fighting a brigade of Irish Jacobites at Fontenoy; but the mare won the day with a rosary looped through her bridle. Oliver Goldsmith had been in no doubt of the political subtext, sarcastically recording 'a benevolent subscription on foot among the nobility and gentry of this kingdom, who are great patrons of merit, in order to assist Black and All Black in his contest with the Paddereen Mare'. (*Paidrín* being Irish for rosary.) The story was evoked many generations later, when Orby won the 1907 Derby at Epsom for 'Boss' Croker of Tammany Hall. His Irish trainer was accosted by an old lady, who exclaimed: 'Thank God and you, sir, we have lived to see a Catholic horse win the Derby!'

But the unprecedented, non-violent mobilisation of the masses under Daniel O'Connell had been complemented, in the years following the 1829 Act, by new self-respect among Irish horsemen. In 1834 the English were obliged to salute both a jockey and a horse from over the water: first Pat Conolly rode the winner of the Derby, and then Bran became Ireland's first Classic runner-up in the St Leger. The training grooms of the Curragh, little more than lodge-keepers when compared to their celebrated peers in England, were also beginning to achieve greater professional standing. Rossmore Lodge, for instance, had been built for Baron Rossmore but was soon to be leased to a fiery rider and breeder from Ulster, Tom Ferguson.

It was here that Sir Hercules was making a brief sojourn while his owner, Baron Langford, prepared to sell off his entire stud in response to a lawsuit by his estranged wife. Sir Hercules had started off back in Co. Meath as an itinerant country sire, walked between fairs and markets to cover farm and hunt mares at a fee of 5 shillings plus a glass of whiskey for the groom. One of his first thoroughbred partners at Rossmore Lodge was a little chestnut mare, Guiccioli, named after Byron's mistress. Though Guiccioli won several races, she was painfully lacking in pedigree or substance and had at one stage been offered for just £30 at Kilkenny races. One countryman was tempted until a friend intervened. 'Why would you want such a cat of a thing?' he asked. 'She'll never breed hunters.' Eventually she found her way to Brownstown, one of the sporting lodges on the Curragh, where George Knox sent her next door to be mated with the visiting stallion.

The following spring Guiccioli delivered a neat, nimble chestnut colt with a blaze, flecks of grey in his rump and an exceptionally light, buoyant way of covering the ground. Named Birdcatcher, he was in due course transferred to Knox's neighbour, William Disney of Lark Lodge, to be trained. Lark Lodge was an oddity – a Georgian bungalow with its own ballroom and a quaint, circular beehive of a gatehouse – and the regime retained an eighteenth-century aspect, with a groom named Mathew Foley both training and riding the horses.

Foley started off Birdcatcher in a race for two-year-olds, on the track adjacent to his stable in October 1835. Evidently the colt was too green to cope with a filly named Caroline, already a winner and herself purported to be sired by Sir Hercules. Caroline was owned by Edward Ruthven Jr., MP for Co. Kildare. Though Protestant, the Ruthvens were outspoken supporters of the campaign against tithes, the hated agricultural levy for the upkeep of the Church of Ireland. Instructively, pasturage had long been exempted from tithe assessment – a conspicuous boon to the Anglo-Irish stud owners. True, the Irish Turf was not uniformly hostile to Catholic emancipation, Baron Rossmore being one eminent supporter. But there were plenty of bigots at the Turf Club agog when rumours began to circulate that Caroline was a 'ringer' – a three-year-old running in races confined to two-year-olds.

In her next start, Caroline routed a colt owned by Lord Milltown. He immediately asked George Watts – an English vet and breeder, whose status on the Curragh made him the automatic choice for so delicate an assignment – to examine Caroline's teeth (still the standard way to ascertain a horse's age). Watts declined a definitive verdict but tentatively accepted that the filly might be a year older than stated. That was good enough for Milltown, who immediately lodged an objection.

Ruthven, protesting himself the victim of a blatant witch-hunt, claimed to have documentation identifying Caroline as a two-year-old by Sir Hercules. But Milltown received intelligence from England that a three-year-old filly with precisely the same markings had recently been exported by Ruthven. Ordered by the Turf Club to produce Caroline, Ruthven refused 'to submit the filly to the inspection of vagabonds said to be brought from England . . . Ten thousand men could be got for ten sovereigns each to swear that she is not the mare.' Nor did Ruthven himself appear at the inquiry. In their absence a famous Newmarket jockey, Nat Flatman, verified the true identity not only of Caroline but another of Ruthven's recent winners.

Ruthven had already resigned from the Turf Club, ostensibly in disgust over his treatment, rendering his expulsion unnecessary. O'Connell, horrified by the scandal, implored Ruthven to stand down as MP for the 1837 elections. He could not repair Ruthven's name in Ireland, but offered £1,000 and 'the first vacant colonial situation you think worth your acceptance'. Ruthven proved stubborn. 'The people are to a man for me,' he bragged. 'Such is the popularity and influence I possess among them, I could were it wanting or could it be useful, bring twenty thousand labourers who would be guided by me together at any point I wish in any of the five neighbouring counties.'

O'Connell was left with no choice but to endorse the Whig candidates. In a letter to the Kildare electorate, he denounced the owner of Caroline as 'convicted of crimes which were in the eyes, not only of gentlemen, but of every honest man however humble, of the most disgraceful nature . . . nothing short of swindling and false swearing'. The Turf Club had published its findings for circulation among every member of the Commons, daring Ruthven to sue for libel. As it was, Ruthven's spluttering reply to O'Connell did not include a syllable about the Caroline case. On election day, the two Whig candidates received 762 and 728 votes respectively; the Tory, 228; and the incumbent Ruthven, 2.

By the spring of 1836 Birdcatcher had strengthened into a colt full of brio. Two wins at the start of the season established speed as his clear forte, and in a couple of subsequent defeats he was perhaps simply outstayed in heavy going. One way or another, nobody could be prepared for what he did at the October meeting. Taken on by a couple of very useful rivals for the Peel Stakes, over 14 furlongs, Birdcatcher careered so far clear that the winning margin was reckoned 'over five hundred yards'. Foley could not pull him up before the cavalry barracks on the turnpike, nearly two miles down the road. 'Such a performance,' wrote one observer, 'has rarely been seen on any racecourse.'

Unfortunately, Disney rewarded Birdcatcher for this exertion by running him again the next day. It was widely thought that the horse, unsurprisingly too exhausted to show his form, never really recovered from this misuse. Nonetheless, he was able to win twice the following season before a showdown with Harkaway – probably the best race staged, to that point, on Irish turf.

The magnificent sorrel Harkaway was bred and owned by Ferguson, the irascible Ulsterman who had taken over at Rossmore Lodge, a brilliant manipulator of horses and a brazen one of odds.

Ferguson's effrontery extended to decanting Captain Becher into a ditch when riding in the Grand National, his victim forever cementing his name to the 'brook' by declaring water to be 'damned cold stuff without brandy in it'. Ferguson's trainer was evidently every bit as feisty as his master, on one occasion only able to watch a race atop a haycock, disguised as a woman, having ended a binge the previous night by 'wallopin' some Peelers with a flail'.

Birdcatcher squared up to Harkaway over a mile, in the Northumberland Handicap — a type of race increasingly in vogue since the expansion of field sizes. Gradually the concept of using weight to close a gap in maturity or class, long familiar in match racing, had been adapted with increasing intricacy to the sweepstakes model. As Birdcatcher was in this instance carrying 20lbs more than his junior, Harkaway, he could be strictly acclaimed the best horse despite a narrow defeat. His reputation remained such that 'many of the oldest and best judges thought him the fastest horse that ever ran in Ireland'.

Harkaway was all but invincible in Ireland, the occasional reverse likely to have been contrived by an owner who once went so far as to steer a favourite not only off the course but into the sea. Eventually Ferguson tired of Harkaway bullying mediocre horses at unprofitable odds. 'It's just not worthwhile here to rob,' he grumbled. So he took Harkaway to England and won two Goodwood Cups, the former factory apprentice exulting in the humiliation of patrician rivals. One tried to buy the horse, presuming that he could easily buy out this Irish lout. He was soon put straight. 'The price is 6,000 guineas,' Ferguson announced. 'And I hunt him twice a week!'

Birdcatcher was meanwhile retired to stud. Disney's first advertisement was scrupulously restrained: 'likely to turn out as good a sire as his own which is as much as a moderate man can expect'. Yet he was soon promoting 'the best sire in Ireland', one of whose two-year-olds had changed hands for £2,000, an astounding sum for an Irish horse. Birdcatcher was quickly in demand on both sides of the sea, shuttling between the Curragh and a variety of studs in England. In the process, he was to transform perceptions of the Irish thoroughbred.

The contemporary record contains one fleeting suggestion that not everyone was comfortable with the proceedings against Edward

Ruthven. In appearing before the final inquiry, George Watts again only 'partly corroborated' the evidence of a veterinary colleague who had obliged Milltown and the Turf Club with a less equivocal second opinion.

But then Watts was no mere hireling; no meek, middle-class toady, nervous of upsetting aristocratic patrons. Though he testified before the stewards in a professional capacity, he did so as one of their peers. At sixty-three, he was one of the most successful breeders in Ireland and master of Jockey Hall, one of the Curragh lodges neighbouring those of Disney and Knox. He had come a long way since his arrival from England in 1800, as junior veterinary surgeon to the Royal Dublin Society.

His wife, Harriet Mackinnon, had doubtless accelerated their rise in Dublin society. Her brother was a famous general while her sister, having once refused the hand of a young Corsican officer, enabled Robert Southey, in his history of the Peninsular Wars, to confirm as 'one of the redeeming points of Buonaparte's character that he never forgot his attachment to the Mackinnon family'. Napoleon was overcome with emotion on hearing that Major General Henry Mackinnon had been killed in a moonlit assault on the walls of Ciudad Rodrigo in 1812. 'The perfect soldier,' Southey gushed. 'Perhaps this country has never sustained so great a loss since the death of Sir Philip Sidney.'

Watts himself, meanwhile, was soon recognised as an exceptional and innovative equine practitioner. Some lotions and ointments bearing his name were still in wide use at the end of the century. As a breeder, moreover, he had an uncanny knack of bringing together mares and stallions that cancelled out each other's defects.

Soon after the Ruthven affair, no doubt encouraged by his combustible neighbour, Tom Ferguson, Watts paired a mare named Miss Pratt with Harkaway's sire, Economist, a grandson of Waxy. One who happened to be present for the delivery of the resulting foal declared her 'frightful' and Watts plainly agreed. He named her Echidna after the mother of several foul monsters in Greek myth, and vowed on the spot that he would not waste time racing her. As soon as she was three years old he sent Echidna to Brownstown to be mated with Birdcatcher – albeit not before first trying to sell her to a priest for £20. Fortunately he does not seem to have been the most ascetic of clergymen, as he apologised that he needed a rather sturdier mount to convey him on his parish rounds.

Echidna's son, a dark chestnut foaled in the spring of 1842, was given a more flattering name: The Baron. Watts proposed this as a rebuke to a German visitor of that rank, who disparaged the young colt as doomed to obscurity. If not quite as disfigured as his mother, The Baron's head certainly had a looming, clumsy aspect. His feet were prone to abscesses, and his 'savage' temperament required the use of a muzzle. On the other hand, Birdcatcher had stamped his son's shoulders and torso with refinement and quality.

Unraced at two, The Baron thrilled Watts with his preparations for a debut on his home track in the spring of 1845 – so much so that he could not conceal his astonishment, leaning weakly upon a great twisted staff, when the horse finished well beaten. The Baron beat the winner just two days later, however, his tender feet now cushioned by leather pads and his owner's smarting pride by a judicious wager. In his next start, The Baron evoked his sire's landmark performance over the same Turf nine years previously, both his rivals being completely tailed off. Watts could already see that The Baron would never discover his full potential until tried in England.

After all, a brother to Birdcatcher had just given the Irish their first success in an English Classic: Faugh-a-Ballagh, in the 1844 St Leger. Watts was duly emboldened to send The Baron over to Liverpool in July, to test the water. In the stands was John Scott, the most successful northern trainer in history, whose Whitewall stable at Malton had already produced nine St Leger winners in just fifteen years. The Baron arrived on Merseyside in deplorable condition: 'as fat as a bull' in one account, his feet shod to protect 'fearfully festered soles'. Unsurprisingly, he faded at the end of the race. But he had shown enough raw ability, covering the first mile with gusto, to prompt Scott to seek out Watts afterwards. 'If you will send that horse to Whitewall without delay,' he said, 'he shall win the Doncaster Leger for you.'

I I

'I see a rum set in my day . . .
But these beat all calculation.'

PERHAPS JOHN SCOTT had been reminded of Touchstone, a colt he had first seen running down the field at the equivalent Liverpool meeting, eleven years previously. Touchstone was likewise sent on to his stables, but got loose on the moors after his groom called at one inn too many and eventually surfaced in Sheffield. When finally brought to Whitewall, his work was so limp that Scott's brother, Bill, preferred to ride the yard's other runner in the St Leger. Touchstone won at 50–1. While the hot favourite was almost certainly doped, that did not diminish universal astonishment that Touchstone had managed to beat the rest on merit.

Scott had become the first celebrity trainer, whose name outranked those of his patrons. Owners who wished to benefit from his skills had to do so on his terms. At fifty, he had already saddled eighteen Classic winners and would eventually be responsible for forty-one. If Robson had secured respect, Scott was achieving outright veneration.

Yet Whitewall was actually a bastion of the old school. Since Robson's retirement, there had been a widespread retrenchment of the punishing 'sweats' regime he had seemed to discredit – so much so in these parts that they were now known as 'Yorkshire sweats'. Scott's programme, as recalled later in the century by a trainer who learned his trade at Whitewall, was orientated towards substance and stamina rather than speed: 'They used to put three or four heavy rugs over a horse and give him a four-mile 'sweat', and scrape the lather off him in what was called the rubbing house . . . Scott was a great believer in that sort of thing.' Moreover, Scott would carry a lance in his waistcoat pocket and regularly 'take a quart of blood from a horse to cool him down and lighten him up'.

Yorkshire, once the nursery of the thoroughbred, was staging a revival on the Turf. The springy moorland of Middleham and Malton, along with enduring redoubts at Richmond and Hambleton, sustained many of the first great public trainers in a golden era that lasted until the 1870s. Newmarket, conversely, was on the ropes. Between 1788 and 1832, Newmarket had produced forty-two Derby winners; in Scott's heyday, between 1833 and 1862, it mustered three.

Scott was not wholly averse to innovation, laying down a two-mile woodchip gallop over Langton Wold for when the ground dried out in midsummer. And he enthusiastically embraced transportation of his runners by van, and then train, when some old-timers treated 20 miles of road as part of a horse's daily conditioning.

But it was in his professional stature that Scott broke new ground. In the 1830s a typical private trainer was on an annual salary of £200. Scott was able to charge £2 a week per horse in a stable of up to a hundred. His patrons ranged from the 14th Earl of Derby, three times prime minister, to 'Crutch' Robinson, a bookmaker 'blanched by time, shouting out his odds, and dealing in the lowest bitter sarcasm and racing slang, either mounted on a four-legged brute, as rough as himself, or leaning on his trusty crutch'. All ranks dined at the Whitewall table, Scott carving their mutton himself with a knife mounted on the shank-bone of Rowton, the St Leger winner he had trained to beat Sir Hercules: one plate handed to the sybaritic Lord Chesterfield, who required a butler even to hold a telescope to his eye; the next to an old jockey down on his luck, 'who had shuffled up on his arthritic pony'.

Only John Scott could ever have lent dignity to the dastardly partnership of John Gully and Robert Ridsdale, and still preserved so pristine a reputation. Gully had been an unknown, bankrupt butcher when redeemed from jail by Henry Mellish to go sixty-four rounds in the prize ring with Henry Pearce, 'the Game Chicken', before a vast crowd that included Byron and the future King William IV. By the time he retired from the prize ring, he was a national celebrity and able to set himself up as publican and bookmaker in Lincoln's Inn. Working with Harry Hill, a former boot-black and thimblerigger, Gully did not just lay and back horses in his own name but also served as 'commissioner' to place or lay bets on behalf of owners, trainers or jockeys anxious to exploit inside information.

Before the telegraph, knowledge was power in the betting market. The secret trial of a Derby favourite could have explosive consequences: he might set the Heath ablaze, or hobble back to his stable with a tendon injury. Given that trainers, jockeys and grooms were all closer to the action, an owner valued their discretion as highly as their skill. He regarded himself as uniquely entitled to lay 'a dead 'un' and righteously denounced the ethics of touts or bookmakers who beat him to the odds – even as his commissioners were seeking bets from other gentlemen on a horse he knew to be lame. Whatever the substance of the aspersions against some bookmakers, it was only ever 'a battle of kites and crows'.

Few knew better than Gully and Hill how to trace toxic patterns in the market to particular stables or owners; and, conversely, how to cover their own tracks. On one occasion, Hill managed to spread stakes of £46,000 on a Derby colt in just two hours. As a commissioner, it was said, 'you have to hunt betting men in the metropolis as you hunt red deer in the Highlands and must be thoroughly acquainted with their trysting places, hours and habits'.

By 1827 Gully was able to buy Lord Jersey's Derby winner, Mameluke, for 4,000 guineas, and absorb a loss of £40,000 when the horse then failed to win the St Leger. On this occasion Gully was himself a victim of a conspiracy, the starter bribed by Bobby Ridsdale and William Crockford: blubbery, creepy 'Crocky', the former fishmonger who enfolded enough of Gully's money in his flaccid fist – his hands 'entirely without knuckles, soft as raw veal, and as white as paper' – to open his famous St James's gaming club shortly afterwards.*

Characteristically, the hard-headed Gully viewed this inimical demonstration as the cue to enter a partnership with Ridsdale, an ex-stableboy now living a life of luxury, with many of the Yorkshire jockeys reputedly in his pocket. In 1832 Gully and Ridsdale won

---

* Even Wellington would join the club, if only to blackball his son should he apply for membership.

the Derby with St Giles, having squared virtually the entire field with bribes; and later that same season Margrave, trained for Gully by John Scott, won the St Leger. A vivid picture has been preserved of the scene in the betting rooms at Doncaster, on the eve of Margrave's win, a blasphemous cacophony of blacksmiths and black-guards, legs and lords:

> It was said that the old Duke of Cleveland pulled the wires to this sweet *tableau vivant* and to see his white, sardonic countenance, and Gully's threatening, overcharged brow, with old Crocky's satanic smile and working jaw, surrounding the table, as the parties explained, was to view a picture worthy of the pencil of Rembrandt. Old Ord . . . also mounted the table, being howling drunk as usual and unshaved for a fortnight, and denounced the 'whole gang as a crew of robbers and miscreants, for whom the gallows would be too good!' at which the room only applauded ironically, or grinned approval. Then old Jemmy Bland, an atrocious Leg of the ancient, top-booted, semi-highwayman school, and Old Crocky got set by the ears, like two worn-out mastiffs, and had 'a few words' through their false teeth.*

Unsurprisingly, Gully and Ridsdale fell out over their Epsom winnings. The resulting feud reached a highly public climax that winter, after the former prizefighter horsewhipped Ridsdale in the hunting field. A court awarded damages of £500 against the bully, a verdict so popular that even court officials joined the noisy 'view halloo' that broke from the gallery. But Ridsdale was still riding for a fall, eventually found dead in a Newmarket hayloft one snowy dawn, a frozen husk of rags and bone with three ha'pennies in his pocket.

Gully, according to Charles Greville, meanwhile 'gradually separated himself from the rabble of bettors and blackguards of whom he was once the most conspicuous'. The diarist was not deceived, crediting him with a 'system of corruption of trainers, jockeys and boys, which put the secrets of Newmarket at his disposal and in a

---

* The words of *Sylvanus* – along with *The Druid* and *Nimrod*, one of the great nineteenth-century chroniclers of the Turf. All wrote at a time when gentlemen retained sufficient dignity not to put their own names to any such enterprise as the present one.

few years made him rich'. Presented at court and elected to the House of Commons, Gully nonetheless bore himself as though never involved in any dirtier work than was performed by the miners in his new collieries.

John Scott's reputation seems to have been almost entirely uncontaminated by such patrons. A dignified figure, his black coat and spotless white scarf in later years set off by a shock of white hair, he was accounted 'the best and kindest of masters, large-hearted and charitable'. He slaughtered a bullock for the poor of Malton every Christmas and professed no interest in betting, though sensitive to the need for privacy when staging trials. For these his horses were led out in the dead of night and galloped through the dawn mist in front of a privileged posse that would sometimes include Lord Derby, a prime minister delivered by the mail train. And then it was back to the breakfast table for a council of war, invariably chaired by George Anson, Scott's great confidant and counsellor, a man cherished across the English Turf for his discretion and sage judgement.

Whitewall was never the same once Colonel Anson was posted to India as commander-in-chief. Mind you, nor was India. Anson's immaculate manners caused him to avoid the unpardonable solecism of opening a telegram while hosting ladies to dinner at Simla in 1857. As a result, he dismissed all talk of a Sepoy mutiny until finally remembering the envelope he had pushed under his plate. It was a last message scrambled by the Delhi telegraph clerks before they fled the first wave of arson and butchery in the colonial compound.

The Whitewall gallops were patrolled by Scott's celebrated American dog, who had supposedly been trained to hunt down fugitive slaves. He sometimes chased 'touts' literally up trees, though Scott would at least console them with a ration of gin once his horses had been sent back home. Drink would never be in short supply, after all, so long as his brother, Bill, remained stable jockey. By the time The Baron entered Whitewall, however, hard-riding, hard-living Bill Scott was clinging to the last vestiges of the powers he had once used so unsparingly against Sir Hercules on Rowton. After a final falling-out between the siblings, a new stable jockey was appointed at Whitewall: Frank Butler, a nephew of Sam Chifney Jr. and another exponent of the family's trademark 'rush'.

No less than his uncle, Butler knew the risk in always pouncing so late. Granted the endemic venalities of the betting ring at the time, there would always be punters who viewed a narrow failure to catch the leader as the very opposite of a miscalculation. By 1837, *Nimrod* was inclined to a bleak revision of scripture: 'The race not being to the swift, but *to the horse on whom the largest sums stand in certain persons' books* . . . No honourable man can be successful, for any length of time, against such a horde of determined depredators as have lately been seen on our race-courses; the most princely fortune cannot sustain itself against the deep-laid stratagems of such villainous combinations.'

Punters, of course, have always been perfectly capable of ruining themselves on horses trained and ridden with the best of intentions. Berkeley Craven, one of the most cherished members of the Jockey Club, was plunged into such despair by the 1836 Derby – he faced defaulting on £8,000 in bets – that he went home and blew his brains out with a pistol. Nor did this tragedy do much to deter his peers, judging from Disraeli's description of the next Derby in the opening scenes of *Sybil*. On the eve of the race, anxiety pervades Crockford's as a storm threatens to change the going: 'Another flash, another explosion, the hissing noise of rain. Lord Milford moved aside, and, jealous of the eye of another, read a letter from Chifney, and in a few minutes afterwards offered to take the odds against Pocket Hercules.' And then, at the track itself, Disraeli records the frenetic final exchanges in the ring:

> 'Eleven to two against Mango,' called out a little hump-backed man in a shrill voice, but with the air of one who was master of his work.
>
> 'I should like to do a little business with you, Mr Chippendale,' said Lord Milford, in a coaxing tone, 'but I must have six to one.'
>
> 'Eleven to two, and no mistake,' said this keeper of a second-rate gaming house, who, known by the flattering appellation of Hump Chippendale, now turned with malignant abruptness from the heir-apparent of an English earldom . . . He was a democratic leg, who loved to fleece a noble, and thought all men were born equal – a consoling creed that was a hedge for his hump.

For many, this convergence of so many different walks of life was the sport's defining strength. Whatever the moral perils, there was something wholesome about the sight of the Earl of Derby, 'the Rupert of Debate', surrounded at Newmarket by 'a crowd of black-legs, betting men, and loose characters of every description, in uproarious spirits'. Greville describes the statesman boisterously shedding all gravitas as Lord Glasgow, taking pinch after pinch of snuff, sought to win a wager that he would sneeze in a given time. '[Derby] jeered at him and quizzed him with such noise that he drew the whole mob around him to partake of the coarse merriment he excited. It really was a sight to see any man playing such different parts so naturally.'

But others viewed this social flux as a dangerous weir. The young queen had been quick to break up the royal stud, after attending her one and only Derby in 1840. She may have been shocked by rumours that the winner, trained by a wily veteran named John Forth, was a 'ringer' – a mature four-year-old, running in a race confined to three-year-olds. Forth certainly tried to pull off a similar stunt four years later, helping to make a historic nadir of the 1844 Derby.

First Crockford's colt Ratan was 'nobbled'. He was locked away in his stable on the eve of the race as smooth and hard as an ingot; when he emerged next morning, 'his coat was standing like quills on the fretful porcupine, his eyes were dilated, and he shivered like a man with the ague'. It was all too much for the ailing Crocky, who promptly died, though still able to assist in one last fraud, his carcass manoeuvred into a window seat to prevent certain bets being inconveniently voided by his demise. Then the winner, ostensibly Running Rein, was revealed to be a four-year-old named Maccabaeus. The fraud was so widely known that John Scott, among others, had put his signature to an official protest even before the race. Nor was Running Rein the only 'ringer' in the field. Leander, trained by Forth, was hastily buried after breaking a leg in a collision with Running Rein. The following night the Whitewall grooms, having won the Oaks, decided to cap off their celebrations by digging up his remains and assessing the teeth. The discovery that someone had removed the horse's lower jaw permitted only one inference.

Colonel Peel, owner of the runner-up, eventually succeeded in having the winner disqualified after a sensational court case, albeit only after the prime minister's younger brother was famously reproved by Baron Alderson: 'If gentlemen condescend to race with black-guards, they must condescend to expect to be cheated.' And that seemed pretty well to sum up the perdition of the Turf. 'I see a rum set in my day of one sort or another, for I can just remember Dan Dawson and Co.,' Crutch Robinson told *Sylvanus*, looking round the ring of the 1840s. 'But these beat all calculation.'

In time, however, the Running Rein scandal would be perceived as something of a turning point. For the driving force behind the impostor's exposure had been the forty-two-year-old Lord George Bentinck. An heir to Sir Charles Bunbury had finally emerged, a man more than willing to clean out the Augean Stables.

Cussed, sly and domineering, Bentinck could be a dreadful hypocrite. But it was precisely his flair for sharp practice that honed his antennae as a reformer. By getting his own hands a little dirty, he acquired a useful intimacy with the practices and personalities behind the real enormities. While he would soon quit the scene, and drop dead shortly afterwards, the sheer force of his personality was the spur to a far greater sense of purpose – if not yet a consistently enlightened one – at the Jockey Club.

At the very least Bentinck can be credited as the author of a transformation in the public experience of racing, having prevailed upon the Duke of Richmond to build a new racecourse on his estate at Goodwood. The modern racegoer, accustomed to commen-taries, giant screens and loudspeakers, can barely conceive how cryptic proceedings remained at the time. At however primitive a level, Bentinck sought to give spectators a better sense of what was going on: horses were numbered in a racecard that also confirmed the names and silks of their riders; they were saddled and paraded in designated areas; enclosures and landscaped elevations cleared the view; starts were punctual and punctilious; and the numbers of placed horses were mounted in a telegraph frame.

He also performed a great service for the racehorse itself, in 1836 commissioning a prototype horsebox to spare his St Leger candidate,

Elis, the long walk to Yorkshire. Typically, Bentinck had been inspired by self-interest sooner than any regard for the colt's tender hooves. Everyone knew Elis still to be in Sussex a week before the race, and that he could not possibly get to Doncaster in time. That same summer, after all, it had been considered remarkable that John Scott could walk Cyprian from Malton to Epsom to win the Oaks on 20 May, and then 300 miles back north to win the Northumberland Plate at Newcastle on 22 June. But those who blithely laid bets against Elis were astonished when Bentinck's secret new contraption, towed by six post-horses, was unveiled. Elis completed a fortnight's march in just three days. Bentinck won over £15,000, and elite thoroughbreds would never again have to trek the turnpike on their own four feet.

In fairness, many other men of Bentinck's class shared the same double standards: on the one hand, deploying their priceless thoroughbreds for the cheapest subterfuge; on the other, virtuously smoking out the odd plebeian impudent enough to grab a piece of the betting action. But there was something especially maddening about Bentinck, with all his Pharisaic meddling. Just as his physical magnificence was betrayed by an effeminacy of voice and gesture, so his righteous crusades often proved to be animated by some mean vendetta. Disraeli described Bentinck counting 'his thousands after a great race as a victorious general counts his cannon and his prisoners'. In his wagering, no less than in his feuding, Bentinck could never tell vindication from vindictiveness.

Both sides of his character had been magnified by his choice of 'Honest' John Day as trainer. This soubriquet had been bestowed in undiluted sarcasm: a pity, for Day and his sons were exceptional horsemen, building a remarkable record in the Classics both as trainers and jockeys. Day galloped horses up Danebury Hill, near Stockbridge, until he could hang washing from their ribs, but Bentinck had noticed the dividends in those who survived the attrition and invested heavily in the stable. They had won five Classics together when Day's son, John Jr., wrote to Bentinck strongly advising a bet on a horse, even as he wrote to his commissioner urging him to lay the same animal. Bentinck was said to have quit Danebury as a result of these two letters being posted in the wrong envelopes.

Day soon found a new patron in John Gully, but their partnership came to a very similar end in 1845 when the old bruiser discovered that another of Day's sons, William, had sought to nobble his colt, Old England, before the Derby. After admitting to a Jockey Club inquiry that he had wrapped a silk handkerchief round one of the colt's tendons and beaten it with a stick, William was banned from Newmarket – 'warned off', in the lasting vernacular – while 'Proprietors and Stewards of all race-courses where the rules of the Jockey Club are in force' were urged to do the same.*

It was a dispiriting prelude to the first Derby since the Running Rein scandal. In the event, Old England recovered to finish third – an especially good effort, given that he had been obliged to jump the prostrate Frank Butler after John Scott's runner crashed to the ground. There had also been a terrifying accident before the race, described with malicious relish by Bentinck as he peered through his telescope: 'There is a horse on the ground. He is kicking violently, his jockey lies insensible. I believe it is Mr Greville's Alarm.' He was perfectly aware not only that Charles Greville was standing nearby but also that he had backed Alarm to win £40,000.

Bentinck and Greville were cousins and had been confederates in a racing stable until a recent quarrel. Soon afterwards the Days, disgusted with Bentinck's sanctimony over the Old England affair, showed Greville letters their former patron had written during his Danebury years. 'They disclosed a systematic course of treachery, falsehood and fraud which would have been far more than sufficient to destroy any reputation,' the diarist claimed after Bentinck's death. The plots Bentinck had proposed 'were concocted with infinite care and explained in elaborate detail, the whole forming such a mass of roguery that any attempt at explanation, extenuation or palliation

---

* This was symptomatic of the organic development of Jockey Club authority, which had only been officially established over Newmarket Heath. Jurisdiction over disputes elsewhere remained ad hoc, contingent on track stewards formally adopting its rules.

would have been in vain'. Yet that same summer Greville read the following inscription on a silver plate, offered as a prize for the Bentinck Testimonial Stakes at Liverpool, a token of the sport's gratitude for the exposure of Running Rein:

> Honourably to commemorate the public spirited exertions of Lord George Bentinck by whose zeal and perseverance a fatal blow was struck at the late irregularities and growing malpractices of the Turf; a wholesome but unflinching lesson was read to the Owners, Trainers, and Riders of horses; punctuality, order, obedience, and fair play were re-established at the Starting Post, and thus to frequenters of the Race Course, whether attracted to the National Sport by pleasure or speculation, confidence and satisfaction were secured.

Greville did not know whether to laugh or cry.

A Day at the Races

Doncaster, 17 September 1845

Typical Bentinck. There he was, strutting in front of the St Leger field with his big flag: the incarnation of a new vigilance, the only man competent to start such an important race according to the procedures he had himself introduced. Yet nor did he consider himself in any way disqualified from the task by wagering £3,500 on the favourite, Miss Sarah.

The whole stage bore the imprint of his personality. In emulation of his innovations at Goodwood, the betting ring, saddling area and grandstand were now sealed off by a new lawn, enclosed by white railings. The track, meanwhile, was so manicured that 'a horse with blown-glass legs might gallop unscathed'. And it had to be said that Bentinck performed his official duties impeccably.

After drawing lots, to line up in a double row, the jockeys had received a lecture to the effect that he expected clean riding for a clean result. He then took the flag, wheeling the fifteen riders obediently before releasing them in an immaculate cavalry charge, silks shimmering in the September sunshine. A hum of approval filtered through the crowd: Bentinck's predecessor in the role, 'the blundering and discourteous Mr Lockwood', had been rendered 'perfectly ridiculous' by the comparison.

Following his fall at Epsom, Frank Butler was relieved just to be in one piece – never mind having the chance to seal his new partnership with Scott by winning Yorkshire's own Classic on the stable's Irish recruit. Not that many gave The Baron much chance against a filly as talented as Miss Sarah. The word from Whitewall had been discouraging: the colt from Ireland had arrived as 'a very rough and snappish customer' and Scott later admitted that he 'took more work than I ever gave a horse in my life, and required more management'.

As soon as Bentinck let them go, Butler anchored The Baron right at the back of the field. From halfway, helped by the strong pace, he gradually allowed his mount to creep into midfield; a murmur of surprise spread through the grandstand when a seasoned voice suddenly shouted from its top steps: 'The Baron wins, for a hundred!' Miss Sarah, still going strongly, followed The Baron through as Butler challenged on the turn; and for much of the straight the issue remained in the balance. But Miss Sarah could find no more inside the final furlong, The Baron edging a length clear. 'I doubt much,' observed one correspondent of the winner's reception, 'whether the repeal of the legislative union would be hailed more enthusiastically than was this victory by the Paddies assembled at Doncaster.'

Others were taking a more jaundiced view. Scott's involvement notwithstanding, this was a second consecutive Leger for the Irish. It was now muttered that nobody really knew anything about the provenance of these horses. The previous year one magazine had expressly aired suspicions that Faugh-a-Ballagh could be a four-year-old: 'Much fear prevailed amongst the enemies of the Irish horse that he possessed higher qualifications than had been generally believed.' After all, Faugh-a-Ballagh had surfaced in the stable of the notorious John Forth. On the morning of the St Leger, the stewards had been asked by none other than Colonel Anson, the godfather of Whitewall, to verify the Irish colt's age.

Though the bona fides of Faugh-a-Ballagh had been confirmed, that had not prevented similar rumours about The Baron this time. That evening, a dozen aristocrats were passing a bottle of wine round the table of Lord Spencer, one of the stewards of the meeting. They had to miss out Bentinck who, as usual, had fallen asleep. A butler entered the room, with the card of the Hon. Edward Mostyn, whose horse had finished third in the big race. Mostyn was admitted, along with Charles Peck, the trainer of the runner-up. Peck proved too nervous to make himself understood, however, and Mostyn took over. Together they would be obliged if the St Leger stakes were withheld pending an examination of The Baron's mouth.

It was a breathtaking request. Scott, of course, could be easily absolved. Everyone knew that he had never set eyes on the horse until July. But any inquiry could not fail to insult George Watts. He had bred The Baron, not bought him, and had expressly accounted the colt's age in entering him for a Classic. No less than in the Ruthven case – where Watts had conducted himself with such rectitude – the charges were laid conspicuously against an outsider to the presiding establishment. Roused from his sleep, Bentinck shrugged. By all means, The Baron could be examined.

The next morning, the same two vets who had inspected Faugh-a-Ballagh now examined the mouth of The Baron in the stable yard of the Salutation Inn. Both were emphatic: this was a three-year-old, and Watts should be paid his stake at once.

12

'Mr Palmer passes me
five times in five minutes.'

THE 1845 ST Leger had revealed limitations in both the imperial
English racehorse, and the imperial English character. The Baron
had been treated as literally too good to be true. No legitimate
champion thoroughbred, surely, could ever crawl out of the Curragh
bog; and therefore this Curragh vet could be no gentleman. One
sporting correspondent did have the decency to reprimand those
who had doubted the word of Watts. 'An honourable man has more
than once been exposed to a very degrading insinuation,' he warned.
'And out of this practice will yet come grave consequences. I know
what course a high spirit is likely to adopt towards him who, however
cautiously, raise a possible doubt of his honour.' Another, more
typically, wrestled between his contempt for Irish horses and the
invidious conclusions invited 'when we compare the few ragged,
half-stud, half-potato farms over there, with the many princely
establishments amongst us, or . . . count the few score brood mares
they possess, with the hundreds on hundreds that have here found
a name and a place in the Stud-book.'

Such contempt had long been automatic. *Nimrod*, for instance,
had damned Pat Conolly with the faintest of praise: the jockey of
Sir Hercules was strong and level-headed, but had 'a bad Irish seat'.
Yet English horsemen were soon forced to digest an unpalatable
truth. The Irish had come up with an authentic prince of stallions.
The Baron was only the first of seven English Classic winners sired
by a horse they registered, in their bemusement, as 'Irish' Birdcatcher;
one whose racing career had been so insular that he never raced
anywhere but the Curragh. The energies that gave him a reputation
as 'a hard-puller, and very fretful and difficult to train' were being
honed by his stock into a clean edge of speed. Within five years of

his death, one expert would concede: 'It cannot be denied that 'Irish Birdcatcher' has done more for the racehorse than any stallion of modern days – probably than ever was heard of; not alone in speed, but in symmetry of shape and power.' His imprint on the Darley Arabian line was to become so indelible that even today silver flecks in the root of a horse's tail, or sprinkled over its flanks, are known as 'Birdcatcher ticks'.

Sadly, Birdcatcher would share the fate of so many symbols of Irish vitality around this time. As Ireland withered in the Great Famine, the stallion was shuttled to a variety of studs across the water. For many years his principal base was Easby Abbey, just a few miles along the wooded banks of the Swale from John Hutton's old seat at Marske. One of the first colts Birdcatcher bred here, Daniel O'Rourke, won the 1852 Derby; moreover, three fillies from the same crop took the first three places in the Oaks. Even as Irish refugees fled starvation for America – some exporting the ideals of O'Connell to the evolving Democratic Party – so 'Irish Birdcatcher' was creating a diaspora of his own.

Exactly a year after first catching John Scott's eye, The Baron was back at Liverpool. This time he was not even quoted in the betting and ran accordingly. Watts had sold him soon after the St Leger, for £4,000, but his new handlers found the horse too much of a challenge and offloaded him to John Mytton in Shropshire.

Mytton's father, Jack, had died in a debtors' jail at just thirty-eight, his headlong disposal of £500,000 over the previous fifteen years the stuff of shire legend: riding a bear into his dining room, scattering guests onto tables and through windows; screaming with laughter at the passenger in his mangled gig after driving a horse to leap a tollgate; stalking ducks over a frozen lake while stark naked. Once he set fire to his nightgown because he had heard that a shock will cure hiccoughs. But he was 'chased always by a high mad black wind', as Edith Sitwell wrote. 'Let it blow through him and eat him to the bone. He would show how little he cared.' The maniacal exuberance that made him famous eventually boiled down to a morbid, bilious sediment. Jack Mytton and his wife both became fugitives: he from the bailiffs in Calais; she from his violence. A friend reckoned him more or less continuously drunk for the last twelve years of his life. In a final bitter twist, he was obliged to sell off his stud – which once exceeded fifty horses – only for one of the foals to win the St Leger.

Evidently Jack Mytton had bequeathed enough of his temperament for his heir to reprise such follies as he could afford. But The Baron had been a challenge even to John Scott. Clearly the colt's problems were far beyond the competence of his subsequent trainers, in an age when some horsemen still resorted to crackpot methods. (Bentinck's father, the Duke of Portland, liked to have young horses inured to noise by a drum and fife band and detonations of gunpowder.) Fortunately, Mytton Jr. soon recognised the futility of his attempt to renew his father's name on the Turf. For his stud career, The Baron was restored to men who palpably knew what they were doing.

John Theobald's farm at Stockwell, then still a village on the southern fringes of London, had become one of most successful commercial studs in England. This was a lucky break not just for The Baron, but for the whole Darley Arabian dynasty. In those days, it was perfectly possible even for a St Leger winner to slip through the net in retirement. There was no more cautionary example than The Baron's own grandsire, Sir Hercules.

Things seemed to fall into place for Sir Hercules when his son, Coronation, won the 1841 Derby, despite being trained until a fortnight before the race by an illiterate, stone-deaf groom on a farm in Oxfordshire. This triumph of amateurs stunned the great magnates who had lost fortunes trying to win a Derby, and Sir Hercules found himself moving up in the world. After Faugh-a-Ballagh, Birdcatcher's brother, proceeded to win the St Leger, Bentinck complained that he had only been able to book three mares to Sir Hercules for the new breeding season, when he had asked for six. After his grandson The Baron won the same race the next year, the rediscovered stallion was sold for 900 guineas to a man rated a prime minister in the making, and whisked away to one of England's finest stately homes.

Sidney Herbert's interest in racing is instructive of the paradox that its principal patrons were becoming more respectable even as their horses were being manipulated, as never before, by the dregs of society. A generation previously, it would have been Herbert's older half-brother, Robert, who might have made the stud at Wilton a symbol of his dissolution. As it was, Robert had made a callow, clandestine marriage to the widow of a minor Sicilian prince before disappearing to Paris to be fought over by ballerinas; though he still inherited their father's title in 1827, as Earl of Pembroke, everything else went to his staid half-brother.*

Sidney, entering the House of Commons at twenty-two, was soon identified as one of the outstanding prospects of his generation. Handsome, refined and intelligent, at Oxford he had befriended Gladstone and three future viceroys of India. Now, rising in Peel's slipstream, he was repeatedly promoted in both opposition and office. Yet it was Sidney, not Robert, who wanted to start a racing stable.

Unfortunately, he confined his new stallion largely to a few desultory matings with the undistinguished Wilton mares. At the worst possible moment, just as Sir Hercules was achieving a belated distinction, his new owner seems to have become disaffected. For there was another exotic newcomer at Wilton, and their fates would be fatefully entwined.

Herbert seemed to offer the beautiful and brilliant Caroline Norton overdue rehabilitation. For legal purposes, however, she remained the hapless chattel of her violent husband, George. At one stage, egged on by a cabal of ultra-Tories, George Norton had pursued a ludicrous suit against Lord Melbourne for the alleged seduction of his wife. His humiliation completed by failure to prove himself a cuckold, George had maliciously impounded their sons with his relatives. There were beatings: a sickly five-year-old stripped naked, strapped to a bedpost and thrashed with a riding crop. Surprised during a desperate, furtive visit to their nursery, Caroline was forced out of the house in a rolling maul by George's brother and his servants, the terrified screams of her sons fading behind slammed

---

* Robert's temperament was perhaps written in his pedigree, as a grandson of Lady Diana Spencer and Topham Beauclerk; his aunt, indeed, had eloped incestuously with Lady Di's son by Bolingbroke.

Panorama of Aleppo in 1698, four years before Thomas Darley rode through its gates into the desert to seek out a tribe of Bedouin horse traders.

Unnamed portrait at Aldby, the family seat, presumed to show Thomas Darley.

The great patriarch himself: Mr Darley's Arabian. If accurately presented, a decidedly plain animal.

A painting by James Seymour that conjures all the quality and virility of Flying Childers, the champion who created a posthumous vogue for his obscure imported sire.

Lord Portmore, owner of Squirt, appears as the camp figure on the right of this caricature by Hogarth.

Tattersalls horse market opened in 1766 at Hyde Park Corner. Subsequently moved to Newmarket, it remains the premier bloodstock auction in Europe.

Lord Portmore, mounted on the right, watching his horses on
Newmarket Heath in a painting by John Wootton, *c*.1735. The date
makes it possible that one of them is Squirt himself.

Seymour's *Two Famous Running Horses* (1747) demonstrates how fine an imprint has
been made by Arabian stallions on the early thoroughbred.

The Duke of Cumberland. Culloden stained his name for ever in Scotland but prompted a grateful Yorkshireman to send him the sire of the great Eclipse.

'The Betting Post', by Thomas Rowlandson. Dennis O'Kelly is the obese figure in a blue coat on the right.

Rowlandson's *A Sketch from Nature*. Charlotte Hayes had a rather more reliable source of income than her partner, O'Kelly.

Eclipse by George Stubbs. Inside the rubbing house, horses had their sweating flanks mopped with straw after murderous workouts in heavy rugs.

Willoughby Bertie, 4th Earl of Abingdon, portrait by Thomas Gainsborough. The toast of American revolutionaries: 'a man of genius, but irregular almost to the point of madness'

The Prince of Wales connives as jockey Sam Chifney pulls at the teeth of his horse, Escape, while keeping the whip safely clamped between his own. Caricature, *How to ESCAPE Winning*, by Rowlandson.

Lord Egremont, the cherished patron of Turner and many other English artists, shown with a statuette of Whalebone at his elbow.

Frank Buckle, a great jockey and one of unusual integrity for the time, reporting to the pioneering trainer Robert Robson.

The horsebox, typically introduced by Lord George Bentinck only to facilitate a betting coup, relieved thoroughbreds of immense treks between racetracks.

The start of the 1831 St Leger, by James Pollard. The varying degrees of readiness in the field make it easy to judge the possibilities available to a corrupt starter.

Caroline Norton, described by the contemporary wit Rev. Sydney Smith as 'that superb lump of flesh'.

Sidney Herbert forswore racehorses – and Mrs Norton – so that Florence Nightingale could work him into an early grave.

'Mad' Jack Mytton, assisted by a bear, sheds light on his nickname.

doors. Edward Trelawny, the swashbuckling adventurer who famously plucked Shelley's heart from a pyre, even offered to kidnap her children and sail them into exile. Yet she could not afford all-out war, so long as she sought any access to her children from the man still entitled to all royalties from her novels and verse.

One of her most famous poems suggests familiarity with the origin and majesty of thoroughbreds. 'The Arab's Farewell to His Steed' describes the sale of a desert horse to a European prospector in the mould of Thomas Darley. The Bedouin narrator confesses that he has exchanged the contentment of his cherished companion for gold. His horse is to be exiled far away, beneath a 'chill and wintry sky', coarsely handled by men lacking proper empathy for his high breeding and sensitivity.

> *Ah! rudely then, unseen by me, some cruel hand may chide,*
> *Till foam-wreaths lie, like crested waves, along thy panting side:*
> *And the rich blood that is in thee swells, in thy indignant pain,*
> *Till careless eyes, which rest on thee, may count each started vein.*

He repents, flings back the gold: how could anyone ill-use a creature 'so swift, yet easy curb'd; so gentle, yet so free'? But if Caroline Norton admired Sir Hercules, when both found sanctuary at Wilton, both were about to suffer misuse.

Sidney Herbert was one of few members of the cabinet on whom Peel could depend as he laid the ground for a momentous shift in policy. The Corn Laws, protecting domestic grain producers with taxes on cheap imports, had long been propped up by vested interests. Now the free trade lobby, already fortified by industrialisation, had obtained a humanitarian imperative. Potato blight was reducing the staple food of Ireland's poor, in Herbert's own words, to 'putrid slime'. The choice lay between repeal of the Corn Laws, and mass starvation.

Peel anticipated fury within his party. George Bentinck was so incensed that he quit the Turf altogether to head a protectionist rebellion in the Commons. He sold his entire stud for just £10,000 to the same Edward Mostyn who had challenged the true age of The Baron. It included a yearling, Surplice, who proceeded to win

the 1848 Derby. After the race Disraeli found an inconsolable
Bentinck in the House of Commons library:

> He gave a sort of superb groan:
> 'All my life I have been trying for this, and for what have I sacri-
> ficed it!' he murmured.
> It was in vain to offer solace.
> 'You do not know what the Derby is,' he moaned out.
> 'Yes, I do; it is the blue ribbon of the Turf.'
> 'It is the blue ribbon of the Turf,' he slowly repeated to himself,
> and sitting down at the table, he buried himself in a folio of
> statistics.

As his lieutenant against Peel, Disraeli was forever indebted to
Bentinck for his initial breakthrough on the national scene. In the
words of one Tory colleague: 'It was he who gave Dizzy the mount,
it was Dizzy's riding that won the race.' Their call to arms had come
on 4 December 1845, when *The Times* suddenly blared that the
cabinet had approved repeal of the Corn Laws. Peel was appalled.
The story was not just premature; it menaced the entire policy. The
gossips were unanimous: Caroline Norton had sold pillow talk to
The Times. Yet Herbert's commissioned biographer, who declined
even to use her name, would later be at pains to absolve her:
'Injudicious and impulsive her conduct may at times have been, but
selfish or mercenary she certainly was not.'

Herbert recoiled all the same, and just eight months later married
a much younger woman. On their honeymoon, Herbert's devout
new wife introduced him to Florence Nightingale; between them
these pious women appear to have talked Herbert out of frittering
money on a walk of sporting life so pervaded by corruption. Within
four years of his marriage, nothing remained of the Wilton stud.

Although his huge estates depended on countless tiers of labour,
Herbert's loss of interest was culpably reflected in the condition of
Sir Hercules when sold 'for a few sovereigns' to a farmer at Bushbury
near Wolverhampton. Escricke Phillips arranged to pick up the old
horse from a livery yard in a London mews. Though Sir Hercules
was bound to be showing his age at twenty-six, Phillips was still
shocked by his emaciation. A contemporary account relates how

'his feeble legs scarcely sustained his skeleton carcase' to Euston station, 'a sad reverse to the pampered state of his younger days'.

Herbert could hardly be expected to monitor every last oat fed to Sir Hercules, as overwork, despite declining health, hastened him into an early grave at just fifty. Even so, this high-born, high-minded man had only twice risked the disapproval of meaner spirits: once by building up a racing stable, and then in a love affair. He had been rewarded, on each occasion, by the arrival into his life of an exceptional creature. And yet he had ended up nervously washing his hands of both.

In those days the Black Country still pealed with birdsong and hunting horns. Woodland and heath were latticed by training gallops. Expensive horses owned by a Glaswegian ironmaster, James Merry, were putting one local trainer in particular, William Saunders, on the map. And it was another of the stable's patrons who would now do the same, in a macabre sequel to the story of Sir Hercules.

The very first foal born to the ageing stallion after his recuperation at Bushbury was bought by William Palmer, a young doctor from nearby Rugeley. Palmer carefully maintained his profile as hale, affable and prosperous. On the wall of his dining room hung a portrait of Goldfinder, his Chester Cup winner. He boasted of the £12,000 he had landed in bets that day, and returned to his local, the Cross Keys, to buy brandy all round. In reality, he was deep in the clutches of London moneylenders, notably the notorious Henry Padwick. Goldfinder, as a better index to Palmer's true situation, would eventually be found towing an omnibus between Islington and Kennington.

The Sir Hercules yearling was shaping nicely when his owner was charged with the murder of a friend named John Cook. A few days previously Cook had landed some big bets at Shrewsbury races with Polestar, a horse trained for him by Saunders, only to fall sick after celebrating with Palmer. Despite the professional ministrations of his friend over the next few nights, Cook died in racked, wild-eyed convulsions.

Suspiciously, his betting book could not be found. During the post-mortem, Palmer jolted the surgeon just as he took a sample from Cook's stomach. At the inquest, a toxicologist heard a chambermaid describe Cook's reaction to Palmer's pills and declared it consistent with poisoning by strychnine. None had been found in Cook's system, but judicious dosing might leave no trace but death. The bodies of Palmer's wife and brother were now exhumed for analysis, both having died prematurely, and his horses hastily put up for sale. Palmer denied his guilt throughout, albeit with provoking ambiguity. 'I am innocent of poisoning Cook by strychnine,' he specified, walking almost jauntily onto the scaffold at Stafford before a crowd of 50,000 in 1856.

Palmer's Sir Hercules colt, named Gemma Di Vergy, proceeded to win no fewer than thirteen races in his debut season. But Palmer's stain would not wash off. One of the colt's purchasers went out of his mind; another was killed in a hunting accident; another wept and ranted in an uproarious court case to settle a dispute over his ownership. Palmer's curse seemed to extend across the whole racing community, a moralising press exultantly discovering that his gambling debts had obliged him to borrow at a catastrophic 60 per cent. At one stage he had bought a horse, The Chicken, with an insurance claim made on his wife's life. The Chicken, renamed Vengeance by his new owner, now proceeded to win the Cesarewitch Handicap; freakishly, the runner-up was none other than Polestar, Cook's fateful winner at Shrewsbury.

A year after the murderer was hanged, Charles Dickens stood outside the betting rooms at Doncaster and observed 'an awful family likeness' among all classes, united in 'cunning, covetousness, secrecy, cold calculation, hard callousness and dire insensibility . . . Mr Palmer passes me five times in five minutes.' Growing anxiety on behalf of middle-class morality had already been crystallised by a Parliamentary Select Committee on Gaming in 1844, aptly the year of Running Rein. In one typical testimony, the commissioner of the London police avowed: 'I think it is a matter of little importance to hear and know that men of large fortune have transferred from one to the other £100,000; but I think it is a very undesirable thing that mechanics and persons engaged in industrious pursuits should be crowding around thimble-tables and going into gambling booths.'

But these paternalist precepts were betrayed by racecourse managers, who collected fees from the booth operators. The select committee's report, moreover, inadvertently promoted horse racing as a medium of casual gambling for the working man. By urging legislation to prohibit the recovery of gaming debts at law, it placed a new onus on cash betting. This resulted in a proliferation of 'list' houses, where odds were posted for all runners. These first betting shops were pioneered by a former carpenter, William 'Leviathan' Davies, who posted his first list in the Durham Arms, Lincoln's Inn, and was soon turning over hundreds of thousands every year. A ticket from Davies, entered by his clerks in a giant ledger, was reckoned as negotiable as a note from the Bank of England.

Hitherto only a few hundred specialists had either the nerve or the means to enter the magic circle, round the betting post at the track or in subscription rooms at Tattersall's and elsewhere. But this new cash model put betting on large fields, at corresponding odds, within reach of all classes. A link was renewed that had been frayed since the days of the old country meetings, when tiny fields had typically kept odds within the same informal wagering range as prizefights, cockfighting or even a man's prowess.* Off-track betting became so accessible that several of Lord Zetland's servants could afford to leave his service after backing his colt Voltigeur to win the 1850 Derby.

Unfortunately, not all 'list' men proved as dependable as Davies. Further legislation in 1853, to shut down as many as three hundred betting shops in the capital, indulged upper-class, private wagering at Tattersall's while clamping down on those who presumed to bet like their betters. One typical editorial had identified wagering by shopkeepers as 'the macadamized path to the Prison and the Workhouse'. But the new Act succeeded only in driving betting onto the street.

Davies, for his part, moved upmarket. Here he performed another valuable service – by filling the vacuum of trust that had persisted

---

* One London blacksmith wagered that he could drink a butt of porter in six days, the loser to pay for the beer: the equivalent of eighteen gallons a day. 'Extraordinary to say,' reported a sporting magazine, 'he performed the disgusting feat with apparent ease.'

for so long among the 'kites and crows'. All Davies sought to do was balance a book of public money on all runners, and the expanding leisure budget of a new artisan class insulated him from the feints and secret commissions of professional horsemen and their patrons. But if the Turf's landed grandees welcomed this one, incidental benefit of the Industrial Revolution, its more direct effects were being registered with ever deeper alarm.

PART IV

Age of the Iron Horse

Stockwell (1849)
Doncaster (1870)
Bend Or (1877)

13

Full Steam Ahead

THE REPATRIATION OF the Darley Arabian line disclosed profound change in the complexion of Britain's wealth. Sir Hercules, Birdcatcher and The Baron had all been born in Ireland. In the meantime the great shire families of England – typified by those who raised and raced Pot8os, Waxy and Whalebone – had begun to sense the ground almost literally moving under their feet.

Some landed magnates did share in the coal boom, excavating their own fields and parks, but the rest were being exposed by an ancestral distaste for commerce. The tipping point was the repeal of the Corn Laws. Having long preserved its agricultural powerbase by protectionism, the Turf aristocracy now had to punch its weight in the open market with industrialists, merchants and bankers. Horsepower, as such, was not just the standard measure of the engines driving the Industrial Revolution. It would also – through the ownership of thoroughbreds – become a definitive gauge of the resulting flux in social status. No single horse charted this transition better than Stockwell, a son of The Baron who became principal heir to the Darley Arabian line.

He owed his name to his sire's brief stay at the Stockwell stud of John Theobald, himself a self-made man. Born two years after the invention of the spinning jenny, Theobald entered the hosiery business just as it gained fresh impetus from steam power, and regarded even his stud as a purely commercial venture.* But both Theobald and his heir, William, died within a few months of Stockwell's birth in 1849, and the stud was promptly broken up.

---

* By the end of the century, with the value of bloodstock rising even faster than the thoroughbred population, as many as nine in every ten foals would be bred to sell. There were 735 brood mares in the 1822 *Stud Book* but 5,890 in 1900.

For one thing, its paddocks were ripe for development as the suburbs of the capital rapidly expanded; and then there was the extraordinary situation of William Theobald's son-in-law, who had taken charge of the stud. Charles Thellusson was the great-grandson of a Huguenot banker whose will was as notorious in Chancery as the case of *Jarndyce v Jarndyce* in a new novel by Charles Dickens, *Bleak House*. It had stipulated that a trust already worth £600,000 in 1797 be maintained during the lifetime of three sons and their sons; only on the death of the last of these would the eldest male lineal descendants of each son divide a fortune that might easily, by that stage, run into tens of millions. Parliament had quickly prohibited similar schemes in future – but the courts, despite serial petitions, could find no way to set this one aside as cruel or absurd. Thellusson, as son of the last surviving grandson, was set to divide the bounty with just one other beneficiary. The worry now was that the bequest, poked and pulled by so many ermined midwives, might yet be stillborn. Litigation and apathy had been eroding the Thellusson holdings for generations already. As Dickens wrote of his parallel version: 'The little plaintiff or defendant, who was promised a new rocking-horse when Jarndyce and Jarndyce should be settled, has grown up, possessed himself of a real horse, and trotted away into the other world.'

Real horses, meanwhile, promised only to make matters worse. Both Thellusson and his father had a weakness for racing, and could not quite bring themselves to shut down the Theobald stud altogether. But The Baron could certainly go – he fetched £1,010 from the French National Stud – and so could his 1849 foal out of a little mare named Pocahontas. The chestnut colt was not just incongruously large, he was gargantuan, nearly grotesque. Old Theobald had never liked him, and the hulk was allowed to shamble away for 180 sovereigns into the stable of Brownlow Cecil, 2nd Marquess of Exeter.

A small man in his mid-fifties, always dressed in black, Lord Exeter wore so starched a collar that he seemed unable to turn his head without rotating his entire body. They said that he could walk from one end of Newmarket High Street to the other without acknowledging anyone who raised his hat. His dread of change in a world ordered for his benefit even caused him to force a diversion in the proposed path of the Great Northern Railway through Stamford, to preserve the great palace at Burghley from smoke and noise. But there was an unusual precision to the gibe that Lord Exeter 'never forgot by undue familiarity the exalted position to which he was born'.

Exeter's mother had been the famous 'Cottage Countess' Sally Hoggins, a buxom Shropshire lass who had married a mysterious newcomer to the remote village of Bolas Magna in 1790. His new friends speculated that 'John Jones' must be a highwayman, a smuggler, a French spy. It was only on the death of his childless uncle that he revealed himself as Henry Cecil, now 10th Earl of Exeter. His first wife having eloped with a curate, Cecil had disappeared to ride out his humiliation in rural obscurity, while leaving a trusted confidant to collect his rents and pay off his debts. To his credit, he maintained a loyal correspondence with the rustics he befriended in Bolas Magna; and as faithfully ignored the malice of Burghley servants and guests alike at the expense of the new chatelaine's blushing Salopian burr. Their son, unhappily, proved rather less relaxed about his interesting pedigree. Exeter had no memory of his mother, who had the decency to die when he was still an infant. And he made sure that his own choice of bride – an heiress of Cowdray Park in Sussex – could not have been in greater contrast to that made by his father.

Disraeli, in fairness, excused Exeter's hauteur as a form of diffidence: he found him 'shy, but very courteous'. Nor did the company Exeter kept on the racecourse suggest him to be a wholly prosaic character. George Payne, for instance: on the face of it – having blown an inheritance of £30,000 a year on cards, horses and hounds – he was a disastrous throwback. Yet he was adored across the Turf for his integrity and generosity, his sage counsel invariably sought by any gentleman in crisis. Colonel Peel, another of their circle, was so unpretentious that he liked nothing better than to pass a summer evening with Flatman, his favourite jockey, ratting the hayricks round Newmarket. And all three – Payne, Peel and Exeter – were staunch companions of the man whose effective investment as dean of the Jockey Club heralded a new decency in the racing elite.

As a young naval officer, stationed on Saint Helena, Henry Rous had staged the race meetings Napoleon enjoyed from the upper windows of his billet. Otherwise the most conspicuous achievement in Rous's rise to admiral had been to bring the rudderless, leaking frigate, *Pique*, from Newfoundland to Spithead in twenty days. 'I could not go back for repairs,' Rous explained. 'I had to be home for the second Autumn Meeting at Newmarket.'

It was Rous who filled the vacuum created by the abrupt exit of Bentinck. Like his predecessor, he was energetic, resolute and led from the front; but he was a much warmer character, able to rely on candour and incorruptibility to clear the webs Bentinck had sometimes seemed to patrol only as a bigger spider. Rous always stressed the Turf's value in bringing together different strata of society. In *The Laws and Practice of Horse Racing*, he rebuked a foreign writer who had observed a dangerous dislocation between the pastimes of Britons rich and poor. 'There is at least one amusement in which all classes participate,' he wrote proudly. 'One point of contact between all parties, and one source of enjoyment to individuals of every rank.'

Even so, Rous was dismayed by the increased standing of jockeys and trainers, believing that they should conduct themselves – and be treated – as servants not celebrities. But the force of his person-ality, such a double-edged sword in Bentinck, enabled Rous to lead by irreproachable example. He was impartial, diligent and astute. If not peering owlishly through his naval telescope from the stand, he would be riding alongside the track bellowing at jockeys he suspected of holding back their mounts. Equally, any tomfoolery at the start would prompt him to canter down and introduce the riders to some of the saltier argot of the high seas.

Under Rous, the Jockey Club proved rather more inclined to practise what it preached – albeit its powers still tended to be exer-cised with genteel complaisance. Arguably it would be the railways, rather than any sudden moral rigour, that finally spurred regulatory centralisation.

The Iron Horse transformed the horizons of the thoroughbred almost overnight. As early as 1842 it had been reported in wonder that Lord Palmerston's mare Iliona had been vanned to Darlington the morning after finishing third in the Northumberland Plate at Newcastle; reached Euston at 11.30 p.m., to be stabled overnight in the capital; and left Nine Elms Station at 9 a.m. to arrive on Winchester racecourse by lunchtime. The jockey who accompanied her rode in two races that afternoon.

Between 1846 and 1850 the rail network more than doubled, to 6,000 miles. Much cheaper than Bentinck's road-van, rail travel produced a series of auxiliary benefits that hauled the Turf into its modern age. The active racing population, for instance, was greatly expanded by a reduced premium on maturity and stamina: in 1802, just one runner in seventeen had been a two-year-old; by 1860 the ratio was one-in-three, while 730 of 1,514 races were staged at distances below one mile. More runners produced more stakes and more spectators, the latter in a virtuous circle of increased mobility and spending power. Northern and southern circuits were integrated at last, ultimately to the advantage of Newmarket over Yorkshire. Results had previously been distributed by carrier pigeons and coachmen. Now the development of the telegraph, and a sporting press tailored to broadening education and leisure, stimulated the spread of knowledge.

All these changes created a clear need for a more purposeful regulatory framework. After 1870, only those meetings staged under Jockey Club rules were published in official calendars; in turn this facilitated powers of licensing and disqualification. Socially and geographically, the Turf was losing its remoteness; it could no longer be arcane and privileged. As such, the coal that nourished racing's railway revolution could be said to have powered a steam-clean of the old byres of corruption.

This was hardly an overnight process, of course. For the time being, it barely seemed to matter whether the crooks won or lost – so long as they were shown how the game should be played. Lord Exeter himself was described as 'the most honourable, gentlemanlike, excellent fellow on the Turf! He seems like a young Bishop, in mufti; but he dearly loves a race for all its nobler, good-dispensing attributes.' Then there was Lord Eglinton, another 'unimpeachable, bona fide gentleman [who] runs steadily to win; making any accident in his stable instantly manifest in his own hand, to secure the public from robbery'. Eglinton, who owned one of the great champions of the era in The Flying Dutchman, was hailed by Disraeli as 'the most honest man, & the most straightforward, I ever dealt with'.

But honour did not blanch all colour from these men. Over dinner at the Jockey Club Rooms in Newmarket, Eglinton once made an incautious wager that he could hold his champagne better than any man in the kingdom. Sir William Gregory, subsequently Governor of Ceylon, memorably records how the next evening Colonel Peel introduced 'a tall, thin, wiry, long-legged customer, who looked for all the world like a pair of elongated tongs' as his brother-in-law, Sir David Baird:

> The match was to be bottle against bottle: that is to say, when one man's bottle was empty, the other was required to finish his, and then each had to begin a new one. Lord Eglinton took the lead at a tremendous pace, hoping to choke his antagonist before the first three bottles were consumed. Simultaneously he kept on chatting merrily, and laughing, as was his wont, while the novice held his peace, but stuck steadfastly to his task. Soon the ominous silence preserved by the latter, and the perfect ease with which he held his own, without turning a hair, began to tell upon his more loquacious antagonist, who was evidently going in difficulty. At last Lord Eglinton turned as pale as death, and rose slowly from his chair, exclaiming, 'I can do no more!' The struggle was at an end, and the defeated champion retired to bed, while the novice played billiards with Osbaldeston, winning two games out of three against that accomplished player. Next morning I had occasion to be out early on horseback in order to see one of my two year-olds gallop. The first sight that met my eyes on the Heath was Sir David Baird, with a short black pipe full of cavendish between his lips, cantering about the course on a hard-pulling hack, with his face as stolid as usual, and with obviously unclouded brow. Meantime, the unhappy Eglinton was walking about in front of The Rooms without his hat, which he confessed was too heavy for his poor head.

Another Scotsman making a singular mark was Lord Glasgow. He was prone to ordering the summary execution of disappointing horses – as many as half a dozen might be shot after a morning of trials on the gallops – and barely less peremptory in his treatment of servants. Once he set fire to the bed of the Doncaster clubhouse steward, who had the insolence to retire before Glasgow had returned for his nightcap; and he also threw a waiter out of a window of the Black Swan in York, famously telling the manager to 'put him on the bill'. Yet Glasgow also fed the poor of Paisley during a slump and bequeathed his stable to that most winsome of losers, George Payne.

Even eccentrics and spendthrifts, then, were now tending towards rectitude. There were exceptions, naturally. Lord Jersey's brother, a Jockey Club member, fled overseas from gambling debts exceeding £100,000; and Charles Greville deplored his former Turf confederate, Lord Chesterfield, as a wastrel: 'a princely fortune dilapidated by sheer indolence, because the obstinate and spoiled owner . . . lies in bed half the day, and rises to run after pleasure in whatever shape he can pursue it; abhors business, and has no sense of duty.' Over the next decade or so the Jockey Club would still fail to prevent many knavish deceits. But there is no mistaking an incipient 'Victorian' morality in those who, observing the incursions of industrial *nouveaux* on their home Turf, suddenly remembered their birthright as guardians of the public weal.

Stockwell's success in the 2000 Guineas of 1852 came as a literal revelation: Exeter, with a lordly resentment of touts and spies, had built a long covered ride for his trainer, William Harlock, to exercise horses in privacy. Anyone who did manage a glimpse of the maturing monster can only have recoiled from 'the very incarnation of ugliness'. Towering 16 hands high, Stockwell had mean little ears and The Baron's obtuse Roman nose, accentuated by a jaunty white blaze, while one groom accounted him 'a bit of a savage'. But this did not dilute his sheer power. His neck obtruded, short and thick, from a vast barrel of ribs; muscle surged through his back, loins and thighs. His bone had a matching density: knees, hocks, shins all commensurate with their great burden. And though he had failed to win his first three races, this strange, nearly mutant creature had now laid down a marker for the Derby itself. Unfortunately for Exeter, the early favourite for Epsom was owned by a man who confirmed him to be never more vulnerable than through his own snobbery.

James Merry had bought Hobbie Noble, the top two-year-old of 1851, for 6,000 guineas – an unprecedented statement of intent by a man who would soon take a central role in the Darley Arabian story. Merry had made his fortune in a bare-knuckle scramble for the seams of coal that transformed his native parish, Coatbridge near Glasgow, into a crucible of the Industrial Revolution. The stakes of exploitation became so astronomical, so quickly, that the two local families who got their hands dirtiest, early in the century, still bestrode the entire Scottish industry fifty years later: the Bairds owned thirty-five collieries; Merry & Cunninghame, with twenty-three, was nearly twice the size of the next on the list.

When Merry's father had first dabbled in coal, the local river was still furnishing the childhood nostalgias of the poet Janet Hamilton:

> *By fair Rosehall, through greenwood glades,*
> *Thou glid'st through rose and hawthorn shades,*
> *By hyacinth banks, where Monkland's maids*
> *Unbind their dark or golden braids*
> *And lave their snowy feet.*

But a rich band of iron ore was discovered even as canal and railway links opened to Glasgow; and then came the local innovation that changed everything: 'hot blast' smelting of iron, widely adopted from 1830. The idyll underwent an overnight apocalypse. Though three times more efficient than the old furnaces, the 'hot blast' method still devoured up to three tons of coal to make one of iron. And Scotland would need enormous quantities of both for the rest of Merry's life. In 1830, her pig-iron production stood at 37,500 tons. In the year he bought Hobbie Noble, it had reached 775,000 tons. And, with seams of both coal and iron underfoot, thirty-nine of Scotland's fifty-seven active blast furnaces were clustered in and around Coatbridge.

Stunted black trees now slumped along the riverbank, caked in slag and soot; thatched hamlets were overrun by squalid rows of overcrowded, insanitary company housing; feral children in rags wandered among stagnant pools. By 1844 there were 126 shops, 66 selling liquor. Janet Hamilton surveyed the inferno:

> A hunner funnels bleezin', reekin',
> Coal an' ironstane, charrin', smeekin';
> Navvies, miners, keepers, fillers,
> Puddlers, rollers, iron millers;
> Reestit, reekit, raggit laddies,
> Fireman, enginemen, an' Paddies;
> Boatmen, banksmen, rough an' rattlin',
> 'Bout the wecht wi' colliers battlin',
> Sweatin', swearin', fechtin', drinkin';
> Change-house bells an' gill-stoups clinkin'.

Every aspect of life here was controlled by the big firms. The 'truck' system required advanced wages to be spent in the company store. Barely legal as they were, one-third of such shops in Scotland were operated by Merry. Families lived in dread of eviction from their hovels. However dangerous and poorly paid their work, miners were under no illusions. During a strike in 1842, the Dundyvan Iron Works threw nearly four hundred men, women and children out of their homes on Christmas Eve.

No matter how many hands he needed, Merry was never short of cheap labour. Dispossessed crofters and starving Irishmen were imported to break strikes, keep down wages and divide a community that desperately needed solidarity against exploitation. Between 1841 and 1851, the proportion of Irishmen employed in the Coatbridge collieries and ironworks rose from 13 to 49 per cent. The rival communities clustered in ghettoes, convening only to break each other's heads at Orange marches or on St Patrick's Day. One young woman dared to flaunt a rare intermarriage by visiting her husband's neighbourhood. Perhaps she was also parading a pregnancy, for she was pinioned by his sister while his hobnailed father jumped on her belly. During the 1840s, it had remained necessary to bring in the infantry to break up strikes. Now Merry's pits were notorious as the most servile in Scotland.

As he approached fifty, Merry judged his fortune sufficiently secure to start enjoying its fruits. He resolved to upgrade his profile on the Turf and sent Hobbie Noble to be trained by William Saunders at Hednesford. In the process, Merry did not just introduce his name and wealth to the Exeters of this world. In posting a local prizefighter, Tass Parker, outside the stable of the Derby favourite, he also set out the abiding paradox of his racing career. Even as he sought to decorate his new status in society with a stable of thoroughbreds, he suspected the racecourse to be a hotbed of corruption. But that was the whole point. In such an environment, how could a proven streetfighter like Merry fail to show up all these naive patricians?

His paranoia would have been inflamed, of course, had he known more about another patron of the Saunders stable. For it was Hobbie Noble's defeat in the Derby that began the catastrophic freefall of Dr William Palmer. His subsequent infamy doubtless contributed to claims that Merry's colt was doped, but the chances are that Hobbie Noble simply got bogged down on the wettest Derby day in memory. True, he might have been better ridden: it was said that Frank Butler would have won on any of the first four home. As it was, he did so on the son of Birdcatcher, Daniel O'Rourke, trained by John Scott.

Doubts were also raised about the competence and, inevitably, the honesty of Stockwell's rider. Exeter's colt could only finish eighth, gashing his leg when crowded against the rail, but his preparations had also been interrupted by an abscess. One way or another, Exeter was certain that Stockwell had not shown his true colours and was impatient for a rematch in the St Leger. As ever, all roads now led to Doncaster. The only difference, nowadays, was that most people were taking the train.

In the old days, Sheffield men 'thought nothing, year after year, of walking through the night to Doncaster, taking up a good position next to the rails, which they never quitted from ten to five, and then walking the eighteen miles home again'. But now the Great Northern Railway had made it possible to travel up from London in just four and a quarter hours, and had credited a St Leger meeting for its first annual profit.

Increased mobility injected still greater social energy into the racecourse. The tone had been set by the very first Derby special, in 1838, when demand had been hopelessly underestimated and mounted police quelled a riot among the thousands left marooned at Nine Elms. After racing, Doncaster station would be overwhelmed by 'the hardware youths' piling onto the nearest carriage without knowing whether they were bound for Wakefield or London: 'They did not care where they went, as long as they went somewhere.'

Since the rout of the thimbleriggers at this meeting, twenty-three years previously, a new circus of chancers and adventurers – with a core of London pickpockets, the 'swell mob' – had begun to ride, third class, from one racecourse to the next. Its leaders, in the hope of restrained policing, observed a pragmatic etiquette with the other regulars on the circuit. One baronet, robbed at the Derby, had his watch returned by the 'head pickpocket' with a stammering apology for the naive error of a novice. Other itinerants – racecard-sellers and tipsters, whose wares were generally incidental to their showmanship – could even find themselves adopted as lucky mascots. How 'Black Jemmy', in his tartan tie and green cutaway coat, found his way onto this circuit is a mystery; but he was so devoted to Eglinton's stable that he was allowed to precede The Flying Dutchman through the crowd before the 1850 Doncaster Cup, shouting the odds as 'a horse to a hen' in his champion's favour. (Wrongly, as it turned out.)

Even George Bentinck had not been above giving a sovereign for a card – perhaps to the famous Jerry, in a gigantic straw hat, whose 'propensity to cling on to the side of carriages proved fatal to him at last, as one was overturned on to him at the Goodwood Meeting of '48'; or to Sailor Jack, 'with his alarming squint, and his utter disinclination to undergo the slightest examination on nautical matters'. Such celebrities might make £20 in a single day at a meeting like this. Altogether the barnacles picketing a 'race special' ran into many hundreds, both men and women; not to mention a song-and-skit artiste who might be either: 'a thin man of about fifty, who spends his summer in woman's attire, with ribbons in his hair, a faded yellow fan in one hand, and a green and pink parasol in the other'.

For the 1852 St Leger, however, spectators were finding it hard enough simply to identify the chief hope of Whitewall. In such heavy rain, the going was clearly going to suit Daniel O'Rourke – but Scott was also running his Oaks winner, Songstress, causing Charles Dickens to weary of all conjecture on the way north:

> No other business other than race-business any longer existed on the face of the earth. The talk was all of horses and 'John Scott'. Guards whispered behind their hands to station-masters, of horses and John Scott. Men in cut-away coats and speckled cravats fastened with peculiar pins, and with the large bones of their legs developed under tight trousers, so that they should look as much as possible like horses' legs, paced up and down by twos at junction-stations, speaking low and moodily of horses and John Scott.

At the eleventh hour it was announced that Butler would ride Daniel O'Rourke, who arrived in the parade ring with an eye 'as bright as a fiery coal', while Songstress was 'nervous and light, nothing like the animal she was on the Oaks day'. The filly had fluctuated so wildly in the betting that the punters now washed their hands of Scott altogether, and instead made Stockwell 7–4 favourite.

Since Epsom, Stockwell had won twice at Goodwood and also at York. There could be no traffic problems today, either, with just five opponents – the crowd nowadays being restrained at all big tracks not just by ropes but by chains and even solid rails. From the outset, Stockwell was rolling through the mud as implacably as a paddle-steamer; he suffered one or two to lead him through the first half of the race, but was already in command turning for home and reckoned as many as ten lengths clear at the post.

Afterwards the gentry retired to the hotels or the Grand Assembly Room, and the working men to the circus or a freak show of Aztec Lilliputians. Everywhere in the town Dickens heard 'a vague echoing roar of "t'harses" and "t'races" . . . until about midnight, at about which period it dies away in occasional drunken songs and straggling yells. But, all night, some unmannerly drinking-house . . . spits out a man too drunk to be retained: who thereupon makes what uproarious protest may remain in him, and either falls asleep where he tumbles, or is carried off in custody.'

None could now doubt that Stockwell was the outstanding member of the crop. Had circumstances not conspired against him at Epsom, he should perhaps have been the first colt ever to win the Triple Crown – the first, that is, to have both speed and stamina sufficient to win the 2000 Guineas, Derby and St Leger. In the event that distinction would be claimed for Yorkshire a year later by John Scott and West Australian.

It had been a day of sweet vindication, not just for Exeter but also for Leviathan Davies. Though Daniel O'Rourke had taken £80,000 out of his Derby book, Davies had never lost faith in Stockwell and boldly laid both the Whitewall pair for the St Leger. Now he set out to complete his recovery by laying James Merry as much as he cared to wager on Hobbie Noble for the Cambridgeshire Handicap.

14

Old Sweats and New Money

JAMES MERRY CONFORMED to the crudest caricatures of the new smokestack barons. Tall and lean, his very skin seemed to have been stretched in a spirit of cold economy. As a perennial outsider, he trusted nobody and was constantly sacking even the most upstanding trainers or jockeys. If not always wholly groundless, his suspicions reflected an assumption that other men went about their business with the same cupidity as he did his own. You only had to see him at the cockpit. Though cockfighting was by no means an ungentlemanly pursuit, Admiral Rous himself among its devotees, there was something fanatical about Merry's lust for its viscera. He bred gamecocks in their thousands, and thought nothing of wagering 500 guineas a main.

The fact that Merry wanted his horses to run straight gained him due approval from the public, but the same could not be said of his uncouth satellites. Tass Parker, the pugilist originally hired to guard Hobbie Noble's stable, was retained by Merry as a personal bulldog. The ingenuous Parker was at least loyal and free of guile. Merry's racing manager, a Glaswegian wine merchant named Norman Buchanan, deceived only Merry as to his parasitical intentions. The endless dismissal of professional horsemen may well have reflected Buchanan's need for scapegoats when his betting went awry.

It was Buchanan, no doubt, who led an overnight stampede to back Hobbie Noble for the Cambridgeshire Handicap after Merry sent Saunders down to William Day's yard to 'try' the horse against better yardsticks. As a typical instance of the continued indulgence of the Jockey Club, even under Rous, Day had been permitted to start training within three years of a suspension for trying to cripple a Derby favourite. His stable, unsurprisingly, had its own bush telegraph to the betting 'list' houses of London, then in their brief heyday:

> The wild fever among the houses on the Saturday night when Hobbie Noble 'came' for the Cambridgeshire, was such as we can never forget. Every lister seemed to be rushing wildly about, as if some great and long pent-up revolution had burst forth at last; and near Piccadilly Circus, that favoured haunt of the Ring, the delirium raged furiously . . . The news flew like wildfire from house to house, so that a commissioner often found the odds altered long before he had half finished his rounds.

Hobbie Noble might still have won the Cambridgeshire but for 'the execrable riding of poor little Pettit [who] entirely lost his head and rode his horse to a standstill' in heavy going. As it was, the horse only went down narrowly to a rival carrying 23lbs less. Evidently Buchanan had persuaded Merry they would be better off with a useless jockey they could trust, rather than a talented one they might not.

Parker, for his part, was more or less kept on a lead, released to thrash any tout with the gall to spy on Merry's horses on the gallops. The tout, his telescope peering cheekily out of the furze, is a stock character of the Victorian Turf. Living on his wits, he was engaged in a constant game of double-bluff, sieving all the misinformation to determine where and when a trial would take place, sometimes moving directly from one misty field of operation to another: from the fug of a taproom, where a stray remark by a groom might light his path to a gloomy nook of Newmarket Heath at daybreak.

But there was no more precious commodity than information, and its ownership was a clearly defined privilege. It was a tout, not a crooked trainer or jockey, who in 1821 first goaded the Jockey Club into publishing a notice in the Racing Calendar 'warning off' a named individual: William Taylor, alias Snipe, for the heinous offence of 'watching a trial with a telescope' and 'refusing to say who his employers were'. On another occasion a Yorkshire trainer was fined just 2s 6d by a local magistrate for riding his hack over a tout, on account of extreme provocation by one who subsisted by the equivalent of 'stealing copyright'.

All manner of deceits were considered legitimate when it came to tricking touts, right down to the use of paint to disguise horses. At least one subsequent Derby winner was impersonated on the gallops by a lame stablemate, in order to inflate the odds against him. Nor was this culture of mistrust confined to outsiders. Baron Alderson, the judge who presided over the Running Rein trial, noted on a visit to Whitewall how the stableboys' dormitory was locked the moment the horses had been given their late feed, such was the 'state of continual siege and fear of internal treachery'.

George Bentinck, congratulating his trainer on tracing a 'leak' in the yard, ordered that the groom be retained until turned to their own use. 'Now we have found him, we shall be fools indeed if we cannot ruin him and all his gang,' Bentinck wrote. 'Of course we must continue to sham the utmost confidence in him.' Even Jockey Club members had no compunction about laying horses they knew to be lame or sick, much to Baron Alderson's disgust: 'Such is jockey morality – to me, similar to obtaining money by cheating.'

By degrees, however, the sporting press was establishing the right of a newly literate betting public to reliable information. By this time there were reckoned to be between forty and fifty professional touts in Newmarket alone, on retainers of around a guinea per week. One who must have been earning a good deal more was paying the Electric Telegraph Company nearly £300 a year to transmit the results of trials. There was also a resident community of touts in Yorkshire, The Flying Dutchman's trainer counting 'sixteen heads, looking like as many crows in a file, watching the horse from behind a wall near Spigot Lodge as he came out for exercise'. It was hardly as though the tout did not earn his living: he rose as early as any stableboy in all weathers and required unusual skill, at a politic distance, merely to tell one brown quadruped from another – never mind to see through trainers' feints. Sir Joseph Hawley, owner of four Derby winners, grudgingly admitted: 'When the tout leaves Kingsclere, I shall think it time to take my horses away, for I shall know I have nothing worth touting.'

For now there was no more forbidding bastion against the touts than Lord Exeter. He kept trial saddles under lock and key, and weighed the riders on scales sealed from their view. Unfortunately, the one person his trainer really needed to keep away from trials was Exeter himself. He was notorious for having his horses galloped until their eyeballs popped: not averse, if vexed by their performance at the races, to having them thrashed across the gallops that same evening. Though many of his horses broke down or went stale, Exeter could not restrain himself even with a horse as good as Stockwell. On one occasion as many as seven or eight horses were slipped fresh into his path, one after the other. He caught all bar one, who held him off by a neck with three stone less on his back.

The wear and tear was such that Stockwell managed just one start in each of the next two years, and Exeter broke up his stud soon after. As a result, the champion bred by a Skinner Street hosier came bobbing back into the mainstream of Britain's new commercialism.

The metamorphosis in Victorian wealth and values was so perfectly registered in Lord Londesborough that he even changed his name – from Albert Conyngham to Albert Denison – in order to inherit a banking fortune of £2 million from his mother's brother. Curiously, this same uncle had only recently declined him £2,000 to redeem an unfortunate speculation in railway stock, requiring him to flee to Boulogne. Perhaps the idea was that he would grasp the value of £2 million only by learning that of £2,000. On the eve of his first wedding, after all, Londesborough had sat up all night playing écarté with George Payne at Limmer's Hotel, losing £30,000, before adjourning next door to St George's for the service.

Londesborough now remained a rake only in his resemblance to the garden implement: immensely tall and thin, 'all teeth and backbone'. In 1848, he indulged his archaeological kleptomania with a tour of the Mediterranean. In that year of revolution and upheaval across Europe, his journal exudes the confidence of an empire fuelled by industry and innovation – even as he contemplated the transience of others, past and present. At Naples, the king had not been seen in public for a year and his cannon gazed malevolently down upon his own people; at Livorno, Austrian troops had just butchered 500 citizens without trial. Londesborough left 'blessing my stars that I was an Englishman'.

On his return he issued the following invitation: 'Lord Londesborough at home, Monday 10th June 1850. 144 Piccadilly. A Mummy from

Thebes to be unrolled at half-past Two.' After 2,500 years at peace, the body of a princess was crudely eviscerated – her bindings sawn open, the hieroglyphics, papyri and amulets trimmed off like pork crackling – until 'found in a condition so exceedingly brittle . . . that the head came off'. Perhaps his guests at this point averted their gaze to a nearby Canaletto or Brueghel, these soon to be joined by a new purchase, *The Monarch of the Glen*, in the possession of one who baldly confessed: 'Pictures I do not understand.' In such a man, clearly, even an idle interest in the Turf was never going to be satisfied with half-measures.

Londesborough picked out a farm near Tadcaster as the site for what he intended to make the premier stud in the country. By the time he acquired Stockwell from Lord Exeter, one young stallion had already been installed. West Australian would ultimately prove a disappointment at stud; Stockwell, in contrast, began his rise as 'Emperor of Stallions'.

However fitful and petulant his treatment of trainers, the fact remains that James Merry launched the career of two – Mat Dawson and later Robert Peck – who would finally render obsolete the punishing 'sweats' revived by John Scott. With typical gall, by 1880 William Day was nonetheless claiming responsibility for the very revolution that supplanted his family as doyens of their profession. Since virtually every word of his memoirs was written with some self-serving purpose, there seems no basis for believing that 'I may take the credit, I believe, of being the first to discontinue the practice some twenty-eight or twenty-nine years ago.'

Old John Day had undoubtedly been a severe trainer, and William began with much the same reputation before adapting his methods, at least for younger horses. In every other testimony, however, Tom Dawson is universally acknowledged as the first to remove 'sweats' entirely from the training of thoroughbreds. Certainly his brother and former assistant, John, was openly derided for doing so when he first arrived in Newmarket.

Their father, George, had been Merry's first trainer in Scotland and it was here that another son, Mat, learned the ropes. Observing the benefits evident in coach-horses when confined to short stages,

Mat developed an emphasis on sharper work and better nutrition. He also stressed that horses should be treated as individuals, noting how different horses responded to different treatment: 'They are wonderful things to form likes and dislikes, and they, like the elephant, never forget an injury.' Not that the dividends were immediately apparent. In 1840, Mat took the aptly named Pathfinder all the way to Epsom, breaking his journey at Tom's stables in Middleham. 'There goes cocky little Mat to win the Derby!' called his brother as he set off next morning. Pathfinder finished last, 200 yards behind the next horse.

It was Tom who finally confirmed the efficacy of their methods, with Ellington in the 1856 Derby. He won £25,000, only to leave it in a hatbox on the luggage rack after being woken at Northallerton station. After a week, and a journey to Aberdeen, the hatbox was restored to its owner unopened.

Yet all the Dawsons had done is follow Robert Robson's innovations to their logical conclusion. Their success so transformed standard procedures that Scott's regime was renounced almost everywhere within a decade of his death in 1871 – quite possibly accounting for the emergence, around this time, of the slang 'an old sweat'.

The reduced workload of racehorses in training had not yet extended to the track. As late as 1867, the Derby winner contested two races in one afternoon just two days after being beaten in the St Leger. Nor was life much less arduous for stable staff. The power structure in racing yards remained nearly feudal, apprentices serving as the equivalent of batmen to senior grooms. A twelve-year-old arriving in Newmarket in the 1880s found himself stripped and dunked head first in a bucket, as an initiation, and then spent six months polishing boots and dressing poultry before he was even allowed to help brush a mane and tail. Discipline often devolved to the head man, whose tendency to sadistic excess can be gauged from the fact that a fourteen-year-old Yorkshire apprentice, who killed his tormentor by defending himself with a pitchfork, had his legal costs paid by another local trainer.

The opportunities for betterment, on the other hand, were exotically measured by Thomas Ward, who escorted some horses sold to Austria as a fifteen-year-old stableboy. Unimpressed with their new accommodation, he was overheard by their purchaser remarking that 'we would not stand this kind of thing in Yorkshire' and was promptly hired as a jockey, and then head groom. In due course he was appointed junior valet to the Duke of Lucca, a Bourbon prince then resident in Vienna. Ward became fluent in German, French and Italian, and uniquely adept in anticipating the foibles of his master. 'I have had the grooming of him,' he said. 'And it was a wuss job than ever the grooming of his hosses was.'

He proved so shrewd and trustworthy that he was promoted to master of the horse, minister of finance and eventually chief minister. A British diplomat, urging Ward to hold his nerve during the upheavals of 1848, invoked his first vocation: 'Keep your Horse in training and up to the mark, but don't bring him out in public till the day.' Ousted only when the new duke was assassinated in 1854, Baron Ward retired to farm an estate near Vienna and patented a machine to reap two and a half acres in 52 minutes, winning a gold medal at the Vienna Exhibition.

In 1859 James Merry promoted Mat Dawson to supervise his stables at Russley Park in Wiltshire. Dawson knew exactly what he was up against: the ironmaster had fallen out with John Prince, the previous trainer, even though they had just won the St Leger. Moreover, Merry wanted nothing to do with a yearling, Thormanby, Dawson had picked out for him at the same meeting. Typically, he made Dawson keep the colt at his own expense until graciously accepting ownership when he blossomed into a Derby possible.

The 'Glasgae body', as Merry liked to call himself, had by now contrived to get himself elected to Parliament, albeit essentially as an act of malice. The Tory seat he targeted in the 1857 general election, Falkirk Burghs, had long been held by the Bairds – the one family always to have outranked Merry in both trade and parish. As boys the Baird brothers had woken in a garret with snow on their blankets. Now James, the previous incumbent at Falkirk, was in a position to leave £500,000 to the Church of Scotland. (This was described as the highest fire insurance premium ever paid.) George Baird, the candidate this time, now owned 18,000 acres of Aberdeenshire, yet retained great pride in his austere, pious upbringing.

Suffrage remained so limited, and inducements and intimidations so routine, that 30 per cent of results in the previous election were disputed. Sure enough, though a lamentable speaker and said not even to know the Lord's Prayer, Merry harvested 770 votes against Baird's 491. The inevitable appeal established that Patrick Quigley had been bribed with £10; Richard Lyon, with £20; while Thomas Wyse had been offered money through his wife. The result was declared void, although 'it was not proven to the satisfaction of the Committee that these acts of bribery were committed with the knowledge and consent of the said James Merry, Esquire'. The Bairds seem to have been satisfied with Merry's humiliation, a Captain Dalziel filling the vacancy unopposed. Unabashed, Merry was in turn the only candidate when another general election was called the following year. He had also raised his national profile as the sponsor of John Heenan, the American challenger to Tom Sayers in what is generally considered the inaugural world title fight. Merry had his man stripped down in a Newmarket tavern for the wonder of his racing pals. After the fight, a brutal impasse broken up by police after forty-two rounds, his champion was offered beer – 'but no one could find Heenan's mouth'.

Three months later, Thormanby lined up for the Derby as second favourite. Determined to find a jockey beyond the reach of crooks, Merry and Buchanan had summoned Jack Sharpe, then riding in Russia. Warned that Sharpe had a fondness for the bottle, Merry dispatched the faithful Parker to meet him at Brussels. On arrival, Parker suspended his vigilance long enough to take a bath – whereupon Sharpe managed to get hold of a decanter of brandy. Though the consequences were obvious as Sharpe staggered into the parade ring, Dawson had to stand up fiercely to his employer before the teenage Henry Custance, due to ride a pacemaker, was authorised to switch mounts with Sharpe.

Thormanby won easily and Merry gloried in public acclaim – the crowd was reckoned to approach 500,000 – and private gain. He had won bets totalling £85,000. From this bounty he made a present of £100 to the jockey. Buchanan, in full Polonius mode, lectured young Custance not to let Merry's munificence 'turn his head'.

No fewer than six of Stockwell's first eight crops included the St Leger winner. In 1866 Lord Lyon won the Triple Crown by beating other sons of Stockwell into second place in all three legs. (The 2000 Guineas runner-up had been foaled two minutes after Lord Lyon, in an adjoining stall.) The following year, Lord Lyon's sister managed two wins and a second from her own three Classic starts.

Sadly, Londesborough did not live to witness Stockwell's success and nothing was cashed in faster by his heir than the stud. A sale that included Stockwell and West Australian was such a sensation that the Duc de Morny, Napoleon III's half-brother, travelled from France in the hope of upgrading the imperial stable. De Morny did manage to export West Australian for 4,000 guineas, to the consternation of all patriotic Yorkshiremen; but though he tried to buy Stockwell as well, he surrendered to a bid of 4,500 from Richard Naylor. Custody of the Darley Arabian line had been transferred from one banker's nephew to another.

Naylor and his brothers had inherited a banking house founded by Thomas Leyland in 1807. In trafficking over 22,000 Africans to the Caribbean, Leyland had helped to make Liverpool the capital of British slave transportation. (Heckled at the opening of the Theatre Royal in 1772, an actor spat back: 'There is not a brick in your dirty town but what is cemented by the blood of a Negro.') Where other slavers typically expected a yield of 8 or 10 per cent on their investment, Leyland would sometimes achieve over 40 per cent. Though the figures remain contentious, one study alleges that Leyland was still transporting 1.8 slaves per ship's ton after legislation had restricted British traders to 1.03. Three times Mayor of Liverpool, his estate of £600,000 was testimony to the habits of parsimony that would also be inherited by Richard Naylor. On first inheriting, however, Naylor evidently decided that it was high time someone in the family stopped counting money, and started spending it.

A Day at the Races

Epsom, 20 May 1863

No institution of Victorian life took its pulse quite like Derby Day. By mid-century the crowd was typically estimated at between 200,000 and 300,000. William Powell Frith's definitive canvas, unveiled in 1858, showed an Epsom described by Sylvanus as 'the national museum of character; so motley and curious is the vast, heterogeneous crowd . . . specimens of every rank and calling, every phase and shade of character; and these again, from every county, and most parishes in Great Britain.'

In his memoirs Frith recalled his first visit to a racecourse, at Hampton. Peering into a dining tent, he saw a solitary figure round off a day of failures by trying to cut his own throat with a blunt knife. 'The fool lost his money,' the painter's female companion remarked. 'But he won't lose his life; it wouldn't matter much if he did, for he ain't married, and he's an awful rip.' Frith, intrigued, decided to experience Derby Day – and was so mesmerised by acrobats, minstrels, fortune-tellers and pretty ladies that only the intervention of his fellow artist, Augustus Egg, saved him from a hustler in a dog-collar:

> 'Look here,' said the clergyman, 'don't you call names, and don't call me names, or I shall knock your d – d head.' 'Will you?' said Egg, his courage rising as he saw two policemen approaching. 'Then I call the lot of you – the Quaker there, no more a Quaker than I am, and that fellow that thinks he looks like a farmer – you are a parcel of thieves!' 'So they are, sir,' said a meek-looking lad who joined us; 'they have cleaned me out.' 'Now move off; clear out of this!' said the police; and the gang walked away, the clergyman turning and extending his arms in the act of blessing me and Egg.

A visiting Frenchman was astonished by the social promiscuity and licence of the carnival, extending to 'gentlemen' relieving themselves against the *wheels of a carriage containing ladies and young girls. 'On this day we are all things to all men,' he wrote. 'But only for one day, as in the Saturnalia of old. Tomorrow, distinctions of rank will be as rigid as ever.'*

Unfortunately, thanks to torrential rain and 'Crimean' mud, the 1863 race was witnessed by the thinnest crowd in years. The roads from town were reduced to such a state that none would ever again doubt the superiority of the iron horse; never again would the roads from town be lined by spectators, as described by Dickens:

> *Near the favourite bridges . . . clusters of people post themselves by nine o'clock, to see the Derby people pass. Then come flitting by, barouches, phaetons, broughams, gigs, four-wheeled chaises, four-in-hands, Hansom cabs, cabs of lesser note, chaise-carts, donkey-carts, tilted vans made arborescent with green boughs and carrying no ends of people, and a cask of beer – equestrians, pedestrians, horse-dealers, gentlemen, notabilities and swindlers by tens of thousands.*

Gypsy camps and canvas booths around the track sagged into a moat of slurry. In the magnificent 1830 grandstand, which could house 5,000, the gentry 'clung to their balconies like a seaman to a mainyard in the Bay of Biscay'. With that blend of pathos and fortitude unique to the British picnicker, ladies huddled against carriage hoods as their bedraggled consorts fished lobster salad and pigeon pie from Fortnum and Mason hampers.

Nonetheless, this would prove a landmark day in Turf history: the first Derby attended by the twenty-one-year-old heir to the throne. True, the Prince of Wales would soon draw a new set of racy spendthrifts into the sport. But his comfort in an environment so deplored by his mother consolidated a sense that racing was cleaning up its act. The death of Prince Albert, eighteen months previously, had so distanced the queen from her people that she would not even go to Ascot. His very presence, never mind his relaxed demeanour, was a signal that the man known to the Jockey Club simply as 'Bertie' intended a closer bond. A more immediate prompt, however, was the fact that Sir Frederick Johnstone had a runner in the big race.

Along with Henry Chaplin, Freddie Johnstone was one of two sporting tearaways who had rescued Bertie from his gloomy sequestration at Oxford, introducing him to cigars, racehorses and other 'fast' addictions his mother (or her critics) would suggest as the cause (or result) of his isolation from responsibility.

In bringing Bertie to Epsom today, Johnstone and Chaplin quietly opened a new era on the Turf. All three would one day lead in a Derby winner of his own; and, by breaking open the crust of the racing establishment, they enabled Jews and Americans to do the same. And if scandal also beckoned them all, it was only ever in the bedroom — not on the racecourse. Bertie never gambled or drank as heavily as Johnstone. (William Day, who had seen so many of the century's great plungers, said that the stakes laid by the young baronet made his 'blood run cold'.) But this first exposure to the Derby was nonetheless a milestone in Bertie's social education: a lesson in how to keep his bearings in a heady, risky environment.

And the prince had something to offer in return. In exchange for the colour and excitement so lacking in his austere upbringing, Bertie would redress the sport's deficiency in dignity. When the young man chatting in the stand was recognised as the next king — a fleshy, brooding face; hooded eyes; rather peevish lips — a murmur of curiosity spread through the crowd:

> *When, without form or ceremony, he took his seat and lighted his cigar, the people cheered him from the bottom of their hearts, and even the Ring spontaneously ceased betting for a couple of minutes . . . As the Prince gazed on the lot cantering down, and viewed the grouping of the carriages on the hill, and the sea of carriages beneath him, animated with but one hope, he must have admitted that it was a spectacle such as no other country could produce, but the one over which on some distant day he may be called on to rule.*

On the track, also, were signs of transition. The Eaton stud in Cheshire built up by Lord Grosvenor was undergoing a period of neglect under his grandson, the Marquess of Westminster. Following an epidemic of strangles, in 1861 the marquess told his stud groom to sell half a dozen of the debilitated yearlings — and, if nobody could be found to take them off his hands, to have them shot. John Griffiths, hired by Richard Naylor to bed down Stockwell's new home at nearby Hooton Hall, secured the lot for just £700. Naylor's trainer in Newmarket soon advised him to start backing one of these youngsters for the Derby. Naylor did so, at 50–1, and was now sitting pretty after Macaroni had won the 2000 Guineas.

Macaroni still faced a formidable rival in the favourite, Lord Clifden. Escorted into the parade ring by three gamekeepers and 'an Irish gentleman strong enough to shake a nobbler as a cat does a mouse', Lord Clifden was ridden by George Fordham, champion jockey for the last eight seasons. But the race borrowed its timbre from the tempest: thirty-four false starts; three horses sprawled in the mud rounding Tattenham Corner; and a duel as unsparing as had ever been seen for a Derby. For most of the straight Fordham was sitting quietly; Tom Chaloner, in Naylor's silks, seemed all out simply to keep level on Macaroni. In the very last strides, however, Lord Clifden became momentarily unbalanced. It is said that he trod on an orange peel. With one last, desperate surge, Chaloner and Macaroni pounced to win by a head.

In Newmarket the church bells rang to mark the town's return from the brink: the Heath had been perilously out of favour for the preparation of Classic horses. Naylor was said to have won £100,000, but Fordham was inconsolable. Despite credible claims as the greatest jockey yet, his Derby record was becoming a millstone. He knew the kind of thing that was being muttered: Fordham lacked nerve; Fordham panicked on the downhill turn into Tattenham Corner. He could deal with such glib ignorance. But riding to join friends for dinner that night he overheard a stranger complaining that the Derby favourite had been blatantly pulled by his jockey. The righteous thrashing he administered afforded little comfort, and he spent the evening sobbing on the stairs outside the dining room.

15

'She is my brood mare.
The others are my hacks'

RICHARD NAYLOR HAD sealed his status with a colt who could otherwise have been shot by the 2nd Marquess of Westminster, richest of all the landed magnates. Now James Merry was about to launch a champion who would goad Westminster's heir into unprecedented expense, in order to restore the Darley Arabian line to the stud that had housed Pot8os a century earlier.

As soon as he acceded as 3rd Marquess, in 1869, Hugh Lupus Grosvenor set about reviving the derelict Eaton stables and paddocks. His father had allowed the famous yellow and black silks to lapse, reflecting an austere dread of ostentation even as the family's Belgravia and Pimlico estates soared in value. But the ambitions of the new marquess to renew the House of Grosvenor as a force on the Turf did not mean that he was any less determined to efface the stains left by his louche great-grandfather. At forty-four, indeed, he transferred from Commons to Lords as a Whig paternalist so clumsily unreconstructed that he had opened a schism from which his party would never truly recover.

Within months of becoming an MP, at just twenty-one, he had witnessed the same European upheavals of 1848 as Lord Londesborough, his tour of Italy transforming into a political crash course. In Rome he met Sidney Herbert, who assured him 'that the last act of the King of Naples was pulling people's toe-nails out'. In Britain, he decided, the masses should never be so provoked; but nor, reciprocally, should they ever rock the boat. His education continued with a tour of India. 'I think I should like to shoot one elephant, but not more,' he wrote from Ceylon. 'A man killed 17 in three days last week.' Invited to the secret kingdom of Nepal, he saw the pyre where the corpse of a royal wife had just been incinerated alongside two live slaves. Returning through India, six years before the Mutiny, he was appalled by the corruption of local rulers. He returned with an unshakeable faith in the unique competence to rule of his race, in general, and his class, in particular.

In 1866, he led a backbench revolt that would have momentous consequences for Victorian politics. For in denouncing his own leader, Gladstone, he enabled Disraeli to bring the Conservatives back from the wilderness they had entered when Peel, steeled by Herbert, embraced free trade in 1845. During the ensuing industrial boom, a new tier of aspiring artisans had identified themselves with middle-class values: thrift, temperance, self-help. By this time, they numbered at least 800,000 in an adult male population of 5.3 million – and Gladstone was proposing to incorporate half of them into an expanded franchise of 1.3 million. The defection of the future Marquess of Westminster, in ecstasies of dread about the demagogy that had caused revolution and despotism abroad, enabled Disraeli to form a minority government. Gladstone responded at a public meeting in Liverpool, on the doorstep of the stately piles at Eaton and Knowsley – respectively the family seats of the Westminsters and the Tory leader, Lord Derby. He pronounced a plague on both their houses, as bastions of an intransigence that would destroy the very order they sought to preserve. In the event, the Reform Act passed in 1867 was broader than the bill that had fatally sundered Gladstone's support the previous year. Disraeli had artfully perceived a chance to restore the Conservatives as a viable party of government. Gladstone, for his part, never forgave 'the timid men' who had scuttled his ministry from within.

The new Marquess of Westminster consoled himself over these charges of perfidy by raking in £115,000 a year from his London rents alone. He regarded spending almost as a public duty and soon commissioned Alfred Waterhouse to replace the neo-Gothic palace at Eaton, itself completed barely sixty years previously. The result, £600,000 and a decade later, was an eligible contender for the famous critique: *C'est magnifique, mais ce n'est pas la gare*. Certainly all that was lacking was a lost property office and second-class waiting room. But Eaton's ultimate ornament was to be its stud.

★

By 1866, Mat Dawson's reputation was such that he was able to set up a public stable in Newmarket. He would not miss James Merry. Courteous and equable though he was, Dawson would brook no interference. His successor at Russley – another Scotsman, James Waugh – could not hope to cow Merry in quite the same way.

One of the first animals to enter Waugh's care was Marksman, bought by Merry as a yearling in 1865 for 1,000 guineas. The preceding lot through the ring had been knocked down for the same sum to Henry Chaplin, and given the name Hermit. Still only twenty-five, Bertie's friend was suddenly making himself very conspicuous on the Turf – a reaction to the humiliation he had suffered when his exquisite fiancée, Lady Dorothy Paget, bolted with the Marquess of Hastings the previous year. It was hardly a coincidence that Hastings had himself embarked on a giddy spree of spending on bloodstock. When Chaplin gave £11,000 for two Stockwell colts entered in the 1865 Derby, his rival responded by giving the moneylender, Henry Padwick, the preposterous sum of £12,000 for his own Derby entry.

Both young men were disgusted by the performances of their new colts at Epsom, the prize instead claimed for France by Gladiateur, the 'Avenger of Waterloo'. But Hermit proved a much better investment, beating Marksman by a neck in the 1867 Derby. The winner had been fanatically laid by Hastings, who lost £120,000 altogether – including £20,000 to Chaplin. In a celebrated gesture of magnanimity, Chaplin sent Freddie Johnstone round to assure him that payment could be deferred. But Hastings was now in big trouble. It did not help that he entrusted his finances to Padwick and his horses to the Day family. Their unique brand of solicitude so appalled Admiral Rous that he fired off a letter to *The Times*: 'What can the poor fly demand from the spider in whose web he is enveloped?' The credulous fly replied indignantly on behalf of his friends but would be dead before the year was out, at just twenty-six. On a last visit to the seat of his ruined family, he saw a portrait of Chaplin and shot out both eyes with a pistol. Bright's disease was named as the clinical cause, but those who had seen Hastings burn himself out in five short years on the Turf favoured a more moralistic diagnosis:

Betting is said to be the touchstone of the Englishman's sincerity, but with the Marquis a craving for the odds had really become a disease . . . His public coups were often so brilliant that it was hardly to be wondered at that he believed in his own destiny and his power to break the Ring . . . The Ring, on the other hand, marked him out for their own, and never left him. They would cluster beneath the Jockey Club balcony at Epsom, holding up their hands to claim his attention, and catching at his replies like a flock of hungry hawks. There he would stand smiling at the wild tumult below, wearing his hat jauntily on one side, a red flower in his buttonhole, his colours round his neck, cool and calm while 'the talent' made his horse a 'hot favourite' . . . For a while he was a perfect Cocker; but he fell at last in the unequal strife.

His fate was in many minds when another young aristocrat announced himself on the Turf the following year. Archibald Primrose, 5th Earl of Rosebery, had just inherited the title and estates of his grand-father, while still an undergraduate at Oxford. He promptly bought himself a Derby colt for £3,500 – Ladas, trained just up the road on the Berkshire Downs. Rosebery registered his colours, primrose and rose hoops, and assembled Regy Brett, Randolph Churchill and other young bloods to watch Ladas on the East Ilsley gallops. 'Brute of a beggar,' scoffed Churchill.

Rosebery's father had died when he was three, while his mother's subsequent marriage began a lasting estrangement. He found himself with £30,000 a year, 21,000 acres of Scottish Lowlands and a seat in the Lords while yet to shed a chrysalis of precocity and pride. For all his intellect, at Oxford he was soon drawing attention to himself in less auspicious ways: a dandy hurtling around the town in his dog-cart, laughing off £1,000 lost at Northampton races, insolently impatient with petty obligations. Eventually Rosebery was summoned before the dean and advised that undergraduates were not permitted to own racehorses. If unable to defer this indulgence, he could leave the university forthwith. Ridiculously, though he could easily have perse-vered under some *nom de course*, Rosebery refused to yield and was sent down at Easter 1869. 'Dear Mother,' he wrote, 'I have left Oxford. I have secured a house in Berkeley Square; and I have bought a horse to win the Derby. Your affectionate Archie.'

He spent Derby week as a guest of Henry Chaplin. Everyone was curious to see which way the young earl might turn. In the event, Ladas finished tailed off behind Tom Dawson's Pretender. This could not have been a less reliable portent. To this day, Pretender remains the last Yorkshire colt to win the Derby at Epsom; while Rosebery would eventually win the race three times.

Merry returned to Epsom the following season with an odds-on favourite, a son of Macaroni named Macgregor. Even Gladstone came to see him – his one trip to the Derby – only to be refused admission to the paddock by a gateman. But Macgregor and the luckless Fordham could manage no better than fourth behind Kingcraft, trained by Mat Dawson. Typically, Merry divided his suspicions between putative nobblers and the ineptitude of his trainer. At the end of the season Waugh left Russley, and Merry replaced him with a young man steeped in Yorkshire horse lore.

Robert Peck's father had trained the runner-up in The Baron's St Leger, and his mother was a Hesseltine – a name that recurs through the annals of the northern Turf, down to the Bob Hesseltine whose riding for Leonard Childers triggered a duel at York in 1709. As a twelve-year-old apprentice, Peck had ridden a filly named Blink Bonny in her work across the moors above Malton. She emboldened him to the first wager of his life, 5 shillings at 20–1 for the 1857 Derby. On the great day the boy waited for the result at the tele-graph office. The clerk had got no further than 'B – L –' when young Peck raced up to the yard to hoist the flag of victory. The bells of St Michael's rang out, a band paraded in the streets, and the pubs stayed open all night. It was only then that Peck remembered there was also a colt named Black Tommy in the Derby field. True, he was a 200–1 shot saddled by his owner's valet; but young Peck was shaken to discover that Blink Bonny had only just denied Black Tommy in a desperate finish.

Peck implored his new employer to buy one of the last colts sired by Stockwell. Naylor's stallion had died the previous year, his repu-tation such that he had at one stage commanded the mind-boggling fee of 300 guineas per mare. Kept in trim by daily 15-mile walks with his groom, a burly Yorkshireman named Mat Veal, he was often found tethered outside various public houses en route. When Stockwell died, Veal sobbed into his ale for days. 'I'd as soon 'ave lost our 'Ria,' he bawled. (After this tribute his wife, Maria, presumably felt little inclination to console him.)

Naylor had not seemed to derive much joy from Stockwell's success. His son-in-law, the 5th Baron Rossmore, remembered him as ever more 'cross-grained and eccentric'. Rossmore was one of the frolicsome young aristocrats clustering round the Prince of Wales. 'Well, Rossmore,' Bertie would ask, seeing him without a silk top hat at Epsom. 'Have you come r-r-ratting?' Rossmore clearly found Naylor a challenge. In his memoirs he depicts a grasping old man who viewed even his daughters with suspicion, and their young men with loathing. Unfortunately for Rossmore, he reserved a special distaste for Irishmen. Our hero was undaunted. 'It didn't matter to me if Mittie Naylor hadn't a penny in the world,' he wrote. 'I was in love.'

Greater love has no man, clearly, than to miss his own horse winning the City and Suburban Handicap, in order to secure an interview with his prospective father-in-law. Finding Naylor lying on a sofa at his townhouse, 'grousing over himself and pretending to be very ill', Rossmore cheerfully announced that he had just won the City and Suburban. A grunt. Rossmore ploughed on. 'I've come to ask you to allow me to marry your daughter,' he said. Naylor scowled. 'Go away, Rossmore,' he said. 'I tell you I'm far too ill to discuss those sort of things.' Then he suddenly jumped to his feet and asked: 'But have you really won the City and Suburban?' The wedding took place two months later. Bertie roared with laughter when Rossmore recounted the tale: 'How like Naylor!'

Bertie had meanwhile discovered that disapproval of Freddie Johnstone and his other racing chums was not confined to his mother. In 1870, he was hissed at Ascot after an excruciating appearance in the Mordaunt divorce case. Though not named as a co-respondent, Bertie had been among those lovers claimed by Harriet Mordaunt in repentant ravings to her husband. The royal witness was treated with deference in court and widely praised for a manly dignity in denying any improper connection with the lady. Johnstone was not so fortunate, even obliged to deny having a venereal disease that might account for Harriet's hysteria over her baby's health. Though the court dismissed her 'confession' as a deranged fantasy, it had made plenty of sense to her husband. Two summers previously he had dragged Harriet to see her two beautiful white ponies from Bertie's stables at Sandringham led onto the lawn by his grooms and shot. Whatever the facts in this particular case, it was quite plain that Bertie – who astonished the court by disclosing that he often used hansom cabs to pay social calls – was not safe in taxis.

The queen implored Bertie to set an example to a generation that appalled her with its 'frivolous, pleasure-seeking, heartless, selfish, immoral, gambling' ways – even going so far as to compare its decadence with the fuse that lit the French Revolution. To avert some such calamity in modern times, she urged him to distance himself from the ignorance and self-indulgence of his male companions, and young women 'so fast, frivolous and imprudent'.

Respectfully but firmly, Bertie stood his ground. It was far better, he retorted, to exalt the national sport than the mean, Low Church grumbles of its critics. In fairness, Bertie was always a relatively modest gambler. The biggest single stake of his life was £600. Accordingly he begged his mother to spare him an annual wringing of hands over his love of the Turf, to acknowledge his age and experience of society, and allow him to use his discretion 'in matters of this kind'.

It was in his gambols, not his gambles, that he proved reckless. Lord Stanley, who knew him well from the racecourse, feared a genuine republican groundswell. Of course, Bertie's attitude was hardly unusual among men of his class, among whom paternity was often not even skin deep. Lady Moncrieffe of that Ilk launched five daughters into London society with a single golden rule: '*Never* comment on a likeness.' Protesting an essential fidelity to his wife, Bertie borrowed an analogy from his other favourite pastime: 'She is my brood mare. The others are my hacks.'

In 1873 Bertie's secretary asked Rosebery whether he would lend his townhouse for the entertainment of the prince's 'actress friends'. Rosebery's firm rejoinder, that the house was too small and that he did not expect to be approached on the matter again, was an early indication that here was no mere sycophant. He was travelling widely, already celebrated for his erudition, wit and cynicism. Though he had started up a stud at The Durdans, an ivied mansion at Epsom, he immersed himself in racing without ever being submerged. Both Gladstone and Disraeli recognised a star in the making.

It soon became clear which way he was leaning, as when fulminating against the Tory stranglehold on the House of Lords. 'We have no hereditary surgeons, or priests, or soldiers, or lawyers,' he complained. 'But for those to whom we entrust our fates, our fortunes, and our honour, no such training is requisite.' But these emerging Liberal proclivities did not diminish Disraeli's lasting personal influence on Rosebery. In fact, it was Disraeli's wife who first introduced the undergraduate earl to the buxom daughter of Baron Mayer de Rothschild, at Newmarket races in 1868.

Ten years would elapse before Rosebery recognised the destiny latent in that encounter; and many more before the Turf could register its consequences for the Darley Arabian line. In the meantime, the racecourse increasingly enabled both Bertie and the Rothschilds to flout establishment prejudice. Already a friend of Natty Rothschild, Bertie stayed with Mayer for stag-hunts at Mentmore Towers in Buckinghamshire. As with his other racing friendships, there were reciprocal benefits: Bertie was able to reiterate his independence; and Mayer became the first Jew elected to the Jockey Club.

If in doubt, punters had developed a default option: 'Follow the Baron!' This proved a lucrative strategy in 1871, when Mayer won four of the five Classics, his amiable, ursine figure mobbed as he led in the Derby winner. 'The luck of the Baron has certainly been extraordinary, but he is grudged it by none,' remarked one correspondent. 'All honour to such a noble sportsman! It would be well for the best interests of the Turf if all raced as he.'

Bertie could have asked for no more obliging contrast to Rosebery than Christopher Sykes, who hosted the prince and his friends at reckless expense in Yorkshire, for hunting and racing, and in Mayfair, for more metropolitan modes of sport. Though ten years his senior, this pathetic, bibulous dandy routinely submitted to Bertie's most witless degradations. When the prince suddenly poured a glass of brandy over his head, Sykes responded deadpan: 'As Your Royal Highness pleases.' He was baited with cues under the billiard table, or had the royal cigar burned into his hand. One night he was so drunk that he was put to bed with a dead seagull.

But there was one genuine bond between Sykes and Bertie: both were fugitives from parental austerity. Old Sir Tatton Sykes had been ranked with York Minster and Fountains Abbey as one of the three great sights of Yorkshire: an eighteenth-century throwback in dress, diction and stamina. Even in his eighties, he would seize a pick from a roadbreaker and continue the work while his guest was refreshed with ale at the manor house. No St Leger winner in history – and he witnessed 77 of them – was ever received more warmly than the one named in his honour, which he led in himself in 1846. 'From youth to death he never weakened in an almost insane passion for fox-hunting, racing, and the very companionship of horses,' recalled his grandson. 'It formed the whole basis of his life and character . . . Very vain, he exploited the then meagre arts of publicity with shrewdness . . . Ludicrous and yet respected, a char-latan in some ways, and yet a homely, comforting, familiar figure, a symbol and a caricature of England, I dare say he was revered and mocked in equal degrees.' Not so, however, within his own family – where he was feared unequivocally as 'a stone-age tyrant', a sadistic flagellant who 'preserved to the last the more revolting vices of the brutal age that produced him'.

The court fool's brother had dealt with their shared insecurities in a very different way – and, as a direct result, Robert Peck was able to find a Derby colt for James Merry. For the son of Stockwell picked out by Peck at the Doncaster yearling sales had been bred by Christopher Sykes's brother, their father's namesake, who had inherited the famous Sledmere stud eight years previously. Young Sir Tatton was pious and taciturn, petulantly decapitating flowers in cottage gardens with his stick and telling his tenants to grow potatoes instead. Under his father, the stud had been chaotically overrun by 300 horses at a time, many unnamed. Immediately after the despot's death, his heir sold off the whole lot with the exception of one filly, and brought in a handful of new mares including 'the speedy lop-eared Marigold' who had finished second in the Oaks. It was her mating with Stockwell that had produced the colt recommended to Merry by his new trainer in 1871.

Reluctant to back young Peck's judgement, Merry set a ceiling of 1,000 guineas. Luckily his bid of 950 was not countered, and he named his new acquisition Doncaster. The ironmaster badly needed a new champion to varnish the image he had been cultivating between his highland estate, his MP's townhouse in Eaton Square, and the racecourse – even as his reputation sank to new depths among the miners of Lanarkshire.

Though they still relied on the same tools as a century before – pick, hammer, wedge, muscle – advances in drainage, ventilation and lighting had opened ever deeper seams. Output and profits were all soaring to record levels. Scottish coal production had doubled in the previous fifteen years. Even wages were rocketing. In 1869 a Lanarkshire miner would typically earn 3s 6d per day; in 1872, he was expecting nearer 9s. 'The Lord Chancellor now sits upon a bag of wool,' George Stephenson noted. 'But wool has long since ceased to be emblematical of the staple commodity of England. He ought rather to sit on a bag of coal, though it might not prove so comfortable.'

But the boom was a precarious one. The Franco-Prussian War had created an illusory spike in demand, while a glut was threatened by investors seeking quick profits. For the ironmasters there was a new headache as the Bessemer process introduced cheaper steel to the marketplace. Towards the end of 1872, Merry and his rivals agreed to cut wages by as much as 2 shillings per day. There were immediate mass walkouts.

Alexander Macdonald, president of the Miners' National Association, tried to steady the ship. Macdonald had long been mistrusted by militants for his pragmatic, conciliatory approach. But he also rebuked Merry's colliers for their intemperance and political apathy: 'They have lived like the carrion eagle, in the wake of an advancing army, but have fought none of its battles.'

Now he warned his members not to fall into a trap. A strike was just what the masters sought, to break the union. Since prices and profits were plunging it was unrealistic to oppose a fair reduction. The militants reacted furiously: Macdonald would return them to poverty and go off to drink port with the coal lairds. As ever, the masters had divided to rule. Bailiffs from Merry & Cunninghame, who had seen eviction notices coolly torn up in their faces during the first, heady protests, were now enforcing them through the courts. The firm's pits were meanwhile kept open by 'scabs', herded through the pickets by police. The strikers, hungry and demoralised, could not hold out.

It was at this bitter low that Doncaster exalted his owner as the toast of a vast holiday crowd at Epsom. For a long time Peck had been embarrassed by the colt he had chosen. Even in the spring of 1873, he was still making his way over the gallops like a bad-tempered glacier. One morning the despairing Peck decided to ride the colt himself. Hitherto mounted by a featherweight, Doncaster was suddenly roused from his torpor by his eleven-stone trainer. Astounded, Peck dismounted and announced: 'There's the winner of the Derby.' He promptly took 66–1 against Doncaster for Epsom, and told Merry that his colt should make his debut in no less a race than the 2000 Guineas. Unsurprisingly, he was too green to make any real impression, but he did finish nicely enough from off the pace.

As in Thormanby's year, Derby day did not start well. Jem Snowden had promised Peck to give his mount a morning spin over the downs, but simply failed to appear. Alas, Peck could not be surprised. He and Jem had been apprentices together in the same Yorkshire stable. Jem had a nearly ethereal talent. His parents had sold pots and pans from a cart round the Dales, and he learned to ride by 'trying' horses bareback at gypsy horsefairs. In a race Jem was through a gap before other riders noticed it opening. He had been a teenager when winning the 1864 Derby. Nine years on, he was clinging pathetically to the shreds.

His story was hardly unique among Victorian jockeys subsisting on a starvation diet. Bill Scott, for instance, had died barely two years after throwing away the Derby of 1846, his mount veering across the track as though pitching away from the reek of brandy. It was true that many trainers still preferred Snowden drunk to a lesser rider sober: it was not as though drink diminished his pluck. But sometimes he was barely able to hold the reins, and needed other jockeys to prop him up through a race. Snowden would arrive at the starting post, winking and blinking and giggling: 'Just mind us a bit, wilt thou?' During real binges he might disappear for weeks. Checking into a hotel at Chester, to ride for Westminster, he remarked on the unusual lack of bustle for the races – only to be told that he was a week late. After each blowout, it was harder to pick up the pieces; harder to deceive himself with the vows of reformation he made on long marches across the moors. These merely registered the completion of another cycle, the hand of a clock clicking a notch closer to doomsday.

Doncaster's success in the Derby can only have accelerated the ruin of Jem Snowden, who would die in poverty at forty-three. After oversleeping, he was replaced by Fred Webb, a young rider apprenticed to Mat Dawson. Doncaster had seemed a no-hoper, freely offered at 50–1. The Guineas winner, another Stockwell colt named Gang Forward, surely had his measure. Yet Webb soon had Doncaster tracking the leaders and was still sitting quietly at Tattenham Corner, as the other jockeys were beginning to push. In the straight, Webb kicked for home and though Gang Forward followed him through, there was still a length and a half between them at the finish.

Two days later, Peck saddled Marie Stuart to win the Oaks for his patron as well. An attempt then to win the Grand Prix de Paris with Doncaster proved something of a debacle: Peck got on the wrong ferry and ended up in Belgium, and a French farrier was accused of pricking the horse's foot. In September, however, Merry's two Classic winners squared up for the St Leger – at the track for which the colt had been named. All the way up the straight, Doncaster and Marie Stuart were neck and neck, dragging each other clear of the rest; at the post, however, it was the filly who gained the verdict by a head. Stockwell's 1870 crop had engraved a fitting epitaph for their great sire: winning two Classics and finishing second in the other three.

In an era when most top stables maintained long and loyal part-nerships with particular riders, Merry had now won seven Classics with seven different jockeys. The one rider he admired, 'Speedy' Payne, had so few other believers that he eventually gave up and took a post as coachman to an Oxford doctor – who evidently did not think much of him, either. One day Payne drove his employer to a lunatic asylum and checked him in, cheerfully advising his hosts to ignore the patient's delusory claims to be a doctor. 'Don't pay any attention to him,' he said. 'He always says that.'

But the pinnacle only brought Merry to a precipice. Over the next eighteen months he found himself overwhelmed by adversity. His health failing, he quit Parliament, while a public flotation of his mines, coinciding with the fall in prices, backfired disastrously. When the masters reduced wages by another 2 shillings, even the Coatbridge men downed tools. Macdonald joked: 'Surely we are pretty near the end of the world now!' Once again, he urged his men to take a 1-shilling cut on the chin. Once again, militant leaders fired up the rank and file with cries of treachery. This time they lasted five months until worn down by evictions, strikebreakers and starvation.*

Perhaps sensing that the blood was running dry, the leech Buchanan tried one last gamble. Confident that Merry would not want dirty washing examined in public, Buchanan concocted a legal claim for unpaid services on the basis that he would be bought off before the case reached a court. For once his punt paid off. Disenchanted, Merry broke up his stable. Though most of the horses went through the ring, Doncaster was sold directly to Peck himself. Given that he was prepared to pay the incredible sum of 10,000 guineas, Merry must have had a hunch his brilliant young trainer had already secured new backing from somewhere. Sure enough, just a couple of weeks later Peck sold Doncaster to Westminster – recently created a duke – for a record 14,000 guineas. Westminster had pointedly resolved not to deal directly with Merry. When his father had given up the Eaton stud, Merry had promptly registered the lapsed yellow and black Grosvenor silks in his own name. The symbolism could not have been more brazen. As a result, Westminster would sooner give

---

* Macdonald washed his hands of the rebels, his ego instead soothed by the historic distinction – shared with Thomas Burt – of being elected an MP in the 'labour' interest the same year.

Peck a 40 per cent profit than pay a lesser sum into the sooty hands of Merry.

Merry died on 3 February 1877, leaving £680,402 9s 7d. Eight months later, 207 men and boys were killed in the Blantyre colliery explosion, the worst disaster in Scottish mining history. Among those to witness the aftermath was the twenty-one-year-old James Keir Hardie, who would not rest until he had laid the foundations of mass unionism in the next century. William Dixon, the pit owner, meanwhile went to court to evict thirty-four destitute widows from their tied cottages.

A Day at the Races

Alexandra Palace, 1 July 1868

'NB. The Company reserves the right of refusing Admission to any Person they think proper.'

The last line was comically lax: only improper persons, it might be construed, were likely to gain admission. But the advertisement also stipulated a fee of one shilling for anyone attending the first race meeting in the grounds of Alexandra Park. It would be staged 'under Newmarket rules' and Sir Freddie Johnstone was listed among the stewards.

Hitherto racecourses had largely charged only for the privileged vantage of stands or private carriages, and otherwise depended on prize money subscribed by victuallers, hoteliers and the like, and payments from the booth operators. Alexandra Park, named after Bertie's long-suffering Danish princess, still offered seclusion for its more affluent patrons by charging 10 shillings for access to the Grand Stand and £2 for a private box. But the universal entrance fee was a novelty, intended to boost funds and guarantee a more salubrious environment for the new middle classes.

Newspapers reported as many as 40,000 Londoners through the gates on the opening day, 'to sit, and talk, and snooze, and eat, and flirt, and "get engaged"' at the height of a raging hot summer. It had been hoped that Bertie would attend, but he made no show. For the second day of the meeting, even though the hard going had reduced the field for the Grand Prize to just three runners, there was an even bigger turnout. It was as cheerfully bourgeois a pageant as the promoters could have desired.

Even as the big race was being run, however, a commotion broke out in the betting ring.

'Welsher! Welsher!'

The cry electrified the crowd. A welsher, sidling away as all eyes were on a race! These rascals were the curse of the betting arena. They robbed punters of their money, and honest bookmakers – who depended, for their ability to trade, on a bond of trust with the punters – of their reputation. Campaigning journalists rebuked the naivety of 'the holiday-making shoemaker or carpenter' for allowing himself to be duped of his half-crown by such flimsy accoutrements: a stool, a random name stuck in a hat, a money-bag, a pencil and a few slips of paper. One elderly punter did stand his ground when a winning ticket, for a trifling sum, was ripped up in front of him at a phoney betting stand at Lichfield. Beaten unconscious by 'the boys', he woke to find that he had also been relieved of his wallet and watch.

As such, any welsher was thought to deserve whatever he had coming. One Derby evening, for instance, two members of a notorious welshing gang were entertaining themselves by throwing missiles at the gentry driving back to town. One clod of earth achieved a direct hit on an elegantly dressed lady. It is recorded that 'this resulted in a surprising deviation from the usual state of things, and instead of the coachman having orders to drive faster, the horses were stopped suddenly, and out jumped . . . two young swells'. The respective parties immediately recognised each other from a welshing transaction that afternoon, and a crowd gathered to cheer as the two Galahads administered a thrashing to the bullies.

But here was a very different scenario. For a start, this was plainly a lone wolf: a sly, tawdry, smalltime character.

'Welsher! Welsher!'

There he was, in a black wide-awake cap. The usual bookie's satchel slung over his shoulder. A big man, but there was no mistaking the sudden panic in his face as he hastened towards the gate of the enclosure. Too late. A stampede. Dust rose into the hot air . . . A first punch. He spun away, straight into a second one. At every turn, another fist. For a few seconds, he disappeared from view. A pause as he struggled to his feet, replacing his hat as he pleaded innocence or at least for mercy. But the venom had taken hold now. This time when he hit the ground they followed in with their boots, kicking and stamping. Half-rising, he reeled through a gap towards the gate. His face was covered in blood. But now he saw a policeman at the gate. A yelling mob had gathered along the rail. Exultant baying as bloodied hanks of clothing were thrown in their direction: part of his shirt, now his coat-sleeves, his waistcoat. A boot, even. At last the policeman perceived the lesser evil, and let the hunted animal plunge past. But it was frying pan to fire.

'Welsher! Welsher!'

Those who greeted him next had not been able to afford a surcharge to enter the betting enclosure. These men wagered at the 'Judies', betting cubicles outside the ring, so named because of their resemblance to Punch-and-Judy booths. Down he went again, skin and clothes meshed in bloody rags as feet and fists renewed a sickening percussion to the swelling jeers. Only a man who realised that his life was now in the balance could summon the reserves to break free, lurching into a shambling run. But he was quickly knocked to the ground again by a bookmaker's stool. Even now his resistance was not quite spent. Reminding one horrified witness in the stand of 'a rat pursued by dogs', he dived into a hansom cab parked nearby, and cowered as the mob clawed at his limbs, or jabbed him with walking sticks and umbrellas.

Suddenly the shouting took on a new tone. Through the last fog of consciousness, the man sensed a respite: the beating, the pawing had stopped. A mounted policeman had spurred his way alongside the cab. The lynch mob, unabashed, now directed its fury on the policeman himself. The solitary hero was on the point of being hauled down from his saddle when reinforcements arrived.

'Then,' recorded a witness, 'the poor tattered wretch, ghastly, white and streaming with blood, was hauled out and dragged away insensible, with his head hanging and his legs trailing in the dust, amid the howling and horrible execrations of five thousand Englishmen.' Eventually the constables were able to lower him into a cellar. Here he was locked away among crates of empty bottles, his sweat and blood congealing in the cool, dusty gloom. And here he stayed, until night fell on another blazing day, and he could be spirited home. A few days later he died of his injuries.

In the event, this horrifying baptism of London's first 'park' course only accelerated the movement towards enclosures and admission fees. Seven years later the first metropolitan 'club' track, purpose-built and fully enclosed, opened at Sandown Park. Its success was such that imitations proliferated across the country, and Alexandra Palace likewise fenced off the racetrack *from the rest of the park in 1883. Members at Sandown were able to bring ladies as their guests, a boon hitherto reserved for the society meetings at Ascot and Goodwood.*

Today only the infield at Epsom remains open to all-comers. And it was there, in the shoulder of the Downs under Tattenham Corner, that in 1880 they witnessed perhaps the single greatest ride in Derby history.

16

'The lad rode as well as any could'

FRED ARCHER HAD been carried off the gallops like a crippled fledgling in the teeth of a cat. Even when finally dropped onto the turf, he could not pull his arm free of those giant incisors. In fact, the deranged horse was now trying to kneel on his chest.

Muley Edris had always been an unruly animal. In races Archer had blunted all the refinement of his genius – which had already qualified him, at twenty-three, as the most celebrated jockey in history – to propel him by plain crop and rowel. 'Archer never liked the horse,' Mat Dawson admitted later. 'He thought him cunning, and punished him in severe races when he was perhaps meeting a better horse; but this the horse never forgot.' Finally Muley Edris was taking his revenge. He had pounced as Archer dismounted to move a gallops marker, lifting him by the arm and trotting away.

It was the first morning of May 1880. Archer had already been champion jockey six times and ridden ten Classic winners. In three weeks' time he was due to wear the silks of the Duke of Westminster on the hot favourite for the Derby: a magnificent son of Doncaster, named Bend Or. But now Archer braced himself for a mutilation that menaced his very life – never mind his career. He well knew the stories of grooms savaged by stallions. One had been killed a few years previously, both his ears torn off and his chest 'so lacerated that they declared they could see the heart beat'.

In the event, Muley Edris lost his balance even as help arrived. The sadistic creature fled towards the horizon and Archer was brought back to Heath House, the Newmarket stable set up by Mat Dawson after leaving James Merry. Here the famous jockey retained the same humble quarters as when he had arrived as a tiny apprentice, twelve years earlier. Over the days that followed his wounds only festered.

Worse, his weight was soaring. At five feet nine, Archer viewed the scales as the register of a soul-destroying attrition. Eleven stone in winter, he would slough off 35lbs for the season with a bespoke wasting draught so devastating that friends who sampled a spoonful were confined groggily to their beds the next day. Archer would drink it by the glass. But now it seemed by no means certain that he would ever ride again.

Lord Falmouth, his principal patron, secured him an appointment in London with Sir James Paget. Archer watched the famous surgeon carefully salve the suppurating flesh. As he finished binding, Paget seemed quite optimistic. 'Well, I think that ought to be all right in three or four weeks,' he said.

Archer's relief was instantly tempered by a new impatience. 'But shall I be fit for the Derby?'

'Yes, I think you should be able to go.'

'I mean, shall I be fit to ride?'

'Better drive, I think.'

It was only then that Archer disclosed his identity. 'Sir, I must tell you that what you are in your profession, I am in mine.'

Paget was amazed to learn that missing the ride on Bend Or might cost the young man as much as £2,000. His neat, sober attire suggested a bank clerk; his quiet tone and mien, a curate. He even had a slight stoop. 'I only wish that my profession were half as profitable,' Paget remarked drily. He looked again at the face in front of him. It had a haunting quality, with its sharp features, sad blue-grey eyes and sensuous lips. But the fact was that Paget had already done all he could. Only the status of his patient had altered, not his prognosis.

Archer retreated disconsolately to his parents in the Cotswolds. His father had once been a jockey himself, riding a Grand National winner. Squat and bluff, he was of a very different kidney from his son, who sooner owed his slender, melancholy allure to his mother. The Archers ran an inn near Cheltenham, and it was here that a friend recommended a bone-setter named Hutton. Something of a quack, who 'would have been burnt as a witch' in times past – but there was nothing to lose in seeing whether he had anything to suggest.

A few days later Archer contacted Robert Peck, Bend Or's trainer, to confirm that he intended to ride at Epsom. Hutton had bound an iron bar to his arm and padded his palm. To Peck the whole situation reeked of desperation. But the Duke of Westminster had pressed Archer for a commitment to his colt. If Archer insisted he was fit to ride, were they not obliged to let him? On the other hand, the stakes were too high for sentiment. Having made that spectacular profit as middle man in the sale of Doncaster, it was plainly in Peck's interest that Bend Or's young sire was made to look worth every penny.

From Doncaster's very first crop, Bend Or had such quality and character even as a foal that his handlers considered him 'more of a human being than a racehorse'. The golden chestnut with a silver mane was given the name of the arms – *azure a bend or*, blue with a band of gold – forfeited by the duke's ancestors in a fourteenth-century heraldry lawsuit. Sent to Peck at Russley, Bend Or won all five starts in his first season, and was made 2–1 favourite for the Derby even though held up in his training by sore shins. With the going at Epsom very firm, Peck was rubbing brandy into his shins every morning.

The one consolation was that Bend Or's most obvious rival, Robert the Devil, had lost a top-class rider at the eleventh hour. Tom Cannon had been claimed for another runner, and all the other leading jockeys were already engaged. Charles Brewer, the owner of Robert the Devil, reluctantly settled for the second-rate Rossiter. Brewer, as a layer and commission agent, was a prominent figure in the betting ring. His horse was brawny to the point of coarseness, bred from a mare who had been turned out in the Fens to fend for herself: a perfect proletarian foil to the ducal, sweet-tempered favourite.

The febrile atmosphere of Derby day was hardly calculated to calm Westminster's nerves. As usual Parliament had adjourned for the day, by 285 votes to 115, despite Sir Wilfrid Lawson's annual rebuke to members intending to join 'a crowd of bawling blacklegs' in 'an organised system of rascality and roguery'. Sir Wilfrid despaired: even the Lords' Committee on Intemperance, which included two archbishops, had been suspended for a recent meeting at Goodwood. But an opponent reminded him that more than half the Derby runners, not least the hot favourite, were owned by fellow Liberals. It would be another twelve years before Sir Wilfrid succeeded in halting Parliament's Derby holiday.

Westminster's tension must have yielded to downright panic when he saw his jockey. Archer was in a terrible state. He had shed 13lbs in four days, through a reckless escalation in the regime of purgatives and Turkish baths that was already poisoning his mind. To prepare for the most momentous moment in his patron's Turf career, he had dosed himself into a husk. How could he ride a finish with his arm trussed to an iron rod? Now that the moment had come, Archer appears to have sensed his folly. Sullen and captious all morning, he lunched on a biscuit and a sip of champagne. It was hard to say which was weaker: his emaciated body or his giddy, unquiet mind?

The one island of calm was Bend Or himself, strolling serenely among the noisy crowd. Archer, pulling rank as usual, lined up near the inside of the nineteen runners. And it was not just the horses who were now released by the starter's flag. Even an ordinary racing environment transformed Archer into a viper, ruthless and foul-mouthed. Today it was as though the fetters that had tightened round his mind over the past month suddenly snapped, unleashing a surge of adrenaline that would take him to the absolute margin of his genius.

The descent round Tattenham Corner was always going to test Bend Or's shins. As they began hurtling downhill Archer felt his mount yawing and stumbling. This was the crucial point of every Derby, when only those few horses still coping with its demands can respond to their riders. Robert the Devil was one, gliding along in front and poised to break clear in the straight. Bend Or was meanwhile so short of room on the rail that Archer had to hoist his left leg onto his mount's withers, at the base of the neck. So began the defining moment of his career. He was attempting to win the Turf's greatest prize not just with one arm, but with one leg.

Archer was still trying to get back on an even keel – and his specially made saddle, weighing just 1lb, gave him the flimsiest of support – as Rossiter kicked for home on Robert the Devil. But all was not yet lost: slowly but inexorably Bend Or began bearing down on the leader. It was too late, surely, but the gap was definitely closing. With a hundred yards to go, rapt in the moment, Archer forgot about his arm and raised his whip. The pain seared open his hand and the whip catapulted into the air. And that seemed to be that. Stirring as Bend Or's rally had been, Robert the Devil should just hold out now.

But if Archer had exhausted his influence with Bend Or, he still had a residual power over Rossiter. The young rider, his head for heights untested, had sensed a new surge in the din of the crowd. It could only be the favourite closing; could only be Archer. 'The great test of a jockey's nerve is his coolness when he finds himself among the leaders for the Derby, about two distances from home,' pronounced *The Druid*. 'If they have an ounce of flurry in their composition, that moment will bring it out.' Sure enough, like Lot's wife, Rossiter looked over his shoulder – and was petrified by what he saw. Archer was in some mystical transport. His oaths did not seem random, but to summon down specific furies. Rossiter quailed and his mount, sensing a release from duty, faltered even as the post loomed. Kicking and pushing and roaring, Archer urged Bend Or into a last lunge. One horse swaying, the other rampant, they crossed the line together.

Westminster endured an appalling wait for the judge's verdict to be hoisted. Brewer seemed to think his colt had held on. But Bend Or it was, by a head. At once the booing began for Rossiter, the pillar of salt. Archer rebuked the crowd as they returned to weigh in. 'It isn't true!' he called. 'The lad rode as well as any could, met a better horse.' But the fact was that Bend Or, his shins beginning to thrum, was barely able to hobble back to the stables. Surely the cool and seasoned Tom Cannon would have beaten him. Rossiter was sobbing uncontrollably, and his reputation never recovered. Five years later he cut his throat in a coppice besides a gallop in Newmarket. Even his suicide was botched, however, and he was committed to a mental hospital. He recovered to ride in Germany for a couple of years but died in an asylum there in 1889. Yet Archer would have the better of him even in the quest for perdition.

For Westminster, the 1880 Derby triumphantly vindicated the immense sum he had paid for Doncaster. Soon afterwards, however, came the sensational charge that Bend Or was not the horse he was purported to be. Brewer lodged an objection, claiming that Robert the Devil had actually been beaten by a colt registered as Tadcaster. His case was based on the testimony of a groom recently fired from Eaton: Richard Arnull alleged that two sons of Doncaster had inadvertently been mixed up when the yearlings left the stud. Bend Or's mother was Rouge Rose; Tadcaster's, a mare named Clemence. The fact that no deliberate wrong had been alleged was neither here nor there. Here was a bookmaker proposing the word of a groom against that of a duke. Some admired Arnull's courage; others presumed him merely malicious. But a hearing could not be avoided, even if few doubted which side the Jockey Club would favour.

After four protracted sessions of evidence, the stewards required just forty-five minutes to decide that the colt who had won the Derby was indeed the son of Rouge Rose, and the result would stand. Nonetheless their findings were embarrassing. The Eaton paperwork had proved so disorganised as to be nearly worthless. No record had been made of the markings identifying the 1877 foals before they left. But Arnull would certainly have known how to distinguish the two chestnuts – Bend Or was golden, and Tadcaster red – while to this day black markings in a horse's coat are known as 'Bend Or spots'. When Bend Or was eventually retired to stud, Westminster pointedly authorised his mating with Clemence – the dam of Tadcaster. To Arnull, who persisted in his story to his deathbed, this was gross incest. In 2012, scientists took a sample from the mandible of Bend Or, whose skeleton is preserved at the Natural History Museum. Using mitochondrial DNA analysis, they established that his genes were characteristic of the maternal family of Clemence, rather than Rouge Rose. After 132 years they concluded that Arnull was probably right, and that Bend Or and Tadcaster had been confused. Not that the patrilineal continuity between the Darley Arabian and sons of the 1880 Derby winner is affected: both Bend Or and Tadcaster were sons of Doncaster.

Still troubled by his shins, the colt known as Bend Or was well beaten behind Robert the Devil in the St Leger but Peck was much happier with his champion by the time the old rivals squared up for a rematch in the Epsom Gold Cup the following season. Having replaced Rossiter with Tom Cannon, Brewer backed Robert the Devil heavily – only to see Bend Or confirm the Derby form with what Peck accounted 'gentlemanly' disdain. Bend Or, the trainer exulted, was not just 'the best horse in the world' but 'the best ever foaled'.

Peck and Bend Or both retired at the end of the season. Peck was still only thirty-six, and evidently had health problems; on the other hand, he had made so much money backing his own judgement that he could now afford a stud and stable of his own, while also managing the investments of others. Westminster sent his horses to John Porter at Kingsclere, so opening new horizons for one of the most prolific training careers in history, while Bend Or returned to Eaton with a fee of 200 guineas. Westminster loved to take his children and guests to see the benign young stallion on a Sunday afternoon. An American agent asked Westminster to name his price. 'There is not enough money in the great American republic,' he replied, 'to buy Bend Or.' Even the record sum paid for his sire now seemed a bargain. Doncaster, in fact, would soon be usurped by his son. In order to make way for Bend Or, in 1884 he was exported to the Kisber State Stud in Hungary. Bend Or would produce a great champion from his very first crop. Yet the year bestrode by Ormonde would culminate in one of the bleakest tragedies in Turf history.

Fred Archer's status on the track had become so invulnerable that few had any inkling of the corrosion within. But Mat Dawson remembered Tom French, Archer's predecessor as stable jockey, and how the younger man had viewed him as a model in and out of the saddle. French, another exceptionally tall jockey, had also been obliged to 'waste' savagely to keep his weight down. Though he won consecutive Derbys in 1870 and 1871, his entire physique had become atrophied, bringing on a fatal consumption. He died in 1873, at just twenty-nine.

Victorian jockeys typically gained around 28lbs in winter, and would sweat it off in three weeks as Easter approached. Their customary 'riding weight' was also sometimes reduced to meet an especially pressing opportunity. It was common to shed 7lbs in twenty-four hours, and Nat Flatman once lost 4.5lbs in two hours.

One jockey only took the odd bite of an apple for eight successive days to make a light weight for a big race.

Modern diet has prompted a steady elevation in the weights to be carried by thoroughbreds, always with the caveat that the more accessible a riding weight, the more people will become eligible to ruin their health in order to ride racehorses. To this day, the most harrowing cases invariably concern riders towards the upper end of the scale. Frank Butler struggled even to make 8st 7lbs for the last ten years of his career. He was another to numb the pangs of hunger with alcohol, and could balloon 9lbs in eight hours after ending a fast. He gave up after winning the Triple Crown on West Australian, but the damage had been done and he died three years later at thirty-eight.

Even those jockeys who could manage their weight comfortably tended to confine themselves to scraps. In the old days, after a breakfast of tea and one piece of toast, they would swaddle themselves in 'five or six waistcoats, two coats, and as many pair of breeches' – essentially borrowing the 'sweats' regime of the horses themselves – and walk ten to fifteen miles. Now that trains permitted them to ride daily at remote parts of the country, however, many favoured salts and purgatives instead.

'Wasting'. The very word was dolorously expressive. And the cold lineaments of Archer's public personality, which presented him as aloof and stingy, sealed a seething, suffering core. Women had always sensed as much. The ageing Duchess of Montrose surrendered to a pathetic infatuation. People said that she nearly persuaded Archer to marry her, though almost forty years his senior. It sounds far-fetched, but the fact is that the flame-haired, hot-headed widow eventually filled the vacancy with a a gentleman still younger than Archer. Registered as 'Mr Manton', she was one of the first women to breed and race horses on a large scale and matched manly ferocity with the sulkiness of a cocotte. When her vicar had the temerity to pray for fine weather for the harvest, she stormed out of the church and threatened to cancel his living: he knew perfectly well that her St Leger horse preferred soft going.

In the event, Archer ended up marrying Mat Dawson's niece, Nellie, in 1883. Their new home, Falmouth House, was named after his first and most faithful patron, whose original £100 retainer remained unchanged at Archer's insistence. By now, in contrast, Westminster was obliged to pay £1,000 even for a third claim on his services.

Viscount Falmouth was certainly a model owner, immune to tantrums. In twenty-six years he had just two trainers: John Scott, until his death in 1871; and Dawson. The only bet he ever struck was for a sixpence with Mrs Scott, who received her winnings set in a diamond brooch. Archer was grieved, then, when Falmouth sold off his stud after a narrow defeat in the 1883 Derby. It was rumoured that Archer had held something back in a close finish to favour a rival trained, and heavily backed, by his brother – to no avail, if so, as both were edged out by St Blaise, a colt trained by John Porter for Freddie Johnstone.

The mutterings about this ride, though wholly inconsistent with Archer's known character, were by no means confined to those who had waited to discredit the phenomenon who ended the year with 232 winners. Yet even without the Falmouth horses Archer would set another new record in 1884 – the year illuminated by St Simon. The best horse Dawson ever trained, and perhaps the best of the Victorian era, he won the Ascot Gold Cup by twenty lengths (though Archer missed the ride that day, being unable to make the weight).

Archer had just ridden his 241st winner of the year when he received a telegram at the Liverpool weighing room: Nellie had safely delivered a daughter. When he got home to Newmarket, all seemed well. The next morning, in fact, he decided to celebrate with a day's hunting. He had just finished dressing when his sister rushed in: Nellie was suffering a sudden seizure. Racing into her room, Archer was in time to see his young wife die in unseeing convulsions.

For a time he was inconsolable. But a long tour of America, facilitated by Rosebery, seemed to help. The press especially savoured his visit to Yseult Dudley, jailed for her attempt on the life of the Fenian exile, O'Donovan Rossa.* On his return, Archer seemed to

---

* Archer accounted Miss Dudley one of the most beautiful women he had ever seen. 'She told me that she would next come across to England and shoot Gladstone,' he said. Was she insane, as the embarrassed British government claimed? 'Not a bit of it.'

retain all the diabolical intensity of old. Among those assisting his rehabilitation was Robert Peck: they shared much success on the track, and a warm friendship off it. The 246 winners Archer rode in 1885 would not be surpassed until Gordon Richards, with infinite logistical advantages, managed 259 in 1933.

On the face of it, it seemed that riding winners could still sedate the anguish gnawing at Archer's enfeebled physiology. But that fiction was exposed the following year by a Triple Crown winner from Bend Or's first crop. Perhaps it was precisely the realisation that even a champion like Ormonde, trained by Porter for Westminster, could no longer relieve his melancholy that finally plunged him into its fatal depths.

That autumn Archer agreed to ride a horse set just 8st 6lbs in the Cambridgeshire, though drastic wasting was required even to manage 8st 8lbs. Friends warned him that he already looked dreadful, yet Archer immured himself in Turkish baths and guzzled his potion. He got down to 8st 7lbs and, lightheaded as he was, just failed in a desperate finish. In his debilitation, Archer contracted a chill and then a raging fever. The doctors diagnosed typhoid but were satisfied by steady improvement in his condition. Mentally, however, the last stake had been wrenched from the palisade that had kept his demons at bay.

On 8 November 1886, two years and one day after the death of his wife, the thirteen-times champion jockey asked his sister to send the nurse from his room so that he could speak to her in private. She did so and, turning round, saw Archer with a revolver in his left hand. The poor woman wrestled with her brother, his right arm round her neck, even as he placed the muzzle in his mouth and pulled the trigger. He was exactly the same age as Tom French.

During the last summer of his life Archer won a four-runner maiden, round the enclosed 'park' at Sandown, on a filly named Counterpane. This was Bertie's first acknowledged success on the Turf. Archer was wearing the silks of the prince's great-uncle, George IV: purple jacket with gold braid, scarlet sleeves, black cap. Bertie was now prepared to defy his ageing mother to the extent of maintaining a Flat-racing stable of his own. Counterpane was one of two fillies – both daughters of Chaplin's Derby winner, Hermit – Bertie had bought as potential foundation mares for a new stud at Sandringham.

On the eve of the Sandown race Bertie had written to his former mistress, Lillie Langtry, to tip Counterpane as a likely winner, although he dared not let himself be '*too* sanguine'. Both had moved on to new amours, but remained on affectionate terms and Langtry's move into theatre had coincided with an increasing enthusiasm for the Turf. It was common for Bertie's circle to keep the ladies sweet by placing indulgent little wagers on their horses. Chaplin had continued placing bets for his former fiancée even after she ran off with Harry Hastings. Lady Lonsdale, the lovely daughter of Sidney Herbert, would often be pleasantly surprised to learn that Chaplin had backed a winner on her behalf. 'I should like to be "on" if you know of a really good thing,' she wrote. 'But it seems to me that in this style of betting the advantage is always on my side, for you never tell me what I lose!'

No doubt Langtry reinvested her winnings when Counterpane contested the Stockbridge Cup a couple of weeks later, but unfortunately the filly dropped dead of a heart attack just as she was coming through to win. Replying to a letter of commiseration from Chaplin, Bertie shrugged: 'I must bear it with philosophy as I know what the glorious uncertainties of the Turf are.' Sure enough, a mare he bought for 900 guineas the following year – Perdita II – would eventually transform his fortunes.

The 1887 Derby, the first since Archer's suicide, had a hollow feel. It was contested by a poor crop of three-year-olds and won by one whose owner, George Alexander Baird, used the occasion to flaunt his contempt for the racing establishment. Robert Peck, who supervised Baird's stable, must have wondered what his old boss, Merry, would have said, had he lived to see this young man slouching and yawning against the rails, refusing even the coveted privilege of leading his Derby winner into the winner's circle.

Three of the seven Baird brothers had bequeathed their estates to young George, who had grown to despise the dynastic precepts of thrift, piety and industry. 'A good judge of horses, but a damned bad one of men', he surrounded himself with 'the worst crowd in Europe'. Langtry endured an affair with him on the premise that he apologised with a cheque for £5,000 every time he beat her up. Once he pursued her to Paris in a jealous rage and put her in hospital for a fortnight, tearing her flesh with his teeth and blackening her famous eyes. For good measure, he shredded her wardrobe and smashed up her room. The gendarmes did not have to look far when a warrant was issued for Baird's arrest: he was already in custody, after a fracas at a brothel. Even then, Langtry withdrew all charges – in return for a yacht and £50,000.

She was inconsolable when his short and useless life dwindled to a miserable end in a New Orleans hotel, burnt out and febrile after a terminal binge – not so much because he was dead, at thirty-one, as because she had been omitted from his will. Approached by his executors, Langtry indignantly refused to return one of the horses Baird had given her, and set up her own stable in Newmarket. As trainer she hired Fred Webb, who had been obliged to quit riding on account of his increasing weight. Merry would have been tickled to see the jockey who won him the Derby on Doncaster now profiting from the Baird millions through this scandalous woman – a nexus that perfectly condensed the changing face of the English Turf during the Industrial Revolution. Now, its volatilities seemingly exhausted by the tragedy of Archer, it would stretch into a lightsome meridian.

PART V

The Fast Set

Bona Vista (1889)
Cyllene (1895)
Polymelus (1902)

17

'My God, Berkeley, this is too hot!'

NOBODY KNEW QUITE what to make of Lord Rosebery. One moment, you could be bathing in those blue eyes and sparkling eddies of conversation; the next, his gaze would become translucent and frigid, his sensuous lips pinched into stone. And for a man of such intellect, such charisma, to demean himself as breeder of 500 racehorses! Typical Rosebery, unravelling in dilettantism those strands of character a firmer hand might have woven into greatness. Some political enemies went so far as to dismiss his entire sporting career, stretching half a century, as a populist affectation. For the philistines of the Marlborough House set, equally, it was unnerving to see this cerebral creature so stimulated by the pleasures they paraded in token of their own frivolity.

As a young man, Rosebery was reputed to have professed three ambitions: to win the Derby; to marry an heiress; and to serve as prime minister. This manifesto is surely apocryphal, being wildly lacking in Rosebery refinement. Yet it is worth noting how each aspiration, though satisfied, ultimately brought him new sadness – and that only one schooled him properly in irony and disillusion. Nothing complemented Rosebery's quixotic nature better than his horses. It would strike him as apt, certainly, that he should be honoured for securing the most potent bloodline in Turf history with a colt he discarded as a yearling.

Bona Vista represented an unexpected windfall from the stupendous dowry of Hannah de Rothschild. During the eighty years since her grandfather had quit the Jewish ghetto in Frankfurt, Hannah's family had built up the greatest fiscal empire in Europe. Within fifteen years of his arrival in Manchester, as an obscure cloth merchant, Nathan Mayer Rothschild was financing Wellington's armies on the continent; his son, Lionel, proceeded to fund war in the Crimea and Disraeli's purchase of Suez Canal shares; while Lionel's son, Hannah's cousin Natty, would in turn become the backer of Cecil Rhodes in southern Africa. Despite this seismic influence on the geopolitical landscape, it took Lionel from 1847 to 1858 to establish the right of a Jew to sit in the House of Commons; while Natty would not breach the peerage until 1885.

Though heartbroken by the recent loss of both parents, Hannah at least found herself free to make her own choice of husband. Even her equable father had joined the family ballyhoo when a niece married outside the religion in 1873. With a trousseau of £2 million and estates yielding £80,000 a year, Hannah's betrothal to Rosebery stung the *Jewish Chronicle* into scriptural transports of anguish: 'If the flame seized on the cedars, how will fare the hyssop on the wall: if the leviathan is brought up by the hook, how will the minnows escape?'

Hannah was more Juno than Venus. One contemporary dignified her with 'a kind of Semiramis profile' but Henry James reckoned her 'large, fat, ugly, good-natured, sensible and kind'. Either way, only a couple genuinely in love could have prevailed against such uniform discouragement, public and private. (There was little hostility among Hannah's cousins and uncles, who knew him well from the Turf, but Rosebery's anti-Semitic mother was even more livid than the *Jewish Chronicle*.) The fact was that Hannah – level-headed, modest, warm and diplomatic – redressed all the most glaring deficiencies of her fiancé.

Disraeli gave the bride away and Bertie proposed the toast. The honeymoon was at Petworth, Rosebery's sister having married Lord Egremont's grandson. From his wedding bed, Rosebery was able to survey the park once patrolled by Whalebone. Little could he realise, returning to Mentmore, that one of the matings he arranged that same spring would give the Whalebone line a foothold into the next century.

The stud at Mentmore was perhaps the single most gratifying item in Hannah's marriage settlement. Quite apart from all the mares bred by the late baron, there was Macaroni, recently acquired from Richard Naylor. One of the first mates Rosebery chose for the stallion was a daughter of King Tom, Stockwell's half-brother. The result, in the spring of 1879, was a filly he named Vista.

Though nominally Liberal, by dint of the imperative for Jewish emancipation, the Rothschilds had always been on the same imperialist wavelength as Disraeli. Natty, now head of the family, was therefore dismayed to see Gladstone's barnstorming Midlothian comeback of 1880 sustained by the hospitality of his cousin, at Dalmeny House, and the oratory of her husband. Inspired by a visit to a Democrat convention in New York, Rosebery was the architect of an electoral campaign that marked a sea change in British democracy – and left his party and monarch no choice but to restore Gladstone as premier.

Rosebery's political career, admittedly, remained becalmed: he was constantly declining or quitting junior government posts for reasons so varied that Gladstone suspected the only consistent factor to be conceit. Only when embarking on his third ministry, in 1886, did Gladstone accept that he could no longer afford to hold back his obvious heir. Rosebery, still just thirty-eight, was appointed Foreign Secretary.

Gladstone had resolved to go for broke on Home Rule for Ireland. Unfortunately, as with his Reform Bill twenty years previously, he was too far ahead of his time for the Duke of Westminster, who inaugurated an Irish Loyal and Patriotic Union. Richard Pigott, a nationalist renegade, was hired to dig up evidence connecting Parnell to crime. This ended in shambles when *The Times* published forged letters, supposedly written by Parnell. Pigott fled to Spain and shot himself, and Parnell was applauded in the Commons as he returned from a successful libel suit. Nonetheless, Westminster was joined by more than ninety rebels to see off the bill, and the consequent general election cemented a terminal division in the Liberal Party.

Westminster brazenly supported the Tory candidate in Chester, resulting in a bitter public exchange with Gladstone. The fact was that they were always very different personalities. In his long life Gladstone attended a single Derby, on sufferance. For many, he was a prophet dishonoured by his own country; to Westminster, he had become a raving old man. To his credit, 'as a neighbour and friend'

Westminster still sent his customary gift of flowers from the Eaton hothouse for his seventy-seventh birthday, but Gladstone had run out of patience with his self-importance and lack of imagination.

Rosebery was one of few to step from the wreckage of the ministry with his reputation enhanced. Gladstone publicly anointed the youngest member of his cabinet as 'the man of the future'. It was a curse Rosebery would never live down.

Westminster's mood was not improved by Ormonde proving a dreadful anti-climax at stud. The last champion ridden by Archer had made his final public appearance at a Jubilee garden party at Grosvenor House. Walked through town from Waterloo by John Porter, he was petted by Bertie and fed carnations by the Queen of Belgium. After mustering just eight foals in his first two seasons at stud, he was sold to Argentina. Westminster was censured over the sale but claimed that he would do the British breed a disservice if permitting Ormonde to reproduce weaknesses in his wind and fertility. As things turned out, the horse could still claim an indirect role in maintaining the Darley Arabian line. For it was the Ormonde formula that inspired Rosebery to send Vista to Eaton for a date with his sire, Bend Or, in 1888. Ormonde's mother had also been a daughter of Macaroni; it made sense, then, to see whether the same cocktail might work with Vista.

The result was a chestnut colt so handsome that Rosebery was reluctant to include him among the yearlings sent from Mentmore to the Newmarket sales in 1890. The operation of twin studs at The Durdans and Mentmore required a degree of streamlining: numbers would otherwise become absurd. But Rosebery set a prohibitive reserve of 1,200 guineas, evidently half-hoping that fate would return the colt to be raced in his own name. He was to be disappointed. At 1,200 guineas, the gavel hovering, the auctioneer spotted one last bid. Vista's son was sold, to Charles Day Rose, for 1,250 guineas.

Yet Rosebery could only wish the colt's new owner well; as a man of such ingenuous enthusiasms, Rose is said to have inspired the character of Toad in *The Wind in the Willows*. His most tangible inheritance had been from his father, a Scots-Canadian diplomat and financier; but perhaps Rose owed an equal debt to the winsome genes of a mother whose beauty in 1838 triggered the last fatal duel on Canadian soil, aptly enough at the Verdun racetrack in Montreal. For the Turf was just one of a series of manias to consume Rose: yachts, automobiles, eventually politics and finally aircraft. He even set a record for the half-mile in snowshoes. The mares Rose kept at Hardwick, his Tudor mansion on the Thames, were expensively accommodated in a new Arts-and-Crafts stableyard; while various mistresses were stowed in different cottages around the park. Nothing, certainly, was going to stop him bidding that extra 50 guineas for the Bend Or yearling. He was still smarting over his failure, a few years previously, to make one more bid for the young St Simon.

Within weeks, Rosebery's regret was placed in perspective by the loss of Hannah, at thirty-nine, to typhoid and Bright's disease.* His wife's anxiety to please had sometimes brought out the worst in Rosebery, who was once alleged to have remarked: 'I am leaving tonight; Hannah and the rest of the heavy baggage will follow later.' But he had become wholly dependent on her for intimacy and ambition, and now seemed to renounce both for good.

Lord Charles Beresford, a swashbuckling Anglo-Irish naval officer, was the showboat of the Marlborough House set. Summoned to dinner, he cabled Bertie: 'Can't possibly. Lie follows by post.' For £5, he once hijacked a pig to ride down Park Lane: 'As I turned down Piccadilly, the swineherd caught me a clout on the head, knocking me off my steed, but not before I had won my wager.'

His eldest brother, the Marquess of Waterford, was badly smashed up in a hunting accident and loathed racing. Even so, for the next three Beresfords it was a governing passion. In 1874, William, Marcus and Charlie contested the 'Three Brothers' Steeplechase at Waterford:

> No racecourse in Ireland, except Punchestown and Fairyhouse, ever had more people on it. Old men and women who had never before

---

* It was said that a mournful bark, through the night of her death, corroborated a Dalmeny legend about a hound that would portend dynastic tragedy. This curio was apparently shared by Rosebery with Arthur Conan Doyle, who subsequently transferred the tale to the Baskervilles of Dartmoor.

seen a race came 50 miles. The city was as deserted as if plague-stricken. Away they went, boot to boot. The pace was a cracker from the start, all three girth to girth most of the journey, and at no time did two lengths divide the first and last till just before the finish . . . Fence after fence was charged and cleared by them locked together, and it was not till [Charlie] was beaten, just before the last, they separated. A determined struggle between Woodlark and The Weasel then ensued; and, after a desperate finish, old Judge Hunter gave the verdict to the former [William] 'by a short head'.

William would add to his laurels a Victoria Cross in the Zulu Wars; Charlie, for his part, became a national celebrity for audaciously slipping the gunship *Condor* beneath fixed artillery fire when bombarding the fort at Alexandria in 1882; and then redeemed the disastrous attempt to rescue Gordon from Khartoum three years later by sharing an immortal resolution with Lieutenant Dawson of the Coldstream Guards: it would be too hard to die, they famously agreed, 'without knowing who had won the Derby'.

But 'Charlie B' was also a barefaced bounder. Nothing pleased him better than to make a woman cry: 'such fun to hear their stays creak'. A seasoned corridor-creeper at country houses, he once sidled into a dark room and leapt onto the bed, shouting 'Cock-a-doodle-do!' When the light was turned on, he found himself between the Bishop of Chester and his wife. In 1889 Charlie found himself in a still more excruciating situation when his wife, Mina, opened a letter from the delectable Daisy Brooke, bizarrely accusing him of betraying her with his own wife. Daisy had been nauseated to learn that Mina, though older and less attractive, was pregnant. Mina placed the letter in the hands of a lawyer and Daisy, panicking prettily, implored Bertie to intervene. That he did so – arriving on the lawyer's doorstep at 2 a.m., forcing him to show the letter; and then ordering Mina to return it, ostracising her when she declined to do so – was an abuse of his position that plainly anticipated Daisy's readiness not to confine herself to the fluttering of eyelashes at her royal benefactor.

Daisy had once been favoured as a suitable bride for Bertie's brother, Leopold, but instead opted for Lord Brooke, heir to the Earl of Warwick. The queen seemed grateful for the reprieve when observing from behind a curtain Daisy's departure from Windsor, before breakfast, already in a scarlet hunting coat. 'How fast!' she muttered of this double solecism. 'How very fast!'

Charlie B, deprived of both his dignity and his mistress, had a blazing row with Bertie. Daisy claimed that the future king concluded the interview by throwing an inkstand at his old friend's head, but fortunately hit the wall instead. Soon afterwards, Henry Chaplin mischievously sent Bertie a hoof of Hermit, who had just died, mounted as an inkstand.

But if Charlie B was now out of favour, it was not as though Marlborough House was going to run out of extrovert boors. Bertie's companions for the 1890 St Leger meeting included Sir William Gordon-Cumming, a hard-swearing, florid veteran of Ulundi and Abu Klea, rated by the *Sporting Life* as 'possibly the most handsome man in London, and certainly the rudest'. Bertie, Gordon-Cumming and the rest of the royal party were hosted by Arthur Wilson, a Hull shipowner, at his gaudy Italianate mansion, Tranby Croft. With his mother denying him the slightest responsibility, the prince was making a stand both in his choice of companions – male as well as female – and in favouring race meetings for their assembly.

He had spent much of the year in the company of Baron Maurice de Hirsch, a Jewish railway tycoon who laid out the Orient Express line. Like Natty Rothschild, who had recently made Bertie a cash loan of £100,000, Hirsch gave him financial assistance on indulgent terms. (In the end it is said that his executors were ordered to waive debts of £600,000 owed by Bertie.) That summer, egged on by Bertie and bidding through Marcus Beresford, Hirsch spent 5,500 guineas on a filly from the royal stud – then a record for an untried yearling. When the auctioneer exhorted three cheers for Hirsch, one sporting correspondent responded with three sneers: 'We do like to see people spend money, and if we think they are spending it rather foolishly, why, we cheer the louder.' Yet the fact was that Hirsch donated all his stable's prize money to London hospitals, with no deduction for costs.

Bertie showcased the generosity and flair of international Jewry, even as a poisonous tide of anti-Semitism was inundating the continent. Hirsch's most lavish philanthropy was reserved for Jewish refugees from the pogroms of Eastern Europe, while the Austro-Hungarian archdukes, who would not receive him at court, were outraged to see Bertie and Henry Chaplin arriving in their backyard for vacations at Eichhorn, the baron's vast sporting estate.

Even some of Bertie's own set were uncomfortable with his challenge to their prejudices – Daisy Brooke among them, despite subsequently reinventing herself as a radical. 'We resented the introduction of the Jews into the social set of the Prince of Wales,' she remembered later. 'Not because we disliked them individually, for some of them were charming as well as brilliant, but because they had brains and understood finance. As a class, we did not like brains. As for money, our only understanding of it lay in the spending, not in the making of it.'

It is not hard to imagine, then, how Bertie's behaviour went down with the xenophobes and snobs of his mother's court; or how they all crowed, when he found himself up to his neck in the 'Tranby Croft scandal'. Though baccarat was strictly illegal, Bertie himself was acting as banker when the Wilsons' son, convinced that he had seen Gordon-Cumming cheat, whispered to his friend: 'My God, Berkeley, this is too hot!' Rashly, though he had seen nothing untoward, Bertie agreed to witness an undertaking extracted from a livid Gordon-Cumming – vowing 'never to play cards again as long as I live' – as the price for his accusers' silence. Even hopeless Christopher Sykes had enough nous not to sign this incendiary document.

The following January, Bertie, Henry Chaplin, Daisy Brooke and her complaisant spouse – in her memoirs, she wryly observed how Bertie 'liked my husband's repose of temperament' – were staying with Hirsch in Norfolk when news arrived that Gordon-Cumming was to sue five of Bertie's fellow guests at Tranby Croft for libel. Desperate to spare him another court appearance, Bertie's courtiers did their utmost to head Gordon-Cumming off but succeeded only in goading the press into a righteous disgust.

The trial began four days after a colt named Common won the Derby for Freddie Johnstone. Bertie was required not only to take the stand but also to hear his inner circle accused by the solicitor general of sacrificing the reputation of an old friend 'to conceal the foibles of a prince'. The jury needed just thirteen minutes to dismiss Gordon-Cumming's complaint. Their verdict, deplored by modern experts, prompted hissing in court and catcalls as Bertie arrived at Ascot the same afternoon. He was relieved, however, by a generous ovation when his own horse, The Imp, won the last race – and even had humour enough to chide the crowd: 'You seem to be in a better temper now than you were this morning, damn you.'

Bertie would enjoy no such clemency in the editorials and sermons that now stoked up the moral indignation of the bourgeoisie. Yet disapproval of gambling was not widely shared among the working class, while the Tory press stood up lustily to ultra-moralists who demonised betting. Though Acts of 1867 and 1872 had prohibited the back-alley and pub bookmakers, sporting 'clubs' (equivalent to speakeasies) squeezed through statutory loopholes, while policemen generally needed only a little encouragement to turn a blind eye to bookie's 'runners' working their own beat of tobacconists, pubs and barbershops.

To emerge as an everyday motif of urban life, street betting required precisely those virtues – trust, honesty, accountability – supposedly endangered by Bertie's example. With no hope of legal redress it was the bookmaker himself who was most exposed to corruption – as when sporting newspapers in 1898 gullibly reproduced 'results' sent from a bank holiday hunt meeting at Trodmore in Cornwall. By the time it was discovered that Trodmore did not exist, bookmakers had already paid out on a 5–1 'winner'.

On the racecourse itself, meanwhile, consecutive scandals had prompted the Jockey Club into its boldest show of strength since Charles Bunbury coolly scolded his future king a century before. In both cases, the nettle was grasped by the young Earl of Durham. In 1887, he instigated the exclusion from the Turf of one of his own class – albeit a callow, disreputable idiot, in Lord Ailesbury – over the running of a horse at York, while restricting the punishment of the jockey to a caution. To recognise that an adolescent rider of humble origins had little choice regarding the instructions of a marquess must be credited a significant departure, and greatly to Jack Durham's credit. Then, two years later, he targeted bigger game:

a former senior steward of the Jockey Club, and a champion jockey.

Riders had finally been prohibited from betting in 1880 but Fred Archer's breezy disregard of the new rules had discouraged their enforcement. Now that Archer was dead, however, 'Determined Jack' set out to tackle the flagrant dishonesty of Sir George Chetwynd and Charley Wood. First he set an obliging newspaper onto Wood, who had just won his first championship after six times finishing second to Archer. A libel jury awarded damages of one farthing for the suggestion that, in stopping a particular horse, Wood had 'nearly pulled its head off'. Durham then made a speech that prompted Chetwynd into a lawsuit of his own. Having sought £20,000, he too was obliged to settle for a token farthing. 'Damned short odds!' he grumbled.

For all that he was contributing at least as much as Jack Durham to the improving reputation of the Turf, Tranby Croft left Bertie exposed on both flanks. On the one hand, the middle classes were wallowing in the unworthiness of the next king; on the other, those who considered Bertie a red-blooded sportsman felt he had behaved like a cad to Gordon-Cumming. In his mortification, Bertie urged the Archbishop of Canterbury to distinguish his love of sport from all the insinuations raised by Tranby Court:

> I have a horror of gambling . . . and should always do my utmost to discourage others who have an inclination for it, as I consider gambling, like intemperance, is one of the greatest curses a country can be afflicted with. Horse-racing may produce gambling, or it may not; but I have always looked upon it as a manly sport which is popular with Englishmen of all classes . . .

Though Common had proceeded to complete a second Triple Crown for John Porter, just five years after Ormonde, the great trainer was still struggling to find a decent horse for Bertie. In 1892, the Classics again seemed likely to be dominated by horses trained at Kingsclere – but Orme, a brilliant colt salvaged from the feeble first crop of Ormonde, was owned by the Duke of Westminster; while the stable's top filly was La Flèche, Baron Hirsch's record-breaking yearling purchase, who duly maintained her unbeaten record in the 1000 Guineas.

The 2000 Guineas and Derby, however, were both blown wide open when Orme was poisoned with mercury. Though nobody claimed the £1,000 reward offered by Westminster to identify the culprit, Porter suspected enough to fire one of his grooms anyway. In the absence of the hot favourite, those with a feasible chance in the Guineas included Bona Vista, the colt sold by Rosebery to Charles Rose. Sent to William Jarvis in Newmarket, he had landed a gamble on his debut the previous year but had subsequently fallen a little short of the best of the crop. Regardless, Rosebery remained too immersed in his grief over Hannah to heed the colt's progress too closely. Sleepless and depressed, he had largely withdrawn from public view. It was only when Bona Vista won the Guineas that Rosebery had to face the possibility that his reject might very well win the Derby. He resolved not to make the same mistake with Vista's latest foal, Sir Visto, and sent him to Mat Dawson.

In the event, Bona Vista was beaten out of sight in the Derby, which should have been won by La Flèche. Unfortunately her jockey, the eccentric George Barrett, held up the filly at the rear, shouting and gesticulating at the other riders, and turned his attention to the business in hand just too late.*

Bona Vista, meanwhile, was found to have injured a tendon after another disappointing run at Ascot, and Rose retired him to the stud at Hardwick. Rosebery did not forget the horse, though then much preoccupied. Salisbury's Unionist government fell that summer and Rosebery, after the usual prevarication, agreed to join Gladstone's last ministry. Bertie had intimated that Rosebery back at the Foreign Office was all that could relieve his mother's despair at the return of the old fanatic. But his return to public life was not helped by an extraordinary business with the Marquess of Queensberry.

Queensberry's eldest son, Viscount Drumlanrig, was a secretary at the Foreign Office. Though only twenty-six, he had been offered a

---

* La Flèche was eventually sold to Christoper Sykes's brother. Young Sir Tatton, having neglected to set a ceiling on his budget, was so incensed that Marcus Beresford had bid 12,600 guineas on his behalf that he initially refused to have her unloaded at Sledmere station. Had the stationmaster not fed her from his own allotment she would have starved in her carriage, but after a fortnight Sir Tatton relented. He went on to sell six of her foals for £21,000.

peerage to bolster Liberal representation in the Lords. The promotion was received as a calculated affront by Queensberry, a Scots peer only, who had plainly suffered one steeplechase fall too many and fired off a series of bloodthirsty letters to Rosebery, Gladstone and the queen in the hope of forcing some kind of public showdown. 'I presume the savoury odour of your Jew money bags has too delicious a fragrance to allow me to expect any justice in high quarters,' he ranted to Rosebery. 'I would prefer having 15 minutes with your fat self in a 16 foot ring & hand gloves to being created an English Duke or even a Bishop.' Eventually this torrent of vitriol swept Queensberry to Bad Homburg, where Rosebery was supposed to be on a rest cure. An audience with Bertie, who also happened to be in town, proved sufficient to coax the crackpot back onto a train. As will be seen, however, there would be a tragic sequel.

The eighty-four-year-old Gladstone, at loggerheads even with the faithful core of the party he had divided, finally stepped down the following March. To the next generation – men like Henry Asquith, who had come to notice as a silk for the defendants in the Tranby Croft case – Rosebery remained the only feasible successor. But it would have taken a leader of monumental conviction to seize the moment and cajole the Liberal Unionists back into the fold. As it was, all Rosebery's frailties now came to the fore. As prime minister, even his supporters found him flippant, unseasoned, touchy. His tenure spanned just two Derbys – and he won them both. Yet nothing measured the disillusion of the Rosebery premiership better than the dismal contrast in the way these triumphs were received.

Ladas II lined up for the 1894 Derby just three weeks after his owner had taken office. Against only six rivals, he was the hottest favourite in the race's history. It was thirty-four years since Mathew Dawson had first won the Derby, for James Merry, but he still maintained a small stable for Rosebery in the hope of winning the race for 'the first gentleman in Europe at the present day'. At seventy-four, with a mane of white hair, Dawson confessed: 'I am afraid if I don't do it this time, I never will.' Ladas II he considered the most handsome thoroughbred he had ever seen; and had already won the 2000 Guineas that spring.

By this stage Dawson's gout was such that he had to supervise gallops from the window of his brougham. Unable to make the journey to Epsom, he entrusted the saddling of the favourite to his assistant, Felix Leach. Leach had been much agitated by letters warning that Ladas II would be nobbled, and installed himself with a stack of novels in a hayloft above his stable at the racecourse. Suddenly he saw a face looking over the door with the most extravagantly waxed whiskers he had ever seen: a palpable disguise. He 'promptly seized hold of the moustache by the two ends, when its owner remarked that he was a detective come to look after Ladas'.

Rosebery watched the race with a glass of champagne alongside Regy Brett, later Lord Esher. That perceptive observer of so many unusual deeds and men, who had once watched the original Ladas snorting up the hill at East Ilsley, now admired this new incarnation gliding clear of Freddie Johnstone's Matchbox with a slick, daisy-cutting stride. 'At last!' the prime minister exclaimed, and the crowd unmistakably shared his joy. At odds of 2–9, their enthusiasm could for once have no mercenary taint. 'A happy and blissful pandemonium broke forth,' recorded one correspondent. 'Not the work of a hundred men, nor double nor treble that number, but the work of a multitude. There was no claque here, no leader to give the signal; the countless throng which poured on to the course gave it themselves.' The police barely secured Rosebery a passage as he descended, unusually flushed, from the Jockey Club Stand to lead in the winner. Rolling breakers of noise multiplied as Ladas II was taken back through the rain to The Durdans. Rosebery conceded to his diary that his success had been received with 'delirious enthusiasm, I scarcely know why'.

Bertie hosted a celebratory dinner at Marlborough House that evening, and the next day Rosebery, in exuberant spirits, was discovered by Brett 'standing on his head on a rug, a queer attitude for a Prime Minister'. Among the telegrams was one from Chauncey Depew – the American politician who once defined a pessimist as a man who thinks all women are bad; and an optimist as one who hopes they are. It read: 'Nothing left but heaven.'

Yet when Sir Visto won the race, twelve months later, nonconformists and temperance campaigners only rebuked Rosebery for his frivolous example; and political enemies sneered at his stable as a Whig pose. Everyone knew that the genuine grandees of the Turf, like the Duke of Westminster, had disowned the Liberal Party. 'The Newmarket Lord Rosebery is an artificial creation,' spat one magazine. 'He wanted to win the Derby and did win it, but only as a man wants to possess and does ultimately acquire a first folio Shakespeare.' Unlike the regal Ladas II, Bona Vista's half-brother's success was attributed primarily to the weakness of his rivals.

Days later, after a trivial reverse in the Commons, the government seized the pretext to resign. Its hold on power had proved too tenuous to endure the narcissistic tantrums of its leader. 'Pascal said that the happiest life – the life he would choose – begins with love and ends with ambition,' Brett wrote. 'R. has reversed the order. He has – while in the prime of life – everything that men toil for, wealth, power, position, everything. Yet he is a lonely sleepless man.'

Things had reached a nadir when Drumlanrig, newly engaged, was killed by his own gun during a shooting party in the Quantocks. Though his brother, Bosie Douglas, arrived next evening to hear the coroner pronounce a tragic accident, attempts have since been made to suggest some scandalous connection between Rosebery and a suicide. There were certainly rumours, credited by one racing peer to 'the Newmarket scum', that the prime minister's name might be dragged into the case against Bosie's lover, Oscar Wilde; while Bosie himself viewed Wilde's persecution as a means to restrain 'maniacs of virtue' from tearing down a curtain over the establishment. Yet all evidence purporting to show Rosebery may have led a double life invariably supports a more prosaic reading.

The Liberals suffered the heaviest electoral defeat by either party since 1832. As such, the prime minister who bred Bona Vista curiously evokes the one who bred Whalebone. Both were cut adrift in the unnavigable wake of a giant: Rosebery, following Gladstone; Grafton, Pitt. Both embraced duty only as the corollary of privilege. At heart, dismayed by the pettiness and cant of daily politics, both yearned only for a library, a racing stable, a few trusted intimates. But Rosebery was a far more complex and captivating figure, who actually had a deeper affinity with Grafton's nemesis – his own biography of Pitt describing a 'haughty, impossible, anomalous' premier who finished up 'distempered if not mad'. As Winston Churchill cutely remarked of his father's old friend: 'He would not stoop; he did not conquer.'

Two years later Rosebery and Bertie were among the pallbearers at Gladstone's funeral. Rosebery must have felt as though he had been shouldering the same burden for years already, always rated too flighty and fragile to fill the shoes of the ascetic old dynamo. In fusing the twin peaks of his ambition – as a prime minister who owned consecutive Derby winners – he had found the view from the top obscured in a fog of insomnia and solitude. Unsurprisingly, he was never again avid for new heights.

Bona Vista's first crop had just ventured onto the racecourse, in 1897, when Charles Rose sold him for 15,000 guineas to Prince Louis Esterhazy on behalf of the Hungarian government. The young stallion was exported to the Kisber State stud, where his grandsire had died in 1892. Esterhazy obviously recognised the potency of the Doncaster line. Rose, for his part, had come within an ace of siphoning it out of the breed's genetic mainstream, once and for all.

Bona Vista would seal a golden age on the Hungarian Turf, and an umbilical connection to England first established by its founding father. As early as 1815 Count István Széchenyi had identified the thoroughbred as a symbol of the political and industrial model he sought to import from England. Over the next two years he imported thirty-nine of them, together with an English trainer. Horses, after all, were integral to the heritage of the Magyar plainsmen. Széchenyi believed that breeding elite Hungarian racehorses would ventilate the national culture against the suffocating influence of Vienna.

The whole process echoed the importation of Ottoman stallions to England two centuries previously. Of the sixty-six sires listed in the first Hungarian stud book, in 1832, fifty-seven originated in England. English trainers and jockeys were also imported, including Robert Hesp, who trained the magnificent Kincsem to go undefeated in fifty-four races including the Goodwood Cup.

The Toad-like whims of Charles Rose were never going to with-stand a frontal assault by Prince Esterhazy. Lillie Langtry remembered the charming military attaché outshining even the Kaiser at Queen

Victoria's funeral: 'When General Prince Louis Esterhazy rode by on a restless thoroughbred hack, which he controlled with great ease, we all thought him the most resplendent figure in the cortege.'

Langtry was escorted round Bona Vista's new home by Esterhazy. Each of the enormous paddocks contained a hundred mares. 'I felt my nerves rather tried when the mares came tearing along from all four corners, stopping suddenly when they were within a yard or so,' she wrote. 'A lot of mutual biting and kicking went on . . . and perhaps I did not inspect them so carefully as I might have done.' To the extent she did, she reckoned them generally 'rather characterless and light of bone'. Nor did she think a great deal of the seven or eight resident stallions.

Yet Bona Vista represented a genuine chance of fulfilling Széchenyi's vision. 'One hundred years of English experience is ours to have overnight,' he had urged. Thereafter, advantages of economy, climate, soil and horsemanship could exalt the Hungarian racehorse to global primacy: 'Some day we will raise better horses than the English.' And it might well have happened, had Bona Vista not left an heir hidden in the rushes of the Thames.

A Day at the Races

Ascot, 17 June 1897

Heir to an imperial throne, uncle to both the Tsar and the Kaiser, Bertie seemed chronically lacking in substance. When invited to the opening of the Kiel Canal in 1895, he asked whether the ceremony could be postponed as it clashed with Ascot. The canal, linking the Baltic and North Seas, represented an important strategic initiative for a nation still viewed as a likely ally in any war between the Powers. But Bertie could not be wrenched from self-indulgence.

For a long time his horses seemed to reflect their owner: they were well bred but flimsy. After eight years, with around a dozen in training each season, they had won an aggregate of just £5,904. At the end of 1892 Bertie removed his horses from Kingsclere. The official explanation was that Richard Marsh's stable in Newmarket was more convenient to Sandringham, but the fact was that the prim and stubborn Porter had never been on the same wavelength as Bertie's racing manager, the livewire Marcus Beresford. Marsh, in contrast, was at ease shooting at Sandringham and credited by the Earl of Durham with 'the gift of dealing tactfully and circumspectly with all sorts and conditions of men'. Typically, Marsh was at pains ever after to credit Porter for recommending Perdita II for the royal stud. The next spring the mare delivered a foal, Persimmon, whose success in the 1896 Derby changed everything for Bertie.

Rosebery fretted whether cynics might suspect the other runners to have been restrained in deference to the royal colt. 'No doubt,' his valet replied. 'But I am bound to tell your lordship that many people thought the same when Ladas won!' As it was, Bertie received an ecstatic reception at Epsom – and now, a year on, Persimmon had the chance to consolidate this new empathy between Bertie and his future subjects in the Ascot Gold Cup.

Beresford had written to Marsh hinting that the queen might even deign to attend, in her Jubilee year, if Persimmon could be more or less guaranteed to win. Marsh set Persimmon the most exacting of trials, over the full Gold Cup distance of two and a half miles. Persimmon carried 9st 12lbs, his lead horse just 6st 3lbs, while others were used to maintain the pace. When Persimmon finished around three hundred yards clear, Marsh advised that the monarch might be 'safely' invited.

Yet she could not bring herself to suspend her hostility to the Turf. The previous autumn she had been incensed when Bertie left Balmoral early to see Persimmon run at Newmarket, when she was still entertaining the young Tsar Nicholas. (Her guest, it must be said, was heartily relieved to be spared any more of Bertie's stag hunts in the rain.) The ageing matriarch still failed to grasp that the transformation of the Turf, under the benign attention of her son, was a wholesome template for his future reign. In a speech this same year, Rosebery felt able to declare the sport 'never better or purer than at this moment; never more honest in its followers'. In 1858, the wife of Admiral Rous had counted herself among perhaps fifteen or twenty ladies at Ascot; her niece, in 1875, reckoned there still to be 'not more than a hundred'. By now they ran into thousands. Things had reached the stage that General Williams, trying to reach the paddock, was stabbed in the cheek by a red parasol, which had also made his horse rear. 'It's perfectly scandalous,' complained the owner of this object, 'that horses should be allowed here.'

It was a flawless summer afternoon, and Marsh produced the favourite in corresponding condition. One highly qualified witness recalled: 'When Persimmon was stripped for the Ascot Cup he stands out in my memory as the most perfectly trained horse I ever saw.' Only three rivals dared to take on the favourite, but each was accomplished: Love Wisely had won the race the previous year; Limasol had just won the Oaks; while the famously astute Captain Machell had struck a £100 match bet with Marsh on the Irish raider, Winkfield's Pride. But the moment his jockey produced the royal colt from the rear, on the last turn, Persimmon went careering eight lengths clear of Winkfield's Pride. Long before he reached the line, the stands were cheering themselves hoarse. 'The demonstration was, in its way, as remarkable for its spontaneity and its warmth as that which attended his Epsom triumph,' The Times reported. 'For the whole of the vast multitude turned, as with one accord, to the Royal Enclosure, cheering, for several minutes. The Prince came forward to acknowledge the compliment, and the cheering was continued until Persimmon had been led back to scale and his jockey duly weighed in.'

Captain Machell sought out Marsh and offered his hand. 'I don't know what sort of horse yours is,' he grumbled. 'I did not think it possible for you to beat me, but you beat Winkfield's Pride as if he had been a common hack.' Marsh had never felt so proud. Bertie, for his part, was aglow with the redemptive power of his first champion. There was no muttering about Tranby Croft now.

After Daisy had left the royal box – she was now Countess of Warwick, on account of her husband's accession to the family title – Bertie was approached by Marcus Beresford. He had a great favour to ask. Bertie immediately assured his friend that he would be delighted to oblige in any way, and was astonished to see tears running down the man's cheeks. Might Bertie be so good as to allow his brother up to offer his congratulations?

Charlie B! After a seven-year silence! Bertie had been infuriated at the previous year's meeting when ostentatiously cut dead by the great sailor. However taken aback, Bertie saw that the moment demanded magnanimity. Charlie was duly produced for an awkward handshake, refusing to replace his hat until urged to do so by Bertie. They spoke blandly of the racing only for sufficient time to achieve the purpose of the ordeal, Charlie exhibiting a humility so uncharacteristic as to be almost unbearable.

Both Bertie and Daisy had now moved on to new lovers, but they remained intimate. That night, he scribbled her an account of an 'unpleasant & unexpected' episode, and anxiously sought her approval. 'I had no alternative but to say yes,' he stressed. 'My loved one, I hope you won't be annoyed at what has happened & exonerate me fr. Blame.'

In the circumstances the Marlborough House set must have especially enjoyed one reporter's attempt to do justice to the prowess of the prince's colt. For the great thing about Persimmon was his 'fire and vitality . . . when he gets his clothes off and knows that business is meant'.

18

'He is far ahead of the lot,
even with all his faults'

So THIS WAS the famous little Yankee. Bertie noticed at once how Tod Sloan contrived a dandyish flair even in slipping a coat over his riding silks. If anything, the summons he had received in the changing room at Newmarket only exaggerated the bumptious swagger that set Sloan apart from the local jockeys almost as radically as his riding style. But there was something cold about his look, as well: something pursed and steely, a hint of scepticism in the arch of his brows. As Bertie extended a hand, plainly fascinated, Lord William Beresford made the introductions: 'Mr Sloan, sir . . . Mr Sloan, His Royal Highness the Prince of Wales.' One 225lb barrel, just 67 inches tall yet with a circumference of 48; and one little big man, 90lbs of all-American nerve, verve and invention.

It is feasible to argue that this encounter, in October 1898, brought together the two men who contributed most to the evolution of the Victorian sport into the one we know today – Bertie, off the track; and Sloan, on it. But Bertie was creating his legacy in increments, dismantling gender, social and ethnic barriers even as new enclosures and regulations raised standards. Sloan was authoring an overnight revolution.

Bill Beresford, brother of Marcus and Charlie, had been first of the believers on this side of the water. The hero of Ulundi had done much to upgrade Indian racing when posted to the Viceroy's staff, and since his return had formed a racing partnership with an American tobacco tycoon, Pierre Lorillard – himself already a trailblazer, having sent Iroquois over the Atlantic to win the 1881 Derby. Lorillard's trainer had bemused Newmarket's professionals by galloping Iroquois 'against the clock'. Even his Derby success was not enough to win over the locals, and to this day American trainers place far more faith in the stopwatch than their European counterparts. But now Bill Beresford, Lorillard and a Wall Street magnate, James R. Keene, were sponsoring a more provocative variation on standard practice, and the English jockeys would have to adapt or die.

In fairness, English jockeys already permitted their mounts relative freedom of movement, holding the reins loose and stretching their boots languidly into long stirrups. Yet here was this American rebel, so wary of interfering with his mount's elasticity that he hitched up his stirrups and perched so far above the withers that he seemed to disappear into the mane. A sporting correspondent remembered his first sight of the Yankee, riding work on the Heath, and asking a local rider if he could account for the mysterious apparition:

> He told me it was an American jockey named Sloan; that he had adopted that extraordinary seat, which was, of course, quite preposterous; and he gave me an imitation of the invader, clutching his reins within a few inches of the bit and explaining that it afforded you no sort of power over your horse. 'But all the same he can ride!' my perceptive friend observed.

At first, the natives viewed Sloan's style as merely ludicrous: he looked like 'a monkey on a stick'. But when he introduced it to the racetrack, with spectacular results, a defensive acerbity infected the criticism. Sloan was guilty not only of an aesthetic desecration but of forfeiting all the control, all the horsemanship of riders such as Morny Cannon, doyen of the old school.

It is no coincidence that Sloan exploded onto the scene just as the English were beginning to phase out flag starts, in favour of the new starting barriers developed in Australia and then America. Race after race, Sloan was stealing prizes from superior horses by dint of a fast break and deft management of his horse's reserves. His pursuers let him go, presuming he had lost control and that they would reel him in as the tearaway's exhaustion told. But Sloan, taught to ride against the clock, was never flat out. By always keeping something up his sleeve, he was able to kick clear just as the others tried to close the gap.

After a brief reconnaissance the previous year, Sloan had returned to ride twelve winners from sixteen mounts at Newmarket's first autumn meeting. Even now, the traditionalists refused to accept the obvious inference. Perhaps they were remembering the African American jockey Willie Simms, who had caused a brief stir with a similar style in 1895. By the end of his visit, the *Sporting Life* found it 'both amusing and instructive to see, when pitted in a finish against such a master of the art as Morny Cannon, how bunched up and helpless to assist his mount the darkie was except by needless punishment of the whip'.

Fifteen of the first twenty-eight winners of the Kentucky Derby, between 1876 and 1902, were ridden by eleven African American jockeys. Before the Civil War many featherweight jockeys had been slaves, a virtue made of their malnourishment as they were promoted from menial work in stables. By 1896, however, and the landmark case of *Plessy vs Ferguson*, African American riders were being driven off by racial segregation. Sloan had been among the white riders to profit from the resulting vacuum.

Though not the first American to crouch above a horse's withers, Sloan was also benefiting from a national mythology that celebrated the lone pioneer. The fact that the 'monkey seat' had been coined collectively in his homeland, probably by stableboys riding at county fairs with minimal tack, was never going to prevent Sloan accepting its authorship. At the very least, he can be credited as the rider who popularised the new style in England. Unlike Simms, Sloan forced an admission that the game was up. Already his style of breaking clear from the gate had entered Cockney rhyming slang: anyone out 'on his own' was 'on his Tod' [Sloan].

He produced the crowning example on a colt named Caiman in the Middle Park Stakes, often a signpost to the following season's Classics. The favourite, Flying Fox, was ridden by Cannon in the Westminster silks and would go on to win the Triple Crown in 1899. There was no way on earth Caiman should have been able to beat him. Sloan recalled this ride as his career masterpiece, a daylight robbery:

> The other jockeys let me make my own pace, 'Morny' holding off on his crack until the place at which he generally began his run. We went slower and slower till we got almost to a walk just before striking the

rise out of the last dip. I was watching him and saw him preparing to come along. So I shot mine out before he got moving and stole the race, Flying Fox, although going great guns, not having quite time enough to get up. I hope it does not seem that I am claiming for myself too much judgment at the expense of others, but without any brag or bounce I must say that there was such a hopeless ignorance of pace among the majority of those riding in the race, that I suppose I managed to kid them and so got where I did.

It was not just the betting public that became infatuated. 'Socially he is the lion of the hour,' reported a New York newspaper proudly, moreover saluting him as a 'well balanced young person, quite capable of holding his equilibrium in any and all circumstances.' Unfortunately this verdict would prove too sanguine. For now, however, anyone who observed Sloan's introduction to the future king could barely know which of the pair considered himself more honoured.

With his tremendous white moustache, Charles Rose wanders across the annals of the Turf like Mr Toad after seeing his first motor car. Cyllene, in particular, smacks of the purest serendipity. One of Bona Vista's first matings had been with an undistinguished mare named Arcadia. Rose named the resulting foal Cyllene, after the Arcadian birthplace of Hermes, but decided that a colt born as late as 28 May would be too backward to enter for the Classics. As soon as Rose sold Cyllene's sire to Hungary, however, his duckling began a startling trans-formation. In his prime not even Sloan could find a way to beat him.

The American was now riding regularly for Bertie, and joshing him with a familiarity that offended even the Beresfords. On one occasion Bertie stopped him on his way into the paddock, and asked how he liked his chances. Sloan told him that he was confident, prompting Marcus Beresford to scoff that he had no chance against Dundonald. 'Never you mind what Lord Marcus says,' the little imp told Bertie. 'You can be a plunger here and have a bit on me.' Bertie bet £700 to £200, and joshed his racing manager mercilessly after Sloan prevailed in a desperate finish with Dundonald.

His success was such that Sloan did not return to America for the 1899 season. He won the 1000 Guineas for Bill Beresford, but his Derby mount broke a leg when looking sure to win and left the way clear for Flying Fox – a parting glory for the Duke of Westminster, in the final year of his life. It was not just in the span of years that Westminster, a page at the queen's coronation, represented the Victorian age. For half a century he had stolidly demarcated the limits of the Whig conscience under the impatient prodding of Gladstone, prompting Rosebery to sum him up as 'a very good noble fellow, but a spoilt child'. Seen as rather a cold, remote figure, he showed characteristic acidity in his drollery after a niece married Henry Chaplin: 'When our Harry is broke, which is only a question of time, all the crowned heads of Europe ought to give him £100,000 a year in order that he may show them how to spend their money.' On the other hand, it was typical that the prize money won by Westminster's last champion should have been donated to a hospital at Rhyl – a gesture commemorated by a weathervane in the shape of a running fox. For all Rosebery's magnetism and oratory, *The Times* contrasted the public connection achieved by the pair: 'The nonconformist conscience which was so much disturbed by Lord Rosebery's racing successes, never, so far as we know, resented those of the Duke of Westminster . . . He could pass from a racecourse to take the chair at a missionary meeting without incurring the censure of the strictest.'

The dukedom now passed to a twenty-year-old grandson, an infant when Bend Or won the Derby and known ever after as 'Bendor'. Most of the stud was auctioned off. A filly out of Ormonde's sister was sold to a gambler and adventurer named Bob Sievier for 10,000 guineas, a new record for a yearling; while Flying Fox was sold to France for the unprecedented sum of 37,500 guineas. Both the great white hopes for the Bend Or line, Bona Vista and Flying Fox, had now been lost abroad. Everything now seemed to depend on Cyllene.

Fortunately, he proved better than ever in 1899, winning the Gold Cup at Ascot by eight lengths. 'Cyllene was essentially of the Bend Or type, all quality, and he struck one as being so sensible and game,' Richard Marsh remembered. 'No horse could have looked better than he did on the day he won the Ascot Gold Cup.' Having won from five furlongs to two and a half miles, Cyllene looked admirably equipped to compensate for the brevity of his sire's own stay there when in turn retired to the stud at Hardwick.

★

The last year of his mother's reign found Bertie consolidating a new public confidence both in his credentials as a future king and the sport he had come to personify. Five days after one of his steeplechasers won the Grand National, Bertie survived a point-blank assassination attempt by a fifteen-year-old anarchist at Brussels station. Less than a month later, Bertie strengthened his growing bond with the common Englishman by approving Marcus Beresford's suggestion that his volatile colt, Diamond Jubilee, be ridden in the 2000 Guineas by an obscure, teenage work-rider named Herbert Jones. A brother to Persimmon foaled in 1897, Diamond Jubilee had proved impossible for more seasoned riders to control. One morning he had even tried to savage Cannon, much as Muley Edris had Fred Archer. But Jones was able to sweeten him on the gallops and together they won the Guineas in great style.

A couple of weeks later Bertie and his wife were at Covent Garden for Wagner's *Lohengrin*. At the end of the second act, a voice shouted from the gallery: 'Mafeking has been relieved!' The whole house rose to its feet, cheering wildly, and belted out 'God Save the Queen'. A similar delirium still infected the crowds at Epsom, where several thousand patriots responded to a premature rumour that Lord Roberts's army had entered Pretoria by singing the anthem before the royal box. Riding this tidal wave of jingoism, Jones steered home Diamond Jubilee for Bertie's second Derby success. It was the first time a starting gate had been used for the race, and confirmed Bertie's renaissance as a king fit for a new century.

Pretoria did fall soon afterwards but those killed on the great march from Bloemfontein included Ernest Rose, a captain in the Blues, and one of two sons lost in the space of five weeks of the Boer campaign – the other to enteric fever – by the owner of Cyllene. According to a regimental history, 'a braver or better soldier never breathed'. Yet Charles Rose would find his patriotism hurtfully impugned that autumn, when putting his name forward as the Liberal candidate for the Newmarket constituency of East Cambridgeshire.

He had past form with the Conservative incumbent, Harry McCalmont. Seven years previously, Rose's Ravensbury had maddeningly finished second in all three legs of the Triple Crown to

McCalmont's great champion, Isinglass. Evidently their old rivalry still rankled. Unfortunately for Rose, his opponent could trump even a visit to the distant graves of his sons: Colonel McCalmont was himself serving in Africa.

Though largely confined to garrison duties, McCalmont's absence from the hustings showed an unanswerable patriotic zeal. At thirty-nine, and a reliably cheerful presence in Bertie's clique, he was admired as a man of action. When winning this seat he had rattled through an 87-mile coach tour of the constituency on polling day. Left £4 million by an eccentric great-uncle, he had built an enormous neo-Palladian pile outside Newmarket and, dressed in a Tyrolean hat and checked suit, hosted the best shooting parties of his day. One guest remembered the universal satisfaction when the papers arrived, shortly before McCalmont's departure, reporting that Winston Churchill had been captured by the Boers. 'Caught him, have they?' said one sportsman. 'By Jove! I hope they'll keep him!' McCalmont had also started a sporting magazine, its first two numbers featuring C. B. Fry on 'Hard Wickets' and Major R. S. S. Baden-Powell on 'Pig-sticking'.

Heavy wagering was soon reported on the East Cambridgeshire poll, although voters were 'troubling themselves very little about politics so long as they are represented by a thorough going sportsman, which they are certain to be'. In the event, McCalmont was returned with an increased majority. Even without his opponent's peculiar advantages, Rose could hardly hope to stem the national tide of a 'Khaki Election'. During the campaign, one Unionist cartoon even showed him helping President Kruger tear down the British flag – a remarkably insensitive image, considering his family's recent sacrifice.

Barely a year after his return, McCalmont dropped dead of a heart attack. Much of his stable was bought up by Lord Howard de Walden, a rare sporting aesthete whose apricot silks were recommended by Augustus John to offset the green of the turf.* And the vacancy in the Commons was filled, in a by-election, by Mr Toad.

*

* It was de Walden's son who would famously knock down a pedestrian when motoring through Munich in 1931; had he been driving a little faster, Adolf Hitler might not have brushed himself down to quite such tiresome effect.

Sloan's astonishing results in England prompted several compatriots to follow him across the Atlantic in 1900. At Royal Ascot, sixteen of the twenty-eight races were won by American jockeys: six by Sloan, seven divided between the two Reiff brothers, three for Skeets Martin. After this rout, the native riders raised a white flag. 'Some of our own riders for a time went almost farther than their models,' lamented one sporting magazine. 'Herbert Jones used simply to flatten himself on [his mount], his attitude being much that of a toboggan coming down the Cresta Run.' Morny Cannon held out longest, but in the end even he grudgingly hitched up his stirrups a hole or two.

In time they settled on a hybrid style, their initial conversion to the precarious American seat causing an epidemic of accidents over the undulations of English tracks. As late as 1925, Richard Marsh was still clinging to the wreckage of the classical school, complaining of 'a demoralizing effect on horses . . . scurried from pillar to post'. Yet Marsh had adapted his own methods to absorb the principles of the American jockeys. For his was the generation that finally completed the work of the Dawsons and Peck, relieving the thoroughbred once and for all from the intensive training of the old masters.

Mat Dawson had died the summer after Sloan's first transatlantic foray, succumbing to a chill after being detained in a long chat by Bertie on the Heath. Sir Visto, in following up his Derby win in the St Leger, was the last of Dawson's twenty-eight Classic winners. His legacy, by then, was secure. And Marsh saw that the modern thoroughbred had now been refined in such a way that trainers needed to match the new finesse of jockeys. One principle he borrowed from Dawson was that good horses should only be led in their work by lesser ones. Marsh's maxim was that 'vitality makes the racehorse'. A trainer's job was to preserve that 'supreme nervous energy, which must be nurtured and never sapped . . . Better to send your horse to the post short of a gallop [i.e. workout] than with one too many.'

Marsh suspected that the proliferation of the Darley Arabian line was creating a genetic powder keg: 'Slavish adherence to the outstanding winning strains of the last quarter of a century is producing a horse more inclined to live and race on his nerves than on the constitution.' The twentieth-century racehorse was no longer as robust as its predecessor, mentally or physically, and so required a more indulgent regime. Trainers had to be guided by temperament and pedigree in judging how far to push their charges. 'The horses that stand the strong work are those which come of stout lines and take only a minimum out of themselves,' Marsh wrote. 'With horses of delicate temperament the art was to hide from them the fact that they had done a gallop.'

Focusing on the raw energy of the modern thoroughbred was a logical development of the principles introduced by American jockeys. Unfortunately, a less edifying innovation was being credited to some of the American trainers who now began to arrive in their wake. One, Enoch Wishard, became the leading trainer of 1900 with fifty-four winners; while his former assistant, William Duke, weighed in with twenty-nine. The pair had arrived the previous summer with a medicine chest full of 'tonics' and set about ruthlessly exploiting local naivety over doping.

Hitherto it had been assumed that racehorses could only be 'stopped' by drugs. The notion that they might respond to artificial stimulants had been confined to such picturesque experiments with port or whisky as were openly attempted by John Scott or Mat Dawson, whose 1885 Derby winner was declared by his jockey to be 'quite drunk' when beaten at Newmarket the following year. One north country vet boasted that he had been injecting cocaine-based 'speedy balls' for some years already, but it was the Americans who began producing 'horses who were notorious rogues running and winning as if they were possessed of the devil, with eyes starting out of their heads and the sweat pouring off them'. One doped horse, having won his race, careered into a stone wall and killed himself.

In 1903 the Jockey Club published a notice that trainers would be banned if found to have used drugs 'for the purpose of affecting the speed of a horse'. The clincher had been an audacious experiment by Jack Durham's brother, George Lambton, who expressly forewarned the stewards that he intended to dope five of his worst horses. Durham was uneasy about the experiment, and made Lambton promise not to stake any bets. Lambton, who lamented that the charming Wishard might have confirmed himself 'somewhat of a genius' without ever resorting to dope, then paraded four winners and a second.

Though no saliva test would be developed before 1914 – and even then a positive result would not give rise to a ban until 1930 – William Duke took no chances and hastily removed himself across the Channel to win the French Derby three times in four years.

Not every American trainer was tainted. John Huggins, for instance, was scrupulously clean. Asked whether there were many rogues and thieves in his homeland, he replied: 'There is not one. They have all come over here.' Sloan, strutting his way between Bertie and John 'Bet-a-Million' Gates, the high-rolling industrialist, was himself allowing his trademark freshness to slide into rank bad manners. He even left Bill Beresford obliged to pay a waiter several hundred pounds to hush up an assault with a champagne bottle at Ascot. But perhaps Bill and his brother should have intervened at a more fundamental level, as one sympathetic observer remarked:

> Young, brilliant, generous, extravagant and vain, Sloan found himself
> with a fortune in the bank after a couple of seasons' riding, and
> quickly became the mark of all the 'boys' on the Turf. He was
> surrounded by bad-hats and by pugilists and toughs of every descrip-
> tion. He was made a tremendous fuss of by the female sex . . . In
> a foreign country, who was there to guide him, to give him a steadying
> word in season, to beg him to avoid this gang, to discountenance
> the advance of those sharps? Nobody.

Instead Sloan was insisting on suites in the best hotels, tables on the Deauville seafront, the biggest cigars and the boldest wardrobe. On the occasion of his Ascot fracas, for instance, he had somehow upholstered himself in a braided white yachting suit and cap. And, disastrously, his arrogance now extended onto the track itself. So blithely did he flout the rules against betting that he stood to win $350,000 in the 1900 Cambridgeshire. In the event, he finished second. But things were coming to a head.

On the face of it, Sloan could be excused for fancying he had soared beyond the reach of petty regulators. Towards the end of the season Bertie sent Marcus Beresford round offering a 6,000-guinea retainer to ride in the royal silks in 1901. They had just agreed terms when Bill Beresford appeared with a cable from the American tycoon William Collins Whitney: 'We must have Sloan, get him at any price, he is far ahead of the lot and worth anything for big races even with all his faults.' Though dismayed to find that his brother had beaten him to the deal, Bill offered Sloan 3,000 guineas for a second claim on his services.

That same autumn, however, Jack Durham broke ranks to rebuke the Jockey Club for its indulgence of rule-breaking by American riders. He was doubtless irritated by the way Sloan had traduced a courageous declaration of faith, just two years previously, when everyone else was still furiously insisting on the superiority of the classical English style. Durham now felt impelled to stop Bertie embarrassing himself. The queen's steepening decline was widely known. Sloan had suited Bertie's cosmopolitan style, but could not hope to ride for a king – or anyone else – until learning some respect.

Sloan was advised not to bother seeking a licence for the following season, and never rode in England again. He was stunned by the suddenness of his downfall. His career had followed an immaculate trajectory of the American dream: the country boy from Indiana, more or less abandoned by his family, who had started out working for a stunt balloonist on the fair circuit and ended up 'dressed in flaming raiment, with a cigar a foot long between his teeth', feted by society beauties and hobnobbing with a prince. In his memoirs he would recall Bertie with a pathetically instructive analogy: 'I can tell you that although I come from democratic America, there was a wonderful impression left on me by the great personal attraction of that royal gentleman,' he wrote. 'It sort of drew me to him in the same way that a magnetic crane in all its strength will pick up scrap iron.'

Descending via vaudeville, bookmaking and billiard halls, he would become a poignant curiosity of the Depression. At one stage Damon Runyon found a chubby Tod Sloan working as a gateman at Tijuana racetrack in Mexico. His last job was as a barman in Los Angeles, where he died in a charity ward from cirrhosis of the liver. He was fifty-nine.

The same clear-out that cost Sloan his career also resulted in bans

239

for Otto Madden and Fred Rickaby, who rode for impeccable establishment figures in Richard Marsh and Lord Derby. That these jockeys could be punished for association with persons of bad character, without the slightest slur on their employers, was a measure of the growing confidence of the Jockey Club. Yet the autocratic treatment of Sloan also showed the progress it still had to make. His nebulous offences were never subjected to any kind of due process, and he was certainly young enough, at twenty-six, to merit the second chance soon granted to Madden and Rickaby.

At least the louche ambience of the Turf in the first half of Victoria's reign had now been fumigated. To a degree, the process had been driven by steam: the railways, having greatly enhanced its commercial potential, made the sport's regulation at once more important and more practical. But it had also been assisted by a prince and a prime minister, the flaws of each redressed by the strengths of the other. Mat Dawson had identified Rosebery, not Bertie, as 'the first gentleman in Europe'. Rosebery's friendship with Danny Maher, an American jockey of high integrity, was dignified, faithful and touching; Bertie, in contrast, had been seduced into a whirlwind, high-risk relationship by the gaudiness of Sloan. Yet it was precisely in his lowbrow imperfections that his future subjects found the warmth, the humanity, they had craved in his mother. For all his pulsating oratory, Rosebery proved too refined and remote to claim the hearts of a nation.

But nor, critically, had the example of these distinguished men rendered the Turf wholly antiseptic. If no longer synonymous with corruption or profligacy, racing remained much too 'fast' for the prigs. For this happy medium, the sport is indebted to this day to both Bertie and Rosebery. How fitting, then, that both men should have basked in the crepuscular glow of this golden era with a third Derby winner apiece.

On the evening the queen died, Winston Churchill wrote to his mother and speculated how Bertie would go about things now. 'Will he sell his horses and scatter his Jews?' he asked. 'Will he become desperately serious?' In the event, Bertie's accession would bring the English Turf to its Elysium.

Regy Brett traced 'a St Martin's summer' in Bertie's public life to the day he had led in his first Derby winner. 'The outburst of popular goodwill on that occasion seemed to transfuse into his blood a new resolve,' he wrote. 'In years the Prince was long past middle life. But age fell away from him . . . The aura of coming Kingship flickered about him.' His racehorses were no longer mere agents of rebellion; they had opened an artery of public affection long clotted by his mother.

Disraeli had tried to explain this to the queen back in 1878. After the Congress of Berlin, he told her of a conversation over dinner with Bismarck. The German Chancellor had asked whether racing was still encouraged in England. With Bertie doubtless in mind, Disraeli assured him that it had never been more so.

> 'Then,' cried the Prince [Bismarck] eagerly, 'there will never be Socialism in England. You are a happy country. You are safe, so long as the people are devoted to racing. Here a gentleman cannot ride down the street without twenty persons saying to themselves, or each other, 'Why has that fellow a horse, and I have not one?' In England the more horses a nobleman has, the more popular he is.'

When the queen had implored Bertie to quit the Turf, over thirty years previously, she had predicted that as king he would belatedly find himself embarrassed by the friends he had made there – and that he would then 'break with them all'. But this Hal, on acceding, saw no need to cut off his Falstaffs. True, poor Christopher Sykes had not lived to see a coronation, departing in 1898 in scenes of predictable bathos. When the time came to lower the old beanpole into the ground, it was found that no allowance had been made for the abnormal length of the coffin. After the failure of various desperate tilts – side to side, up and down – the vicar indicated that the coffin should be left resting above ground while the rites were completed. Bertie buried his face in his handkerchief as a paroxysm of coughs testified to the true nature of the tears, whimpering and shaking of shoulders round the graveside.

Freddie Johnstone and Henry Chaplin, the men loathed by Bertie's mother for leading him astray, remained intimates of the new king. There had been a temporary rift with Johnstone after a boisterous exhibition in the billiards room at Sandringham. 'Freddie, Freddie, you're very drunk,' Bertie had reproved. His tone was amiable but Johnstone, poking the royal gut, not only used a nickname absolutely proscribed in Bertie's presence but also mocked the curious Germanic residue in his accent: 'Tum-Tum, you're ver-r-ry fat!' Bertie promptly ordered an equerry to pack Johnstone's bags and he slunk away before breakfast next morning. But the froideur did not endure, and Bertie remained a regular guest at Johnstone's villa in Monte Carlo and his house near Ascot.

Chaplin had an increasing parliamentary profile as a diehard Tory protectionist, a monocle glinting atop his enormous bulk like a telescope seeking land from the crow's nest. Though matching Bertie's expanding girth, in other respects he had been tightening his belt. 'Horses were not only his pride, they were his ruin, for the time came when the race-course broke him, as it has broken so many,' Daisy Warwick remembered. 'The only difference was that other men go under.'

The author of this charming back-handed compliment had by now been succeeded in Bertie's affections by Mrs Alice Keppel.* For a time Daisy turned her heaviest erotic artillery towards Rosebery instead, though it remains unclear to what extent his defences may have been breached. Widowed so young, there were always rumours about possible matches for Rosebery, though the most authentic was scotched by Bertie himself: a Liberal politician, however noble, was out of the question for his daughter, Princess Victoria. The fact was that Bertie and Rosebery, whatever their common ground on the racecourse, were always very different characters. In 1903 the new king was given lunch at Rosebery's villa on the Bay of Naples, and found both the food and his host out of sorts. How, Bertie grumbled afterwards, could anyone enjoy prolonged solitude out here? The diplomat who accompanied him shrugged: 'He is a strange, weird man, sir.'

Though Hardwick House was the undisputed model for Gardencourt in *The Portrait of a Lady* – Henry James, a distant relative, had visited

---

* No doubt Bertie viewed his introduction to Mrs Keppel, at Sandown Park in 1898, as due reward for making the racecourse a suitable venue for a lady.

Rose there – its claims as the original Toad Hall appear to be more contentious. What is certain is that Kenneth Grahame wrote his Edwardian idyll when a regular guest of his fellow banker, often found recumbent by the willows and tall grasses, musing upon the waters idling by. And Rose's resemblance to Toad (or vice versa) was only increasing with the years.

In 1904, four years before the publication of *The Wind in the Willows*, he acquired an enormous Mercedes tourer. Rose delighted in scattering terrified pedestrians as the silver monster roared through the narrow lanes. Impatient with a short walk to his real-tennis court, he took advantage of his wife's absence on holiday to build a new one on the site of her rose garden. But all these restless and expensive enthusiasms were putting pressure on the stud.

Cyllene's first yearlings generated little interest at the sales. His mother was too obscure; his father had vanished. Few had any inkling that Bona Vista was flourishing in Hungary, where he began four seasons as champion sire in 1902. The one man who did show faith was Rosebery. In his second season at stud, Cyllene was favoured by a visit from one of the most precious mares at Mentmore: Gas, a half-sister to Ladas II. And Gas was followed to Hardwick that same spring by a mare named Maid Marian, owned by Rosebery's new son-in-law, Robert Crewe-Milnes, 1st Marquess of Crewe.

Despite holding junior office for the same party, Lord Crewe had never aligned himself politically behind Rosebery. It was on the Turf that Crewe had sooner commended himself to the father of the eighteen-year-old Peggy, whose loveliness thawed even this notorious cold fish, a longstanding widower of forty-one. Certainly Crewe seems to have heeded Rosebery's counsel regarding Cyllene: since Maid Marian's sire was also the grandsire of Gas, the resulting foals would have very similar pedigrees.

Both mares produced a colt in the spring of 1902. Rosebery sent Cicero to Percy Peck, son of the man who had trained Doncaster and Bend Or; while Crewe asked the ageing John Porter to take in Polymelus, named after a Trojan warrior. Polymelus would fall a notch below the best of their generation; but Cicero, ridden by Maher, won the 1905 Derby in a record time.

What did his fellow diners think, as Rosebery was toasted by the king at Buckingham Palace that evening? 'The great Sphinx' remained as inscrutable as ever. And racing, so he grumbled, had always devoured his time and money at a hopeless rate. Yet there were valid consolations: companionship, above all; the enchanting tableau, summer after summer, of mares and foals grazing a park; and always the grail of the next 'horse of the century'. The names of great racehorses, he noted, endure for generations. 'How many poets, how many philosophers, aye, how many statesmen, would be remembered 150 years after they had lived?' Yet their breeding depended, not on any 'abstract theory and historical law', but on 'the Goddess of Fortune'. Sure enough, he was about to compound his error with Bona Vista on behalf of his son-in-law. With Cicero sidelined by injury, Polymelus was able to finish second in the St Leger and then rounded off his campaign, in the Gatwick Stakes, as the final winner ever saddled by the great Porter. But both Peggy and her father now prevailed upon Crewe to sell his colt for £3,000. At first, it seemed the right call. Polymelus proved largely disappointing in 1906 and his new owner hastened to offload the horse in a sale at Newmarket – with a reserve of £4,000 – the moment he offered a glimpse of his old form. The sequel would be agonising. 'Polymelus,' Peggy grieved years later, 'would have been a gold mine.' She chose her words advisedly.

19

Jewels in the Crown

THE GREATEST SCRAMBLE in the history of capitalism was
begun by an itinerant pedlar, wandering a cindery plain on the
northern fringes of the Cape Colony in 1867. Calling at a lonely
farmhouse, he was hospitably received by Schalk Van Niekirk, who
showed him an unusual stone he had noticed local children using
in a pitching game. The pedlar agreed to take it to the next town
and eventually had it identified as a 21-carat diamond worth £500.
For now, there was no undue excitement. But the following year
Van Niekirk was shown another odd stone by a Griqua shepherd.
It proved to be an 83-carat white diamond, and sold for £11,200.

This sensation reached the ears of adventurers the world over,
and many left their drinks unfinished on the bar. Farmers pegged
out the grey scrub in claims of 30 square feet – ten times the size
of your grave, cynics said – initially let at 7s 6d a week. As more
and more gems appeared on the sorting tables, these spiralled dizzily
in value – one, typically, from £20 to £4,000 in a year. In all, the
58 square miles encompassed by three farms would yield £40 million
worth of diamonds over the next two decades.

By 1871, 10,000 men were encamped in the shanty town that
would become Kimberley. Twenty miles from the nearest river, the
parched diggers swarmed like ants over the partitioned hollows. All
human life was here: veterans of the Australian and Californian
rushes; Fenians and deserters, swindlers and impostors, gamblers and
whores. By day, dust smeared the brutal sunlight over the sifted
claims; by night, hundreds of paraffin lamps smoked eerily over a
city of canvas and corrugated iron. The air seethed with raw sewage
and cupidity. A harlot stood on a crate in a canteen and auctioned
her company for the rest of the night. Everyone was either living

on his wits, or losing them altogether. One man so despaired of a dud claim that he tried to sell it for 15 shillings, only to find a £10,000 'whopper' the next morning. A former army captain placed his last ten pounds on red at a roulette table; the ball snagged in a black groove, and he plunged palely into the street pursued by callous jeers. Moments later a shot rang out.

The wheel turned rather more kindly for David Harris, a young Jew from London. Watching a friend gambling in Dodd's Canteen, he had no intention of placing a bet until the croupier made a pointed remark about the glass of champagne he was enjoying on the house. He placed a token sovereign on 13, was paid out at 35–1, and left several hours later with £1,400.

His cousins, Harry and Barney Isaacs, were suitably impressed when Harris made a triumphant visit home to the slums of Spitalfields. Before his departure, he had worked as a ledger clerk at 15 shillings a week. Now here he was in a smart new suit, buying drinks all round at the pub run by Harry and Barney's sister, Kate Joel.

The stagehands who drank at the King of Prussia had so taken to the landlady's young brothers – both had that bit of spark to them, a bit of plausibility – that Harry's conjuring act had begun to appear down the bill in local variety shows. Myopic Barney played his straight man. And it was their stage name, Barnato, that they now took with them to the Cape: first Harry, then Barney. They would miss their family, especially their sister's three lads. Barney was more like a brother to them, really, only nine years older than even the youngest of his nephews, Solly, when arriving in Cape Town, at the age of seventeen, with £30 and forty boxes of mephitic cigars. Paying £5 to load his luggage on a bullock wagon, he trudged alongside for 700 miles to Kimberley. The trek took two months.

Barney arrived to find that Harry – 'Signor Barnato, the Great Wizard' – was already a popular figure in the corrugated theatre huts, smashing watches in his handkerchief before returning them intact to astonished members of the audience. Entering partnership with Lou Cohen, to whom he introduced himself by sneezing soup all over the counter of a bar, Barney started out as a 'kopje walloper'.

The wallopers traipsed round the sorting tables trying to buy diamonds direct, as middlemen to big European buyers. It was thirsty work, and the novice often had to learn by expensive mistakes. But it was also conveniently close to the action. The walloper, in one contemporary account, would 'haunt the edge of the mine . . . sometimes on the chance of buying a diamond cheaply, trading on the ignorance of the finder, but generally with the view of tempting sorters to steal'.

As the Big Hole deepened, floods, collapsing shale and a harder bedrock all tended to impel amalgamation of claims. But company mines would have no need for small-time, scrounging brokers. It was a critical moment. Pooling their resources, the Barnato brothers mustered £3,000 to buy four claims in 1876. Five years later they were able to buy another half-dozen, in cash, for £180,000, and open a dealership in London. Barney took to wearing a pince-nez, starched collar, bow tie, spats and a flower in his buttonhole. As soon as they were old enough, he summoned his nephews Woolf, Jack and Solly Joel to come and share in the booty.

Yet no matter how they prospered, the Barnato brothers – and, by extension, their Joel nephews – were unable to shake off rumours about their rise. The fact was that the ever more draconian supervision of native workers, and punishment of petty pilferers, was doing little to stop a thriving and fairly brazen trade in stolen gems. One suspected dealer was searched thoroughly before riding out of town. As soon as he crossed the Transvaal border, he dismounted, shot his horse and cut a bag out of its intestines. Such men were known to trade in particular hotels. One landlady earned her customers' gratitude by scooping up their wares in a tablecloth as a policeman walked in, only to express bewilderment when they thanked her afterwards. She assured them that she had found nothing but breadcrumbs in the tablecloth. Another notorious clearing hotel was owned by Harry Barnato. Finally, in 1884, a fearless detective dared to challenge the untouchables: he charged the eldest of Barney's nephews, Jack, over the possession of unregistered stones. Jack jumped bail and fled home, never to be seen in Kimberley again.

Meanwhile the Big Hole gradually swallowed almost all the dreamers who had begun the deepest excavation in history. By the time it had reached 3,500 feet by a quarter of a mile, the last men standing were Barney Barnato and Cecil Rhodes. Both were to claim victory in the 1888 De Beers consolidation that hoarded every diamond in Kimberley for a company set up by Rhodes, backed by Natty Rothschild, in which Barney now had the biggest stake. It was a textbook example of keeping your enemies closer. 'Rhodes had a stone in hand,' Barney boasted, using the racetrack vernacular. 'But I won in a canter!'

He then sent young Solly to a new boomtown, Johannesburg, and placed him in charge of a frenetic spree of investment in mines, utilities and property. But if the goldfields of the Witwatersrand made Solly's reputation, it was the English Turf that would seal it.

By the turn of the century a stable of thoroughbreds had become the classic hallmark of a new, international plutocracy. Some of its members had become cogs of imperial statecraft, like the Rothschilds; others, symbols of the social polity projected by Bertie. Competition with princes and prime ministers for Classic races dating back to the 1770s helped to certify the status of Americans, Jews and other outsiders who had scrapped their way to the top of a global economy. In effect, they bought into the English Turf in much the same way as the daughters of New World tycoons married titled aristocrats: Jennie Jerome and Consuelo Vanderbilt, for instance, who respectively married Lord Randolph Churchill and the 9th Duke of Marlborough. The fathers of both these brides were founders of the American Jockey Club, and helped to build opulent racecourses in New York fit for the Gilded Age.

Barney Barnato appointed Marcus Beresford, Bertie's racing manager, to manage his string for much the same reason as he built himself a mansion on Park Lane. Yet he never felt accepted, instead becoming ever more prone to paranoia, insomnia and bouts of heavy drinking. Solly was relieved to find his uncle more like his old self during a voyage home in 1897. Over lunch, he had enjoyed chatting with George Lohmann, who had taken eight wickets for seven runs for England at Port Elizabeth the previous year. Afterwards, however, Barney suddenly asked the time, jumped out of his deckchair and began scrambling over the rails. Solly yelled for help but only managed a brief hold on his uncle's trouser leg. One of the ship's officers heroically threw off his jacket and dived after him, but to no avail. An inquest returned a verdict of 'death by drowning while temporarily insane'.

Its distressing end, at forty-four, was hardly likely to disperse the innuendos about the incredible career of Barney Barnato. As they took charge of the family firm, Solly and his brothers decided there was no better place to shake the dust of the veldt from their soles – together with anything more incriminating – than the racecourse. Solly had already established a racing stable on the Cape. At Epsom and Ascot, he knew to expect snobbery and anti-Semitism: the ostentation and ruthless ambition of the 'Randlords' put them largely beyond even the embrace of Bertie and his set. But if Solly could not join them, he could at least beat them.

He certainly looked the part with his flamboyant wardrobe and whiskers. If he was never going to be wholly respectable, he had the personality to shrug it off, toting colossal cigars in Riviera casinos and at bloodstock auctions. In the shanty days of Kimberley his uncle had once tried his hand as a bookmaker, in one story even trusting that a horse would run faster than the paint that disguised him. Now Solly embarked on a sibling rivalry with Jack, with all the rollicking, lordly sportsmanship of the Beresfords themselves.

One of Jack's earliest purchases, in fact, was a horse named Democrat from Bill Beresford's stable. Unfortunately, this animal's deterioration was such that he eventually surfaced for an unexpected day in the sun, as Lord Kitchener's charger in Curzon's vainglorious Delhi Durbar, in 1903, to celebrate Bertie's accession. That same year, however, Jack won the Oaks – his first Classic – while Solly acquired a fifty-bedroom mansion at Maiden Erlegh, near Ascot, planting 20,000 flowers in his racing colours. He filled its paddocks with mares, and its marble pool with chorus girls. (One visiting troupe was kindly loaned swimming costumes only to discover that the material dissolved in water.)

Whatever corners they may have cut, there was an undeniable Midas touch to the Joel brothers. Sifting the debris of the Turf, Solly now picked out a drab stone, Polymelus, and had him polished up into a priceless gem by Charles Peck – son of the man who

trained the horse's great-grandsire, and brother of the trainer of
Cicero. Rosebery, Crewe and Peggy watched aghast as Peck achieved
a transformation in the horse as rapid as it was dramatic. Starting at
white-knuckle odds of just 11–10, Polymelus became perhaps the
most popular winner in the long history of the Cambridgeshire
Handicap. Solly and his pals landed over £100,000, while countless
working men followed them in with smaller wagers.

The acclaim for Polymelus was in gratifying contrast to the thun-
derstruck silence that had greeted Solly's biggest winner to date,
earlier that season, when Peck saddled Bachelor's Button to administer
the sole defeat of a great public favourite, Pretty Polly, in the Ascot
Gold Cup. Polymelus represented a turning point for the Joels:
within five years, Jack would be cheered as he led in the winner of
the Derby.

In doing so he matched the recent examples of W. C. Whitney;
'Boss' Croker, of Tammany Hall; and Alfred Cox, who had won a
share in a dusty Outback sheep ranch when playing poker on the
boat out to Australia, and found himself sitting on the Broken Hill
silver mine. Six of the first seven Derbys after Bertie's accession,
meanwhile, were won by American jockeys. The English Turf, in
other words, was already reflecting trends the colonial powers stubbornly failed to recognise. Had they paid closer attention to
Edwardian Derby results, they might have understood that the profitable exchange of culture and capital no longer depended on military
bondage; that the Industrial Revolution had created a global
economy, itself contingent on the increasing affluence of those who
manned its machinery; and that territorialism would only produce
instability. Instead these lessons would have to be catastrophically
amplified in a world war.

By this stage, the Hardwick stud was resembling Toad's boathouse
and gypsy caravan in its gradual dereliction. Shortly before Cicero
won the Derby for Rosebery, Charles Rose was offered the terrific
sum of 30,000 guineas for his sire, Cyllene, by William Bass, the
young beneficiary of a brewing fortune. This time, acknowledging
the cost to the English Turf of Bona Vista's sale to Hungary, Rose
stipulated that Cyllene be kept on home soil until 1908. As soon as

that clause lapsed, however, Bass sold Cyllene on to a stud that had long led the way in grafting an Argentinian version of the European thoroughbred.

Ojo de Agua was founded in 1873 by Santiago Luro, whose father, Pedro, had left the Basque country for Buenos Aires in 1834 and, just like Alfred Cox, traced his fortune to a card school *en voyage*. In his case, he won enough to buy himself a cart, two oxen and some goods to hawk to homesteaders in the interior. By the time he died, his estates exceeded 100,000 acres.

According to family legend, Pedro found many settlers so cowed by fierce native reivers that they were ready to sell their ranches at a loss. He hired gauchos to guard his cattle and bought a horse, El Moro, fast enough to outrun any ambush. Vast swathes of savannah were certainly staked out, around this time, by prospectors emulating their contemporaries in North America, bloodily skirmishing with aboriginals along a western wilderness. But smaller ranchers tended to be too lacking in influence or means, never mind ammunition, to resist the claims of big speculators.

A final extermination of the tribes in the 1870s – celebrated as the Conquest of the Desert – opened up virgin prairies just as refrigeration, railways and steamships created a new export market. Nowhere in the world was land so fertile, so close to great ocean ports. Suddenly this backwater was registering growth seldom matched in any modern economy: wheat exports in 1882 were valued at 60,000 gold pesos; a decade later, they had reached 13.6 million. Glamorous *estancieros* began to surface in Paris to complete a cosmopolitan education and pay for champagne.

These European connections heightened tensions between the *porteños* of Buenos Aires, inclined to liberal secularism, and the conservative aristocrats who dominated the political machinery. And the hub of *porteño* life was the Jockey Club of Argentina, founded in 1882 by a young politician named Carlos Pellegrini. Six years previously he had attended the French Derby at Chantilly and vowed, dining with friends that evening, to upgrade the Argentinian race-horse. British expatriates had imported thoroughbreds at a desultory rate for a generation or so, many then cross-bred with creole mares. But now Pellegrini, as its first president, and Santiago Luro, as treasurer, determined – much like the Hungarians – to make their Jockey Club a symbol of national modernisation.

It was no longer 'enough to breed from pure blood – the horses should be select types, of noble blood'. In a culture where the young W. H. Hudson saw even beggars on horseback, the sight of nouveaux *estancieros* leading the equivalent of Grand Prix cars into the winner's enclosure at Palermo made the most obvious of statements to the newly confident Argentina. Even a sudden economic and political crisis, in 1890, found its solution at the Jockey Club, which loaned Pellegrini for two years to preside over a regime of austerity and protectionism.*

By the turn of the century there was no better measure of fiscal recovery than a series of stallion imports from Europe, crowned by Diamond Jubilee, a royal Derby winner for £30,000, and then Cyllene himself. Many years later, when breeders in the Northern Hemisphere found themselves producing too many horses of style without substance, they would be relieved to discover in Argentina and Chile a precious repository of bone and brawn, stamina and grit, tracing to the Classic families of late Victorian and Edwardian Britain. And it would then fall to the Luro family, once again, to brand the Darley Arabian line with the stockmanship of the Pampas.

Even as Polymelus sealed their arrival on the Turf, the Joels were still being discomfited by their past in the Cape. Not long after their uncle's death, Solly's brother Woolf had been shot dead by a German conman calling himself Baron Von Veltheim. His real name later proved to be Kurtz – and he was every bit as disquieting a European adventurer as his contemporary namesake in *Heart of Darkness*. At his trial Kurtz claimed that he had been last to go for his gun, but quickest, and the Transvaal burghers on the jury took three minutes to acquit him. Now Kurtz had resurfaced, demanding payment for silence over the outlandish political intrigues he ascribed to the

---

* The City of London was badly spooked, Barings Bank being disastrously exposed to Argentinian debt, and the diamond trade also suffered. But Solly Joel remained ebullient. 'Women are born every minute,' he shrugged. 'And as long as women are born, diamonds will be worn.'

family in Africa. In 1908, as Polymelus began his stud career at Maiden Erlegh, Kurtz was tried for extortion at the Old Bailey. This time, his story was dismissed as preposterous and he was packed off to jail.

Having triumphantly exorcised one spectre, the Joel brothers now decided to clear their name once and for all. Kurtz may have been a low-life fantasist, but he was genuinely sinister. They could surely make short work of a cheap scribbler like Bob Sievier. Jack had been feuding with Sievier for years. It was Sievier who had paid a record 10,000 guineas for a yearling filly at the dispersal of Westminster's stud; and who then found himself short of cash even as that filly, named Sceptre, somehow made herself look a bargain. At some stage Sievier had asked Jack for a bailout, and then accused him of exploiting his predicament with an insulting offer for Sceptre. Jack responded by poaching Sievier's trainer, Charles Morton, to run his own stable. Though it meant missing out on Sceptre's sensational Classic campaign in 1902 – Sievier ran her in all five Classics and she won four – Morton would be handsomely vindicated for transferring his allegiance to Jack. His new patron proved loyal and astute, and together they would win eleven Classics over the next twenty-three years. Sievier meanwhile ran Sceptre into the ground, and eventually had to sell her anyway.

But then Sievier never knew when to stop. 'I was born in a hansom cab,' he began his autobiography. 'And have been going on ever since.' He, too, had set out for the Cape as a teenager, just too late for the diamond rush; instead he volunteered to fight the Xhosa. Then he tried his luck as an actor in Bombay and a bookmaker in Australia, where it was said that a man had been found dead under the balcony of his house after a card party. Sievier was utterly fearless, whether his fortune depended on the tip of his billiard cue or that of his pen.

He started a magazine, *Winning Post*, in which he gleefully eviscerated the hypocrisies of the establishment. His motto was aptly borrowed from Voltaire: *I possess no Sceptre but I do possess a pen.* As circulation soared to 50,000, bookmakers, private eyes and pornographers rushed to advertise to a market they could not reach elsewhere. There were salacious 'Tabasco Tales' and an especially incendiary series, *Celebrities in Glass Houses*. It was rumoured that Sievier would send his next subject two drafts, and invite payment to spike the more scabrous version.

When it came to the turn of Mr J. B. Joel, Sievier was exultant to discover the skeleton in his subject's cupboard. Nobody, until now, had known the circumstances of Jack's flight from Kimberley twenty years previously. When Jack did not take action, Sievier fell into a habit of casual vilification. Jack was 'the notorious dealer in illicit diamonds'. Readers were invited to perceive a literal contamination of the stones that had made him rich. 'The Kaffirs were bribed to swallow the "booty" before leaving the mines,' Sievier claimed. 'In what circumstances they passed on the "precious" stones to the purchaser of stolen property history leaves us to conjecture . . . many of the sparkling ornaments which at this moment adorn the neck of a beauty have been subjected to this procedure. If they could speak!'

It is impossible to know where the lies stopped between Sievier and the Joels. Sievier went for broke when claiming that Jack had attempted to hire a former pugilist to attack him with acid. Solly's biography, published by his son after all the antagonists had died, in turn describes the tycoon coolly disarming an assassin hired by Sievier. The scene was pure Hollywood: the parting of curtains by a gunman in the French window, Solly at his desk producing a bankroll of £3,000 to pay off a shamed hireling. Perhaps, as so often, the root of the discord was an uncomfortable similarity. How the shanty days of Kimberley would have suited Sievier! As born gamblers, both Sievier and the Joels tended to exempt themselves from scruple as a refuge of the meek.

Soon after the Kurtz trial, Sievier was arrested in the parade ring at Sandown. The warrant alleged an attempt to extort £5,000 from Mr J. B. Joel by abstaining from the publication of a libel. Back in the Old Bailey however, Jack found the going a good deal heavier than against Kurtz. It emerged that he had discussed a loan to Sievier, to end the vendetta, but then tried to set him up for a blackmail prosecution, concealing a detective behind false panels when a negotiator named Mills arrived. Unfortunately Mills was trying to play the adversaries off against each other: Sievier thought he was getting a loan of £5,000 from Mills, and Jack that Sievier had demanded £5,000 for his silence. Jack proved a desperately lame witness, admitting the failed entrapment to have been 'a very dirty business on my part'. Sievier's counsel did not mince his words, raging at 'the power of money in the hands of an unscrupulous person'.

When the verdict came, cheers spread from the court into the street outside. Strangers shook hands and slapped each other on the back. The news was wired to Goodwood, and rippled through the enclosures. Rosebery had never seen anything like it on an English racecourse. Bertie asked what had caused the commotion, and it is said that he was not displeased when told that the jury had found Bob Sievier not guilty.

In his final spring at Hardwick, Cyllene had been mated with a mare belonging to another of the big brewers, Colonel Hall-Walker. A fanatical astrologist, Hall-Walker chose mates and races for his horses according to the horoscope, and even installed skylights in their stables to expose them to the influence of moon and stars. At the same time, he may have been aware of earthier forces at work: his wife had a habit of entertaining Bertie to tea in a perfumed suite with the curtains drawn tight.

Bertie's stable was going through a long period in the doldrums, even though he had doubled its strength since becoming king. As a result, Marcus Beresford arranged for the lease of half-a-dozen youngsters from Hall-Walker. These included his Cyllene colt. Named Minoru, he won both the 2000 Guineas and the Derby in 1909. It was a desperate finish at Epsom, and not everyone was convinced that the judge called it right, but there was bedlam when Minoru's number was hoisted into the frame. A police cordon was swamped by a tide of silk hats bursting onto the track to converge with one of bowlers and cloth caps. 'But the King did not hesitate a moment. With perfect calm he went through the gate of his enclosure and into the seething mob.' The first reigning monarch to win the Derby waved off the constables and plunged cheerfully among his jostling subjects. That evening, he told the Jockey Club dinner that one man had slapped him on the back and exclaimed:

'Well done, Teddy! You've won the Derby, now turn out your damned Government.'

Incredibly, Minoru was only the first of three Derby winners from the last four British crops of Cyllene. Added to Cicero, these took the exported stallion level with his ancestor, Waxy, as sire of four Derby winners. As the scale of his loss to the English Turf became clear, the government was said literally to have sent a blank cheque to Ojo de Agua for his repatriation. It was returned with a simple message on the back: *Cyllene no está en venta y no tiene precio* – 'Cyllene is not for sale and has no price'.

In fairness to Bass, who had sold him, even the most scientific of stockmen require luck as well as judgement. And it would be too condescending to rebuke Rose – who had consecutively let Bona Vista and Cyllene slip through his grasp – as a mere faddist, when he had persevered in a pastime as discouraging as the Turf for over twenty years.

Rose had proved a popular MP, affectionately known in the Commons as 'the Member for Horses and Horseless Carriages'. On the stump, he would address fenland labourers from an old farm wagon, reiterating the mantra: 'Tories for the little loaf, Liberals for the big loaf.' The regard of his constituents was fortified by annual banquets for Newmarket stable staff. Once he fed 612 men in a marquee on his trainer's paddock – a gesture typical not only of his expansive nature but also of an unreconstructed approach, among all parties, to expanding suffrage. Those who worked for the local squire, for instance, were expected to vote Tory as a condition of employment. Gifts of herrings or blankets helped them to concentrate. Failing that, toughs were sent from Newmarket to block the lane to the polling station. At one election, labourers intent on voting for Rose fought the 'jockeys' with sticks, killing one and tossing his body over the churchyard wall. A Baptist minister was among several men jailed, and it was said that Rose personally maintained the families they left behind, otherwise facing destitution.

Curiously, the last absolute majority won by a Liberal government included three men who had all jettisoned future mainstays of the Darley Arabian line: Rosebery discarded Bona Vista; Rose, Bona

Vista and Cyllene; and Crewe, Polymelus. Crewe was flabbergasted when Polymelus, rather than one of Cyllene's four Derby winners, emerged as principal guarantor of the line. Standing at 300 guineas, he was five times champion stallion and his five Classic winners included two for Jack Joel and one for Solly. Today his skeleton is displayed in the Museum of Zoology at Cambridge University as the epitome of anatomical adaptation to speed.

Polymelus might have gone a long way to saving estates that dwindled sharply under Crewe's supervision. Much of his father's historic library – which had included a copy of *Les Annales d'Aquitaine* in which Philip Sidney had scribbled a poem in his own hand – ended up mouldering in stables. But if Crewe raced only a handful of horses after Polymelus, the Jockey Club stewards invariably sought his counsel in times of crisis.

Herbert Asquith described him as 'the most under-rated man in England'. Crewe's oratory was measured to a nearly sadistic degree – when Peggy was going into labour, Rosebery hoped that 'her delivery will not be as slow as Crewe's' – but he was a steadying hand on colleagues of greater dash and distinction. It was Crewe who presided over a constitution for the Union of South Africa, and in 1909 he was chosen as ministerial representative for a state visit to the Kaiser. It was a trying excursion. Testy and bronchial, Bertie kept falling asleep at public events – a poignant symbol of the somnambulism that alone united the royal kinsmen of Britain, Germany and Russia in the last years of peace.

Perhaps Hall-Walker was right. Perhaps it really was all in the stars. The king did not live to see another Derby. His last words were prompted by congratulations offered on the success, that afternoon, of one of his fillies at Kempton. 'Yes, I have heard of it,' Bertie said. 'I am very glad.' Marcus Beresford comforted Marsh with 'the extra satisfaction of having been the means of giving him a pleasant thought to finish up his great life'.

Henry Chaplin mourned 'the oldest friend perhaps that I had left, and certainly the kindest that I ever knew'. Whatever his flaws, Bertie had always raced his horses in the best spirit. When Persimmon was beaten on his first start after the Derby, Leopold de Rothschild had been amazed by the warmth of Bertie's handshake. As Rothschild himself attested, Bertie's example had 'done much to remove the impression that racing cannot be conducted in a healthy manner, in the spirit of pure sport'. The *Sporting Life* agreed: 'Within living memory the term "a racing man" was practically synonymous with that of "vagabond" in the minds of the middle classes, and it is largely due to the late King Edward that the idea that the racecourse is nothing more nor less than a sink of iniquity has been removed from the minds of all but a few irreconcilables.'

It would be ridiculous to ascribe the rehabilitation of Kipling's 'corpulent voluptuary' among his future subjects solely to his Turf career. But three Derby winners had surely helped to turn things round after the Tranby Croft trial, when Bertie told friends at Ascot that even the defence lawyer was predicting 100,000 extra radical votes at the next election. At that stage the monarchy had seemed almost irreparably damaged by a morose, invisible queen, and an heir consumed by sartorial protocols, gourmandise, baccarat and the cuckolding of courtiers. By the time he died, however, the epoch had obtained a sepia glow.

Charles Rose, one of its most characteristic figures, did not long survive the king. His extravagant lifestyle reached a crisis with a stock-market slump in 1912: much of the Hardwick estate was put up for sale, along with the house in Newmarket and various yachts and motor cars, while the rest was remortgaged. It was announced that Rose would not be defending his seat in Parliament. But Mr Toad hardly dwindled into some reclusive Badger, and remained an enthusiastic chairman of the Royal Aero Club. In April 1913, aged sixty-six, he was piloted above the aerodrome at Hendon: a seven-minute tour in a Farman biplane, ambling barely seventy feet above the airfield. He was abuzz afterwards – too much so. When his chauffeur opened the car door outside his townhouse, Rose fell black-faced into his arms. The coroner cautioned the newspapers that flying was not a suitable pastime for anyone getting on in years.

Rose was buried in the riverside churchyard at Mapledurham. His only surviving son would be killed the following year, in one of the first cavalry charges of the war. Innocent of the gathering storm, men from many different worlds – politics, aviation, yachting, motoring and the Turf – stood in the cemetery listening to the spring birdsong and the faint roar of the weir. The Royal Automobile Club laid a harp with a broken string by the grave. 'He was eminently one of those personalities whom it is a delight to know,' remarked the official magazine of the Royal Aero Club.

A few weeks later George V, having taken over his father's stable, went to see Anmer run in the Derby. The death of a suffragette under his colt's hooves marked the end of a halcyon era. That November, Crewe's fellow guests at a Windsor shooting party included the Archduke Franz Ferdinand. Between them they slaughtered over 5,000 gamebirds in four days. A single shot, in Sarajevo the following summer, would transform that unthinking fusillade into a portent of catastrophe. By 1916 Hall-Walker was donating his stud to the Crown to bolster a cavalry being blasted to ribbons in France. Minoru, its most famous graduate, had been sold to Russia as a stallion but would disappear during the Revolution. He was last seen being coupled to a cart alongside the 1913 Derby winner, Aboyeur, for a 900-mile evacuation from Moscow to the Black Sea.

PART VI

War Horses

Phalaris (1913)
Pharos (1920)
Nearco (1935)

20

'All their young men are killed'

WHEN RAYMOND ASQUITH made his first visit to Mells, in the summer of 1900, life seemed to stretch cloudlessly before him. He was twenty-one years old and, according to Edward Thomas, 'watched over alike by the Muses and the Graces'. How could he know that so few wisps of care might one day pack into the dark cumulus of war? As it was, delighted by this redoubt against bourgeois convention, the Balliol undergraduate poured his brilliance into sunlit impressions of a country house party in the Mendip Hills.

His hostess, Frances Horner, had been a famous beauty, her golden hair and ghostly eyes lovingly preserved on canvas by Edward Burne-Jones. Robert Browning had shown her the frescoes in Florence; she dined with Ellen Terry and Henry Irving after the theatre; her entire family went to court to root for Ruskin when sued by Whistler.* Frances belonged to a clique whose salons and intrigues set a foil to the horse-racing philistines clustering round Bertie. It was thanks to Charlie Beresford, in fact, that they had become known – somewhat to their distaste – as 'the Souls'. Invited to stay by the Tory leader, Arthur Balfour, he had snorted: 'You do nothing but sit and talk about each other's souls.'

Mells was one of their quirkier outposts. It was a constant struggle to keep the place going, and Jack Horner was a genuine oddball. But James Barrie recalled a debate, among his most luminous peers, whether it would be worse to be known as a bore or a cad. Someone suggested that it depended on who called you either. 'Suppose Sir

---

* Ruskin had written: 'I have seen and heard much of Cockney impudence before now, but never expected to hear a coxcomb ask 200 guineas for flinging a pot of paint in the public's face.' Whistler was awarded damages of one farthing.

John Horner called you a cad?' There was an immediate chorus of horror: 'Oh, my God! That *would* do for you!'

For Raymond, the Mells idyll was crowned by his hosts' two daughters. In a letter he described the formidable Richard Haldane – a political ally of his father, Herbert, the rising star of Liberalism in the wake of Rosebery's abdication – splashing among the water lilies with seventeen-year-old Cicely. 'To see this vast white mass with the brain of Socrates and the shape of Nero executing his absurd antics from a thin plank which bent double under his weight and sporting fantastically in the water with a divinely beautiful girl . . . recalled the sunniest days of the Roman decline.' Haldane then emerged from the bushes, wearing a towel and a panama hat, to extol the superiority of Buddhism over Christianity to a tea party of local spinsters. 'Hey nonny nonny!' Raymond concluded. 'I like this life.'

But it was Cicely's younger sister, Katharine, who would enchant Raymond with her magnolia skin and huge, long-lashed eyes that could 'draw a limpet off a rock'. Their courtship was necessarily a leisurely one: Raymond first had to make his way at the bar, and she would still only be twenty-two when they married seven years later. In the meantime he became the dominant personality of 'the Coterie' – as the children of the Souls, courting equal disfavour among prudes and boors, in turn found themselves styled. Decades later, John Buchan remained infatuated with their leader: 'Most noble in presence and with every grace of voice and manner, he moved among men like a being from another world, scornfully detached from the common struggle.' Outsiders could recoil from his astringent pronouncements on the mediocre or the facile. But intimates like Buchan, who modelled the hero of an early novel on Raymond, knew the warmth of humanity within. In a village inn, pretending to be American tourists, Buchan once watched Raymond berating the locals on the virtues of abstinence. 'It was the most perfect parody . . . and completely solemnized his hearers,' Buchan remembered. 'Then he ordered beer all round.'

Raymond and Katharine's wedding reception in 1907 was held at 11 Downing Street. Though the groom's father was now Chancellor, the Souls spanned the political spectrum and Balfour gave a toast. Afterwards Katharine admitted a poignant presentiment. 'I think I am happier than anyone has a right to be,' she wrote. 'I am only afraid of some jealousy of God.'

The following summer, Cicely found herself staying with the same friends for the York Ebor meeting as George Lambton. He was tall, which always helped in measuring up to the Horners; his wardrobe was as immaculate as his manners; and he was a brother to the Earl of Durham, that noble scourge of villains on the Turf. But he was also twice her age, at forty-seven, and devoted to the thoroughbreds he trained for the 17th Earl of Derby.

Many in the Coterie owed their impression of Lambton's world to the royal swanks they despised – whose lowbrow principles were gleefully espoused by Daisy Warwick:

> We acknowledged that it was necessary that pictures should be painted, books written, the law administered; we even acknowledged that there was a certain class whose job it might be to do these things. But we did not see why their achievements entitled them to our recognition; they might disturb, over-stimulate, even bore. On rare occasions, if a book made a sufficient stir, we might read it, or better still, get somebody to tell us about it, and so save us the trouble.

But even Cicely's most bohemian friends soon repented of any dismay prompted by the announcement of her engagement. Lambton charmed men and women of every stamp. Even the Duke of Portland, who fell out bitterly with Jack Durham, willingly attested that 'ladies and children, horses and dogs, all seemed to love [Lambton], and I can well understand their doing so.'

Trainers had continued to enhance their status since the days when Mat Dawson was paid just £5 a week as private trainer to James Merry. By the turn of the century, the operators of public stables were living in grand houses with 'fine gardens, trim lawns for croquet and lawn-tennis, billiard-rooms, and cellars containing choice vintages . . . You will not meet with elsewhere a better-groomed set of men, with whom it is quite the ordinary thing to be tall-hatted, frock-coated, kid-gloved, patent-leathered-booted, instead of breeched and gaitered.'

At the same time, many trainers owed their expertise to parents or grandparents who had first entered stables as refugees from poverty. 'The Honourable George', as Lambton was known across the Turf, represented a singular departure: a dapper, quizzical aristocrat who had received a gold cup from the king on his wedding day. Everyone knew the social and moral inviolability of the man who had famously unmasked the American pharmacist trainers. Richard Marsh recognised the same integrity in his rival trainer as in Jack Durham. 'If they believed themselves to be in the right they cared for no man,' he wrote. 'It is a Lambton trait.' But Marsh had equal regard for Lambton's professional merits, rating him the best trainer of his time. 'I always admired the way his horses were turned out so hard and well trained . . . lasting and fighting it out to the finish.'

Lambton had entered the profession at the suggestion of Regy Brett, who sent him a couple of fillies to train after his career as a dashing amateur jockey was ended by a bad steeplechase fall in 1892. Soon afterwards he was approached by Edward Stanley, heir to the 16th Earl of Derby, who was eager to revive the derelict family stud. The Duchess of Montrose had just decided to quit the Turf and Lambton suggested that Stanley recruit her groom, John Griffiths, who had supervised Stockwell for Richard Naylor at Hooton. Griffiths recommended a yearling filly from the Montrose dispersal, for 1,800 guineas, despite a temper inherited from a sire so irascible that he had smashed his own skull against a brick wall. Canterbury Pilgrim proceeded to give the new team a Classic success in the 1896 Oaks, and became the foundation of a stud that would remaster the thoroughbred for a new century.

None of the Coterie can have been more comfortable with Cicely's choice of fiancé than her brother. Edward Horner had a passion for riding and gambling, and sooner matched his sisters in looks than brains. 'Six foot four inches in height, broad-shouldered, lithe and muscular, with a superbly shaped head and neck, he was a picture of radiant masculine beauty,' F. E. Smith would remember. Yet he had 'a caressing and sympathetic charm which was entirely feminine'.

He was also wild and unsettled. Always affectionate, always

indulged, the teenage Edward was said to have seduced Lady Cunard's parlourmaid after a luncheon party. 'It was as impossible not to be recurrently angry with him as to be angry with him for long,' remembered one contemporary. 'He came back, after each scolding, with the affectionate eyes and caressing ways of a faithful dog who has been beaten . . . He had no ambition but to sip honey.'

Having scraped through Oxford, Edward had somehow contrived a place in F. E. Smith's chambers. One friend thought him more eligible as 'hereditary posset-bearer to the King at £10,000 a year'. No doubt Cicely, herself not averse to a bet, maintained some excitement in Edward's life with tips from her husband's stable: perhaps Canterbury Pilgrim's son, Swynford, before he won the 1910 St Leger. But George Lambton performed a still greater service for Derby, that same year, when he recommended that he buy a mare named Bromus. Her dam had never won a race; and Bromus, with a solitary success from ten starts, was the only one of her offspring to have done so. In the spring of 1912, even so, her new owner sent her to Solly Joel's Maiden Erlegh stud to be mated with Polymelus.

Edward's only real aspiration remained Diana Manners, the angel on the prow of the Coterie, whose coruscating beauty was the agony of countless men. (Not that any of her suitors, in her view, compared to the one man she could not have: his fidelity to Katharine did not prevent an ardent correspondence between Diana and Raymond.) Soon after Diana turned twenty-one, in the last summer of peace, their friend George Vernon took a palazzo on the Grand Canal. Their revels would prove the final flourish of the Coterie. There was dancing, champagne, amateur prizefighting, kissing on moonlit balconies. They dressed Raymond's father, now prime minister, as a doge for his birthday. Amid frenzied wagering, Duff Cooper and Denis Anson swam the canal in their evening clothes.

The following July, Edward hosted a party on a Thames cruiser. Around 3 a.m. Anson decided to reprise his performance in Venice, but was instantly in trouble in the strong currents. His body washed up three days later near Lambeth Bridge. The popular press made hay after the inquest, deploring the irresponsible, hell-raising swells. Osbert Sitwell looked back on Anson's loss as an equivalent symbol, for 'his generation, kind and coterie' to that offered – as a broader token of the approaching apocalypse – by the sinking of the *Titanic*.

They were standing in aisles and stairwells and doorways and they spilled into St Anne Street. Inside the drill hall, the summer night pulsed with the zeal of men whose lives of shared drudgery seemed to gain thrilling new meaning with every word they heard. From time to time the rapt silence yielded to sudden roars of approval. 'This should be a battalion of pals,' they were told. 'A battalion in which friends from the same office will fight shoulder to shoulder for the honour of Britain – and the credit of Liverpool!'

The speaker was a tall, imposing man in his fiftieth year. The 17th Earl of Derby exuded energy, warmth, candour, and wore a moustache of corresponding gusto. In this company he permitted extra rein to the brusque Lancashire cadences that inflected his highborn tones. 'I don't attempt to minimise to you the hardships you will suffer; the risks you will run,' he said. 'I don't ask you to uphold Liverpool's honour; it would be an insult to think that you could do anything but that. But I do thank you from the bottom of my heart for coming here tonight and showing what is the spirit of Liverpool – a spirit that ought to spread through every city and every town in the kingdom!'

When Lord Derby named the new battalion commander as his own brother, Ferdinand Stanley, the hats flung into the air seemed to bob upon the swelling ovation. The men broke into spontaneous chorus: the earl was a jolly good fellow, and God save the king.

It was just over three weeks since war had been declared, and Liverpool proudly viewed itself as the hub of the threatened empire. At a time when British ships carried more cargo than all other maritime nations combined, Merseyside's 30,000 dockers handled one-third of the nation's exports. And, as the fifteenth member of his family to serve as Lord Mayor of Liverpool since 1568, Derby had a genuine relish for his civic obligations.

Ever since losing his Commons seat to a carpenter in 1906 – two years before acceding as earl – he had been careful not to take hereditary influence for granted. So while one guest at Knowsley disdained its 'dreary' park grazed by 'sooty red deer', Derby liked to be reminded he was tied to the surrounding factory towns by more than rent rolls. As a result, 'no bazaar or fete was too remote for him to attend, no foundation stone too small for him to lay'. In a city where Tory support was poisoned by Unionist and anti-Catholic bigotry, his mediation soothed many simmering sectarian and industrial disputes. Earlier in 1914 one Irish Nationalist MP had even commended Derby as an eligible prime minister. At one Grand National, the head of the dockers' union won £15 after betting 10 shillings on a tip from another guest in Derby's box: the king. Only Lord Derby, perhaps, could have hosted such an encounter.

While he may not have come up with the concept, Derby was first to use the term 'Pals' Battalion' and was soon saluted by Lloyd George as 'the most efficient recruiting sergeant in England'. By mid-October, he had raised a fourth battalion of Pals, bringing them up to brigade strength. Some were initially trained on Hooton Park racecourse but all were soon encamped on Derby's own estate at Knowsley. He emerged from the great house to present each recruit with a cap badge: a silver eagle and child, his family crest. One looked so absurdly young that Derby felt compelled to ask his age. 'Nineteen, sir.' 'You liar!' the magnate grinned. 'But best of luck, son!'

When ready for advanced training, the Pals marched through the city to the station. A holiday atmosphere pervaded the streets. 'Will we win?' shouted one voice, in what had become a ritual. Hundreds chorused back: 'Rather!'

Raymond Asquith's sense of the ridiculous, unsurprisingly, had withstood the tide of patriotic hysteria. 'The atmosphere here is appalling,' he wrote to Diana Manners in the first days of the war.

> The crisis has brought out all that is best in English womanhood. Katharine still keeps her head. But Cicely Lambton and Frances Horner have sunk all political differences and are facing the enemy as one man. They have cornered all the petrol, sold all Charles Kinski's hunters, knocked off two courses at dinner, and turned Perdita's pony-cart into an ambulance. Cicely thinks that everybody ought to give up everything except racing, which (she tells me) has ceased to be a sport and has become an industry, and that everyone

should enlist at once except George because the whole of Cambridgeshire depends on George continuing his industrial career at Newmarket.

Raymond put his name down for the London Volunteer Defence Force, on the premise that it did not yet exist. 'No member,' he noted, 'can possibly be killed before Goodwood 1915 at the earliest.' But the emergency was perfect for Edward Horner, who wasted no time in joining up – taking with him two of Cicely's hunters, a valet and a cook. 'He was full of zeal but, poor fellow, rather feckless,' recorded Raymond's father, after lunching Edward at Number 10. He was soon home again with a shrapnel wound to the kidneys. Diana, racing to France with his parents and a private surgeon, had found him in narcotic serenity, lying like a crusader with his curls upon a white pillow, 'very, very ill and looking ecstatic'. As they crowded tearfully round, he saw Diana. 'Oh darling, this is heaven,' he said.

Despite the mechanisation of slaughter, horses were still being enlisted in large numbers – 8,684 hunters being donated to the War Office in the first two months of the war. The *Sporting Life* did report that the 1914 Derby winner, owned by an American and trained in France, had been exempted military service by both sides after his 'Negro groom wrapped the Epsom hero in an American flag and covered his horse-cloth with a placard which read as follows: "This is Durbar II, the Derby winner. He is neutral."' But those racehorses that remained in training were widely deplored as symbols of a tasteless levity. Hostility in press and Parliament prompted races to be reduced in number and confined to Newmarket. For the rest of the war, the sport would only be permitted in fits and starts.

Lambton recalled later how difficult it was to find anyone prepared to risk the odium reserved for 'a man so lost to all sense of decency that he could give his mind to horse racing while his country was in the throes of such a desperate struggle.' Along with his brother Jack Durham, he became one of the most vocal exponents of the Jockey Club position. In one letter to *The Times*, Lambton rebuked his own brother-in-law, Lord Robert Cecil, for asserting that football

Three great trainers: John Scott
(*above right*), Mathew Dawson (*left*),
and Robert Peck (*below right*).

Fred Archer. On his suicide, *The Times* declared: 'A great soldier, a great statesman, great poet, even a Royal prince, might die suddenly without giving half so general a shock.'

Yankee Doodle Dandy. American jockey Tod Sloan, all dressed up but ultimately no place to go.

Lord Rosebery leads in his first Derby winner, Ladas; still the mask does not slip.
Illustration for *The Graphic*, 16 June 1894.

Minoru, with Herbert Jones up: the only Derby winner raced by a reigning monarch.
Edward VII is flanked by Marcus Beresford, with trainer Richard Marsh nearest the horse.

Lord Derby (*left*) and George Lambton:
having kept the show on the road in
1914, despite indignation in press and
Parliament, they were vindicated by
the wartime emergence of Phalaris –
subsequently sire of the century.

Cicely Horner: the future Mrs Lambton
struck Raymond Asquith as 'about as
perfect a specimen of female beauty as I
have ever seen'.

But it was Cicely's sister, Katharine, who would love and lose Asquith,
tragic symbol of a doomed generation.

Federico Tesio (with bow tie) escorts Nearco after the Grand Prix de Paris in 1938. His jockey is about to enrage the local crowd with a fascist salute.

Horatio Luro:
el gran señor.

Northern Dancer wins the 1964 Kentucky Derby – a turning point
in the history of the thoroughbred.

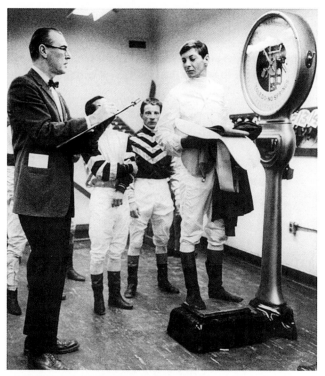

Bill Hartack does not need to stand on the scales to
look down at officialdom.

Vincent O'Brien, Robert Sangster and John Magnier: ready for a last roll of the dice at Keeneland in 1985.

Sheikh Mohammed assesses a Northern Dancer yearling at the same sale. Finding himself bidding against the colt's breeder, the sheikh dropped out at $7.5 million, leaving his opponent stranded with a record 'buyback'. The sheikh later agreed a private deal for the horse, subsequently the champion sprinter Ajdal.

By 1976 Bobby Frankel (wearing stripes) had made a sufficient name for himself to be training for the film star James Caan, here disdaining the informality of his entourage in the winner's circle at Hollywood Park.

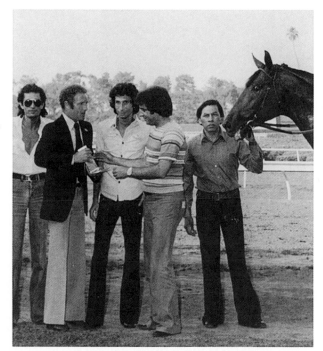

The Darley Arabian line entered the twenty-first century in the best of hands. Henry Cecil with Frankel, a potential fount of future champions.

and horse racing should be treated alike. 'Football is played with a ball and 22 strong and sturdy young men,' he wrote. 'Racing is played with horses, ridden by small men, the majority under 8st.' Rosebery wrote to the same newspaper, observing that a Derby had been staged ten days before Waterloo and that the Epsom result, during the Crimean War, had been given out in the day's General Orders. But the strongest argument concerned continuity of pedigrees. 'Make no mistake, if our races are to cease, our thoroughbred horses must disappear,' Rosebery stressed.

As it was, Lambton was able to race Phalaris, the son of Polymelus and Bromus, through the war. After an impressive win in the autumn of 1915, he decided to prepare Phalaris for the 2000 Guineas the following spring. In the event, Phalaris seemed to lack stamina even at a mile. It looked as though he was a pure sprinter. Raymond, having soon abandoned his pose of apathy to join the Grenadier Guards, sent a sardonic note of sympathy from France to Katharine, who was staying with Cicely and George in Newmarket. 'I am extremely sorry about Phalaris,' he wrote. Having said that, it was 'terrible to think of your being in a house with so many pictures of horses.'

As the volunteers dried up, Derby found the heady optimism of the war's early days hard to sustain. Promoted as Under-Secretary to Lloyd George at the War Office, after Kitchener was drowned in 1916, he eventually found himself presiding over a painful transition to conscription as his Pals, sailing out of Folkestone, passed a boat carrying troops home on leave. 'Are we downhearted?' a voice shouted across. 'No!' responded the Pals lustily. 'Well, you bloody well soon will be!'

They began in a quiet sector of the Somme, welcomed apologetically to scenes of atrocious mud and rain by George Lambton's brother, Billy, who happened to have command of their division. By 1 July, they were ready to join the 'big push'. 'Of course I had to be in my dug-out and wait for messages, so had to miss the most glorious sight imaginable,' General Stanley complained to his diary. 'Those who saw it say that it was quite wonderful, and it must have been quite a ceremonial performance. Those miles and miles of men just went steadily forward with our artillery pouring shells in front of them . . . everything went like clockwork.'

The realities of the front line were better conveyed by Raymond Asquith, who that same day wryly commended Katharine for going up to town from Mells: 'I too am getting rather tired of country life.' The playful tone he tended to maintain for his wife, anxiously raising their young family, was evidently a calculated one. He reserved a less sparing description for Diana:

> Craters swimming in blood and dirt, rotting and smelling bodies and rats like shadows, fattened for the market moving cunningly and liquorishly among them, limbs and bowels nestling in the hedges, and over all the most supernaturally shocking scent of death and corruption . . . The only dug-out turned out to be a 'dirt trap' if not a death trap, awash with sewage, stale eyeballs, and other debris . . . And in a fortnight or so I suppose we shall have won the war.

The trouble was that the generals nearly believed as much. That September, Lloyd George, touring the front before a renewed offensive, asked Haig and Joffre the purpose of the cavalry squadrons he had seen clattering towards the front. Haig enthused that the cavalry would pour through the gap opened by the Guards in the imminent attack. Lloyd George watched sceptically as those same Guards, Raymond among them, marched in a long column through the valley.

At 6.20 a.m. on 15 September, Raymond led his men over the top through clearing mist. Seventeen of the twenty-two officers in his battalion were about to be killed or wounded. Raymond was probably the first, hit in the chest as he cleared the parapet. He lit a cigarette as nonchalantly as he could. A medic arrived with morphine. By the time he had been stretchered to a dressing station, he was dead. A private in his platoon avowed: 'There is not one of us who would not have changed places with him if we thought that he would have lived.'

Rushing down to Mells, Diana found Katharine crouched numbly over a fire in a dark room. To Duff Cooper, her future husband, Diana admitted: 'I don't think you know how I adored Raymond

. . . Had you not known him his loss might have been your gain
– but knowing him there is no gain in possessing the world if he
is not in it.' Winston Churchill wrote to Katharine, sharing her grief
over 'the loss of my brilliant hero-friend . . . These gallant charming
figures that flash and gleam amid the carnage – always so superior
to it, masters of their souls, disdainful of death and suffering – are
an inspiration and an example to us all. And he was one of the very
best.'

Lloyd George was still in France when he learned that the attack
had failed and that the prime minister's son was among the dead.
Yet when he ventured to Joffre and Haig his 'doubts as to whether
cavalry would ever operate successfully on a front bristling for miles
. . . with barbed wire and machine guns, both Generals fell ecstat-
ically upon me.' Soon afterwards Billy Lambton wrote to Jack
Durham: 'Net result of two weeks fighting – a gain of about 400
yards on a 400 yard front which has cost me, I suppose, 3,000
casualties.' Lloyd George considered Asquith's morale terminally
damaged by Raymond's death, and three months later replaced him
at Number 10.

In the spring of 1917 the government yielded to the anti-racing
lobby and suspended the sport altogether. Billy Lambton, on the
front, was unimpressed. 'As far as I can make out it is due to faddists
and anti-sports and not to real shortage,' he wrote to Jack Durham.
'We seem to be much upset by submarines and losing our heads.'
Jack joined the heavyweight deputation to Lloyd George – including
both Derby and Rosebery, whose respective daughter and son had
married in 1915 – that succeeded in revoking the ban. Racing would
be permitted at Newmarket and a handful of other tracks but the
number of horses in training, already down from 4,014 in 1914 to
2,124 two years later, would be capped at 1,200. Derby's reward was
the continued blossoming of Phalaris, who had hit form in the
second half of the 1916 season. Though only 390 races were staged
in 1917, he won seven in a row, including a handicap in which he
had to concede between 15lb and 47lbs to his fifteen opponents.
He was sent off favourite for the Cambridgeshire, but that race was
always bound to stretch his stamina and his spree came to an end.

By this stage, even the most momentous shifts in the wartime landscape seemed to slough back into the abysmal stasis of mud and blood. On the one hand, the Americans were on their way; on the other, the Eastern Front was convulsed by revolution. Having promoted his deputy to replace him at the War Office, the new prime minister discovered that Derby had a tiresome loyalty to the generals he blamed for escalating the carnage. Now all those connected with Phalaris – the families of his owner, trainer and jockey – were about to be drawn into the inferno.

First came the death of Neil Primrose, Derby's son-in-law. Like Cicely Lambton, Primrose had linked Derby to an alien circle of the Liberal intelligentsia: he had inherited to an uncanny degree Rosebery's looks and rich, measured voice. Though appointed Under-Secretary at the Foreign Office after his marriage, Primrose soon renounced the security of a desk job to rejoin his regiment. In 1917 he was posted to Palestine where his brother, Harry, was already serving as military secretary to General Allenby.*

Fighting the Turks near Gaza that November, Neil was killed instantly by a bullet to the head. His cousin Major Evelyn de Rothschild was lost in the same engagement. Derby could not 'but feel the glory of his death, an example to many men of his age who ought to be fighting'. Rosebery pretended no such comfort. 'Neil was everything to me,' he admitted to the king. 'He had become my greatest friend and confidant. But I have no right to complain. Hundreds of thousands of others have borne and are bearing the same.' One of these, Raymond's father, struggled in the House of Commons to find words adequate to the silent communion of their suffering. 'I only trust myself to say this,' he said. 'That there are few who can realise better than myself how much of hope and of promise there was for his future.'

The following day, over three hundred new tanks achieved a spectacular breakthrough towards Cambrai. Once again the generals

---

* It was Harry who lent T. E. Lawrence his 'red tabs' so that he could enter Jerusalem with Allenby as a staff officer. Lawrence, needless to say, had arrived from the desert in Bedouin rags and had to beg and borrow a uniform, piecemeal.

had persisted in their anachronistic delusions that the Hussars could follow through the tanks' gains. So it was that Edward Horner and his squadron were found, on the second morning of the offensive, setting up a Lewis gun on the corner of the square in Noyelles. There were still enemy troops in the village, and the advance was being held up by snipers.

It was just a potshot that got Edward. He was hit in the groin and died that evening. One friend mourned a man 'without an achievement to his name except his gallant death, [as] one of the most remarkable figures of his time . . . free-handed to the point of extravagance, and in everything absolutely fearless, or audacious; adored by servants and tenants, and delighted in by everyone who valued salience above convention.' Diana knew his strengths and weaknesses to be more or less the same. 'He could not bear to be humdrum . . .' she concluded. 'He thought life could do more than it can.' Duff Cooper remembered motoring to Venice in 1913. All four of his companions on the journey were dead: George Vernon, Denis Anson, Billy Grenfell, now Edward. 'I begin to feel that the dance is already over and that it is time to go.'

The very same day, though fully aware that Lord Derby was grieving his son-in-law, one MP could not resist a little fun at his expense in the House of Commons. Henry Watt was never averse to the limelight – his 'stage bookie' attire typically extending to 'a flower in his buttonhole the size of a small cabbage' – and asked the president of the board of trade, George Wardle, whether a special train had recently been provided 'from Liverpool Street to Cambridge for a Mr Rickaby, who had a contract with the Secretary of State for War to fulfil there, namely to ride his horse Phalaris for the Cambridgeshire?'

Wardle assured him that the Great Eastern Railway Company denied this. Watt quickly resumed his feet, asking: 'Will the honourable gentleman say whether it was the action of his Department, in preventing the train being utilised, that led to the fact that this horse, which was largely backed by the Government Department, was last in the race?'

Wardle, himself a Labour man, had to deadpan on behalf of the

Tory grandee. 'I have no knowledge,' he replied, 'either of the train or the horse.'

But now a Scottish Presbyterian, James Hogge, eschewed all mirth: 'How is it that Lord Derby can get permission for a man training in this country to ride a horse, when soldiers fighting on the West Front have great difficulty in getting leave?'

Not long afterwards Rickaby, a dispatch rider for the Royal Flying Corps, was transferred to the Tank Corps. It seems inconceivable that the exchange in Parliament could have been disregarded by his superiors.

Derby paid no heed to the persiflage. Primrose's death had filled him with ennui. 'I am very tired of things, and should like to have done with it all,' he told Regy Brett. 'I nearly did so this week, but a talk with the P.M. made me much happier about things.' This was typical. Derby had a tedious addiction to theatrical but half-hearted resignations, and would soon be offering three in twenty-four hours as Lloyd George – infuriated by the failure to see through the tank breakout at Cambrai – continued his machinations for change among the top brass.

Derby's reaction to the unnerving German offensive of March 1918 was the final straw. 'He was not at his best in a crisis,' Lloyd George wrote later. 'In an emergency leaders who sweat despondency are a source of weakness.' He dispatched Derby to Paris as ambassador, feeling 'he would render greater service to this country in a position where it would not be obvious that his bluffness was only bluff'. These bitter words followed publication of Duff Cooper's *Haig*, in 1936, when Lloyd George was appalled to discover the extent of his War Minister's 'clandestine' assistance to the generals in resisting 'efforts to avert or abate the tragic carnage of the Passchendaele campaign'.

Nobody ever doubted Derby's motives. Raymond's father had concluded that he 'had the best intentions, but unfortunately was short of brains'. And blood was now on so many hands that all causation and responsibility seemed to be absorbed into a blind, drooling destiny. Even General Stanley had been dismayed by some of his orders. Nearly 500 Pals were lost in a single calamitous manoeuvre that had guaranteed to expose their flanks. On another occasion, he was appalled when a fresh attack was ordered where his own men had just been mown down by machine guns in open ground. By the end of the war, Derby's brother had been eased out of his command and the original Pals' battalions were so depleted that they had been merged and regrouped beyond recognition.

Billy Lambton, nourishing few illusions about the mayhem enveloping his men, could well have featured in Lloyd George's restructured command. He had, after all, maintained a candid private correspondence with the king, who mistrusted sanguine official briefings. But his mare put her foot in a hole in September 1917, broke her fetlock and rolled over her rider. It was touch and go for a while, and George Lambton and Jack Durham hurried to their brother's bedside near Arras. They felt touched to find doctors, nurses and all ranks eager to talk horses, all grateful for the continued distraction of a sporting press.

Derby was soon crossing the Channel himself, to take up his new post in Paris. He would prove a surprising success as ambassador. Regy Brett had spent much of the war in Paris and literally marked Derby's card with a 'form guide' to various embassy staff, politicians and soldiers he would encounter. Derby would find his military attaché, for instance, 'a certain winner if ridden in a snaffle'. The role of English milord was hardly an alien one, and his execrable French did not prevent Derby dismantling cultural barriers much as he did social ones. He viewed his principal obstacle as the Foreign Secretary: the 'Soul' George Curzon. On one occasion, Derby began a dictated letter thus: 'My dear Curzon, I have always known you to be a cad. I now know that you are a liar.' A new aide wisely elected to 'miss' the last mail that night, and next morning Derby agreed to start afresh: 'My dear George, You and I have known each other too long to quarrel over so small a matter . . .'*

Both the initial impetuosity and the change of heart were typical. Haig himself, for all the loyalty he had been shown, privately dismissed Derby as 'a very weak-minded fellow, I'm afraid, and, like the feather pillow, bears the marks of the last person who sat on

---

* The young officer who acted so astutely in this instance was Malcolm Bullock; in 1919 he married Derby's daughter, Victoria, the widow of Neil Primrose.

him.' Others detected a faux bonhomie. Clementine Churchill pulled no punches. 'People think he is bluff and independent and John Bullish,' she confided. 'But he is really a fat sneak.'

George Lambton meanwhile kept the home fires burning in Newmarket. Phalaris contributed another four wins from five starts in 1918, now ridden by Brownie Carslake. After his embarrassing appearance in *Hansard*, Rickaby had been dispatched to France. Just twenty-three, and already winner of five Classics, Rickaby would never see his two young sons again. He died a month before the Armistice, of wounds suffered in the final offensive at Cambrai, and was buried a dozen miles south of Edward Horner. Joe Childs, another jockey who had secured dispensations from the Royal Flying Corps, was still bitter in his 1952 reminiscences: 'If it had not been for a certain Member of Parliament, Fred might still have been with us today.' But Derby himself remained wholly unwitting of his inadvertent agency in the tragedy. 'Poor little Rick,' Derby wrote to Lambton from Paris. 'It was very sad indeed his death. I had no idea that he was even in France.'

There would be memorials, of course. Frederick Lester Rickaby's sister, Iris Piggott, gave his middle name to the son she delivered in 1935. Nor was that all he inherited: one day Lester Piggott would ride some of the greatest champions descended from Phalaris. But the fact remained that men like Raymond Asquith and Neil Primrose had been raised as the elect, eligible to assume leadership of the nation from the 'Souls'. And instead they had been herded into a charnel house by Herbert Asquith, Balfour and the rest. Doubtless Rosebery cast his mind back to Raymond's visit to Dalmeny, as an undergraduate, and guiltily remembered the impression he had made. Raymond had extolled his host as his 'ideal of what a man of 50 should be – clever, cynical, sensual, and wonderfully witty . . . frankly cynical about politics and completely disillusioned about everything else.' How ingenuous his worldliness seemed now! What might Raymond have made at fifty, or Neil? An alternative Chamberlain, a Churchill? Rosebery shrank into himself. Days before the Armistice, he suffered a stroke, and his movement, sight and hearing remained impaired through a pathetic final decade.

'All their young men are killed,' wrote Edwin Lutyens to his wife, returning from Mells in August 1919. As a friend of Frances, he had promised a pedestal for the magnificent bronze by which Alfred Munnings commemorated Edward. In its way, the noble figure of a young cavalry officer would suggest undiminished faith in a chivalrous ethic of sacrifice. The last thing Edward's own sister could imagine was that she might help to make the horse itself, rather than its tragic rider, a valid symbol of continuity.

A Day at the Races

Epsom, 6 June 1923

As the runners cantered to the start, Lord Derby could not hide his nerves. 'Have you had a stiff dose of brandy?' a friend asked. Derby smiled and mutely shook his head.

His grandfather, the fourteenth earl, had served as prime minister three times and led in four Classic winners trained by John Scott. None of them, however, had won the Derby. Now, at last, it seemed possible that the seventeenth earl might satisfy the dynastic craving for a new Sir Peter Teazle. That colt had won the eighth running of the race named after his owner, in 1787, from a son of Eclipse owned by Dennis O'Kelly. The closest the family had come since was in 1911, when Stedfast gave the rest a hundred-yard start, whipping round at the gate, before reeling in twenty-four of his twenty-five rivals – the exception being Jack Joel's Sunstar. George Lambton had also saddled the runner-up for his patron in 1920, but now they were beginning to hope that the house of Stanley had finally found the colt to go one better.

Pharos was one of the first foals sired by Phalaris, who had retired to stud in Newmarket at the end of 1918. Luckily, a projected sale of the young stallion to Australia had fallen through – and his popularity, at 200 guineas per mare, represented a striking vote of confidence in the future of an industry that staged 277 days' racing in 1919, up from fifty-three the previous year.

Derby had also come within an ace of culling the dam of Pharos. Scapa Flow, racing at the height of the war, was beaten in a Stockton 'seller' and was about to be taken home for just £50 by a Scottish trainer when reclaimed at the last minute for Stanley House. Her first foal, Spithead, was so game a winner of the Chester Cup that Lambton recalled how he even won over a mob blocking traffic through the Potteries during the General Strike: 'When the occupant of the box was discovered, he was not only allowed to go on but received with cheers and the slogan "Pass on Spithead" through all those turbulent towns.'

Scapa Flow's second foal was Pharos, whose arrival at Epsom represented another step towards Derby's accession as 'Uncrowned King of Lancashire' and doyen of the English racecourse. Since his return from Paris, Derby had remained a figure of sufficient substance to make a bizarre incognito mission, as 'Mr Edwards' and escorted by a Liverpool parish priest, to meet De Valera in Dublin. At fifty-eight, however, he was ready to renounce affairs of state and return to his roots. As 6–1 second favourite, Pharos offered him the perfect chance to consolidate his image as the toast of every working Lancastrian.

Even before the race, surveying the charabancs and open-topped buses parked along the rails, Derby must have felt a great sense of vindication for his role in keeping the show on the road during the war. After all, the sire of Pharos had only been able to make his name because of the skeleton race programme he had fought to maintain with Lambton, Rosebery and Jack Durham. And the thronged Downs testified that the Derby, likewise, had weathered its loveless wartime exile to Newmarket. As many as 250,000 people milled among bookmakers and beer tents, coconut shies and cauldrons of eels.

Derby and Lambton nursed only two reservations about Pharos. One was the stamina deficiency presumed in sons of the speedy Phalaris. Pharos had managed a couple of wins over a mile and a quarter, but would now be entering uncharted territory. 'It was quite recognised in the stable that a mile and a half was beyond his best distance,' Lambton recalled. 'But so well did he thrive on his work that it was hoped that his pluck and condition might get him home.'

The second doubt was closely related to the first. To get Pharos home would require nuanced, fuel-saving tactics. But owner and trainer had both lost confidence in their latest stable jockey, Eddie Gardner, and were particularly anxious about of their colt's tendency to boil over without quiet handling. Pharos had seemed noticeably more relaxed when worked by young Tommy Weston. But when Lambton confided his belief that Pharos would win at Epsom if they removed Gardner, Derby could not bring himself to be so heartless.

In contrast, there was one jockey in the race who automatically increased his mount's chance. Steve Donoghue had been champion jockey for nine years, and after winning two wartime Derbys at Newmarket had shown his mastery of the Epsom switchback by winning the latest two runnings there as well. In 1921, indeed, he had wriggled his way out of a retainer to ride for Lord Derby in order to win the race in Jack Joel's silks on a Polymelus colt, Humorist.

This year Donoghue had again extricated himself from another lucrative contract – which committed him to an outsider – so that he could partner the fancied Papyrus. He exuded confidence as he strolled into the parade ring, even though one of his eyes was closing up after a flint had been kicked into his face in the first race. When the Prince of Wales asked whether he was going to win his third consecutive Derby, Donoghue replied with total conviction: 'Yes, sir.'

Donoghue knew that Papyrus had abundant stamina; and, conversely, that the strong pace would expose any soft underbelly in Pharos. As they careered downhill out of the mist and into Tattenham Corner, he threw down the gauntlet to the hapless Gardner and broke clear. Gardner's best chance of getting his mount home was to delay his challenge before throwing everything into a late burst of acceleration. Once seeing Donoghue kick for home, however, he dared not wait. He sent Pharos in immediate pursuit. With two furlongs still to go, he was already engaged in a desperate duel – and each stride now took Pharos into the unknown.

Pharos did get his head in front, with the winning post looming just 300 yards away. But Gardner had gone too hard, too soon. Gradually Donoghue and Papyrus clawed their way back alongside and edged a length clear inside the final furlong.

Lambton was doubly aggrieved. The great prize had slipped through his fingers twice over. The Aga Khan, who had been introduced to her brother-in-law by Katharine Asquith, would later claim that Lambton had talked him out of buying Papyrus as a yearling. And then there was the gossip that Gardner had been seen out dancing late the previous night. The jockey would lose his position soon afterwards. But Derby proved magnanimous in defeat. As Donoghue returned to unsaddle, he smilingly extended a hand and said: 'Stephen, if they had kept you in that ambulance room another half an hour I should have won the Derby.' His tone was so warm that Donoghue, who had denied one of the richest men in the empire in the silks of a former draper's assistant, almost felt guilty.

As things turned out, Derby only had to wait another year to return not only with an eligible colt, but also with an eligible rider. Tommy Weston had not long before been sharing a stableboys' dormitory in Yorkshire with another aspiring jockey named George Formby. Whereas rising weight forced the latter to try vaudeville, Weston was toting two stone of dead weight in his saddle as he rode Sansovino clear in the 1924 Derby. The colt's owner received a terrific reception, oblivious to the downpour as he dazedly shook hands all round.

Yet this, its apparent climax, would ultimately prove only a footnote to a Turf career better defined by the colt who had failed Lord Derby the previous year. For it was Pharos who helped to register the transformative potency of an apparently pedestrian sire, Phalaris; and Pharos who would do most to extend it to future generations.

21

'I have no method. Method is imitation. I invent.'

A S TRAINERS, ONE had reached the beginning of the end; the other, only the end of the beginning. That much was obvious. But any who witnessed Italy's premier race of 1932 was bound to mistake the respective destinies of Federico Tesio and the dashing young Count Visconti di Modrone.

On the face of it, the Grand Premio di Milano confirmed the decline of Tesio as not just poignant but inexorable. At sixty-three, the colossus who had won the Italian Derby ten times between 1911 and 1923 – as both breeder and trainer – had plainly lost the Midas touch. Tesio seemed increasingly overmatched, his one-man, boutique Dormello stud struggling to compete with a new generation of Milanese industrialists.

A filly named Nogara had restored some respectability, the previous year, to a win ratio that had plunged to just three of the last twenty Italian Classics. Tesio adored Nogara, bred from a mare he had bought in England during the war for just 75 guineas. 'Look at her!' the little man would exclaim as she bounded through her workouts. 'Look at the power behind! There is no deviation, no waste. It's all propulsive force.' Nogara was not a typical Tesio horse: she was all about speed, not stamina, winning the two shortest Classics over a bare mile. But she had covered a multitude of sins. Tesio saw that it was no longer enough to rely on unique horsemanship. He needed investment and approached a young aristocrat, Don Mario Incisa della Rochetta, to invite him into a partnership.

Even as the Tesio–Incisa firm appeared on the racecard, however, Dormello was menaced with a terminal humiliation. The previous year Tesio had culled from his stable a son of Papyrus with brittle hindlegs and a big, hollow fuselage. Tesio had managed to get Sanzio onto the track to win one race, but decided that he would never repay perseverance and sold him for just 1,500 lire to Count Visconti.

There was something about Sanzio's new owner that appealed to Tesio. Perhaps he was reminded of his own bachelor days, when he too had first swaggered onto the racecourse as a young cavalry officer. Orphaned early, Tesio had boarded at an elite Barnabite school until presented with 500,000 lire by the trustee of his parents' estates, who then left him to dispose of it as he saw fit. Yet while Visconti was plainly in a position to treat his stable as a playboy indulgence, he was taking the whole thing very seriously. On the training track he would be seen listening intently to lengthy disquisitions from the maestro, who others found only terse or sarcastic.

At twenty-five, Visconti was impossibly glamorous: dark, sleek and rich. The marriage of his parents had been a classic match of cash and kudos. By the suitably brisk agency of a castor oil laxative, his mother's family had risen from street vendors to industrial magnates; her beauty and music, both exquisite, had soothed all social queasiness in her ducal father-in-law. The count and his siblings had been raised in a baroque palazzo, just round the corner from La Scala, identified by the family crest: a viper swallowing a Saracen. Divas, composers, painters and playwrights ascended the marble stairs daily. But it transpired that certain guests did not always follow the others down at the end of the evening. There was a scandalous breakdown in his parents' marriage – his father evidently as tempted by Adam as Eve – and Visconti ran away on several occasions, once tracked down to the monastery of Monte Cassino. It was decided that he could benefit from military regulation, and he was sent to cavalry school. Only it was not the army who taught him discipline: it was the horses.

Certainly they appealed to his vanity, as the perfect accoutrement to his uniform and dainty moustache. The swells in his regiment included Prince Umberto, heir to the throne. On one occasion, a princess sent a liveried chauffeur to convey the count to her hotel in a Rolls-Royce. Unfortunately he steeled his nerves with so much champagne that he threw up all over her. This misadventure was presumably a symptom rather than a cause of his subsequent sexual preference for men. Either way, the count was for now preoccupied by an awakening of another kind. If horses had initially assisted a life of frivolity and extravagance, they soon engendered a capacity for sobriety, diligence and professionalism.

The turning point came in 1929. Already he had announced himself by riding a winner over the frozen lake at St Moritz. It seemed a highly fitting marker: a Corinthian accomplishment in the most fashionable of settings. In the same spirit, he bought himself a Lancia Spider. One morning he decided to test the machine round the racing circuit at Monza. He ordered one of the family retainers, Macerati, to accompany him and was incensed by a show of reluctance: it was foggy, his son was ill, did it have to be today? Visconti furiously told him to be ready in fifteen minutes.

His driving doubtless reflected his irritation. He knew it had been unreasonable to turn an idle whim into a test of authority. Suddenly, rounding a bend, a cart loomed out of the fog. Visconti swung wide, the wheels slewed. A pole protruding from the cart caught Macerati in the throat and he died a few hours later.

The count did not drive for the next twenty years, and after his death it was discovered that he was still supporting Macerati's family. He hired a Tuareg guide as the only concession against two months of expiatory solitude on the Saharan plateau. Returning to Milan, he immured himself in his new stable complex, and a life of spartan ritual. Rising before daybreak, he supervised daily ceremonies of feeding, cleaning, exercising, grooming. 'It was a bit like a retreat in a monastery,' he acknowledged later. 'I began at four o'clock in the morning. I inspected the horses one by one. By eight o'clock in the evening I was in bed.' A friend remembered those years as devoted to *ascetismo*, Visconti poring over breeding manuals and 'lost in arcane discussion with Federico Tesio'.

He hired a steeplechase jockey from Tuscany, Ubaldo Pandolfi, to help around the stables. Pandolfi was impressed by his young employer's hunger for knowledge. The very opposite, in the words of Visconti's brother, 'of people like the Aga Khan, who went to see their horses at 11 o'clock in the morning, getting out of their Rolls in raccoon coats'. Visconti began to upgrade the quality of his bloodstock: from Lord Derby he imported a mare who had finished third in the Oaks, and in 1931 he bought a couple of rejects from Tesio himself.

One, Sanzio, had failed to cope with the exacting regime of his first owner, who treated each crop he bred as a programme to produce one champion. Unlike other trainers, obliged to coax dividends from different horses owned by different patrons, Tesio would sometimes employ even Classic winners as mere pacemakers on the gallops. Once any horse had established its limitations, it could be pressed into the service of one that was yet to do so. All the horses were worked on the principle of 'make or break'. Only those who matched raw ability with toughness merited a stallion career. As a result, he was prepared to write off even lightly raced horses. Sanzio had not only lacked the physique to break through the ranks, he was not even able to serve as a punchbag.

His new owner, however, could afford to give Sanzio all the time and treatment he needed. In effect, he was rebuilt. 'Little by little, the horse gained strength,' Pandolfi remembered. 'Sanzio was a creation of Count Visconti's will.' Before each race, Visconti slept in Sanzio's stable. He had done so five times, and the horse had won four times. Now he had earned a shot at the Gran Premio, and the count once again kept an overnight vigil in the straw. Sanzio retained one unconquerable aversion: heavy ground. The morning was overcast, and the clouds darkened as the first races were run. The count muttered to himself. 'So long as the rain holds off . . .' It did, just. Moments after the race, the storm burst. It seemed an apt portent for the professional demise of Federico Tesio.

'He was seething,' Pandolfi remembered. 'When he sold Sanzio he was convinced he had given the Count nothing but a headache.' Stubborn and obsessive, Tesio refused to accept this was the kind of thing that happened all the time in racing. This was a man known to deny himself cigarettes or even food in penance for a mistake. Head shrinking ever deeper into his sloped shoulders, Tesio's discomfiture was compounded later that summer when Sanzio plundered the Grand Prix d'Ostende, then one of the biggest prizes in Europe. Visconti threw a terrific party to celebrate.

The writing on the wall would only be magnified the following year, when the Prix de l'Arc de Triomphe winner was trained by

Tesio's former assistant. Federico Regoli had almost been part of the family, and for a long time it had been assumed he would take over the stable when the old man retired. But a couple of years previously Regoli and the stable jockey, Paolo Caprioli, awkwardly announced that the Crespi brothers, Milanese industrial barons, had offered to double their salaries. 'There's the door,' Tesio replied. 'Go if you want. But go at once.' His wife, Lydia, burst into tears. Tesio shrugged.

And now a final embarrassment, perhaps a final straw: Tesio's application for Nogara to be mated with Fairway was turned down by Lord Derby's new stud manager. Captain Paine, with his ginger military moustache, surveyed the strange little Italian blankly and apologised that Fairway's book for 1934 was already full.

After the near miss of Pharos at Epsom, Derby had sent Scapa Flow back for another tryst with Phalaris. The resulting colt, Fairway, was of a different stamp from his brother, so much so that he slugged out a win in the St Leger. Given a choice of two young stallions with identical genes, Derby elected to promote the one who had actually won a Classic, Fairway, and exported Pharos to Normandy just three seasons into his new career.

Fairway had been trained by Frank Butters, Lambton having briefly taken a back seat because of health problems, and by 1932 Derby was itching to retire his ageing trainer for good. Apart from anything else, he had come to view Cicely's influence on his stable as intolerable. Of course, Derby was always the type of man who might recoil nervously from the intellect of a Horner female. But he may also have suspected that Lambton, at seventy-two, was only holding out until his adolescent son, Teddy, could take over the yard. Derby prevaricated unhappily and the following year the status quo appeared to be justified by another Epsom success, with Hyperion. Lambton had again been unwell and Cicely must have had a major hand in the colt's preparation. In spite of Hyperion's success, that winter Derby finally informed Lambton that he could not allow him to continue at such risk to his health, and promised him a generous pension.

Lambton was livid. After forty years' service, he had been dismissed with six weeks' notice – 'the knife' delayed until it was nearly too late to set up as a trainer elsewhere. The secret of the partnership's success now accelerated its breakdown. No other trainer could have felt so at ease, socially, with such a patron. But that also meant the sudden rancour between them was dangerously unfettered. 'I doubt if it is possible for any man to know another better than I know you,' Lambton wrote. 'In this instance I say that you have let your weakness control your better qualities.' He hastily set himself up at Kremlin House Stables, and hired Bill Rickaby – son of the ill-fated rider of Phalaris – to ride the lightweights.*

It was in approaching this unhappy crossroads that Derby had appointed Captain Paine to manage his stud. His predecessor knew and respected Tesio, and would surely have found some way to help. As it was, Tesio decided to send Nogara to Fairway's brother, Pharos, who was available in France. And he was delighted with the colt Nogara delivered early in 1935. When he examined the weanlings at Olgiata, Don Mario's estate near Rome, it was impossible to miss the one he had named Nearco. The stocky little fellow would literally throw his weight around, barging into his companions and making them stagger. 'I will make something of this one,' Tesio declared.

Olgiata was one of the principal attractions of partnership with Don Mario. Tesio had been fascinated by the behaviour of his mares when winter crept down from the Alps to Dormello, on the shore of Lake Maggiore. Once they had cropped their autumn pasture, they would loiter anxiously by the southern fence. Tesio was certain the paddock rails had intruded on a primal instinct towards migration, and viewed a southern annex for the stud as the chance to restore a natural cycle, and bring forward the spring bloom in his horses.

That was typical Tesio. He had developed a curiosity about animal behaviour during extensive travels as a young man. (His flight had been prompted, in the first place, by unwarranted optimism in

---

* Bill did not last long in the post, evidently due to his influence on Teddy. Their hell-raising adventures climaxed in a chaotic tour of Cambridge in Bill's new sports car, with a young woman firing blanks from a revolver at terrified pedestrians. Lambton was not amused when bailing his son and jockey out of custody.

climbing through the hotel window of a married woman.) He rode in pony races in Peking, and one autumn encountered 20,000 bison on a Canadian prairie – heading south, of course. He rode with gauchos from Buenos Aires to Patagonia, with thirty-nine colts and a single mare to keep them together across the trackless plain. 'We travelled like mariners,' he remembered. 'By compass and the Southern Cross.' Here he saw wild horses broken; and saw, also, the intuitions they retained: lying down in the grass before the first gusts of a tumultuous *pampero* blew out of the still air, or taking an unerring shortcut across unknown country to a spring.

On his return, Tesio resolved to put his observations to the test. In 1899, the same year that another Piedmont cavalry officer founded the Fiat car factory, Tesio began to assemble Dormello from a series of crumbling smallholdings. He would gesture towards the distant summits of Monte Rosa and claim that his soil bore minerals of the same glacial moraine. There was even gold up there, he said. Some of his theories were hopelessly unscientific. He loved the story of Cavaliere Ginistrelli, who had moved his stable from Naples to Newmarket around 1880. Ginistrelli noticed how his champion filly, Signorina, and a mediocre, nine-guinea stallion named Chaleureux would both neigh wildly whenever she was led past his paddock. 'They love!' pronounced the romantic Cavaliere. Forfeiting an appointment with Cyllene, standing at 300 guineas, he took his mare straight to Chaleureux. The result was Signorinetta, 100–1 winner of the 1908 Derby. But when a repeat mating was arranged, a couple of years later, it was a routine business: Signorina took her place in the routine presentation of mares and the foal proved useless. Tesio explained that their first encounter had been charged with an eroticism that suffused the resulting foal with a productive nervous energy. It was on this profoundly speculative basis that Tesio opposed artificial insemination.

Then there was the case of Brunelleschi, a young stallion sold by Tesio, who betrayed a mysterious aversion to his mares. He was on the point of being castrated and expelled to a cavalry regiment when Tesio's counsel was sought. 'Go and fetch the ugliest, dirtiest, most disreputable-looking mare you can find,' he ordered. 'Plaster her with mud. Then leave her with Brunelleschi.' Unchaperoned, the stallion surreptitiously mounted the mare. Tesio had remembered that Brunelleschi, in training, had been chastised for showing excessive libido and simply needed to overcome that sense of taboo. 'I was pronounced a wizard,' he wrote. (And indeed he was: on the Italian Turf they called him *Il Mago*.) 'But all I had done was to realise that a horse is capable of intelligent and complex reasoning.'

Tesio seldom indulged Don Mario with consultation. His instincts went unchallenged. Some matings were conspicuously inbred, especially to St Simon; others were wholly outcrossed. There was no pattern, there could be no imitation. The only tool of his trade was a shooting stick, upon which he perched for hours observing the behaviour of his horses. 'I copy no one,' Tesio would tell his partner. 'I have no method. Method is imitation. I invent. And because the others have never seen what I do before, they say I am mad.'

An accomplished painter, who named all his horses after artists, Tesio explained that imitation became decadence. 'Look what happens in art when an original style becomes fashionable,' he said. 'Some painters even imitate their own work if it is successful: Boldini, Sargent, Whistler . . .' If there were no experimentation on the Turf, nothing would have changed since Eclipse: 'Horses would still be running in four heats of three miles at 15 miles an hour!'

Nonetheless, Don Mario did observe a few basic tenets. Tesio was always refreshing the stud's female blood, wary of stagnation. He seldom kept his own stallions, lest he divert mares from more suitable partners. Above all, he set his gold standard as Classic blood – a principle preserved by Don Mario in a famous axiom: 'The thoroughbred exists because its selection has depended not on experts, technicians or zoologists, but on a piece of wood: the winning post of the Epsom Derby.'

Every year, the Tesios and the Incisas wrote down the name of one of their yearlings and sealed it in an envelope, to be opened two years later. Invariably, Don Mario and the two wives picked youngsters of outstanding conformation and pedigree – and failed to find the champion nominated by Tesio. None of them, however, could fail to see the potential of Nearco.

Nogara's promising son was only one symbol of *Il Mago*'s revival since entering partnership with Don Mario. Donatello, for instance, won the Gran Premio ten days after Nearco won his first race on the San Siro racecourse. The following weekend Donatello ran in the Grand Prix de Paris, but was trapped on the rail before hurtling into second. Nearco meanwhile had a busy and prolific autumn, winning six more races including the Premio Chiusura, in which the best juveniles could test the water against older horses. His time in that race would stand until 1970.

It did not matter what Tesio asked him to do. Nearco soaked up every workout, every weight and every pacemaker with equal indifference. Eventually Tesio even began to find himself a little vexed. Priming Nearco lacked the precarious margin of danger he explored with other horses, pushed to breaking point. He was barely a challenge at all, somehow immune to the setbacks that disturb the mental and physical equilibrium of a thoroughbred at fever pitch. Where other horses lost their appetite or temper, Nearco would cheerfully empty his manger and take a siesta. As a three-year-old, he proved so superior to the Italian crop that his brilliance seemed almost mechanical. One witness of Nearco's Derby Italiano attested that it would 'remain forever the supreme yardstick of dynamism and grace combined'.

But would his freewheeling approach last in the Grand Prix de Paris? Tesio arranged a trial over the full distance, just short of two miles, with two specialists. One, a stayer carrying 11lbs less than Nearco, escorted him from the outset; they were joined at halfway by a top-class sprinter. It was an exorbitant challenge. No other twentieth-century trainer would have dreamed of pushing a champion so hard without prize money at stake. Yet Nearco shrugged off both horses. And just a couple of days later he cruised clear of his pursuers in the Grand Premio di Milano.

Finally Tesio had a horse that might even allow his long-suffering wife to make sense of all their sacrifices. Daughter of a Dalmatian shipowner, Lydia saw nearly every lira immediately diverted to the stud; the household was permitted one servant, their meals also served by the chauffeur. This was the faithful Zibra, an atrocious driver whose duties also extended to carrying Tesio's binoculars at the races. As his master's sight failed in later years, he would peer through them himself and attempt to convey what might be happening. Meanwhile Lydia, tall and thin and tweedy, was left to redress the solecisms of her husband. 'Donna Lydia was never beautiful,' Don Mario recalled. 'And somehow her dentist had managed to accentuate her resemblance to an old horse. But she had great *style.*'

So now this exotic entourage proceeded to Paris, to announce Italy's new champion. Tesio's every superstition had to be scrupulously observed. There could be no coffee at lunch, lest a stain darken the tablecloth. Black cats would cause Zibra to stop, ignoring the horns of traffic behind, until the street had been 'cleansed' by a pedestrian moving in the opposite direction. On one occasion, a priest had reproved Tesio that no sensible Christian could find a bad omen in thirteen sitting down to dine together. Tesio nonetheless remained a bundle of nerves. (The priest himself died the next day. As Tesio put it: 'Luckily, he settled the matter quickly.')

But this was 1938, and Italy under Mussolini was no longer supposed to be prey to such primitivism. For many compatriots, in fact, Nearco represented something very different – a eugenic masterpiece, physically magnificent, invincible.

The Parisian sporting public had only had a week to digest an unpalatable exhibition of Italian fascist machismo. Having won the 1934 World Cup on home soil four years previously, the Azzurri had come to France and retained the trophy with a pointedly martial approach, their Roman salutes before a game signifying their discipline and aggression.

Il Duce's preference was for such sports as fencing, or the shining modernity of motor racing. But the popular appeal of football provided a valuable exercise in mass psychology and fascist mythology. The 1934 tournament, staged in neo-Roman stadia, had been his Berlin Olympics. Yet while referees had then been conspicuously obliging, no such grumbles seemed possible this time round. The fascist press saluted the world champions as 'pure thoroughbreds . . . a symbol of the overwhelming march of Mussolini's Italians.' Now, in Nearco, they hoped to vaunt the moral implicit in the Italian word for thoroughbred: *purosangue*, literally 'pure-blood'.

Tesio had little time for politics, albeit his appointment to the senate in 1939 at least implied a reliable orthodoxy. Essentially he was too obsessed by his own small world – he worked seven days a week for six decades – to concern himself with the one beyond its walls. If anything, he exhibited a distrust of the establishment, depicting himself as a maverick needling the pompous Italian Turf hierarchy.

But nobody else, in France or Italy alike, would be treating the success of Tesio's champion in Paris as a purely personal vindication. Partisan emotion ran high when, for the first time in his life, Nearco was unable to open up in the middle of the race. Entering the straight, he was still being harassed by four horses. Pietro Gubellini, his jockey, hesitated a moment, but then decided to ask his mount an unprecedented question. In the somewhat excitable estimation of Tesio's biographer, he administered 'the most fateful whip-stroke in racing history'. Nearco exploded clear.

In the stands Tesio watched in silence. As a rule he was wary about taking horses outside his homeland. Though he raised perhaps a thousand horses in all, he won only a dozen races abroad – and these mostly relatively minor affairs. When his champion passed the post at Longchamp, then, Don Mario was astonished by the roar that issued from a man who stood no more than five feet five inches. Tesio's bellowing, he remembered, evoked Attila the Hun 'when, having raped, pillaged and plundered, he decapitated with one stroke of his scimitar the bishop who knelt begging him to spare the cathedral'.

And Gubellini, it transpired, had a corresponding sense of theatre. As Tesio led Nearco back to be unsaddled, they were jeered by the crowd. Gubellini, incensed by this unsporting reception, gazed down like a cavalry general receiving a white flag, and gave the fascist salute.

To Count Visconti, Paris had meanwhile come to symbolise something very different. On the whole, the Italian aristocracy considered Mussolini a necessary evil. However puerile, however crude, he had at least brought the workers to heel. At the same time there was something stifling about this industrious, puritanical Italy. As Tesio regrouped after the Sanzio debacle, his young rival began to feel restless.

At first, he travelled on the pretext of attending bloodstock sales in France and England. In Paris, however, he found the kind of cultural experimentation that had been asphyxiated at home – above all, in the works of Salvador Dalí and Luis Buñuel. Coco Chanel, captivated by the glorious young Italian, introduced him to Jean Renoir. Visconti's name appeared, as third assistant to Renoir, on the credits of *A Day in the Country*. 'I realised that the love of horses was not enough any more,' he said later. 'I had to express myself some other way.'

In 1932, the year of Sanzio, Visconti had saddled twenty-eight winners from only eighty-one starters. Just two years later, he was largely confining himself to breeding.

In later years, Luchino Visconti would say that it had been thoroughbreds who taught him how to work with actors; how to bend them to his will, how to mould their personalities to a specific role. It is not hard to see how the theatre of the Turf had engaged a mind like his: its pageant of silks, its patient rehearsal of a fleeting performance. And *The Leopard*, of course, is worth a thousand Sanzios. But cinema's gain was undoubtedly the Turf's loss. Pandolfi, Visconti's assistant, insisted that his employer was the only man Tesio ever feared as a genuine competitor. 'Federico Tesio was Italian racing,' Pandolfi said. 'And he still is. For all that, the Count might have been his equal.'

The morning after Nearco won in Paris, as the press at home exulted in this equine incarnation of the new Italy, Tesio received an offer for Nearco to go to stud in England. Don Mario was dispatched overnight to Newmarket, where he was received by a bloodstock agent representing Martin Benson, a bookmaker. There was £60,000 on the table for the unbeaten son of Pharos. Nearco's career was over. Tesio would always say that the horse had untapped depths nobody else had ever glimpsed.

Benson would soon set to work on a bomb shelter for his precious new stallion. In the event, Nearco's impact at stud was barely delayed by the war. The last of the Derbys transferred to Newmarket, in 1945, was won by his son, Dante; and he had already produced Nasrullah, whose own considerable success at stud would also vindicate the provision, once again, of an emergency racing programme.

Nearco's grandsire had provided the ultimate proof that at least one national heirloom, the thoroughbred racehorse, should not be melted down in wartime. For Phalaris had become the unexpected tinderbox of a twentieth-century explosion in the range of the Darley Arabian blood. Quite apart from maintaining the central trunk, he established a parallel branch that still flourishes via Native Dancer; while his grandson, Nearco, would do the same via Bold Ruler. As such, there is a strong case for identifying as sire of the century a sprint handicapper who picked his way modestly across the few duckboards permitted him through the First World War.

With age, the two stubborn men who produced Phalaris gradually overcame their differences. Derby's trademark energy ebbed into infirmity and melancholy, the resumption of war in Europe finding him isolated and out of touch. Already losing mobility to bulk and rheumatism, he was further debilitated by a car accident and did not see Watling Street, trained by Walter Earl, win him a Newmarket Derby in 1942. Characteristically, he instead went to open a gymkhana in the Lancashire rain.

Churchill found time to send a telegram of congratulation, and George Lambton wrote as well. When Lambton succumbed to a final illness, shortly before the end of the war, his son Teddy assumed control of his stable. Derby made a significant gesture of contrition in a letter of condolence to Cicely. 'I wish his licence to train could have been continued to you,' he wrote. 'As you certainly thoroughly deserved it.'

'Mechanical war is brutal, cruel and ruthless,' Lambton had written, not long before. 'When it is over we shall all look forward to a world of sanity and peace; but that will not easily happen if we become mechanized body and soul.' He commended the old sports and pastimes as the best insurance, and racing for its historic capacity to unite all classes. Post-war capitalism, however, would no longer sustain the conservative view of a stud as a symbol of landed stewardship. A new, commercial synergy would instead develop between professional breeders and international plutocrats; between the lore and the profits.

PART VII

Raising the Stakes

Nearctic (1954)
Northern Dancer (1961)
Sadler's Wells (1981)
Galileo (1998)
Frankel (2008)

22

'Chuck, what I tol' you?'

A YOUNG MOTHER HAD fainted, so Eddie Taylor carried her baby onto the lifeboat. The infant was protected from the perishing wind by a cardboard box; Taylor, by silk pyjamas and a duck-hunting jacket. He did have a matching pair of trousers, but had been unable to unpack them because of a snagged zip. It was only because his wife had been so alarmed by Lord Haw-Haw's latest rant, on the eve of the voyage, that he had consented to buy a survival suit at all. The renegade broadcaster had promised the *Western Prince* the diligent attention of U-boats on her way from New York to Liverpool, causing some passengers to wait for another crossing. Taylor was not so inclined to mock their timidity now.

Woken by the impact of the torpedo, he had hastened through a netherworld of corridors, half-lit by emergency generators, on to the deck. A cold, wet December dawn was breaking over the North Atlantic. All drills were mutely observed. It helped, no doubt, that professional sailors outnumbered passengers by nearly two to one. The *Western Prince's* principal cargo comprised food and base metal, priceless succour to the British in their solitary stand of 1940. The U-boat chivalrously waited for the lifeboats to draw clear before finishing her off with a second torpedo. Along with her captain, and two hands who had winched down the last lifeboat, she was consumed by the heavy swell in barely a minute.

Numb and nauseous, the survivors began to row mechanically in the vague direction of Iceland, 200 miles away. Those who could not row, bailed. At thirty-nine years old, over six feet tall and fifteen stone, Taylor was one of the ablest passengers. In his flimsy pyjama trousers, even he was menaced by hypothermia. It was only a week to the winter solstice; night would soon return. Fortunately he was unaware that British merchant vessels had been forbidden to respond to any humanitarian summons in waters known to be patrolled by U-boats – which were, of course, precisely where a Mayday was most likely to be heard. It was a ruthlessly utilitarian calculation. Britain's lifeline to North America was already so stretched that it could not be frayed or tangled by diversions in the name of pity. An exception might have been made, admittedly, had it been possible to specify that those in peril now included C. D. Howe, Canada's minister of munitions and supply, and his right-hand man, Edward Plunket Taylor. Their agenda in London included establishment of a Joint Air Training programme, providing 120 new airfields in Canada for the training of 131,000 air crew. But it was a bit late for special pleading now.

After six hours of rowing, somebody in Howe's boat casually remarked that he thought he had seen a ship. Another peered towards the horizon, and demurred; a third thought it might be. Then someone stood up. 'Yes,' he murmured. 'It's a ship, all right.' As Howe recalled: 'Nobody said another word. They just calmly waited – as if they did this kind of thing every day.'

Captain Lachlan Dewar, a commander in the merchant navy, had seen the distress flares and could not bring himself to ignore them. Carefully he ranged his grimy collier between the lifeboats and the wind; rope ladders were lowered, and a basket for the baby. Even now, at the very brink of salvation, there was one last disaster: a lifeboat capsized, and one of Howe's executives was never seen again.

Captain Dewar surrendered his cabin, wardrobe and whisky to Howe and his two surviving colleagues. Four days later, newspapers reported their arrival at Greenock 'unshaven and in borrowed clothes, but in good health'. After their return, Canada would contribute 12,000 aircraft to the defeat of Hitler. But their reprieve would also have one less obvious dividend many years later: a new global paradigm for the thoroughbred racehorse.

Born in 1901, E. P. Taylor belonged to a generation of Canadians that later caused his son, Charles, to look back in wonder at their 'heady self-confidence [and] almost unbridled optimism . . .' One morning, as a freshman at McGill University, Taylor's impatience to get on extended even to his breakfast toast. Vexed by waiting, he asked himself whether a machine might be devised to grill both sides simultaneously. Soon afterwards he licensed a prototype for royalties of 40 cents apiece. Next he took an old truck chassis to a foundry and drove home-made buses along a neglected streetcar route. By twenty-one, he was on the board of his late grandfather's brewery.

After moving to Toronto the young dynamo made a study of the Ontario brewing industry as Prohibition was relaxed. He found it to be fantastically inefficient, divided between as many as thirty-seven rival firms while operating, in 1930, at just 25 per cent capacity. He began a precarious series of acquisitions, amalgamations and closures, often persuading vendors to accept shares in lieu of cash. By the time war broke out, he had condensed fifteen breweries into six and controlled 35 per cent of the Ontario market.

In the meantime, as an enjoyable means of circumventing a ban on the advertising of alcohol, he had decided to start a racing stable in the name of his latest brewery acquisition, Cosgrave. He took a chance on Bert Alexandra – a trainer constantly at loggerheads with officialdom, but with a history of turning up bargains. Once, admittedly, he had claimed a horse in Chicago without realising it was owned by Al Capone. He moved his entire stable out of town at sundown. This fly-by-night quality amused his new patron. At their first meeting, Taylor warned that his budget was limited: their recollections would vary, but it was no more than $7,500. Two days later Taylor received a telegram from Maryland congratulating the Cosgrave stable on its first success there. Soon Alexandra resurfaced in Toronto, at the old Woodbine racetrack, with half-a-dozen horses. Each won at least once – within the week. Soon posters of Taylor's best horse, bearing the Cosgrave legend, were adorning bars throughout Ontario.

By the time of Pearl Harbor, Taylor was supervising every ounce of transatlantic relief to Britain. But if he was in the eye of the storm, another unusually talented forty-year-old found himself tiresomely becalmed. Horatio Luro sat in a hotel room in Miami Beach wondering how on earth he might go about paying the bill.

Though born within a month of Taylor, Luro belonged to another era. He was a grandson of Pedro Luro, pioneer of the Pampas; and his family had founded the first great stud of Argentina, Ojo de Agua, where Cyllene had arrived in 1908. Horatio Luro's father, Adolfo, owned 50,000 cattle and became president of the Buenos Aires Jockey Club. But Adolfo's twin, Rufino, was a playboy who had dissipated his fortune – and Horatio had the potential to follow the footsteps of either. He was six feet three inches, with a moustache that made Errol Flynn look like Groucho Marx. Swiss watches have been assembled more casually than Luro knotted his ties. He abandoned a motor-racing career when one of his brothers was killed in the same race, but that just left more time to pursue chorus girls. Luro had even fought a duel. With swords.

He once rebuked a reporter for telephoning the morning after he had won a big race: 'Sundays are for laauving . . .' Yet it was a failed engagement, failed marriage and failed affair that had sent him back and forth between Paris and Buenos Aires, selling Chryslers and playing polo, before finally discovering his vocation. He had adored thoroughbreds since boyhood, and now began learning the business properly on the family's El Moro stud. In 1937 Luro and a partner took four cheap horses on the seventeen-day voyage to New York.

Their first runner, in Chicago, had been bought in Argentina for $800. He won at 25–1, and was sold for $25,000 to Joe E. Brown – subsequently renowned for declaring that 'nobody's perfect' in the fadeout of *Some Like It Hot*. Luro was beginning to look like an exception to that rule, the three other horses taking aggregate profits on a $7,000 investment to $85,000. Returning home to restock, he again had spectacular results. The second wave of imports included Ligatori, who raced for Bing Crosby and ran the great Seabiscuit to a nose in a match at Del Mar. But then came the war. His assistant, Charlie Whittingham, joined the marines and Luro gradually ran out of horses, patrons and money.

Now, as he sat glumly in the little hotel in Florida, the only solution that suggested itself was an ignoble one. Before going out to dinner, Luro silently ransacked his own room. When he returned, he announced that he had been burgled. 'This is a serious situation for me,' he told his landlady. 'I had some cash hidden and it is gone.

I'm afraid I will not be able to pay you for a while.' The story made the local press, and sympathetic friends sent him cash. But whether he had reached the limits of his conscience or his invention, Luro knew that he had to find backing from somewhere – and quickly – or his American adventure was finished.

Then, at a cocktail party in Palm Beach, he ran into Audrey Emery. When Luro first met her, in Paris, Audrey had been married to the Tsar's cousin, Grand Duke Dmitri Pavlovich, described by one historian as 'a Romanov Hamlet'. He represented both the old order and the new chaos: his own family wiped out by assassinations and executions, while he himself was complicit in the murder of Rasputin. Banished to the Persian front, he had been able to slink away to France when the Revolution took hold. Dmitri briefly found succour in Coco Chanel, but she soon despaired of these handsome, hollow Russians: 'They drink just not to be afraid.' Marriage to Audrey, daughter of a Cincinnati industrialist, could not prevent the tide of his life running ever lower.

As her husband receded from society, stranded on the mudflats of his lassitude, Audrey became restless – and in Dimitri Djordjadze, a Georgian prince and man of action, she discovered a seductive contrast. Curiously, Djordjadze had also been able to flee the Bolshevik carnage by dint of his role in a notorious homicide – he had been posted to a Black Sea port after killing a fellow aristocrat, apparently in self-defence – but embraced his new life in exile with rather more gusto. After working as a movie stunt rider, Djordjadze won the Grand Prix de 24 Heures at Spa and was soon restoring Audrey to a life of adventure. One day they were on the terrace of an Austrian hotel when a group of surly young men in leather jackets arrived. Everyone stood up except Djordjadze's party. He would never forget Hitler's glower, likening it to the stare of an animal trainer. But now they had been forced to pack their bags, as the tyrant brought Europe under his heel, and struck Luro as being desperately in need of new stimulation

He talked them into a racing partnership, and they claimed a horse for $2,500. It was typical of their incendiary relationship that both Luro and Djordjadze would later claim credit for discovering Princequillo, who went on to win a series of big races. Perhaps they simply had too much in common. Physically, they might have been brothers; while Djordjadze likewise prided himself on his horseman-ship, learned from Tartars. Confronted with another exotic in Luro, it was perhaps not so much his ego that was at stake, as his very identity. What is certain is that Princequillo, in saving his new trainer's career, proved unable to perform an equivalent service for his owners' marriage. Djordjadze disappeared to sell horses in California, soon a familiar face on the Hollywood scene as he strolled around arm-in-arm with George Brent and Clark Gable. (When they ran into Ronald Reagan, Brent exclaimed: 'Hello farmer!') But nor would he be able to shake off Luro even here.

Princequillo, the trainer's breakthrough champion, had secured plenty of orders: the war was over, optimism was in the air, and his old assistant had demobbed from the Marines. Charlie Whittingham later proved an outstanding trainer in his own right, and always stressed his debt to *El Gran Señor* for teaching him patience – to ignore impatient owners and accountants and heed only the horse itself. Whenever this forbearance paid off, Luro would turn to his lieutenant and say: 'Chuck, what I tol' you?'

It was time for the most ambitious raid yet on South America. Luro took Lana Turner along for the ride, and came back with a boatload of champions. Their success created a vogue for South American horses, in general; and for Horatio Luro, in particular. *El Gran Señor* dancing the tango was now the validating watermark of a Hollywood party. Luro attended Basil Rathbone's masquerade as the Devil, with Loretta Young on his arm as Joan of Arc. And while he settled down in 1951, to a long and happy marriage with a Southern Belle, his erotic career still had one last boon to bestow.

During the 1940s Luro had a tumultuous affair with his most glamorous client. Liz Whitney had screen-tested as Scarlett O'Hara in *Gone with the Wind* – not simply because the film was largely financed by her then husband, but also because she had an authentic blend of feistiness and femininity. (Once, surprising a thief, Liz jumped onto a horse and hauled him down with a lasso.) Having remained on civil terms with Luro – at least sporadically – and solicitous for his ever fragile health, she recommended the profes-sional services of her next husband, a fashionable surgeon. It would prove a fateful introduction. For when E. P. Taylor was confronted by a problem in his own stable, in 1956, he cast his mind back to the charming Argentinian trainer he had happened to meet in the waiting room of a New York clinic.

After the war, many of Canada's leaders anticipated trouble for an economy that would have to absorb an influx of demobbed manpower. True to form, Eddie Taylor took a different view. His service under C. D. Howe had forged priceless connections with other men of can-do spirit, who had, by 1945, turned the backward, agricultural Canadian economy of 1939 into the fourth most powerful in the free world. Now, diversifying into lumber, food, chemicals and property, Taylor teamed up with some of them to form the Argus Corporation: an engine room of an unprecedented boom in North American consumerism.

At the same time Taylor began to apply his tried-and-tested principles of expansion and consolidation to his stable, and to Canadian horse racing in general. Ontario had too many tracks, most of them dilapidated and poorly regulated. He persuaded the Ontario Jockey Club to buy them all, refurbish a couple that might be rendered efficient, and sell off the rest for malls or housing. The proceeds could then be invested in a new, flagship racetrack, something to make the world sit up and take notice. The old hands of the Bluegrass had always told Taylor that he could never rear a top-class thoroughbred in the frozen north. But Bert Alexandra told him a Kentucky Derby winner could be raised on the corner of Queen and Yonge Streets in downtown Toronto – 'provided you spend enough money, and have a lot of luck'.

At this point Canada's wretched prize money and facilities were matched by the mediocrity of her bloodlines. The average Canadian yearling fetched around $1,500. So Taylor got busy addressing the pedigree deficit, too. Windfields, his suburban homestead in Toronto, expanded into a sprawling stud farm of nearly 1,000 acres, grazed by dozens of mares. In 1950, he established a new wing at Oshawa; and, on Alexandra's retirement, also hired a new trainer, a taciturn horseman of the old school named Gordon 'Pete' McCann.

McCann had started out riding at harvest fairs and had been

champion jockey of Havana in 1926, when still only eighteen. He made a flying start for Taylor, winning the premier prize on the Canadian Turf, the King's Plate, in 1951 and 1953. But Taylor was prospecting new horizons. He wanted horses good enough to compete south of the border. If that was to happen, he would need a trainer prepared to risk – and relish – taking them there. And McCann, who generally found it easier to communicate with horses than people, was never comfortable away from the sanctuary of stud or stable.

Not that this seemed likely to become an issue, unless Taylor upgraded his stock. Unlike some great breeders he believed that the female blood contributed most; that if you mated the world's fastest stallion with a slow mare, you would get a slow horse. He instructed a British bloodstock agent, George Blackwell, to find the very best mare in the 1952 December sale at Tattersalls. It did not matter how much she cost, so long as she brought authentic Classic genes to Windfields. They settled on Lady Angela, a mare being sold by Martin Benson and in foal to his stallion, Nearco.

The following summer Lady Angela was winched out of the hold of a ship onto the quayside at Montreal. In the crate with her was Harry Green, Taylor's stallion manager. Green had rushed aboard after the mare had started to go berserk, slipping and sliding over the steel surfaces. She could easily have broken a limb, and that would have been that. Green immediately identified the cause of her anxiety. The stevedores had been trying to unload Lady Angela first, and she had panicked about leaving her foal behind. Green calmed her down before accompanying her colt into the crate. The crew were dubious but Green knew what he was doing. Sure enough, once Green returned for Lady Angela, she was eager to take her turn.

Lady Angela had been culled from Benson's stud after producing two duds to the stallion he had acquired at such expense from Federico Tesio. Nor would her little colt do much to improve Nearco's record with Lady Angela. Yet Taylor had nonetheless stipulated, as a condition of her purchase for 10,500 guineas, that Lady Angela have one final tryst with Nearco before leaving Newmarket. The result, on 11 February 1954, was a very dark, sturdy colt with a small tick of white on his forehead. Nearctic, as Taylor called him, represented a priceless transfusion of Classic blood from the Old World: Lord Derby's foundation mare, Canterbury Pilgrim, surfaced on one side of his sire's pedigree and both sides of his dam's.

Not even McCann could soothe Nearctic's aggression. The tighter you gripped the reins, the more he tossed his head. McCann rode him with a curb bit and an extra set of reins. The ebony colt emanated a restless power. In May 1956 Nearctic won two sprint races at the Old Woodbine Park, on the city waterfront. In the first, his jockey tried to focus his attention with a couple of cracks of the whip even as he careered clear of his rivals. McCann was livid. The last thing he wanted was to sour the volatile colt, and a different rider was hired for his second start.

A fortnight after the opening of the $14-million supertrack at New Woodbine, Nearctic produced a performance in keeping with the stage: six lengths clear into the stretch, ten clear at the line. He scalded his pursuers with speed. Within nine weeks of his debut, he had won five races. They were beginning to talk about Nearctic as the best horse ever foaled in Canada. For Taylor, that meant only one thing. He had to go to Saratoga, and be measured against the leading young colts in the United States.

But McCann either could not or would not go with him. Between the yearlings on the farm and the racing string on the track, he was nurturing over fifty horses. Long before daybreak, he was in the barn mixing feed. And that was when he was happiest. Even a horse as good as Nearctic could not justify the ordeal of an entire August alone among the East Coast's social elite, as they gossiped and tinkled ice on clapboard verandas.

Nearctic was driven to Saratoga and lodged in the barn of a trainer named Charley Shaw. He also had a new jockey, who tried to restrain Nearctic in the early stages of his first race there. They fought each other to a standstill and the Canadian raider dropped right out. It was a sobering moment. Things went better next time, as Nearctic tore into an enormous lead by halfway – albeit he only just held out after veering across the straight. Tried in the Hopeful Stakes, climax of the juvenile programme at Saratoga, he again hurtled clear; and again started wandering in the straight. Whether he was tiring himself out, or in some kind of discomfort, he could finish only fourth.

Briefly restored to McCann, Nearctic boosted his confidence by thrashing Canadian rivals back at Old Woodbine. But he was then sent back to Shaw, now at Belmont in New York – even though he was suffering a quarter-crack, a split in the wall of his hoof, that should really have been given time to heal. Instead he was asked to race twice in eight days against a champion in the making, Bold Ruler. Nor was he given time out when returned to McCann. A silk purse was being turned into a sow's ear. It was then that Taylor remembered Horatio Luro.

It was not as a racehorse, but as a sire, that Luro would ultimately make Nearctic's reputation. When the colt arrived at his barn in California that winter, he brought so many problems with him that he could not run for eight months. Yet it is not hard to see why Luro appealed to Taylor as the man to solve the Nearctic riddle. From Princequillo onwards, he had proved especially adept in drawing out the staying power of horses. And here was one gluttonous for speed, apparently far too headstrong to fulfil his talent. Luro remembered watching Shaw detonate Nearctic into lightning workouts in Saratoga. When Nearctic arrived at Santa Anita, Luro resolved to keep a lid on his fires with a regime of longer, steadier exercise.

Rae Johnstone, rider of over thirty Classic winners in Europe, happened to be wintering in Los Angeles. The Australian was famous for his patience. Every morning he appeared at Luro's barn in a cashmere turtleneck, jodhpurs and gleaming leather boots; every morning, reins loose and stirrups long, he would hack Nearctic quietly among the vines and trees beside the track. Hack, walk, stand, jog. Once sensing sufficient docility in his mount, Johnstone would be able to gallop Nearctic round the track.

Unfortunately, just as Nearctic began to respond to the therapy, his quarter-crack reopened. They could now forget any fantasy about the Kentucky Derby. As it was, Nearctic eventually surfaced for a couple of ring-rusty starts at Belmont in the summer, and was returned to McCann to renew his confidence and fitness. Though he started climbing back up the ranks, neither trainer seemed able to get him past a certain plateau in 1957. After trying to eyeball Bold Ruler at Belmont, Nearctic staggered home in last place.

The following season Nearctic was a different proposition: Horse of the Year in Canada, winning nine races in all. Though largely confined to his home beat, McCann still being happiest at places like Fort Erie and Old Woodbine, he managed a surprise win in the Michigan Mile. At the time, it was the richest race won by a Canadian horse. A fortnight later, Taylor went to the yearling sale at Saratoga and decided to ride his luck. In Luro he had found a trainer equal to his ambition. But he still needed better horses. Already he had seventeen stallions and eighty mares. Once again, he sought out George Blackwell and asked him to find another Lady Angela. And the catalogue again contained one outstanding candidate: a bay filly, with a white star on her forehead, from the third crop of Native Dancer.

Native Dancer, another conduit of Phalaris blood, was the first horse-racing idol of the television age, barrelling his way through nearly every crisis – he suffered his only defeat in a photo for the 1953 Kentucky Derby – as a mirror of the invincibility and prosperity of post-war America. The filly's mother, for her part, would again introduce Classic European blood: she was by Mahmoud, whose record time in the 1936 Epsom Derby would stand for fifty-nine years.

Taylor got the filly for $35,000, named her Natalma and sent her to Luro. After winning her first two starts at Belmont, she was first past the post in the Spinaway Stakes at Saratoga – a performance that identified her as potentially the best filly of her age in North America, albeit she was relegated to third for hampering a rival. More vexing than the loss of the prize was the thrashing from her jockey that caused her to run so waywardly in the closing stages. When Luro returned from his annual retreat to France, he found that Natalma was refusing to set foot on the racetrack, and so becoming impossible to train.

Just as he had with Nearctic, Luro found a way past Natalma's insecurities. Dosing her with a mild tranquilliser, he had her ridden every morning on an idle tour of the Belmont backstretch, up and down the warren of stabling, sometimes pausing to graze or simply to relax as her rider chatted with friends. Eventually Luro coaxed her into a state of such narcoleptic calm that she allowed herself to be ridden gently round the track again.

The following spring, Luro was increasingly optimistic that he could win Taylor not only the Kentucky Oaks, with Natalma, but also the Kentucky Derby itself with Victoria Park, who had broken the track record at Hialeah, in Florida. But Natalma broke down after a dazzling final gallop, while Victoria Park was beaten into third. Nonetheless, he was the first Canadian horse to make the podium in a Triple Crown race.

Natalma had chipped a bone in her knee, and this would cause her to sit out the rest of the year. The alternative, though extremely late in the breeding season, was to try rushing her into foal. Taylor had a rookie stallion who was proving very fertile: Nearctic. An eleven-month pregnancy would condemn Natalma to a May foal, likely to be behind his peers from the outset. Taylor debated the dilemma with his team, and they decided to take a chance. On 27 May 1961, Natalma delivered her foal – and triggered a revolution in the international breeding industry.

His 'dollar a year' wartime service should have left no doubt of Taylor's public spirit, and he had since devoted much time and energy to philanthropy. Yet even his sporting success, itself the result of patriotic investment in Canada's scorned racing and breeding industries, was now corroding his reputation. In 1961, the first four home in the Queen's Plate had all been bred at Windfields. In the next running there was uproar when the Texan-owned favourite was ruled ineligible at the eleventh hour, on a technicality. As Taylor's eighth Queen's Plate winner returned to be unsaddled, booing could be heard – and it only increased as the Canadian Croesus, big and bald and bespectacled, accepted the customary purse of fifty sovereigns. It was not just in brewing, many felt, that Taylor was trying to corner the market.

Even a sympathetic editorial around this time noted that Taylor was 'having problems with the size of his shadow . . . its size throws people into a panic.' The value of the Argus portfolio, $15 million at its inception, was approaching $140 million. Turnover in 1961 equated to around 4 per cent of Canada's gross national product. Yet the real E. P. Taylor, a pipe between his teeth and a twinkle in his eye, was 'known, trusted and liked by a very large number of unimportant people . . . as honest, friendly, good natured and superbly confident.' Certainly he was exactly the same talking to the queen, hosting her to the centenary Plate in 1959, or a stable boy. This was particularly vexing to his brother, Fred, an ex-communist living in an artists' colony in Mexico. During the war Fred had been commissioned by C. D. Howe to paint the working-class heroes of munitions factories, mines and shipyards – only to find himself poignantly lacking the common touch. Of late, however, the family's cold war had begun to thaw. Taylor had even begun supporting the Art Gallery of Toronto. Not that he was going to pretend that Fred's mystifying world made any more sense to him now. 'Too bad some of the parts fell off,' he said, as the gallery's first Henry Moore was unveiled. 'I hope it's insured.'

A few weeks after the birth of Natalma's foal, a lumber and steamship magnate named George A. Pope Jr. sent a neurotic young colt named Decidedly to Horatio Luro. He had a terror of the starting gate, and Pope hoped that his old polo buddy could somehow persuade Decidedly he was a racehorse.

Once again, Luro showed his intuition with a maladjusted thoroughbred. Himself a victim of chronic stress, perhaps he felt a personal empathy with such animals. By surreptitious degrees Decidedly was taught to enjoy the training environment. Eventually Luro considered him ready for a race. Next morning, an irate Pope was on the phone. He did not appreciate his horses winning at 24–1 without being advised to have a bet. Luro soon hosed down the flames. Pope should be positive: he might just have a smart horse here.

This was trademark Luro. John Fulton, one of his later assistants, would loiter around the barn after his shift purely to hear his boss on the phone. 'It was a work of art,' Fulton said. 'By the time the call was finished, the owner would almost be apologising for his horse taking up a stall.' He remembered only one occasion when Luro was lost for words. A filly had been lined up for a gamble at Atlantic City, and all was going according to plan as she galloped clear in the stretch. Suddenly, between reaching for his jacket and leaving for the winner's circle, Luro found that she was nowhere to be seen. For some reason – Fulton thought a duck might have wandered onto the track – the filly had abruptly jumped the hedge, discarded her rider and fallen into the infield lake. Unbelievably, her tangled tack dragged her under barely three feet of water, and her thrashings proved fatal. Luro was incredulous. 'So what am I supposed to tell my owner?' he asked. 'Sorry, we didn't win the bet. And oh, by the way, your filly drowned.'

Decidedly's preparation for the Kentucky Derby, the following spring, was one of his trainer's masterpieces. Luro confined him to very light workouts, short and sharp. He wanted to keep the horse hungry for action. This represented a departure from the alien methods Luro had imported from South America, which tended to build stamina with longer, steadier workouts. In his warm-up races, he asked his jockey to conserve Decidedly's energy until closing up late from the rear. In his famous axiom, Luro did not want to 'squeeze the lemon dry'.

There were a lot of fast horses in the Derby that year, and Luro intended to let them burn each other out before Bill Hartack pounced late on Decidedly. And while Hartack was a rider who seldom held his tongue, Luro could trust him to hold his nerve. Sure enough, as the front-runners imploded, Decidedly came bounding through from nowhere to take a full second off the race record. Hartack proved sour as ever. His principal satisfaction was the defeat of the favourite, a horse he had ridden until sacked by its owner. Invited to smile for the cameras, Hartack scowled. 'I never smile over a Derby,' he said. 'In fact, I never smile over anything.' Then he grinned. Luro, likewise, chose his moment of triumph to reiterate his maverick status. 'Some people laugh at me because I do things in the Argentine manner,' he said. 'But the Señor, he gets the job done today.'

In his own way, Northern Dancer was also out of step with convention. In any orthodox judgement, Natalma's foal was far too small to develop into a top-class racehorse; some 40lbs below the average as a yearling, when nobody proved willing to meet Taylor's $25,000 reserve. But he was well put together, full of character and, of course, had that very deep pedigree. Sent to Luro's satellite barn in Toronto, supervised by 'Peaches' Fleming, his initial progress was retarded by a cracked heel. That suited Luro. The colt was still raw, he needed time. Leaving for his August holiday in Europe, he told Fleming to keep Northern Dancer under wraps until his return. But Taylor noticed newspaper reports of his workouts and ordered Fleming to bring forward his debut. Northern Dancer would end up being given nine starts in just four months.

Both the horse and his handlers were slow to learn about the best use of his energy. He was racing very aggressively – showing the trademark Nearctic dash – and was worn down in the closing stages of two early races. But there was no doubting his raw class, notably when cutting loose from halfway to win Canada's richest juvenile prize at Woodbine in October by half-a-dozen lengths. Next tried in New York, he made all the running in a race that often produced a Kentucky Derby colt. It seemed that this little bundle of muscle could have a legitimate shot.

Nonetheless, Luro was alarmed. Northern Dancer would never last the extra distance in the Derby unless he learned to restrain himself. Worse, he was showing signs of the same hoof problem that had hindered his sire. And a horse only ever gets one chance at the Kentucky Derby. (All Classics are confined to three-year-olds.) Then, fortuitously, Luro read an article about a Californian blacksmith who had pioneered a new treatment and had him flown across the continent. After a seven-hour operation, Northern Dancer was pronounced fit to begin his Derby preparation in the Florida sunshine. Now that his hoof was sorted, all that remained was to send for the Shoe.

Bill Shoemaker seemed born to ride the little horse. He had arrived into the world weighing 1lb 15oz, and only survived because his grandmother put him in a shoebox on an open oven door. Raised in a sharecropper's shack, he was eight years old when he flung down a hoe in the Texas dust and announced that there had to be a better way to make a living. Now, all of 4ft 11in and 95lbs, he was a Goliath of the Turf, the number one rider in North America: top earner for the sixth year running. If Northern Dancer was going to punch above his weight, the Shoe was the obvious man to have in his corner.

In January 1964, Shoemaker agreed to ride Northern Dancer in his main Derby trials. Luro was delighted by the way the colt was training: so obliging, so hardy, that he could be treated like a trireme oarsman. Had Luro put Decidedly on the same schedule, the horse would have dug a tunnel out of the barn. But Northern Dancer just came back for more. In each of his three races before his last big rehearsal, the Florida Derby, he won more impressively. Luro was burnishing this little nugget brighter every day.

Yet on the eve of the Florida Derby months of patient planning seemed to be squandered in a bare minute. Northern Dancer's regular exercise rider was unavailable and his replacement was overwhelmed – either by the responsibility, or by the sheer gusto of his mount. Either way, what was supposed to be a single pirouette suddenly turned into a full-blooded Charleston: 5 furlongs in 58 seconds. Though Northern Dancer still managed to win the next day, Luro was adamant that he had done so on half a tank of fuel. The time was mediocre, and Shoemaker seemed sceptical. It turned out that he had already made discreet soundings about Hill Rise, the principal Kentucky Derby hope of California. He now decided to make the switch.

Hill Rise was the perfect foil: a burly, raking animal with a relentless stride. Out west they were talking about him as a monster. In his own key trial, the Santa Anita Derby, he had devoured his field by six lengths. And if it was bad enough for Luro to lose his jockey, what made things worse was the fact that Hill Rise had once been sent to his own barn – and Luro had sent him straight back. Like Decidedly, Hill Rise was owned by Pope. Luro had been invited to pick out a two-year-old from his paddocks and opted for a precocious little chestnut. When the lorry arrived, however, it contained a big, backward bay. Luro saw at once that it was the wrong horse, and told Pope's men to return him to the ranch. Hill Rise was instead sent to a veteran trainer named Bill Finnegan. 'Hill Rise may not have impressed Luro when he got out of that van last year,' Pope said after the Santa Anita Derby. 'But he probably scared him to death today.'

Pope's one concern was that Don Pierce, his rider, might suffer an attack of vertigo on Hill Rise. He had never ridden for such high stakes. And now here was the Shoe himself, telling Pope that he wanted to ride Hill Rise. Pope decided that he could not afford to be sentimental. Pierce was shattered – and so was Taylor. Shoemaker's defection was a massive blow to morale. But Luro comforted him that there was an obvious replacement. For the thought that he might win the Derby on a horse rejected by Shoemaker was enough to make even Hartack smile.

His mother died on Christmas morning. The brakes on a truck coming the other way had failed. Bill Hartack was five years old. The following year, their house burned down. It was not insured. Rural Pennsylvania lay bleeding under the weight of the Depression. Later in life, Hartack said he was grateful for the severity of his upbringing: everything thrown at him then made the rest of his life a walk in the park. 'I used to take the stick a lot to Billy,' his father would remember proudly. 'I don't believe in letting no kid have his way. He'd do anything I tell him. He had to.'

Hartack and his two sisters were raised in a cabin without heating or electricity. They had a few chickens and pigs, the odd cow; a patch of corn, another of potatoes – all tended by the boy, before and after school, while his father toiled in the mine. Later on, Hartack would show uncharacteristic warmth when working with boys' charities. It was as though he were trying to retrieve a lost childhood. Few kids at school had been forced to grow up as fast, and they found Hartack wary and introverted. Smart as well, but college was obviously out of the question. Even so, he had to get away somehow. Anything but the mine.

He was very small, barely 7 stone, and someone suggested he might find work on a racetrack. An outlandish notion: there was no racing anywhere round there, and Hartack had reached eighteen without knowing the first thing about thoroughbreds. He took the bus to Charles Town, where there was a half-mile 'bull ring' huddled in grimy snow. The first race he ever saw resulted in a six-horse pile-up on a frozen track. Yet Hartack felt immediately at home. The trainer who took him on, Junie Corbin, not only showed him the ropes as an exercise rider, but at last provided him with something resembling paternal affection.

For the next couple of years Hartack enjoyed the nomadic life of the stable, moving from one leaking barn to the next, the arrival of the racing circus enlivening provincial towns in Maryland, Ohio and West Virginia. Corbin realised the kid had a natural touch; you could put him on anything. The very idea of racing petrified Hartack, but his third mount was a winner. It was amazing to have someone believe in him the way Corbin did; his counsel stayed with Hartack for ever. Ride on your wits. Look for the rail. And stay honest. 'If you do your best on every horse you ride, no matter where you finish, you'll never have to worry about looking somebody in the face,' he said.

That first winner was in October 1952. He was not quite twenty. In 1955, Hartack rode 417 winners – a tally only reached once before, by the inevitable Shoemaker a couple of years previously. Hartack had a demonic drive, and never merely hoped to win. He spoke contemptuously of all the people he had seen living on hope, on dreams. He *made* things happen.

Many felt that his astonishing rise brought out the worst in him. They found him so lacking in respect or modesty that he seemed almost to relish disfavour. In his eyes, he was simply being true to himself – and to Corbin. 'Don't take a stand on anything unless you're sure,' his mentor had said. 'If you're not sure, say you're not sure. But if you believe something to be a fact and you back down, you're gonna be just like everybody else. Make them prove you're wrong.'

It was the same with the stewards or the press. Sure, he could butter up ignorant scribblers for the sake of his image. But who cared about image? He knew who he was. Cold-eyed, his lips curling, he hoarded clippings in which he had been misquoted. Nor did he stifle his waspish intensity even with owners and trainers. If losing made him mad, well, that was exactly why they should hire his services. Not because he was a nice guy. And, of course, if the horse was no good, or lacked courage or condition, he would not pretend otherwise. If that caused a trainer a problem with his owner, so be it. His agents did not tend to last very long. They were either peremptorily fired, or quit in despair. Said one: 'I spend most of my time trailing around after him, apologising.'

There was something heroic about Hartack's obstinacy, his refusal to dissemble. He confessed himself no stylist, a Marciano not an Ali. 'He looked like hell on a horse,' remembered one old hand. 'But they sure ran for him.' Needless to say, he fell out with many rival jockeys. Hartack, said one on retiring, 'doesn't have a friend in the jocks' room'. Nothing suited Hartack better than the fact that his Kentucky Derby breakthrough, on Iron Liege in 1957, had been achieved at the expense of Shoemaker, who was beaten by a nose on Gallant Man after momentarily mistaking the finish line.

Whenever things went against him, Hartack's enemies exulted. He would read sanctimonious commentaries in the press about all the bridges he had burned. In 1963, a year after Decidedly had become his third Kentucky Derby winner in six runnings, he could not find a mount in any Triple Crown race. It was payback time. 'Whatever Happened to Bill Hartack?' exulted one magazine.

But Luro knew that nothing is as fierce as a cornered tiger. He had fallen out with plenty of people, including some of his biggest patrons. If an owner tried to interfere with a horse's programme, he was liable to draw back the curtains one morning and find the animal grazing his front lawn. Jockeys knew his wrath, too. Once Luro set up a horse for a bet at Saratoga, and told his jockey to come with a late run. He watched in amazement as the horse was gunned into the lead until folding, exhausted. When the rider returned, and began his excuses, Luro grabbed him by the throat in full view of the stands. He was suspended for thirty days. 'Gentlemen,' he told the stewards, 'I am a lover – not a fighter.'

Hartack had been made to fight for everything and fed candidly off his hate. It was a form of honesty. 'Don't try to get me to compromise,' he said. 'Because if you do, you're gonna get nothing. I don't care if I ruin myself.' Whatever else that made Bill Hartack, it made him a very dangerous adversary.

A Day at the Races

Churchill Downs, 2 May 1964

*Kids had been pouring into the infield since 8 a.m. During the 1950s, this
had remained a leisured haven of mint juleps, picnics and parasols. Year by
year, however, an occasion long redolent of the Old South was being infil-
trated by the heady reek of unrest and hedonism among the young. This
was the first Kentucky Derby since the assassination of President Kennedy,
and the hordes pullulating behind an eight-foot chain-link fence were exper-
imenting, socially, in a spirit of rebellion that would one day culminate,
politically, in race riots and draft-burning.*

*Like its Epsom template, the race had become a window on national life.
One reporter, touring the infield at a typical Kentucky Derby of the 1960s,
observed: 'There is probably no place in America where ladies and gentlemen
at their tea, a dowager reading a novel in a lounge chair, gaudily clad bandsmen,
soldiers in combat clothes, kids perched on 12-foot ladders, the beatnik fringe of
the college set and lanky young men in ten-gallon hats could merge and mingle
so freely.' By the end of the decade, the scene would be rendered immortal by
Hunter S. Thompson in a magazine article that became a primer in gonzo
journalism: not so much a stream of consciousness as a trickle of viscera. But
such lucidity as Thompson could salvage from his bourbon-stained notes became
a lasting monument to what he dismissed as a 'jaded, atavistic freakout with
nothing to recommend it except a very saleable "tradition"'.*

*Many of the 100,000 who flocked to see Hill Rise and Northern Dancer
experienced this historic day in the same haze. Let us follow them, then,
out of Louisville:*

Out to the track in a cab, avoid that terrible parking in people's front yards,
$25 each, toothless old men on the street with big signs: PARK HERE,

321

flagging cars in the yard. 'That's fine, boy, never mind the tulips.' . . .
Sidewalks full of people all moving in the same direction, towards Churchill
Downs. Kids hauling coolers and blankets, teenyboppers in tight pink shorts
. . . black dudes in white felt hats with leopard-skin bands, cops waving
traffic along.

Plunge after them into the clubhouse bars:

Along with the politicians, society belles and local captains of commerce, every
half-mad dingbat who ever had any pretensions to anything at all within
five hundred miles of Louisville will show up there to get strutting drunk
and slap a lot of backs and generally make himself obvious.

And then out into the mayhem of the infield:

Total chaos, no way to see the race, not even the track . . . nobody cares.
Big lines at the outdoor betting windows, then stand back to watch winning
numbers flash on the big board, like a giant bingo game. Old blacks arguing
about bets; 'Hold on there, I'll handle this' (waving pint of whiskey, fistful
of dollar bills); girl riding piggyback, T-shirt says, 'Stolen from Fort Lauderdale
Jail.' Thousands of teenagers, group singing 'Let the Sun Shine In,' ten
soldiers guarding the American flag . . . Far across the track the clubhouse
looks like a postcard from the Kentucky Derby.

This time there was a rebel out on the track as well. Seventy of the previous
eighty-nine Derby winners had been bred in Kentucky. To Bluegrass professionals, Northern Dancer had emerged from the Arctic. The little horse was
also trying to unravel the physical stereotype for a Classic winner. Factor in
Hartack in the saddle, and it was an outliers' convention.

Northern Dancer, moreover, was all about speed. He won his final
rehearsal with such breezy insouciance that people wondered whether his
greatest asset would also be his Achilles heel. For when he tried that extra
furlong for the first time, Hill Rise would really be rolling.

During the week, the atmosphere had been febrile. Luro did his best to
contain his colt's simmering energies, sometimes even producing an impostor
when photographers clamoured for a picture. Luro derived great satisfaction
from extolling the physique of a plain old hack, while his real champion
– the jaunty little character with a blaze skewed impudently aslant his face
– tore quietly at his hayrack. He was also indebted to the placid influence

*of Northern Dancer's groom, Bill Brevard, who had been with Luro since
the Princequillo days.*

*Not that the reporters were too bothered about seeing a horse, when his
trainer was so exotic. Luro was now sixty-three, his hair thinning, but still
cut a dash in his tweed hacking jacket and cap, set off by a shirt of pink
or yellow, as he picked his way through the Derby week parties like a
nineteenth-century general at a cavalry ball. Nor did he disguise his confidence. For months, every step taken by Northern Dancer had been dictated
by a single imperative: to reach the limit of his capacity at 4.30 p.m. on
this afternoon, and not a moment before.*

*The eleven runners were led through the tunnel onto the track, and the
band struck up the race anthem: 'My Old Kentucky Home'. Northern
Dancer responded with a spirited buck. The mighty Hill Rise, his black
coat gleaming like a snowy peak, was hot favourite at 7–5; Northern Dancer
next at 3–1. There was a fleeting moment of alarm at the gate, as the little
horse backed off, but again he was just reminding everyone of his rights. A
moment later, he strolled into the gate on his own terms – and suddenly
his ears filled with the metallic call to arms, the shrill bell and clattering
gates, and the little Canadian speedball was rolling.*

*Hartack dropped onto the rail, a good five lengths off the lead; Shoemaker
ranged alongside on the big horse. Up front, they were smoking. Northern
Dancer had settled beautifully. In the back stretch, still five furlongs out,
Hartack made a critical manoeuvre, breaking wide while he could. He did
not want Shoemaker to trap him on the rail. Instead it was Hill Rise who
would be briefly short of room, hampered as one of the spent front-runners
dropped out. Swinging into the stretch, Hartack seized the moment. He
knew he had a start on his big rival, and would now try to kill him off
by detonating a burst of speed. Northern Dancer hurtled through the ninth
of the ten furlongs in eleven seconds, his squat frame barrelling forward on
that choppy, dozen-a-dime stride. Hill Rise, in contrast, needed a moment
or two to gather his long limbs into top gear. One slap on the shoulder,
another on the rump, and suddenly Northern Dancer's brisker gait had
carried him two lengths clear.*

*But Shoemaker was after him by now, and there still remained that
uncharted tenth furlong. Gradually but inexorably, Hill Rise was eating into
Northern Dancer's advantage. A hundred yards out, it was down to a length.*

Hartack first sensed his challenger through the crescendo from the stands. This was it: high noon, the showdown everyone had come to see. Now Hartack could hear Shoemaker's whip; now the snorting of Hill Rise, this outraged giant, bearing down on the insolent runt who had broken out of his herd. As the post neared, Hartack sensed that there was nothing left. They drifted towards the rail; it was just a case of trying to hold him together. Hill Rise plunged his long neck alongside Hartack's heel; the next stride, it was past his knee. In the corner of his eye, Hartack sensed Shoemaker throwing everything at one last effort. Both men shared a single thought: 'Nearly there.' And then one of them was.

Eddie Taylor proudly led Canada's champion into the winner's circle. The molten duel with Hill Rise had forged a new record time: for the first time ever, the race billed as 'the most exciting two minutes in sport' had actually been run in two minutes flat. And Northern Dancer had held out by a neck.

It was Hartack's fourth Kentucky Derby success from just six rides, not one of which had started favourite. Shoemaker, stuck on two winners, had now been beaten on the favourite for the fourth time. Yet he was not ready to repent of his defection. Hartack had enjoyed all the breaks. He insisted that Hill Rise was still the best horse, and next time he would prove it.

The rematch would take place just a fortnight later, in the Preakness Stakes. This time Hill Rise never picked up and was ultimately caught for second. 'Northern Dancer is just too much horse,' Shoemaker conceded. Yet Hartack confided that his mount felt 'dead tired' by the line, and Luro promptly astounded Taylor by declaring that Northern Dancer would not bother with the final leg of the Triple Crown. At a mile and a half, the Belmont Stakes would be too brutish a test of stamina. There was uproar. The Triple Crown was the defining quest for any American thoroughbred, and had not been won since 1948. Taylor quickly overruled Luro. But the fact was that Northern Dancer had only got away even with the Derby distance through Hartack's masterly tactics; and had since soaked up another draining experience in the Preakness. Hartack, for once, seemed wholly resigned after Northern Dancer duly failed in the Belmont.

But Northern Dancer bounced back just a fortnight later to perform his civic duty in the Queen's Plate. To be fair, he was so superior to his indigenous rivals that it amounted to little more than a lap of honour. Having been issued the key to the city of Toronto — carved from a large carrot — the hometown champion coasted home by seven and a half lengths. Taylor, deeply hurt by his hostile reception the previous year, was now warmly acclaimed for the glory he had bestowed upon the Canadian Turf.

Soon afterwards Northern Dancer developed a tendon problem, and was retired to Taylor's Oshawa farm for a fee of $10,000. There would be no such fresh start for Hartack. The 115 winners he rode that year represented his lowest tally since his debut season. By 1969, he was reduced to 55 – yet these included a fifth Kentucky Derby in just nine attempts, on Majestic Prince. Eddie Arcaro, the only other man to reach that mark, needed 21 rides. At $250,000, Majestic Prince had been the most expensive yearling in history. Yet he proved to be worth every cent. Not so much because he won over $400,000 in prize money, as because he was then syndicated as a stallion for $1.8 million. In Ireland, an ambitious young stud manager took note.

23

'Bang him on the nose early, Bobby. Make his eyes water.'

JOHN MAGNIER WAS son-in-law of arguably the most accomplished trainer of all time, in Vincent O'Brien; and together they would build the greatest commercial stud in history. But it is instructive of the industry he transformed that Magnier, a freak of acuity, should ultimately owe so much to a chaotic chancer like Billy McDonald.

Short and chubby, eyes clenched in a grin, McDonald was forever on the point of some triumph or disaster. A life-changing prize always tantalised him at the end of the highwire: a bet, a woman, a champion racehorse. McDonald reeled uproariously forward, balanced by a bottle of champagne in each hand. Before pronouncing himself a bloodstock agent, the Ulsterman had sold Rolls-Royces. Both vocations helped to establish him as a Hollywood court jester. Friends are adamant that it was McDonald, not Don Rickles, who made Frank Sinatra promise to come over to his table and say hello, in order to impress his date – only to turn round and say: 'Not now, Frank, can't you see I'm busy?' McDonald was even indulged with a small role in a forgotten racetrack comedy, *Let it Ride*.* On one occasion, having hired a yacht to dazzle a couple of girls, McDonald discovered that the friend he relied on to carry off the stunt was likewise wholly ignorant of sailing. His lovely guests sobbing in terror, McDonald wrecked the yacht on Alcatraz.

Yet here he was, in the spring of 1976, scouting the Bluegrass with Magnier and O'Brien: two of the very greatest horsemen in Irish history, engaged in a high-stakes experiment that would

---

* Though not, sadly, as the punter who exclaims that he would stake his life on a horse – only to be admonished that the minimum stake is $2.

revolutionise the modern Turf. True, McDonald was along for the ride principally as sidekick to Robert Sangster, the English tycoon bankrolling an imminent raid on the yearling sale at nearby Keeneland. But as they inspected the lots to be sent up from Kentucky's premier nursery of champions, it was McDonald who stumbled across the combination that would open up the genetic safe. Claiborne Stud had recently lost both its formidable patriarchs: 'Bull' Hancock and Bold Ruler. The latter, the outstanding American stallion of the 1960s, shared a grandfather with Northern Dancer: Nearco. Bold Ruler and his sons between them produced seven Kentucky Derby winners in the 1970s alone, including the great Secretariat. But Bold Ruler had died in 1971; and the farm's owner followed abruptly the next year.

Within weeks of taking over, at just twenty-three, Hancock's son Seth had arranged the unprecedented $6 million syndication of Secretariat to stand at Claiborne when his career ended. (And that was *before* he won the Kentucky Derby.) Then, bringing his first batch of yearlings to Keeneland that summer, Seth set another record: one of the last sons of Bold Ruler became the most expensive horse ever sold at auction. This colt, in turn, proved a fateful spur to the men now examining Claiborne's latest crop of yearlings. He had been top of O'Brien's shortlist at Keeneland that year, and Magnier provisionally valued him at $500,000. Sangster proposed a neon statement of intent: they should blow everyone out of the water by making that their opening bid, just $10,000 short of the all-time record. But Sangster was then bewildered when a rival syndicate promptly answered this show of machismo with a bid of $600,000. O'Brien urged his men to call their bluff, to try one more, but found Sangster staring at the floor in mute terror.

It proved a lesson bitterly learned. His purchasers named the colt Wajima, and Magnier watched him develop into the perfect prototype for his masterplan. It was irrelevant that even the big races subsequently won by Wajima did not quite cover his cost as a yearling. Instead it was his syndication for stud, at $7.2 million, that made him a bargain – even at a price never paid before. And they had passed him up.

So here they were again, back at Claiborne. Sangster watched in fascination as the master stockmen, Magnier and O'Brien, murmured remarks that might render something of their ineffable intuition to the layman. But McDonald cut to the chase. He sought out the yearling manager, Gus Koch, slipped him a couple of bills, and asked which *he* reckoned best of the crop. The answer was as surprising as it would prove inspired: 'The little Bold Reason filly, every time.'

Shortly before the Keeneland auction that July, Sangster celebrated his fortieth birthday. At the same time he received the final third of his inheritance as only son of a pools magnate. When first introduced to Magnier, in the bar at Haydock Park five years previously, Sangster had suddenly realised how little he really understood about the hobby that had captivated him over the past decade. Though Magnier was then just twenty-three, he exuded preternatural authority.

Horses were in Magnier's blood. His great-grandfather had walked a stallion from farm to farm along the Blackwater Valley in Co. Cork; and his father had turned Cottage, winner of a single race, into a champion jumps sire. If Magnier seemed sage beyond his years, it was hardly surprising: his father's premature death had obliged him to leave school at sixteen, to run the stud. By the time he married, he was beginning to grasp a possible way to dovetail his own genius with that of his father-in-law.

Vincent O'Brien had saddled two of the last four Derby winners, both imported from North America. Sir Ivor had been picked out as a yearling by Bull Hancock, but Nijinsky was found by O'Brien himself. An American platinum magnate, Charles Engelhard, had sent O'Brien to a yearling sale in Toronto to assess a colt by Ribot, the last champion bred by Federico Tesio. O'Brien was not impressed and briefly resented a wasted journey. But then he noticed a big, rangy chestnut from the second crop of Northern Dancer. He was instantly besotted and implored Engelhard to buy this one. The colt cost $84,000 and, christened Nijinsky, in 1970 became the first horse in thirty-five years to win the English Triple Crown. Nijinsky was then syndicated to stand at Claiborne for $5.4 million dollars – and Magnier assured an incredulous Sangster that this represented a bargain.

At that time, stallion syndication entailed the sale of forty shares (thirty-two in North America) each representing one mating per season. The value of these 'nominations' was set at three times the stallion's fee, and your annual breeding right could either be used for one of your own mares or sold to another breeder. If the stallion could maintain his reputation – and so his fee – beyond his third season at stud, each subsequent covering would be pure gravy. In a booming yearling market, moreover, investors might conceivably recover their entire stake in one go. Each share in Nijinsky, for instance, had been valued at $170,000 – based on an opening stallion fee of not quite $60,000. But bigger money was now being paid for yearlings so routinely that E. P. Taylor had willingly spent $340,000 for two of the thirty-two shares in Nijinsky – a colt he had sold for just $84,000 two years earlier.

Magnier had now begun to wonder about the gains available if you could find a stallion before he had even begun to advertise his ability on the racetrack. Even the most expensive yearlings, with top-class genes and physique, cost far less than a proven runner on the track. Inevitably there would be many duds. But the few that did make the grade would generate such astronomical profits – not least with the Irish government now exempting stallion revenue from taxation – they would absorb those losses. All Magnier needed was the right backing.

Every bloodstock professional knows the orthodox prescriptions of equine anatomy, and indulges different blemishes according to his own prejudices and available funds. But the real masters seek something less tangible – something found in no manual, something they could never put into words. Consider how inadequately you would convey the overall éclat of Cary Grant or Grace Kelly, merely by delineating angle of neck or length of limb. The most intelligible shorthand, for the layman, is to seek 'the look of eagles'. But even this has long been worn to triteness.

To Vincent O'Brien, a horse's physical symmetries had to be complemented by something in the eyes and demeanour. McDonald once claimed that O'Brien told him: 'The eyes, Billy, are the mirror of the soul.' If the words seem suspiciously redolent of McDonald's five-leaf clover, O'Brien would certainly stare at a yearling for long minutes until sensing some intimation or deficiency of kindness, courage or intelligence. He especially sought masculinity in the head of a colt: evidence that the animal might stand up to the stress of competition, travel and crowds. And the movement, of course, had to be balletic.

It was an innate gift. His father had a nearly occult reputation as a dealer in Co. Cork. O'Brien started training after his father died in 1943, leaving the family farm to a couple of older brothers. One of his earliest horses was a son of the Magniers' stallion, Cottage. O'Brien sent his brother Phonsie to fetch the youngster off a bog and drive him home in a trap. Named Cottage Rake, he won the Cheltenham Gold Cup three times. A meticulous and guarded nature meanwhile gave such lethal precision to O'Brien's betting that by 1951 he could afford 280 overgrown acres and a dilapidated Georgian farmhouse at Ballydoyle, near Cashel in Co. Tipperary. Here, impossibly, he crowned his career as a jumps trainer by producing a winning ticket for that unaccountable lottery, the Grand National, three years running with Early Mist, Royal Tan and Quare Times.

This was too much for some in the Irish sport, who decided that this provincial interloper must be too good to be true. Summoned before the Turf Club to explain perceived inconsistencies in the running of his horses, O'Brien was suspended for three months. The absence of any coherent case against him convinced him that he was the victim of a jealous vendetta.

When he switched to Flat racing, the cycle soon repeated itself. He achieved immediate, stunning success – notably with Ballymoss, winner of the 1958 Prix de l'Arc de Triomphe – and was soon back in trouble with the Turf Club. This time it was more serious: one of his winners failed a drugs test, and O'Brien was required to hand over the yard to Phonsie for a year. His offence was so opaque that the Turf Club meekly settled his libel suit out of court. Even when he won his first Derby at Epsom in 1962, with Larkspur, O'Brien was dragged from the winner's enclosure to refute some pettifogging suspicions before the stewards. Sometimes he asked himself whether he should have taken up Bull Hancock's invitation to train in America; or just confine himself to a couple of dozen horses for family and friends. But then his daughter's fiancé came up with this intriguing new project. Everyone else thought that the yearling market had inflated into a perilous bubble. Magnier insisted that the real boom had barely begun.

O'Brien had bought a controlling stake in a stud near Ballydoyle from Tim Vigors, who had once shot down a Heinkel while wearing pyjamas and a silk dressing gown. Its name was Coolmore, and this became the banner for an amalgamation with Magnier's own farms. Next they sent out their new backer, Sangster, to recruit other investors.

After the Wajima debacle of 1973, Sangster investigated the subsequent fortunes of the ten most expensive yearlings in each of the last ten years. He calculated that the only way to guarantee a profit, through syndication of those that made the grade, would have been to buy them all. In other words, they had to corner the market – in colts by Northern Dancer, in particular. O'Brien adored the combination of blood and guts in his progeny: they had the genes, and they had the constitution. Northern Dancer's first crop, conceived in Canada, produced sixteen winners from eighteen starters – including, incredibly, ten at stakes level. His very first foal won eight out of eight as a two-year-old. His second starter broke a track record that had stood for twenty-two years at Santa Anita.

Once O'Brien had identified a target they were not to falter – no matter how high the bidding might go. In their opening barrage, at Keeneland in 1975, the new partners spent $1.8 million on twelve lots. Now, returning for the 1976 sale, O'Brien picked out another dozen colts. They bought them all, as well as a handful of fillies with breeding potential. The whole haul was just short of $2.5 million. But one of the fillies cost only $40,000: the Bold Reason filly pointed out to Billy McDonald by Gus Koch at Claiborne. Despite her lack of stature, Koch had noticed that she always outran the rest of the herd when he brought the feed into the paddock: she just behaved like a natural racehorse.

It would be years before anyone grasped the significance of this acquisition. In the meantime, the filly – named Fairy Bridge – amply paid her way on the racecourse, rated the top two-year-old filly in Ireland after winning both starts in her first season. And her mother, Special, also introduced fresh distinction to their family tree by producing an elegant little colt by Northern Dancer. He was a top priority for O'Brien at the 1978 Keeneland sale and, considering how things had gone so far, nothing should have stopped his partners. After all, their 1975 harvest had included a spectacular vindication of Magnier's theories: a Northern Dancer colt out of a half-sister to Nijinsky, bred by E. P. Taylor. Named The Minstrel, he had proceeded to win the 1977 Epsom Derby before returning to Windfields for his stud career – Coolmore banking $4.5 million from Taylor for a half-stake. As a yearling, he had cost $200,000. Then there was Alleged, who had actually been unsold at $34,000 at the 1975 sale but was subsequently traced to California by McDonald, and bought privately for five times as much. Alleged went on to win the Arc twice, and was syndicated for $16 million. Everything was working like clockwork.

But others were cottoning on. The 1978 Keeneland sale registered a 45 per cent hike in average prices – and the Coolmore team somehow missed out on Special's son at $1.3 million. Only one yearling had ever been sold for more but O'Brien scolded his partners that they had vowed *never* to back down. If necessary, they should have gone to $2 million. Sure enough, the little colt had a brief but stellar racing career for a French trainer, as Nureyev, before being syndicated for $14 million.

The consequences of this episode were momentous. On the one hand, it would commit Sangster to stop at nothing – even when the market went haywire. On the other, it gave fresh glamour to Fairy Bridge, who followed her mother for a tryst with Northern Dancer. The resulting foal was unsurprisingly compact: both his parents had lacked bulk. But he strongly evoked his sire – a darker bay, perhaps, but the same sturdy build and a vivid white streak down his face. They named him Sadler's Wells.

Around this time Sangster gave an interview that betrayed a perilous complacency. At forty-two, dimple-chinned and stocky, he was months into a second marriage; Alleged had just won his second Arc. He proudly related how he had decided 'to get hold of the racing business by the neck, and shake it'. He gloated that everyone had waited for him to crash and burn. As it was, Alleged would have an earning capacity at stud of $3 million per annum.

For all his lack of airs – his mumbling tones so different from the clipped enunciations of the English racing aristocracy – Sangster sounded just a little too arrogant when asked about those trying to emulate his success. 'We are light years ahead,' he scoffed. And it did seem as though even the vertiginous cycles of the market remained self-fulfilling. As a result, the ageing Northern Dancer's stud fee multiplied tenfold between 1979 and 1984 – from $50,000 to $500,000 per mare. He had started out, back in 1965, at $10,000.

Though the Keeneland average soared nearly 30 per cent in 1979, Sangster's partnership accounted for almost 20 per cent of turnover. One of their purchases was a Northern Dancer colt out of an E. P. Taylor mare, for $1 million. Storm Bird became a champion juvenile and was hot favourite for the 2000 Guineas when a disgruntled former employee crept back into Ballydoyle and sheared off his mane and tail. Dejected and debilitated, the horse suffered various problems thereafter and disappointed on his only subsequent start. Nonetheless, Coolmore managed to sell a 75 per cent stake for $21 million.

Once again, a single jackpot had covered a multitude of sins. The fact was, however, that the hiatus between The Minstrel and Storm Bird – graduates of the 1975 and 1979 sales respectively – had raised the stakes unnervingly. And the goal posts were about to be moved, for everybody.

In his younger days, Sangster had been an accomplished amateur boxer. Now, at the Keeneland sale of 1981, he remembered sparring sessions in a Soho gym with Freddie Mills – and the old champion's advice about unsettling an opponent short on experience: 'Bang him on the nose early, Bobby. Make his eyes water.' He looked at the ropes round the dais, where each yearling stood to be auctioned. It even looked as though a prizefight was about to be staged. Sangster resolved to remove the gloves.

Just over the road from the sales complex, inside the airport perimeter, a Boeing 727 brooded as symbol of a new threat to his racing empire: the private plane of the Maktoum brothers, sons of the ruler of Dubai. In 1970, oil still averaged $3 a barrel; a decade later it had reached $35. And Dubai's oil production, from an initial strike in 1966, was building to a peak exceeding 400,000 barrels a day. Though only third of the four brothers, there was no mistaking Sheikh Mohammed as their charismatic young captain. It was just four years since he had bought a train ticket from Victoria to Brighton. The racetrack here, high above the sea, still evoked 'Pinkie' Brown and his mob in *Brighton Rock*. Nobody could suspect the opulent background of the anonymous twenty-seven-year-old Arab who greeted a filly named Hatta in the unsaddling enclosure. His first winner had cost him 6,200 guineas.

The Maktoum brothers now intended to raise the stakes. When a brother to Storm Bird entered the ring, Sangster rolled up his sleeves. Sheikh Mohammed's agent, a former wartime spymaster named Dick Warden, found every bid answered so promptly by the Sangster partnership that he ended up offering $3.4 million – doubling the previous record of $1.7 million. But that was not enough. Sangster's man came straight back with a bid of $3.5 million, and this time Sheikh Mohammed walked away: Sangster had slugged him squarely on the nose. Even so, twenty minutes later he came back to buy another Northern Dancer colt, at $3.3 million. If anything, Sangster was the more shaken.

Time would show that the Maktoums had the better of those exchanges. Storm Bird's brother proved disappointing, whereas their colt would win them a first Classic, as Shareef Dancer, in the 1983 Irish Derby. What is more, he was then syndicated for a record $40 million. But Sangster had such a cluster of big winners around this time that he could prolong an illusion of invulnerability. Golden Fleece, a $775,000 Nijinsky colt, was syndicated for $28 million after winning the 1982 Derby; and in the same year O'Brien's twenty-five-year-old son, David, showed an inherited dexterity as a trainer by winning both the Irish and French Derbys with Assert. He had cost just £16,000 – and was syndicated to Windfields for $24 million.

Sangster landed another right hook at Keeneland that summer, forcing the sheikh to surrender a Nijinsky colt for another new record of $4.25 million. But he still had no idea that he faced a rival wholly beyond his ken – in terms of resources and ambition. Together these rendered the sheikh almost immune to the bottom line. The years to come would reveal a man animated by a profound sense

of his cultural heritage: he even named his breeding empire Darley
Stud after the merchant who bought an Arabian stallion from his
Bedouin ancestors.

Sangster's mistake was to presume himself engaged purely in a
test of financial virility. As prices spiralled out of control, spectators
felt the same unease as they might at a real heavyweight bout. They
flinched at the visceral endurance of the ego. They wondered about
the ethics of it, too. How could any horse be worth so much, never
mind one whose ability could only be measured by hunches? But
nobody could look away.

The crowning folly came at Keeneland in 1983. Lot 308, a
Northern Dancer colt out of a mare named My Bupers, needed
just five bids and 45 seconds to set a new record at $4.5 million –
and Sangster's men did not even jump in until $5.3 million. The
auctioneer breathlessly trilled the numbers through the humid air
like banjo notes, up $100,000 a time. The galleries fell rapt, occa-
sionally breaking into a disbelieving roar at some new landmark.
Did these guys realise that the half-grown animal before them had
never even had a saddle on its back?

At $7.5 million, and again at $8 million, Sangster and his team
huddled in ashen conference. Sangster desperately promised to
increase his share: they could not back down. He was a man possessed,
his pride resisting all restraint. He ordered their agent on, all the
way to $9.5 million. Dick Warden rolled his eyes and offered $9.6
million on behalf of the Sheikh. Now Sangster played a last, desperate
card. He stood up and splayed all ten fingers, reaching $10 million
with a single bid of $400,000. And the digital board abruptly went
blank: it could only accommodate seven figures.

The packed arena responded in a tumult of cheers, whistles and
exclamation. These men were thrusting their millions at each other
like bleeding antlers. But if the sheer theatre was intoxicating, some
sensed its essential toxicity. This could become the alarm call to
wake the breeding industry to its untenable foundations.

Sure enough, Sangster's surrender – after Warden tottered back
out of Sheikh Mohammed's corner with a bid of $10.2 million –
spared him only future embarrassment. The colt, named Snaafi
Dancer, never even made it onto a racetrack. 'Nice little horse,' his

trainer concluded. 'But no bloody good.' An attempt to salvage something from his genes at stud proved futile. He was infertile. When that digital display had climbed from $9.6 million to zero, it was far closer to the truth than anyone could have realised.

Signing for the colt, Warden had quipped: 'You'll find ten cents extra a gallon on your petrol for this.' At the end of the sale, the Maktoums had bought twenty-six yearlings for $43 million; Sangster's men had mustered fourteen for $18 million. The men from the desert had drawn a line in the sand. The following year the sale average passed $600,000, up from $53,000 in 1975. The dozen Northern Dancer yearlings in the catalogue sold for an average of just under $3.5 million. And it so happened that two Northern Dancer colts stabled at Ballydoyle were about to rally to the cause. But even these contributed to a sense that Sangster had run out of chips at Keeneland: both were home-bred.

The presence in the stands of the grand old man himself said it all. Still debonair and erect, at eighty-three, Horatio Luro did not need an Edwardian dress code to introduce a vestige of the Belle Époque to the 1984 Derby. Among all the perms and sunglasses, the Señor lent a near sacerdotal quality to his morning coat and top hat. After all, that was exactly why he was here: to preside over a ritual.

For the odds-on favourite, from Ballydoyle, seemed to have been consecrated to this moment since the day he was named: a creature handsome enough to celebrate the man who had trained Northern Dancer. Even if El Gran Senor won, it would still be Luro who dominated the souvenir photographs. John Fulton remembered once joining his boss at a dinner in Paris, attended by royalty and aristocrats from all round Europe. 'But he was the centre of attention,' Fulton said. 'He was the one in the middle, talking four languages. No matter how important an owner might be, it was the owner who wanted to be seen with him . . . Apart from the charm, apart from the impeccable dress, he had that mystique, that intrigue.'

It must be said that even his admirers sometimes found Luro a little sly, and his feuds were Homeric. He faced some of his most important patrons in court – even a past lover, like Liz Whitney. At the same time he inspired great loyalty, in staff and peers alike. No other trainer could have got away with a stately retreat to Deauville or Baden-Baden every summer. But nor could anyone be better trusted to have a horse at its absolute best on a specific day, in six months' time – whether to land a bet or win a Derby. Luro was never hurried. For men and horses alike, it was speed that kills: both, he said, cracked up in 'the mad rat-race to the bank'.

As he watched El Gran Senor strolling the parade ring, no doubt Luro's mind went back to his grandsire. Perhaps Pete McCann had got closest, but E. P. Taylor's men between them plainly never got to the bottom of Nearctic. Northern Dancer had been one of only fourteen foals in his first crop, conceived at a fee of just $2,500. All fourteen won races, five at the elite stakes level. After Northern Dancer won the Kentucky Derby, Taylor was able to syndicate Nearctic for over $1 million to stand at Allaire du Pont's stud in Maryland. Du Pont was another of those gilded women, like Audrey Emery or Liz Whitney, who strolled onto the American Turf as though onto the set of *The Philadelphia Story*. She had even been a pioneer aviator, setting both endurance and altitude records for a female glider. Her Chesapeake City farm would remain home to Nearctic until his death, aged nineteen, in 1973. He sired 345 foals in fourteen crops, a very conservative tally by subsequent standards. (His grandson, Sadler's Wells, would produce over 2,000.) Astonishingly, 87 per cent of the Nearctic colts who made the racetrack were winners.

And now Luro was to anoint the obvious heir to that legacy. The previous month El Gran Senor had pulverised a vintage field in the 2000 Guineas. Form, pedigree and physique qualified him as the obvious replacement for his sire, now twenty-four years old. In fact, a syndicate had offered the mind-boggling sum of $40 million for a half-share. Their only condition was that El Gran Senor first strengthen his CV in the Derby.

Just as everyone suspected, Northern Dancer had indeed produced his principal scion in his 1981 crop. There was just one, critical, misapprehension. As Luro admired the champion elect at Epsom, his true heir was peering out of his stall back at Ballydoyle, wondering where his neighbour – who had been raised in the same paddock – might have been taken for the day.

★

If the roulette wheel had come up with Billy McDonald's number the day he staked a couple of bills on Gus Koch's insight, he never knew when to stop spinning. While he could talk his way out of many obligations, bookmakers and casinos were inclined to be stubborn – and at some stage McDonald had been forced to sell his own share in Fairy Bridge to Sangster. Phonsie O'Brien played his hand very differently, buying into her son after he had won both his first two races by a street – even though the word from Ballydoyle was that Sadler's Wells was never going to achieve as much as El Gran Senor. Both had finished their juvenile seasons unbeaten, but a first defeat was guaranteed for one of the pair when O'Brien decided to run them both in the Gladness Stakes. The very fact that he was pitched against El Gran Senor – and not given an unduly hard race in second – confirmed that expectations remained relatively limited for Sadler's Wells. Indeed, in the Irish 2000 Guineas the stable jockey opted to ride the other Ballydoyle runner. As Pat Eddery ruefully acknowledged in later years, Sadler's Wells was a lazy worker at home. In the event, Eddery's mount finished down the field as Sadler's Wells won by a neck.

Back in third was yet another son of Northern Dancer, Secreto. His trainer, David O'Brien, promptly decided to send his colt over to Epsom to challenge El Gran Senor. There was only one conceivable chink in the armour of his father's champion: stamina. Could a colt who showed such speed over a mile really stretch it over a mile and a half? Everyone expected Eddery to hold him together and pounce late. In the event, however, he let El Gran Senor cruise into the lead over 300 yards out – and was worn down by Secreto in the final strides. A short head had cost $40 million. At the same time, O'Brien could only be jubilant on behalf of David. A Derby photo finish had been contested by two colts born and bred on the same farm, trained by a father and son.

Without ever evincing the same brilliance as El Gran Senor, Sadler's Wells meanwhile continued to show great heart. Despite carrying his chin at a strange tilt, he won the Eclipse Stakes by a neck, and gave his all for podium finishes against top-class colts at longer distances as well. At the end of the year he was syndicated to stand at Coolmore for £20 million, with a starting fee – cognisant of his kinship to Nureyev – of £125,000.

Sangster was still depicting the advent of the Maktoums as a boon: their involvement in the market would simply enhance the value of his holdings. Sure enough, returning to Keeneland in 1985, his partnership spent $13.1 million for a Nijinsky colt. But the under-bidders turned out to be from California, not Dubai – and this latest record would prove a last throw of the dice. The fact was that Sangster had just about reached the bottom of the barrel. The ones containing crude oil, in contrast, never seemed to run dry.

The 1986 sale finally brought the runaway market to heel. No formal truce was ever admitted, after Sangster and Magnier had accepted an invitation to visit Sheikh Mohammed in Dubai. But they granted him a clear run to a brother to Storm Bird, for $3.6 million – and it then emerged that the sheikh would be sending the colt to Ballydoyle. In all, the Maktoums hoarded fifty-seven yearlings – saturated with Northern Dancer blood – for $40 million. Sangster bought three for $3.5 million. The sale average, which had touched $600,000 two years previously, plummeted to $411,755.

So began a nauseous plunge down the lift shaft for those Bluegrass studs that had been deceived by their own greed. Jay Gatsby himself would have blanched at the parties thrown on his farm, during the boom, by Tom Gentry. The entertainers ranged from Bob Hope to Ray Charles; you could ride an elephant, a camel, a Ferris wheel or a balloon. One year Gentry reckoned that 2,500 gatecrashers 'hopped the fence'. He would end up seeing his breeding stock seized by the banks, and serving time in jail.

Fittingly, the mirage began to melt even as its author entered a physical decline. In the spring of 1987 Northern Dancer covered twenty-four mares to produce just two foals. Access to the great stallion was by now likely to cost you $1 million, regardless of whether your mare produced a foal. For the sake of everyone's dignity, not least his own, he was put out to grass. The sire of fifty-four $1-million yearlings, and 147 stakes winners, was remembered by one early handler as barely clearing 15 hands. 'His personality, on the other hand, was bigger than all outdoors.'

Meanwhile cracks had been quietly widening in Sangster's empire, which at its height extended to around a thousand horses as far afield as Venezuela and Australia. Golden Fleece had died only a couple of years into his stud career; and now El Gran Senor was having fertility problems. Of his first fifty mares, thirty-six required reimbursements of his $200,000 fee. Then in 1986 the horses training at Ballydoyle were enfeebled by a virus.

Despite a cluster of Classic winners trained in England during the early 1990s, Sangster gradually became primarily a vendor of bloodstock. He also cashed in Vernons, presciently anticipating a National Lottery that would siphon off its lifeblood: the working-man's dreams of emancipation. (Sangster had been fond of quoting the episcopal minister who had told him: 'We're both in the same business: selling hope.') In his final years, Sangster had a wistful, deposed air. The incorrigible McDonald was lying low: his luck had finally run out in the 1990s, and then his health failed as well. But Sangster could always comfort himself with the fact that he had started something momentous. And he had enjoyed every minute. He died of cancer in 2004, at sixty-seven.

As for O'Brien, it turned out that he had already saddled the last of his sixteen Classic winners in Britain when El Gran Senor had won the Guineas. But he did have one last ace to play. In 1988, O'Brien daringly invested the last $3.5 million subscribed to a failing public flotation – much of it, to his mortification, by small investors – in a son of Nijinsky at Keeneland. Two years later, as Royal Academy, this colt won the Breeders' Cup Mile in New York. He was ridden by Lester Piggott, Fred Rickaby's nephew, and rider in his pomp of Nijinsky and The Minstrel. Piggott was now fifty-four, the creases of his face gouged deeper by a year in prison for tax evasion, and had ended a five-year retirement at O'Brien's request barely a fortnight previously.

O'Brien retired four years later. It was not clear how, or even if, Magnier might replace his irreplaceable father-in-law at Ballydoyle. David O'Brien had abruptly quit training as early as 1988. He had won Derbys in England, Ireland and France by the age of twenty-eight, but was smoking eighty cigarettes a day and seeing little of his young family. Perhaps his upbringing had included a burden nearly equivalent to its benefits. Phonsie, after all, would say of Vincent that if you went up to heaven and brought him down a star, you would be asked why you had not managed to get two or three. His seemed an impossible act to follow. David could hardly be reproached, then, if he preferred to buy a vineyard near Aix. In the end, Magnier would appoint another O'Brien altogether – one who had left school at fifteen to drive a forklift truck at the Waterford Co-op.

24

'They'd run through a wall for you.'

THE BOY COULD never understand why the man in the next furrow was able to fill two buckets in the time it took him to do one. Just seven years old, Aidan O'Brien crouched all day between the endless strawberry rows until numb from ribcage to toes. 'You'd start at four or five in the morning, to get the fresh fruit for the market, up until about eight,' O'Brien remembers now. 'And then you'd pick jam to six o'clock.'

He shakes his head as he surveys the new yard at Ballydoyle, a monument in stone to the regeneration of Coolmore. It represents new English investors, succeeding Sangster; a new champion stallion, in Galileo, heir to Sadler's Wells; and this new O'Brien, to succeed his own namesake. By the end of the 2014 season, John Magnier had broken new ground: *six* Epsom Derby winners standing together on one stud. All sons or grandsons of Sadler's Wells; five had been trained at Ballydoyle.

And here was O'Brien, at forty-five, remembering a Co. Wexford boyhood that promised him nothing while making him equal to anything. Potatoes were worse than strawberries because it was autumn by then, cold and muddy. Even so, O'Brien sometimes persevered until eleven at night. 'I remember the pain in my tummy, from not having had anything to eat. But you had to keep going, had to see it through. No one was going to come and get you. If you needed new clothes, or wanted a bike, that's just the way it was.'

This was a very different kind of hardship from that endured by Bill Hartack. O'Brien cherished his parents as models of humility, sobriety and endeavour. It was just that everyone had to take a hand. And it was soon clear that the boy had an unusual knack for one kind of work in particular.

343

There had always been the odd horse around the place, raw and hairy creatures that might make somebody a hunter or even a point-to-pointer. By fifteen, O'Brien was in charge of six or seven. 'Cheap ponies, problem ponies, bucking and doing all the bad things. And you'd just be trying to make something of them, trying to make a few pounds selling them on.'

He became obsessed by the glossy Coolmore stallion brochures; had a particular fixation with that hardy runner, Sadler's Wells. 'I don't know what it was,' he shrugs. 'He seemed a good horse, rather than a great horse – but whatever it was, I was always fascinated by the way he used to carry his head, point his toe.' O'Brien was nineteen before he realised he needed spectacles. 'Obviously I must have sat in the school my whole life without ever seeing the blackboard. I was in a dreamland, could only think of horses.'

One day, perhaps, he could find a job at Coolmore. He even applied for one, once, as a stud groom. At the time, for various reasons, it didn't happen. As it was, after that spell on the fork-lift, O'Brien found work in a small racing yard before graduating to a post with Jim Bolger, one of the most formidable trainers in Ireland. Bolger's austere regime was also moulding another phenomenon – Tony McCoy, subsequently the most prolific jump jockey in history. Even so, it is said that O'Brien was the only employee whose departure Bolger has ever lamented.

O'Brien was not the only mainstay of Magnier's second empire to have left school at fifteen to work at the Co-op. Michael Tabor did not stay long, either, in his case taking up an apprenticeship as a hairdresser. He remembers reading about the Manchester United air disaster through the froth of shampoo he was working into a lady's scalp. West Ham was his team, though, as an East End lad born during the Blitz of 1941. That same year, the mass extermination of Jews began in the Vilna ghetto, a fate Tabor's family might well have shared had not his grandparents – still Taborosky, in those days – fled earlier persecution. Emerging from the same neighbourhood as the Barnato brothers, Tabor would also prosper in a field of high risk for higher reward.

His father, a glassmaker, had once tried to set up as a bookmaker at a greyhound track, and the adolescent Tabor likewise became intrigued by the louche allure of Hackney, Hendon and White City. When betting shops were legalised, in 1960, he overcame parental objections to undertake a five-year apprenticeship before beginning to take bets at the dogs. Of the first ten dogs he laid, eight won. Bookmaking, it seemed, was like any other business: you could not just career along the crest of a wave, but had to ride out high and low tides. In 1967, he borrowed £30,000 to buy his first two betting shops.

The first Grand National he traded was won by Foinavon, the 100–1 shot who slipped past a pile-up at the twenty-third fence. Tabor cleaned up. But his determination to reduce that chaos factor, to leave no stone unturned, disclosed a residual naivety. In 1970, he was banned briefly by the Jockey Club for paying riders for information. What he did have, from the outset, was the right temperament – whether as layer or backer. He would never dwell on a bad day, never chase losses.

On his return from suspension, Tabor registered his colours as an owner and hooked up with Neville Callaghan, a trainer who loved to goad bookmakers and establishment alike. The seven wins of Tornado Prince, Tabor's first hurdler, were invariably anticipated in the betting ring. Callaghan relished the thrill of sailing close to the wind, and was regularly carpeted by the Jockey Club. 'We'd do it more or less within the rules,' he said on his retirement. 'But racing would lose its sparkle if there wasn't a certain amount of that, wouldn't it?' Though the stakes were always highest for Tabor, he was the only one of Callaghan's patrons who would not be straight on the phone when a punt did not come off. Instead he would leave things to cool off for a few days before a dispassionate consultation on what had gone wrong.

By 1992 Tabor's betting chain extended to 114 shops turning over £70 million a year. He moved to Monaco, and spent that Christmas in the Caribbean. Others hibernating there included Magnier, to whom Tabor had been introduced by the Irish gambler and speculator J. P. McManus. All three were linked by newspapers with the notorious run against the pound that same year, reputedly costing the Treasury over £3 billion in a single day. Soon afterwards Tabor was cashing in his betting shops, for a reported £27 million, and instructing one of Magnier's key advisers, Demi O'Byrne, to invest in a superior grade of racehorse in the United States. One of his first purchases, for some $400,000, was a promising two-year-old named Thunder Gulch. The following May he won the Kentucky Derby.

Magnier bought into Thunder Gulch, who retired to Coolmore's Kentucky farm, and soon took Tabor on board for the yearling sales. After coming away from Keeneland with three of the top four lots, they also paid the joint-top price at Tattersalls that autumn: 600,000 guineas for a colt by Sadler's Wells. Named Entrepreneur, he proceeded to win the 2000 Guineas eighteen months later. But the Midas touch of his new partner was not the main reason why Magnier had climbed back into the ring, five years after Sangster and Vincent O'Brien had thrown in the towel. The real key was the sire of Entrepreneur.

Sadler's Wells had laid down an immediate, unequivocal marker. From his first crop, comprising fifty-five foals, he produced two colts to dead-heat for the premier juvenile race in Britain, the Dewhurst Stakes; another to win Derbys in Ireland and France; and another to win at the Breeders' Cup. A triple Classic winner from his second crop, Salsabil, then secured Sadler's Wells his first sires' championship in 1990. Though edged out in 1991 by Caerleon, another grandson of Northern Dancer standing at Coolmore, Sadler's Wells would reign uninterrupted for the next thirteen years. This unprecedented hegemony would be compounded by sons who themselves developed into top-class stallions. As such, Sadler's Wells not only became the bedrock of a new era at Coolmore; he also transposed the entire balance of power between Europe and Kentucky. The opening phase of Magnier's adventure had been predicated on Northern Dancer pepping up stagnant European bloodlines. By the time Sadler's Wells was pensioned, in 2008, you were far more likely to find a Derby winner in Co. Tipperary than in the Bluegrass state.

In the meantime, by harnessing advances in veterinary science and transportation, Coolmore had made commercial breeding a numbers game. Northern Dancer never produced a bigger crop of foals than the thirty-six he sired in 1974. Sadler's Wells ended up

twice covering 196 mares in a single season. By 2014, six of the
seven busiest Flat-racing stallions in Britain and Ireland represented
Coolmore, each covering over 170 mares. And that is without taking
into account that some of the stud's busiest stallions, nowadays, are
also shuttled to Australia or New Zealand for a year-round breeding
cycle.

It is this inundation of genes from a relatively small pool that has
completed the triumph of the Darley Arabian line. It has also caused
plenty of angst among less commercial breeders, over the extinction
of 'outcross' options. True, a degree of inbreeding has long been
favoured to multiply a dominant gene. Tesio, for instance, included
St Simon four times in the first five generations of Nearco's pedigree.
And Magnier plainly remains unabashed. In the private museum at
Coolmore, a newspaper article recalls a furore at the Thoroughbred
Breeders' Association in 1930. English breeders, outraged that an
Irish stallion had served seventy-three mares the previous year, passed
a resolution urging a limit of forty-five per season. The stallion in
question was Cottage, standing at just 19 guineas for Magnier's father
at Grange Stud in Co. Cork. The article, published in 2000, noted
that the same farm – as Coolmore's National Hunt wing – had that
spring accommodated over a thousand mares between just three
stallions.

The proof of the pudding, of course, is in the eating. The fact
is that Coolmore's stack-'em-high approach is only sustainable so
long as it regularly produces colts of sufficient class to initiate the
next cycle. Galileo himself was the result of the purest eugenics: a
mating in 1997 between the outstanding sire of his day, in Sadler's
Wells, and Urban Sea, winner of the 1993 Prix de l'Arc de Triomphe.
Moreover, Urban Sea's maternal family, from Germany, introduced
valuable genetic variation. She would subsequently produce another
great champion, Sea The Stars, winner of the 2000 Guineas, Derby
and Arc for her owners, the Tsui family.

Galileo was sent into training with Aidan O'Brien, who had arrived
at Ballydoyle after a record-breaking start to his career as a trainer of
jumpers. He had married another precocious achiever, Anne-Marie
Crowley, the first woman to win the jumps training title in Ireland.
They met as amateur riders, circling behind the starting tapes at

Galway. O'Brien was unnerved when his glamorous rival struck up a conversation. 'I couldn't believe it,' he recalls. 'Because who was I, like? And then she spoke to me again. And again.'

After their marriage, O'Brien quit riding to take over the training licence and, approached by Magnier, began to test the water with Flat horses at Ballydoyle. Having cut his teeth with jumpers, just like his predecessor, he made a seamless transition. He won three Irish Classics in 1997, before raiding England for the 2000 Guineas and Oaks the following year. In the meantime, he was still able to produce one of the great hurdlers of the era in Istabraq, himself a son of Sadler's Wells.

By the time Galileo entered his care, O'Brien had just turned thirty and still looked impossibly young: slim, bespectacled, agonised by modesty. But there was something steely there, too; some hint that this was a man who put the grit into integrity. Just as well, really: Ballydoyle was no place for faint hearts, and Galileo was about to intensify a growing hostility between Magnier's new regime and the rivals who had brought down his previous one.

When Vincent O'Brien's son, David, threw open the Ballydoyle succession with his abrupt retirement, as many as twenty-three of the twenty-nine horses in his stable were owned by Sheikh Mohammed. But the rapprochement between the two camps would not last. The year before Aidan O'Brien arrived at Ballydoyle, a filly named Balanchine had kickstarted a quiet revolution for the Maktoum brothers. Purchased from none other than Sangster, after a promising novice season, Balanchine was flown to Dubai for the winter and returned for a season of spectacular success. Sheikh Mohammed, irritated by the complacency of trainers who took his investment for granted, was determined to bring the thoroughbred back to its roots – and to advertise Dubai as a global hub for the next century. Balanchine became a pathfinder for a new stable, an experimental, elite corps dividing its time between the desert and Newmarket; one of its priorities would be the Dubai World Cup, inaugurated in 1996 as the richest race on the planet. Sheikh Mohammed, having already established Darley Studs, invoked another of the founding fathers in naming the new stable Godolphin.

No racing stable has ever been freighted with more political meaning than Godolphin. Turf professionals around the world – a fairly hard-nosed community, on the whole – were bemused to receive branded calendars and merchandise, amplifying the portentous aphorisms of its founder. Every morning in Africa, they learned, a gazelle wakes up knowing he must outrun the fastest lion or perish; and a lion wakes up knowing he must outrun the slowest gazelle or starve. Nonetheless, they found themselves joining the racing public in a growing regard for the sheikh, a previously inscrutable character now showing a vivid contempt for all meanness of spirit or ambition. The young and energetic personnel he recruited for Godolphin were encouraged to challenge him with their own ideas, albeit he invariably got his way in the end. Indeed, 'the Boss' himself took a hands-on role with many of the stable's best horses. Godolphin consummated the innate empathy, both personal and cultural, Sheikh Mohammed has always professed with horses. The injury to his pride was correspondingly grievous, then, when Mahmood Al Zarooni – a young trainer he had promoted through Godolphin – was banned for eight years for use of anabolic steroids in 2013. Much of the romance of Godolphin unravelled overnight.

Back in 2000 the stable seemed only a force for good. All the barriers erected round horses – especially those with a reputation to protect for their stud careers – were to be dismantled. Godolphin's champions would race all round the world, against all comers. Dubai Millennium, moreover, had just sealed his place in his owner's heart by running away with the World Cup. That summer the sheikh dared his old adversaries at Coolmore to a winner-takes-all, $6-million match between Dubai Millennium and their latest champion, a French-trained son of Sadler's Wells named Montjeu. Unfortunately Dubai Millennium suffered a career-ending injury on the gallops on the morning that the *Racing Post* revealed the challenge. But the proposed match, evoking the earliest days of the English Turf, was instructive of the way the sheikh viewed his rivalry with Coolmore.

Magnier, at heart, remained a commercial stockman, his only imperative to make the figures add up. For the sheikh, it was a genetic arms race – a duel for the right to set a defining stamp on the breed. In the event, Dubai Millennium would be denied this chance, too. The following April, halfway through his first season at stud, he was put down after contracting grass sickness, a rare but untreatable condition. Over at Ballydoyle, meanwhile, they were already getting excited about a young colt who would one day achieve everything, in his impact on the breed, that Sheikh Mohammed had dreamed for Dubai Millennium.

Galileo had announced himself the previous autumn with a ridiculously easy win at Leopardstown, on the southern fringe of Dublin. Though the ground was heavy and he led with only 300 yards to go, he suddenly went fourteen lengths clear. In Flat races, a margin of three or four lengths is generally thought comprehensive.

The horse had stood out from the beginning. Even the blaze on his face, a perfect white arrow, seemed to intimate some thrust towards greatness. He was a natural from the day he entered Ballydoyle. Though held up by coughing a couple of times as a two-year-old, he was so obliging that he seemed to get himself fit with no pressure from his trainer. As a result, his ultimate potential remained unknowable. 'He was probably the most athletic horse we ever had here,' O'Brien remembers. 'With his movement and his temperament, you could not do little enough with him really: he came ready to run, and by training him all you could do was damage him.'

The following spring Galileo was given two Derby trials back at Leopardstown. They were intended only to bring him forward in fitness and seasoning, and some people were disappointed by a lack of visual éclat. But O'Brien had no intention of lighting the powder keg before 3.50 p.m. on 9 June 2001. 'The last thing we had wanted was a big, mad impressive trial before the Derby,' he recalls. 'There were knockers as usual, but to me he did it all very easy.' As the day drew closer, Galileo started to pummel his usual sparring partners on the Ballydoyle gallops with new violence. One morning he went barrelling so far clear, fifteen or eighteen lengths, that O'Brien concluded that the others must be off colour. He hoped that Galileo would not go down with the same problem.

There were no qualms over the jockey. Michael Kinane had won the Derby, Arc, Melbourne Cup and Belmont Stakes, and was in his prime at forty-one. 'Mick was granite, mentally and physically,' O'Brien says. 'And Galileo, on the day, was bombproof. Tacking up, he stood like a lamb and there wasn't a bead of sweat on him. He was in a great place.'

Luxuriantly balanced throughout, Galileo knuckled down when asked to stretch halfway up the straight and, hitting overdrive in the final furlong, went bounding three and a half lengths clear. Though the early pace had been relatively pedestrian, the final time was the second fastest in Derby history; even the understated Kinane reckoned he had ridden 'undoubtedly one of the best Derby winners ever'.

The previous day Sadler's Wells had been responsible for all the first three fillies in the Oaks, so matching his ancestor Birdcatcher in 1852. Now, after five runners-up in the Derby, he had redressed one of the few remaining omissions in his record. Tesio's 'piece of wood' had finally signposted an outstanding heir for the breed's ageing potentate.

After Galileo followed up in the Irish Derby, the stage was set for the champion three-year-old to take on the best older horses in the King George VI and Queen Elizabeth Stakes at Ascot in July. Here Galileo was obliged to dig deep as Fantastic Light followed him through for Godolphin. But he never looked in danger of defeat and ultimately imposed himself by two lengths. Sheikh Mohammed spoke generously in defeat. 'I respect the courage of the other team in coming here,' he said. 'They were the ones with something to lose, but they were not afraid to find out just how good he is.'

Six weeks later, Fantastic Light took on Galileo once again – this time over a shorter distance in the Irish Champion Stakes. The hometown champion started at odds of just 4–11. But the Irish were in for a shock. It was not just that Fantastic Light won. What was more injurious was the sense that the Ballydoyle team had somehow been beaten at their own game: that they had been outsmarted by the sheikh.

Both camps deployed a pacemaker. Galileo was always going to profit from any extra emphasis on stamina, but the Ballydoyle pacemaker went off so fast that he became irrelevant: none of the other jockeys was ever going to be seduced into such a reckless tempo, and Kinane found himself tracking the Godolphin 'rabbit' instead. At the critical moment, Fantastic Light was obliged with a gap between his pacemaker and the rail; Kinane was forced to wrench Galileo round the outside. That allowed Frankie Dettori to steal a decisive advantage on Fantastic Light and, though Galileo gradually wore him down, in the final strides it was obvious that he was held. Kinane suspected that Galileo would not have been caught so flat on a softer surface. But the exultant sheikh left no doubt as to his personal authorship of the winning tactics. 'The race got very messy,' O'Brien concedes ruefully.

Undaunted, Magnier and his team tried one last gamble: to give Galileo his final start in the Breeders' Cup Classic, against dirt specialists in New York. This, according to O'Brien, showed his patrons to be just as open to adventure as the sheikh – partly because Tabor and Derrick Smith, another new investor with a bookmaking background, are more animated by racing than breeding; but also because Sadler's Wells and his sons have produced potential stallions so reliably their limitations can be discovered on the track, rather than at stud. One such in the progeny of Sadler's Wells appeared to be that they did not handle dirt courses. But the audacity of the enterprise would allow Galileo to be pardoned if beaten, while success would throw open the American market when he was retired to stud.

As it was, Galileo finished well beaten. 'He came in and he was crying, poor fellow,' O'Brien recalls. 'Damnedest thing I ever saw. He was so genuine, he ran the whole way with his eyes open, and came back with them full of muck. Most horses would shut their eyes and not face it, would duck and pull back . . . It was as if he ran the whole race in the dark. It wasn't that his heart was broken, but he had given his all. All he knew was to keep going.' But it was in this, his only humiliation, that Galileo disclosed the kernel of his future greatness.

O'Brien ended the year with a record twenty-three Group One winners, and the following season produced another son of Sadler's Wells, High Chaparral, to win the Derby. He also saddled the runner-up, the pair a dozen lengths clear of the rabble.

Galileo meanwhile started out at Coolmore with a fee of

Ir£50,000, not outrageous for a Derby winner of such pedigree. He duly entertained as many as 157 mares in his first season, and these produced the colts who went on to finish first, second and third in the 2006 St Leger. His second crop included an unbeaten champion juvenile, Teofilo, bred by O'Brien's mentor, Jim Bolger. As a breeder, Bolger had bet the bank on Galileo and would now reap spectacular rewards.

The emergence of Galileo – not to mention Montjeu, sire of four Derby winners in eight years – heightened a growing disparity in standards between Ballydoyle and Godolphin. Once the Maktoums began pointedly ignoring yearlings by Coolmore stallions at the sales, it was difficult to know whether Godolphin's deficiencies should be blamed on breeding or training personnel. The only certainty was that détente between the superpowers was over. In 2006, at a sale in Florida, Magnier and his partners even allowed themselves to spend a record $16-million dollars to deny Sheikh Mohammed a flashy two-year-old of modest pedigree. The Green Monkey was retired without a win after just three starts.

Bolger accepted big money from Sheikh Mohammed for Teofilo; and then he promptly did the same with another son of Galileo, New Approach, who proceeded to win the 2008 Derby. Teofilo and New Approach both retired to Darley Stud, giving the Maktoums precious access to the blood of Galileo – without having to pay Coolmore.

Not that Magnier needed to worry. By the time Galileo's fee was listed as 'private' in the Coolmore brochure, it was said to have reached €300,000. Of course, many of his matings are with Coolmore mares – enabling O'Brien to observe better than anyone the replication of Galileo's trademark assets. 'Of all the horses we had here, ever, what made this horse different was his will,' O'Brien explains. 'And he passes it on, puts it into all his stock. It's the one thing you can't see until you go and train them – what's inside, in their minds: that they won't ever give up. And that's everything in a horse, so long as you don't destroy it. And the difference, in Galileos, is that it's very hard to destroy. Because they just keep giving. They'd run through a wall for you.'

O'Brien always felt he had to be careful with the stock of Montjeu.

They needed protection from experiences that might unnerve them. Galileos need protection, as well – but only from themselves. 'If you overwork them, they won't stop,' O'Brien cautions. 'So if they're not ready physically, they'll hurt themselves. Most horses, if you work them before they're fit enough, or when they're feeling any pain, they'll stop – and they will never give you their all again. But Galileos never question anything they're asked.'

It is surely no coincidence that Bill Hartack, who rode Galileo's grandsire to win the Kentucky Derby, remembered Northern Dancer as almost too game for his own good: 'too willing, too generous . . . If you'd ask him to run, you might not be able to stop him.' But it is, of course, a two-way process: the genetic transmission from stallion to stallion can always be broken if a trainer is on the wrong wavelength.

'What we try to do with the horses is get them to develop a personality,' O'Brien explains. 'Because they have to get so that they can make their own minds up, to a point. So before you start working them you ask them to do little things; and you'll see a response, you'll see a confidence develop. But if you treat them like machines, they will always be machines: when you work them, they'll overwork or underwork. When you have their trust, and they have their personality developed, they'll know how much to do.'

Galileo very nearly died in the autumn of 2008. On Christmas Day, three months after his surgery, the scars were still bleeding. Many horses would have been killed by his first bout of colic; the complication of a second attack, two days later, should absolutely have finished him off. Much credit for his survival went to Niall O'Riordan, a groom who for weeks tended Galileo round the clock. But O'Riordan describes how world-class veterinary surgeons were asked to step aside for the local priest, Father Tom Breen, to bless the stricken horse with holy water. They found it hard to disguise their contempt for this superstitious ritual. To O'Riordan, however, the horse's return from the brink unmistakably began at that moment. Soon afterwards, he left Coolmore for a seminary.

It was a critical moment for Coolmore – Sadler's Wells, at twenty-seven, had been retired four months previously – and, conceivably, for the Darley Arabian line. For Galileo's principal heir may yet turn out to be one of the champions conceived after his reprieve. One of the next two Derby winners, perhaps: Ruler Of The World, or Australia. On the other hand, it could be a foal who had spent three months that spring in a paddock at Coolmore.

He was one of ten bred annually by Coolmore stallions from mares owned by a Saudi prince, Khaled Abdullah. In a foal-sharing arrangement, standard across the industry, the stallion fees are waived in exchange for half the resulting foals. In 2008, by the agency of some forgotten toss of the coin, it happened to be the turn of Abdullah's men to have first pick. So it was that the son of Galileo and a mare named Kind entered training, not at Ballydoyle, but with Henry Cecil in Newmarket.

25

'I'd be surprised if there's
ever been a better horse'

WHEN BOBBY FRANKEL threw $20,000 in bills over her bed, his mother thought he must have robbed a bank. They had never imagined anything like this, when first taking him to the track: harness-racing, at the Roosevelt Raceway on Long Island. But before long he had found a store in Far Rockaway that took delivery of the *Daily Racing Form* at 8 p.m., and was spending the night studying for his bets the next day. And here he was, twenty-one years old, his grin and flashing dark eyes half hidden by the bills floating towards to the bed. He had started the day with $40.

That was 1960. Later, as a trainer, Frankel liked to say that his only connection to horses was a grandfather who had been in the Russian cavalry. (His parents had a kosher catering business.) But that was also how he accounted for his success. 'You don't get things set in your mind, ideas you grew up with,' he said. 'You make your own judgements. I've heard things at the racetrack that have been passed down from era to era that are pure bullshit.' He lasted one day in college; got in a fight and cleared out. He followed the horses down to Florida, scraping together a few dollars in the mornings on building sites or valet parking or, best of all, hotwalking. The hotwalker leads horses round and round the barn after their exercise, cooling them off: the hamster wheel of a deadbeat. But a racetrack pass saved him three dollars a day in parking and admission. He watched and learned. As a gambler, he had an instinct for the right level for a horse. In 1966, he started to buy the odd one out of claiming races, the bargain basement of the sport. Frankel's new recruits seemed to improve at an astounding rate and, venturing to California, he maintained a win ratio of one-in-three. Too good, many suspected, to be true. He was not just a novice, remember, but an outsider. 'Everything I ran, they tested,' he recalled. But there was no test for the edge that set Frankel apart: nous, nerve, panache.

Soon he was training for the big players, for tycoons and Hollywood stars. Eventually, in the 1980s, he was sent horses bred by Juddmonte Farms, the breeding empire established by Khaled Abdullah. It was a classic showcase for the land of opportunity: a Jewish kid from Brooklyn, training for a Saudi prince. Their crowning moment together was the 2003 Belmont Stakes – somehow, Frankel's one and only success in a Triple Crown race. As one of twenty-five Grade One winners for his stable that year, Empire Maker helped to beat the record set just two years previously by Aidan O'Brien.

Plenty of people on the American Turf will tell you that Frankel's teak veneer was no veneer at all. He candidly preferred horses and dogs to people. Falling out with Frankel could be thermonuclear, according to two ex-wives and a daughter who complained of his neglect. But he inspired exceptional loyalty in his staff, and the reclusive and courteous Abdullah was devastated when his brash, foul-mouthed trainer fell victim to lymphoma. After Frankel's death, in 2009, Abdullah asked his men to reserve his name for the best specimen they could find among Juddmonte's 170 yearlings.

On the face of it, Henry Cecil and Bobby Frankel could hardly belong to the same species – never mind the same profession. You can just imagine Frankel's incredulous mutterings whenever this fey, patrician flâneur made one of his reluctant forays to the United States for the Breeders' Cup. Cecil's long limbs would be upholstered in some exquisite concession to the democratic ethos of this alien environment: Armani jeans, and maybe something in suede or leather. He smoked, yes, but it was like watching the Marlboro Man slide open a silver cigarette case. Every morning, during the week leading up to raceday, Cecil held frivolous court down by the quarantine barn where the European runners were stabled: tilting his head, answering press questions with a drawled question of his own, always playing a part: 'Here for the shopping, don't you know.' Moving on to Bobby Frankel's barn, the same reporters would then record some rasping invective about the CIA – and marvel that paths so very different could converge in the same walk of life; and in the service, moreover, of the same patron.

Their antecedents could not have been more different. One of Bobby Frankel's former assistants placed his legacy at the heart of national mythology: 'He proved you don't have to grow up on a [stud] farm or be somebody's kid to make it.' Cecil, in contrast, was the stepson of one pillar of the Newmarket establishment and son-in-law to another. He was born in 1943, ten minutes before a twin brother, David, and four days after news had arrived of their father's death, with the Parachute Regiment in North Africa. Their mother, Rohays Cecil, then married Cecil Boyd-Rochfort, a strait-laced royal trainer considered, at fifty-seven, an impregnable bachelor.

Rohays was glamorous and vivacious but also had an edge of danger, specifically regarding drink, that would recur in both her twin boys. While at agricultural college, Henry and David once reassembled an old Morris on the principal's bed; on another occasion, they painted daffodils red, white and blue on the eve of a royal visit – a nearly literal case of gilding the lily.

On his stepfather's retirement in 1968, Henry took over the training licence and then married the daughter of Boyd-Rochfort's greatest rival, Noel Murless. In 1976 he took over the Murless yard at Warren Place, soon emerging as the most flamboyant and successful trainer of his generation. For all his advantages, his touch seemed wholly untutored, wholly intuitive. He seemed to cultivate these highly strung thoroughbreds largely as a matter of aesthetic sensibility, much as he did the roses in the famous Warren Place garden. Lord Howard de Walden, one of his principal patrons, reckoned that Cecil trained horses literally by personal charm. At Ballydoyle, Aidan O'Brien monitors workouts with GPS tracking. Cecil never even used a stopwatch. Asked about timing horses, he would roll his eyes, pull down his mouth and say that it could only be of use to people cleverer than he was. One way or another, horses blossomed in his care. There were ten training championships between 1976 and 1993, during which time Cecil became an indispensable asset for Sheikh Mohammed in his rivalry with Coolmore. But an acrimonious rift between the pair in 1995 exposed the first fissures in the ornate surface of Cecil's life. Over the next few years, one thing followed another. There was a disastrous second marriage. Though David Cecil eventually overcame his alcoholism, he died of cancer in 2000. His surviving twin, inconsolable, turned to drink himself but only exacerbated his solitude and bitterness. As late as 1999, he had come within a neck of winning the first four Classics. But his career now entered what seemed a terminal decline. Without the Maktoums, Warren Place was badly exposed by the decline of the old English studs. Jim Joel, son of Jack, had died in 1992; Howard de Walden followed in 1999. In 2005, the stable that had turned out 180 winners in 1987 mustered a bare dozen all season. The pain seemed to gnaw at Henry Cecil's vitals. So the doctors looked into his stomach, and found the same disease that had killed his brother.

One morning on the gallops he overheard a young trainer whispering to a patron: 'That's Henry Cecil. Should have retired years ago.' He was furious. Then he thought of David looking down on the wreckage of a twin who should, in fact, be living his life for him. And he realised that if you feel shame, then at least you still have pride. Cecil's renaissance would become so closely identified with one horse that it is worth reiterating how its initial impetus came from within. The season after beginning his chemotherapy, he ended a seven-year drought in the Classics by saddling Light Shift to win the Oaks. Cecil was touched by the reception of the crowd at Epsom. 'Three cheers for Henry!' It would become a familiar refrain during his return from the wilderness. But he could not fail to notice a subtext of condescension. Good old Henry: he was not going to go out with a whimper, after all. But nobody doubted that he was still going out.

Cecil hated people feeling sorry for him; hated being an 'also-ran'. Determined not to let his sickness become an excuse, he scheduled his chemotherapy around work mornings and dragged himself onto the gallops no matter how vile he felt. Cecil, who had spent his boyhood summers at a family castle in Scotland, proved himself every bit as tough as Bobby Frankel, the street-smart son of Brooklyn and Queen's.

It helped that he had restored domestic stability: his third wife was proving a rock, understated and protective. And then, in January 2010, arrived a colt known to the Juddmonte stud grooms as 'Bobby'.

When first tried on the gallops, Frankel exhibited a manic tendency to run before he could walk. For a while Cecil doubted whether the horse would ever manage to harness his raw, physical ability. But gradually it dawned on his work-riders: Frankel had such a prodigious stride that when you urged restraint, he lost his temper. Most horses that want to go too fast are literally on the run, gasping, neurotic. Frankel was simply straining to explore the full ambit of his freakish capacity.

Rumours began to filter out of Warren Place that the old master, now sixty-seven, had a monster on his hands. In the circumstances, everything Frankel did already seemed drenched in greater meaning. Even his induction as a two-year-old – a 'maiden' race at Newmarket in August 2010 – would acquire a retrospective significance. The runner-up was another son of Galileo, named Nathaniel. The following summer this same colt won the King George VI and Queen Elizabeth Stakes at Ascot.

By that stage, Frankel's extraordinary exhibition in the 2000 Guineas (described in the Introduction) had secured Cecil the twenty-fifth Classic of his career. Abdullah indulged his friend by delaying Frankel's retirement to stud for another season and, by the time he returned to Ascot the following summer, the horse had achieved full equilibrium. He always had it physically: a rolling, buoyant rhythm, which combined balletic grace with murderous, animal power. In maturity, he had now achieved a corresponding mental balance, between ease and exuberance. An eleven-length success in the Queen Anne Stakes had the same, vaulting extravagance as his Guineas performance but this time, by consenting to kindle by degrees, he was able to burn brighter for longer.

Frankel's three remaining starts would all be at venues cherished lifelong by his trainer: Goodwood, York and Ascot. In the first he faced three rivals, including his own pacemaker, at odds of 1–20. (To win £10, in other words, you had to stake £200.) The distance – for the seventh time running – was a mile.

Only then, in his penultimate appearance, did the champion try something new: he ran an extra two furlongs at York. But his superiority was so established that all he had to do was remain relaxed, and another lap of honour was guaranteed. Yet if anyone really wanted to measure his reach, even now, it would not have been difficult. He could have run in the Prix de l'Arc de Triomphe or at the Breeders' Cup. Perhaps he could even bid to avenge the 'tears' of his own sire, by trying an alien surface in the Classic. Dirt racing, after all, is all about rhythm: Frankel, with his relentless dynamism, would surely have lapped them. And, if not, who would sensibly think less of him? At least he could be saluted as a champion who went looking for trouble. As it was, in his entire career he never spent a single night away from Warren Place.

For three seasons, to be fair, Frankel had kept Cecil together, body and soul. By now, however, there was a harrowing decline in the trainer. Tottering on a stick round the parade ring at York, Cecil was a wraith, his strange, hangdog glamour withering into sallow folds. The insidious sickness had renewed itself in his chest, reducing his voice to a ghastly, dry hiss.

Still he retained his dignity, wryly reproaching himself for vanity over the loss of his hair. But when Frankel made his final start, at Ascot that October, a corresponding dread compounded the mood of valediction. How long could Cecil conceivably last, once Frankel had been retired? There was an answering mournfulness in the damp, grey air. The going was horrible. As a result, Frankel was going to be asked a new question after all: could his flair still gleam through all this mud? Well, of course it could – although this time, in conditions that suited the top-class Cirrus des Aigles, he had nothing in reserve as he won by a little under two lengths. If we never discovered just how good Frankel was, we now knew his limits in heavy ground.

'I'd be very surprised if there's ever been a better horse,' Cecil whispered. He was Sir Henry nowadays, but he had always been a natural chevalier, at ease with men of every station. As Boyd-Rochfort's stepson, he had tea with royalty even as a child; yet the approaches of north-country working men at the races were not just tolerated, but warmly reciprocated. Cecil transcended class as he did time. In some ways, he belonged to another era: he adored tradition, and deplored the confusion between innovation and progress. He didn't even have a pair of binoculars, standard issue at the races, never mind a mobile phone. But he had few of the fetters of times past, either.

For all the incorrigibility of his wild or sad times, he was an innocent. Even his naivety would become a strength. After bidding farewell to Frankel, Cecil drew up a business plan with a tailor to start a clothing label. Not that he was in denial. That winter, in Dubai, he bought himself a tie with a motif of skulls. He died the following June.

And now the sons of Frankel stroll around the sales rings, round and round, circle after circle as though tracing the rings of an ancient oak. Here they are, a fresh cross-section of the modern thoroughbred after three centuries of cyclical endeavour by breeders: twenty-five generations back to the arrival of the Darley Arabian in English pasture; and countless generations beyond, lost in the treeless desert.

Even in retirement, Frankel retained his theatricality. His first foal offered at public auction was afforded an unprecedented stage: the Orangery at Kensington Palace. Bidding for the little colt, sold along with his mother and a sibling in utero, opened at £1 million. Five minutes and another £150,000 later the package was the property of Coolmore – represented by Magnier's son 'M.V.'.

Bull Hancock, doyen of post-war Kentucky breeders, had a saying: 'A good bull is half of a herd; a bad bull is all of it.' In other words, if you have a top-class stallion you have half a chance; and a good mare gives you every chance. But if your stallion is no good, even the best mare is no good. Perhaps the ultimate successor to Galileo will be some other son, unsuspected or as yet unborn. But an heir will be out there somewhere. Between them – himself and all those who have gone before, the Tesios and Derbys and Graftons and Cumberlands – Magnier thinks they are inching forwards. There is just one caveat. 'I'd say the breed is improving,' he says. 'But whether that's by accident or design, I couldn't say.'

And who would want it any other way? What chance could you otherwise have given all those different characters, from Mr Toad to Dennis O'Kelly, who have somehow preceded Magnier to the middle of the maze? Those who ineptly sold their stallions abroad, or bred them with mares unable to bear a country priest round his parish? Tesio himself, remember, only put Nearco's parents together because his application for another stallion had been rejected. The fact that Magnier keeps getting it right shows that there is a strong element of design. But it is the chapters of accident that give everyone a chance – and that keep everyone interested, rich and poor alike, in the thoroughbred racehorse. After all, once wealth can buy anything nothing has any value. But you can spend as much as you like on the finest pedigrees and still end up with rubbish. 'And that's what makes this game so interesting,' Magnier says. 'A yearling that costs five thousand could beat the one that costs five million. Horses don't know what they cost.'

It so happens that Cirrus des Aigles, the horse who pressed Frankel so hard on his final bow, represented one of the last residues of the Byerley Turk bloodline. But he was also a gelding: castrated in his youth, he had no prospect of a stud career. Horse by horse, day by day, the Turf is a crucible of humility. If the Darley Arabian story tells us anything, it is that you are as likely to miss your only chance by a deliberate decision, as seize it by an oversight. That is why Bobby Frankel had a favourite axiom, picked up from a veteran trainer of the old school. 'It's not who's best,' he would say. 'It's who lasts.'

Acknowledgements

M R DARLEY'S ARABIAN has needed the help of many different trainers, riders and grooms to reach the finishing post, and I am extremely grateful for their collective patience and expertise.

In the first instance, Catherine Clarke, my agent at Felicity Bryan Associates, made sure the horse was saddled and shod in the best of stables.

And then Georgina Laycock, my editor at John Murray, somehow kept faith that *Mr Darley's Arabian* was worth steering through numerous extra circuits in heavy going.

Several of her colleagues also provided skilled assistance in getting the horse across the line, without recourse to whip and spurs, notably Caroline Westmore, as managing editor; while Martin Bryant's copy-edit brushed through every tangle in the draft with the most meticulous of currycombs. Any remaining knots or flaws are, of course, my own responsibility. Many thanks also to Alice Laurent, Juliet Brightmore, Amanda Jones and Douglas Matthews.

The horse depended for daily sustenance, throughout, on the staff and benefactors of the Bodleian Library in Oxford – but the diet was transformed, at a critical stage, by an invitation to Lexington, Kentucky, to browse the extraordinary collection of books, newspapers and photographs that qualify the Keeneland Library as an unrivalled resource of the international Turf. Many thanks to everyone who made my ten days in the Bluegrass as enjoyable as they were rewarding: notably Becky Ryder, the infinitely painstaking and enthusiastic director of the library; Bill Thomason, Keeneland president, for inaugurating the scholarship programme; Rogers Beasley and Jacqueline Duke, for their charming hospitality; and Ed Prosser, for enlisting all these and many other good people to so undeserving a cause.

Fortunately researchers in Britain have another remarkable Turf library rather closer to home, which was shared with his usual generosity by Tim Cox – to whom, along with Helena McGrath, I extend additional thanks for reliably astute remarks on an early draft of the opening chapters.

For primary sources regarding Thomas Darley, I am indebted to the archivists at Northallerton (North Yorkshire County Records) and Kew (National Archives); and also to George and Sara Winn-Darley.

Many thanks for time and insight to Aidan O'Brien, in particular; also John Magnier, Richard Henry, John Fulton, Lady Cecil and Sir Julian Rose. And for the provision of wheels, digs and much laughter, as ever, Eddie Wiley.

Lastly, and most importantly, the race could never have been run at all without the support from the grandstand (heckles notwithstanding) of three generations of Willis-Bunds: Jane; Jo; Fred, Johnnie and Stella; nor without a sire and dam, Michael and Karin, to eclipse every other pedigree in the story.

Illustration Credits

Glossary

Backstretch: in America, a complex of communal stables – hired out to trainers for the duration of a meeting – generally sited along the far side of the track.

Backward: of a horse, immature or unfit.

Barb: sometimes, in the eighteenth century, any highly bred racer; specifically, one tracing its roots to North Africa.

Bit: a bar fitted through the mouth of a horse, fixed to the bridle and reins, to assist the rider in control and steering: the 'snaffle' is a basic model; the 'curb' a very severe one.

Blackleg: often abbreviated to 'leg'. A forerunner of the bookmaker, as the first to make a living by taking bets against a horse – though only specific horses, as opposed to trying to balance bets on the whole field. Distrust of his motives increasingly lent the word a pejorative flavour.

Break down: of a horse, to suffer a career-ending injury while galloping.

Broodmare: a female horse retired from racing to breed.

Claimer: a race in which the weights carried are determined by the value of each horse, as decided by its owner, each then eligible to be 'claimed' after it has run. The cheaper the price you set, the less weight your horse has to carry – and the more likely you are both to win the race, and lose your horse. By definition, a race for dispensable animals.

Classic: one of five historic English races confined to three-year-olds, notably the Derby; or an overseas imitation.

Cocker: strictly, an enthusiast of cockfighting; though sometimes applied to some zesty, high-rolling fellow.

Colt: a young male horse, ungelded, specifically one not more than four years old.

Commissioner (sometimes 'commission agent'): in the nineteenth century, a gambling expert hired to take the best odds on behalf of a principal who generally wished to remain anonymous – either because of aristocratic dignity or professional prudence. If a commissioner was historically associated with a certain stable, his enthusiasm to lay bets against one of its horses would cause panic in the market.

Conformation: the degree of correctness, against textbook ideals of angle and proportionality, in the muscular and skeletal assembly of a horse.

Covering: the mounting of a mare by a stallion.

Crop: can refer to a whip, but in this text often denotes a generation of foals produced by a horse in a particular breeding season – the word applied in the sense of harvest or yield.

Dam: a horse's mother.

Damsire: a horse's maternal grandfather, the sire of its dam.

Destrier: a brawny medieval war horse, bred to bear the immense weight of armoured knights.

Filly: a young female horse, equivalent to a colt – that is, no more than four years old.

Furlong: one-eighth of a mile, or 220 yards.

Galloway: an extinct breed of hardy pony, predominantly bred in Scotland; sometimes the term was applied indiscriminately to early sport horses of limited stature.

Gelding: a castrated horse. Young horses whose potential seems limited by other distractions are very often gelded – though promptly ineligible not only for a stud career, but even to run in the Derby.

Grandsire: a horse's grandfather, the sire of its sire.

Grass sickness: a rare but very often fatal condition that attacks the nervous system of horses, typically manifested by paralysis of the digestive tract.

Guineas, the: one of the first two Classics of the season, run over a mile at Newmarket in the spring; the 1000 Guineas is confined to three-year-old fillies only and the 2000 Guineas is open to three-year-old colts and fillies.

Hack: an everyday, utility mount, simply for getting around, though often cherished for long service.

Handicap: a race in which horses are allotted weight according to an official assessment of their merit, the objective being to secure a competitive race between horses of varying ability.

Heat: one of three legs contested, on the same day, to determine the winner of a single prize – a format very popular in the eighteenth century even though race distances then were much longer. If the same horse won the first two heats, there was no need to stage a third.

Hedge: to take out a bet as insurance.

Hobby: an extinct Irish breed of horse, prized as a nimble, agile mount.

Jennet (sometimes 'genet'): a historic breed of saddle horse, tracing to Spain, valued for the smoothness of its gait.

Juvenile: a two-year-old racehorse (though see 'yearling').

Lay: to oppose a horse in a race by accepting a bet on it winning.

Leg: common abbreviation of 'blackleg' above.

Length: standard measure in determining margins at the end of a race, multiplied according to the number of times a horse's length – head to tail – might notionally be interposed between winner and runner-up. In closer finishes, three-quarters and half a length will reduce to a neck, a head, a short head, a nose and, if too close to call, a dead heat.

Macaroni: a Francophile enslaved by an eighteenth-century vogue for overblown, effeminate fashion, extending from coiffure and wardrobe to speech and gesture.

Maiden: a horse yet to win a race; or a race restricted to such horses.

Main: a cockfight between teams, typically gentlemen of one county against another, comprising the same number of birds to be paired in matches.

Match: a race arranged between two horses, with the stakes, weights carried and distance run negotiated between their owners.

Nobbler: one who drugs or injures or otherwise interferes with a horse to prevent it running, or at least showing its best form.

Odds-on: odds so short that your stake, which is returned to you if successful, is greater than your potential winnings.

Outcross: a choice of mate that improves genetic diversity, when a particular bloodline is considered too dominant.

Pacemaker: a front-runner ridden to guarantee a strong gallop in the interest of a fancied runner from the same stable; sometimes, a horse designated the same role on the gallops.

Paddock: often refers to fenced-off pasture on a stud, but can also denote a racecourse parade ring.

Plunger: one who fearlessly risks enormous wagers.

Postilion: the rider of a horse in a pair or team drawing a coach.

Pull: to describe a jockey deliberately restraining his mount from winning; sometimes 'stop'.

Ring, the: only in later years a betting enclosure; originally the community of aristocratic gamblers, together with lowborn 'legs' and 'commissioners', who together comprised the metropolitan betting market.

Ringer: a horse deviously entered for a race under the name of another – often more mature than the animal he is purported to be, and invariably faster.

Scope: the physical reach and range of a horse, specifically its ability to stretch and jump with little evident effort.

Seller: a bargain-basement race in which the winner is put up for auction in the unsaddling enclosure, all other runners meanwhile available to be bought at a stipulated price.

Sire: a stallion; or, when related to a specific horse, its father.

Sorrel: variation on the more conventional 'chestnut' (also 'chesnut') to describe a horse of copper-red coat.

Stakes: in everyday usage, the sum committed to a wager; also the entry fee for a race, pooled for prize money. In modern blood-stock circles, however, a 'stakes' performer or race is formally identified at an elite level of the sport.

Stud: a horse breeding farm, generally with a resident stallion.

Stud Book: a register of pedigrees to authenticate the breed.

Tailed off: to describe a horse that has dropped right away from the back of the field.

Thimblerigger: operator of a primitive version of the three-card trick, using three thimbles and a pea; generally of a build and disposition to discourage questions about his integrity.

Tonic: in former times, a brew or recipe to provide a horse with a boost.

Tout: a gallops spy, who sells information to gamblers about the quality or otherwise of a horse's work.

Turf, the: the horse-racing community and environment – enabling Jack Leach, a former jockey and trainer, to give his memoirs the immortal title *Sods I Have Cut on the Turf*.

Turkoman: a breed of horse tracing to the Central Asian steppes, its powers of endurance belied by a lean, refined physique; forefather of the modern Akhal-Teke and also an influence on the early thoroughbred.

Walkover: a victory by default, when all scheduled opposition has forfeited, nonetheless requiring the 'winner' to appear at the appointed time and place to be ridden past the post.

Warned off: banned by the Jockey Club. Originally the prohibition was confined to its formal jurisdiction, over Newmarket Heath, but was later extended to all courses.

Waste: of a jockey, to sweat off or purge weight.

Welsher: a defaulting bookmaker, who typically disappears during the running of a race.

Withers: the ridge behind the neck and between the shoulders of a horse, traditionally the point at which its height is measured.

Yearling: a horse in the second calendar year of its life, all thoroughbreds being deemed for administrative purposes to be born on 1 January.

Bibliographical Notes

It soon became evident that a conventional bibliography would be highly impractical for a panorama stretching over three centuries and four continents. The alternative may still seem wildly uneven, books cited under one chapter often being no less pertinent to another, but I hope that it might at least be vaguely coherent. The following sources were invaluable throughout:

Oxford Dictionary of National Biography
Roger Mortimer, Richard Onslow and Peter Willett (comp.), *Biographical Encyclopaedia of British Flat Racing* (Macdonald & Jane's, 1978)
Websites www.bloodlines.net; www.tbheritage.com
The various histories of Newmarket: Richard Onslow, *Headquarters: A History of Newmarket and its Racing* (Great Ouse Press, 1983); Frank Siltzer, *Newmarket: Its Sport and Personalities* (Cassell, 1923); Laura Thompson, *Newmarket: From James I to the Present Day* (Virgin, 2000); R. C. Lyle, *Royal Newmarket* (Putnam, 1945); J. P. Hore, *The History of Newmarket and the Annals of the Turf* (A. H. Baily & Co., 1886). A lavish new gem is David Oldrey, Tim Cox and Richard Nash, *The Heath and the Horse: A History of Racing and Art on Newmarket Heath* (Philip Wilson, 2014). Also consistently useful, in broader terms: Roger Mortimer, *The Jockey Club* (Cassell, 1958); Theodore Andrea Cook, *A History of the English Turf* (Virtue, 1905); J. C. Whyte, *A History of the British Turf* (Henry Colbourn, 1840); Theophilus Taunton, *Famous Horses, with Portraits, Pedigrees, Principal Performances etc.* (Sampson Low, Marston, 1901); Roger Longrigg, *The English Squire and His Sport* (Michael Joseph, 1977); Mike Huggins, *Flat Racing and British Society 1790–1914* (Cass, 2000).

Chapter 1: 'The most esteemed race
amongst the Arrabs both by Syre and Dam'

Thomas Darley's letter is at the North Yorkshire County Record Office in Northallerton (DAR.CP1) – a moving document for any man of the Turf to hold in his hands. The Darley family archives there also feature several items relating to the dispute with Marriott's executors, one noting that Thomas's estate included 'an Arabian Horse worth three hundred pounds' (ZDA DDDA/3).

The National Archives at Kew hold extensive records of the Levant Company in Aleppo, including several tantalising glimpses of Thomas Darley. He first appears as early as November 1685 – SP 110/73 (5:2) and is repeatedly referred to as 'Capt' or 'Cape' Darley. (The unnamed portrait at Aldby does show an expatriate wearing some kind of military coat.) His letter home suggests that Darley may have bought his colt around April 1702, when a Company correspondent writes: 'Am just now mounting with Cape Darley to Kifreen & those parts for 4 or 5 dayes' (SP110/22.141).

Captain Wakelin's log is also at Kew (ADM51/479:6) and describes taking merchant vessels under his wing as the convoy overcame tempests and French privateers before reaching Kinsale on 12 May.

Darley's death is recorded as the result of 'a fall from his Horse' (SP110/23.73) but 'our worthy friend' is discovered to have been guilty of 'villany' and 'knavery' in the paperwork he left his partner Marriott (SP110/23.263-268). The latter's misfortunes reach a revolting climax after a riding accident of his own (SP110/23.376).

David Oldrey's unpublished monograph on the Darleys and their Arabian was very useful.

The description of negotiations with Bedouin tribesmen quotes from 'Horse Dealing in Syria, 1854' in *Blackwood's Edinburgh Magazine* (1859).

For Thomas Darley's environment, there is no better starting point than Dr Alexander Russell's *The Natural History of Aleppo* (A. Millar, 1756). Other portraits of Aleppo include two by inquisitive clergymen: *The Diary of Henry Teonge, Chaplain on board his Majesty's*

Ships Assistance, Bristol, and Royal Oak Anno 1675 to 1679 (Charles Knight, 1825) and Henry Maundrell, *A Journey from Aleppo to Jerusalem at Easter AD 1697* (7th edition, W. Meadows, 1749). For the curious conduct of the villagers of Martavan see two aristocratic French travellers, Comte de Volney, *Travels Through Syria and Egypt* (C. G. J. and J. Robinson, 1789) and Baron de Tott, *On the Turks and the Tartars* (Jarvis, Becket & Co., 1785).

According to Major Upton in *Gleanings from the Desert of Arabia* (Kegan Paul, 1881), a tradition still survived at the Aleppo consulate that Darley bought his horse from nomads at Palmyra. The merchants' rediscovery of a lost desert city is described in Rev. William Halifax's *A Relation of a Voyage from Aleppo to Palmyra in Syria* and 'An Extract of the Journals of two several voyages of the English Merchants of the Factory of Aleppo to Tadmor, anciently call'd Palmyra', both in *Philosophical Transactions of the Royal Society* (1695–97, 19:215).

For the lives of English merchants: James Mather, *Pashas: Traders and Travellers in the Islamic World* (Yale University Press, 2011); A. C. Wood, *A History of the Levant Company* (OUP, 1935); Ralph Davis, *Aleppo and Devonshire Square: English Traders in the Levant in the Eighteenth Century* (Macmillan, 1967); Gwilym Ambrose, 'English Traders at Aleppo (1658–1756)' in *Economic History Review* (1931, III:2); M. Epstein, *Early History of the Levant Company* (Routledge, 1908). For a snapshot of another younger son, similar to Thomas Darley, see Adrian Tinniswood's *The Verneys: A True Story of Love, War and Madness in Seventeenth-Century England* (Jonathan Cape, 2007).

For an overview of early British travellers' perspectives: Sarah Searight, *The British in the Middle East* (East-West, 1979); Christine Laidlaw, *The British in the Levant: Trade and Perceptions of the Ottoman Empire in the Eighteenth Century* (I. B. Tauris, 2010); Gerald MacLean & Nabil Matar, *Britain and the Islamic World 1558–1713* (OUP, 2011). A valuable local focus is Abraham Marcus's *The Middle East on the Eve of Modernity: Aleppo in the Eighteenth Century* (Columbia University Press, 1989); see also Bruce Masters, *The Origins of Western Economic Dominance in the Middle East: Mercantilism and the Islamic Economy in Aleppo, 1600–1750* (New York University Press, 1988); and Douglas Carruthers (ed.), *The Desert Route to India, being the*

Journals of Four Travellers by the Great Caravan Route Between Aleppo and Basra 1745–1751 (Hakluyt Society, 1929).

For Western vogues inspired by the Ottoman Empire, see Alexander Bevilacqua and Helen Pfeifer, 'Turquerie: Culture in Motion 1650–1750' in *Past and Present* (2013, 221:1). As for the Arabian horse, contemporary sources cited include *Travels of John Sanderson in the Levant, 1584–1602* (Hakluyt Society, 1931); Guy de la Bédoyère (ed.), *The Diary of John Evelyn* (Boydell Press, 1995); Robert Halsband (ed.), *The Complete Letters of Lady Mary Wortley Montagu* (OUP, 1967); Laurent D'Arvieux, *The Chevalier D'Arvieux's travels in Arabia the desert . . . Done into English by an eminent hand* (Barker & King, 1718); William Cavendish, *A new method, and extraordinary invention, to dress horses* etc (Thos. Milbourn, 1667); Henry Blount, *A Voyage into the Levant* (Andrew Crooke, 1636).

For a later, colonial perspective see Austen Henry Layard, *Discoveries in the Ruins of Nineveh and Babylon* (John Murray, 1853) and William Tweedie, a consul at Baghdad, in *The Arabian Horse, his Country and People* (Blackwood, 1894).

For a remarkable study of the horse's emergence from the Steppes, see Miklós Jankovich, tr. Anthony Dent, *They Rode into Europe: The Fruitful Exchange in the Arts of Horsemanship between East and West* (Harrap, 1971).

Some idea of the practicalities of keeping a horse alive at sea was obtained from Greg Bankoff, 'Big Men, Small Horses' in Edwards, Enenkel and Graham (eds), *The Horse as Cultural Icon: The Real and the Symbolic Horse in the Early Modern World* (Brill, 2011); M. Horace Hayes, *Horses on Board Ship: A Guide to Their Management* (Hurst & Blackett, 1902).

Chapter 2: 'The cross strains now in being are without end'

The tangled roots of the thoroughbred generated some fairly bitter polemics, purists stubbornly insisting that the blood of the modern racehorse preserved some undiluted prepotency imported from the east. But while science has confirmed a fairly narrow genetic pool – and the presence of the Darley Arabian's Y chromosome in 95 per cent of modern thoroughbreds, according to E. P. Cunningham et al. in *Animal Genetics* (2001, 32:6) – it has also demonstrated the role of native and cross-bred populations. Such anguished texts as Lady Wentworth's *Thoroughbred Racing Stock and its Ancestors: the Authentic Origin of Pure Blood* (Allen & Unwin, 1938) now seem to have been muted by mitochondrial DNA analysis, notably a paper by M. A. Bower et al. demonstrating the contribution of native British and Irish mares to a heterogeneous bedrock (*Biology Letters*, 2011, 7).

Their findings lend further distinction to Alexander Mackay-Smith for his brilliantly militant investigation of the breed's roots in *Speed and the Thoroughbred: the Complete History* (Derrydale Press, 2000). See also Richard Nash, '"Honest English Breed": The Thoroughbred as Cultural Metaphor' in K. Raber and T. J. Tucker (eds), *The Culture of the Horse: Status, Discipline, and Identity in the Early Modern World* (Palgrave Macmillan, 2005).

Earlier writers who sought to unravel the dogma included C. M. Prior, whose examination of historic stud registers resulted in *Early Records of the Thoroughbred Horse* (Sportsman Office, 1924) and *The Royal Studs of the Sixteenth and Seventeenth Centuries* (Horse & Hound, 1935); and Peter Willett, *The Thoroughbred* (Weidenfeld & Nicolson, 1970). But as Nicholas Russell observed in *Like Engend'ring Like: Heredity and Animal Breeding in Early Modern England* (CUP, 1986), the disparate origins of horses formally labelled Turk, Barb or Arabian meant that cross-breeding was taking place even among those preserved from indigenous stock. The whole process is harnessed to English self-image in both liberty and empire by Donna Landry in *Noble Brutes: How Eastern Horses Transformed English Culture* (Johns Hopkins University Press, 2009).

The historic role of the horse in everyday British life received little attention before Joan Thirsk's 'Horses in Early Modern England: for Service, for Pleasure, for Power' (Stenton Lectures, University of Reading, 1978), but has since been well explored, in terms of economics, by Peter Edwards in *Horse and Man in Early Modern England* (Bloomsbury, 2007) and, culturally, by Anthony Dent in *Horses in Shakespeare's England* (Dent, 1987).

The superiority of Arabian horsemanship had been observed in

Nahum Tate's translation of *The four epistles of A. G. Busbequius, concerning his embassy into Turkey* (Taylor & Wyat, 1694). Evidence that the English were beginning to absorb these lessons comes from Richard Bradley's husbandry manual *The Gentleman and Farmer's Guide for the increase and improvement of cattle etc* (3rd edition, Hodges, 1739), along with the quote in the title to this chapter.

Unlike most of the Yorkshire breeders, the Darleys were Parliamentarians. Useful context was found in Jack Binns's *Yorkshire in the Civil Wars: Origins, Impact and Outcome* (Blackthorn Press, 2004) and *Yorkshire in the Seventeenth Century* (Blackthorn Press, 2007). See also W. Clay, 'The Gentry of Yorkshire at the Time of the Civil War', *Yorkshire Archaeological Journal*, Vol. 23 (1915). For the raid on Aldby and abduction of Henry Darley, see 'Sir Hugh Cholmley's Narrative of the Siege of Scarborough Castle 1644–45', *English Historical Review* (1917, 32:128).

Mackay-Smith credits Fairfax, sponsor of a bloodless restoration, with a parallel continuity in equine bloodlines during the Protectorate. See Philip Major, '"The Fire of His Eye": Thomas, 3rd Lord Fairfax's "A Treatise Touching the Breeding of Horses"', *Modern Language Review* (2010, 105:1).

For the dispute of Messrs Childers and Peirson, see John Orton's *Turf Annals of York and Doncaster* (Longman, 1844).

Chapter 3: A Groom with a View

In April 1739, the *Gentleman's Magazine* objected that 'our noble breed of horses is now enervated by an intermixture with Turks, Arabians and Barbs, just as our modern nobility and gentry are debauch'd with the effeminate manners of France or Italy'. Though the former complaint proved misplaced, it was pardonable to conflate the two in the 2nd Earl of Portmore. His mother, the feisty royal mistress Catherine Sedley, inherited the verve of a man who had typified the Newmarket court of Charles II. See Vivian de Sola Pinto, *Sir Charles Sedley 1639–1701: a Study in the Life and Literature of the Restoration* (Constable, 1927); and *Restoration Carnival: Five Courtier Poets* (Folio Society, 1954); J. H. Wilson, *The Court*

Wits of the Restoration: An Introduction (Princeton University Press, 1948). See also Avril Lansdell (ed.), *The Portmore Story: Four Generations of Colourful Eighteenth Century Aristocrats* (Elmbridge Borough Council, 1975).

Queen Anne's enthusiasm for the Turf is featured by Sean Magee in *Ascot: The History* (Methuen, 2002). Cited on the disrepute of Hanoverian Newmarket: Daniel Defoe, *A tour through the whole island of Great Britain* (Dent, 1962); and John Macky, *A journey through England in familiar letters from a gentleman here to his friend abroad* (3rd edition, J. Hooke, 1723).

The breed's two other founding fathers, the Godolphin Arabian and the Byerley Turk nowadays receive contrasting treatment. See Mordaunt Miller, *The Godolphin Arabian: the Story of the Matchem Line* (Hyperion Books, 1990), and Richard Nash, '"Beware a Bastard Breed": Notes Towards a Revisionist History of the Thoroughbred Racehorse' in Edwards, Enenkel and Graham (eds), *The Horse as Cultural Icon: The Real and the Symbolic Horse in the Early Modern World* (Brill, 2011).

Details for the sadistic training regime come from Gervase Markham, *Cheap and good husbandry for the well-ordering of all beasts and fowls etc* (George Sawbridge, 1676, 13th edition) and *The experienced jocky, compleat horseman, or gentleman's delight* (Whitwood, 1684), while various hair-raising therapies can be found in Henry Bracken, *Farriery improved; or, a complete treatise on the art of farriery* (Frobisher, 1792) and William Taplin, *The gentleman's stable directory: or, modern system of farriery* (Kearsley, 1788).

For the daily life of stableboys see William Hazlitt, *Memoirs of the Late Thomas Holcroft* (Milford; OUP, 1926); also Henry Fielding's *Joseph Andrews* (Penguin, 1983).

For the Harpur family and the beautiful stableyard built shortly before their acquisition of Squirt, see Howard Colvin, *Calke Abbey Derbyshire: A Hidden House Revealed* (Guild, 1985).

A Day at the Races: Outwood Racecourse, Wakefield, 4 September 1745

A German visitor gives a rare early view of a race meeting in *London in 1710: From the Travels of Zacharias Conrad Von Uffenbach* (Faber & Faber, 1934).

For a broader picture of rural fairs: Robert W. Malcolmson, *Popular Recreations in English Society 1700–1850* (CUP, 1973); and, for a more contemporary flavour, Charles Caraccioli's *An historical account of Sturbridge, Bury, and the most famous fairs in Europe and America* (Fletcher & Hodson, 1767).

The evolution of a sporting calendar is charted by Dennis Brailsford, *A Taste for Diversion: Sport in Georgian England* (Lutterworth Press, 1999); and given specific focus by Iris Middleton and Wray Vamplew, 'Horse-racing and the Yorkshire Leisure Calendar in the Early Eighteenth Century' in *Northern History* (2003, XL: 2).

The scene for this meeting, notably its unique value to Lord Irwin, is set by J. W. Walker in *Wakefield: Its History and People* (1939, 2nd edition). See also G. H. Crowther, *A Descriptive History of the Wakefield Battles: and a Short Account of this Ancient and Important Town* (Wakefield Free Press, 1886); and John Stevens, *Knavesmire: York's Great Racecourse and its Stories* (Pelham, 1984).

Chapter 4: 'He won as many hearts in Newmarket as he lost in Scotland'

The literature of the Jacobite risings has made few detours to sample the panic of 1745 in Yorkshire. Foremost is Cedric Collyer, 'Yorkshire and the "Forty-Five"' in the *Yorkshire Archaeological Journal* (1952), while Jonathan Oates includes 'Independent Volunteer Forces in Yorkshire During the Forty-Five' in the same journal (2001) and *York and the Jacobite Rebellion of 1745* (Borthwick Institute Papers, 2005). Archbishop Herring's role is assessed by R. Barry Levis in 'The Jacobite Uprising of 1745 and the Ecclesiastical Province of York' in *Northern History* (2014, 51:1), while his rousing address at York Castle was printed in full by the *Gentleman's Magazine* (1745).

Herring's correspondence with John Hutton appears in the *Yorkshire Archaeological Journal* (Vol. VI, 1881). Hutton's letter about the female jockeys is in the family archive at the North Yorkshire County Records Office (ZAZ/79). The career of the most extraordinary of all the Yorkshire volunteers is preserved in *The Life of John Metcalf, Commonly Called Blind Jack of Knaresborough* (Peck, 1795).

For the broader history see A. J. Youngson in *The Prince and the Pretender: Two Views of The '45* (Mercat Press, 1996); Frank McLynn's *Bonnie Prince Charlie: Charles Edward Stuart* (Pimlico, 2003); and, enjoyably partisan, Charles Petrie, *The Jacobite Movement: The Last Phase 1716–1807* (Eyre & Spottiswoode, 1950).

W. A. Speck attempts an even hand in *The Butcher: The Duke of Cumberland and the Suppression of the '45* (Wiley-Blackwell, 1981) but Rex Whitworth defends 'an honourable man treated with dishonour' in *William Augustus, Duke of Cumberland: A Life* (Leo Cooper, 1992). Cumberland's role in the story of the thoroughbred awaits a fuller exploration, but see Arthur FitzGerald, *Royal Thoroughbreds: A History of the Royal Studs* (Sidgwick & Jackson, 1990); and Robert Black, *The Jockey Club and its Founders* (Smith Elder, 1891).

Chapter 5: 'Eclipse first, the rest nowhere'

The story of Dennis O'Kelly, Charlotte Hayes and Eclipse is told by Nicholas Clee in *Eclipse* (Bantam Press, 2009). Not that fact and myth have been remotely separable since the hasty publication, after his death, of *The Genuine Memoirs of Dennis O'Kelly, Esq, Commonly Called Count O'Kelly* (Stalker, 1788). Other versions include Theodore Andrea Cook, *Eclipse and O'Kelly* (Dutton & Co, 1907); Henry Blyth, *The High Tide of Pleasure: Seven English Rakes* (Weidenfeld & Nicolson, 1970); Bracy Clark, *A Short History of the Celebrated Racehorse Eclipse* (C. Richards, 1838).

The partnership of O'Kelly and Charlotte Hayes is given valuable context by Hallie Rubenhold, *The Covent Garden Ladies: Pimp General Jack and the Extraordinary Story of Harris's List* (History Press, 2005).

For a panorama of the sex trade, see Dan Cruickshank, *The Secret History of Georgian London* (Random House, 2009); Fergus Linnane, *Madams: Bawds and Brothel Keepers of London* (Stroud Sutton, 2005); E. J. Burford, *Wits, Wenchers and Wantons: London's Low Life* (Robert Hale, 1986).

Colourful eyewitness testimony is provided by Monk of the Order of St Francis, *Nocturnal Revels: or The History of King's-Place and other Modern Nunneries* (M. Goadby, 1779); and *The Life of Dick En-l-d alias Captain En-l-d of Turf Memory* (T. Boosey, 1792). See also Walter Jerrold (ed.), *Bon-Mots of Samuel Foote and Theodore Hook* (Dent, 1898); and, for the Fleet Prison, Moses Pitt, *The Cry of the Oppressed* (1691).

For Viscount Bolingbroke's circle, see S. P. Kerr, *George Selwyn and the Wits* (Methuen, 1909); J. H. Jesse, *George Selwyn and his Contemporaries, with memoirs and notes* (Richard Bentley, 1843); E. S. Roscoe and Helen Clergue, *George Selwyn, his Letters and his Life* (Fisher Unwin, 1899); L. Melville, *The Star of Piccadilly: A Memoir of William Douglas* (Hutchinson, 1927); Henry Blyth, *Old Q, the Rake of Piccadilly* (Weidenfeld & Nicolson, 1967).

See also Basil Taylor, *Stubbs* (Phaidon, 1971) and Judy Egerton, *George Stubbs, Painter: Catalogue Raisonné* (Yale, 2007).

Chapter 6: Breeding Discontent

For the exceptionally obtuse characters in the Grosvenor love triangle, see Stella Tillyard, *A Royal Affair: George III and his Troublesome Siblings* (Chatto & Windus, 2006); Charles Neilson Gattey, *'Farmer' George's Black Sheep: The Lives and Loves of George III's Brothers and Sister* (Kensal Press, 1985). Their story scarcely requires the exaggeration of such contemporary accounts as *Authentic and Interesting Memoirs of Miss Ann Sheldon* (printed privately, 1787–8); *An Apology for the conduct of Lady Grosvenor* (T. Walker, 1770); and *Copies of the depositions of the witnesses examined in the cause of divorce between Richard Lord Grosvenor and Henrietta lady Grosvenor* (J. Russell, 1771).

At least the odious Bully introduces us to two richer characters in his wife and her lover, all three well portrayed by Carola Hicks in *Improper Pursuits: The Scandalous Life of Lady Di Beauclerk* (Macmillan, 2001). See also Lord Herbert (ed.), *Henry, Elizabeth and George: Letter and Diaries of Henry, Tenth Earl of Pembroke and his Circle* (Jonathan Cape, 1939); Andrea M. Montague, "'That Insuperable Idleness'": An Account of Topham Beauclerk' in the *South Atlantic Quarterly* (1973, 72:IV).

Bernard Falk, *The Royal Fitz Roys* (Hutchinson, 1950) contrasts the monstrous Duke of Grafton depicted in the *Letters of Junius* (see, for instance, the OUP version of 1978) with the weak, vacillating man of flesh. Neither survives the aridity of Sir William Anson (ed.), *Autobiography and Political Correspondence of Augustus Henry, third Duke of Grafton* (John Murray, 1898). A useful summary is Peter Durrant's 'The Duke of Grafton (1768–70)' in Herbert van Thal (ed.), *The Prime Ministers* Vol. I (Allen & Unwin, 1974), while the ministry's most celebrated bequest is considered by David W. Lindsay in 'Junius and the Grafton Administration 1768–1770' in *Prose Studies: History, Theory, Criticism* (1986, 9:II). For a portrait of Nancy Parsons see Horace Bleackley, *Ladies Fair and Frail: Sketches of the Demi-Monde during the Eighteenth Century* (J. Lane, 1909). The privileges applied to get marriages annulled are measured by Lawrence Stone, *The Road to Divorce: England 1530–1987* (OUP, 1990) and *Broken Lives: Separation and Divorce in England 1660–1857* (OUP, 1993).

Abingdon's own writing is full of gusto: *Thoughts on the letter of Edmund Burke, Esq, to the sheriffs of Bristol, on the affairs of America* (W. Jackson, 1777) and *An Adieu to the Turf* (M. Smith, 1778). That he was considered no mere crank is made clear by G. H. Gutteridge, *English Whiggism and the American Revolution* (University of California Press, 1942); and Paul H. Smith in introducing *English Defenders of American Freedoms, 1774–1778* (Library of Congress, 1972). For a biographical survey see D. McCulloch, 'The musical oeuvre of Willoughby Bertie, 4th Earl of Abingdon (1740–99)', *Royal Musical Association Research Chronicle*, 33 (2000). His row with Dennis O'Kelly at Burford is recorded in the *Sporting Magazine* (1793) and the sale of Pot8os to Grosvenor in William Pick's *Turf Register, and Sportsman & Breeder's Stud-book* (A. Bartholoman, 1803). Abingdon has lost credibility by the time he surfaces in *The Manuscripts and Correspondence of James, first Earl of Charlemont*, Vol. 1 (HMSO, 1891).

See also William Griffiths, Grosvenor's stud-groom, *A Practical Treatise on Farriery* (J. Marsh, 1795).

Chapter 7: The Way Ahead

Enthusiasm for Bunbury in all the Turf histories is not shared by his first wife: Ilchester, Stavor (eds), *The Life and Letters of Lady Sarah Lennox, 1745–1826* (John Murray, 1901); also Stella Tillyard, *Aristocrats: Caroline, Emily, Louisa and Sarah Lennox 1740–1832* (Chatto & Windus, 1994). John Lawrence attests to the great moderniser's aversion to sweat-rugs in *British Field Sports: Embracing Practical Instructions in Shooting, Hunting, Coursing, Racing, Cocking etc.* (Sherwood, Neely & Jones, 1818).

Samuel Chifney Sr. is the first of countless characters introduced to the text via *The Druid*, nom de plume of Henry Hall Dixon – through *The Post and the Paddock* (Piper Stephenson, 1856). This was followed by *Silk and Scarlet* (Robinson & Tuxford, 1859) and *Scott and Sebright* (Rogerson & Tuxford, 1862), three books in six years that brought the Turf to life with a richness seldom matched since. Charles Apperley as *Nimrod* had lit his path with *The Chace, the Turf and the Road* (John Murray, 1843, 2nd edition) while Robert Colton, as *Sylvanus*, produced a one-off classic in *The Bye-lanes and Downs of England, with Turf Scenes and Characters* (Richard Bentley, 1850). Between them, these three writers attested to the maturing skills of a sporting press ever wider in its embrace.

As the first celebrity jockey, Samuel Chifney Sr wrote an auto-biography modestly entitled *Genius Genuine* (Shury, 1803). For the despairing remark about his royal patrons see Countess Minto (ed.), *Life and Letters of Sir Gilbert Elliott, First Earl of Minto* (Longmans Green, 1874). The many versions of the Escape scandal include Michael Seth-Smith, *Bred for the Purple* (Random House, 1969); Amanda Murray, *All the Kings' Horses: A Celebration of Royal Horses from 1066 to the Present Day* (Robson Books, 2006); Vincent Orchard, *Tattersalls* (Hutchinson, 1953).

The little known about Sir Ferdinando Poole we owe to the son of his ward Bessy, as explored by James Bieri in *Percy Bysshe Shelley, A Biography: Youth's Unextinguished Fire* (University of Delaware Press, 2004); there is a glimpse of Poole's charity to the townsfolk in Cheryl R. Lutring, *Lewes Racecourse: A Legacy Lost?* (Phreestyle Pholios, 2013).

A Day at the Races: Epsom, 16 May 1793

Every Derby depicted in this book will have been sketched from *The History of the Derby Stakes* by Roger Mortimer (Michael Joseph, 1973). Further shading came from Edward Moorhouse, *The Romance of the Derby* (Biographical Press, 1908), and Michael Wynn Jones, *The Derby* (Croom Helm, 1979).

The French visitor cited was Pierre Jean Grosley, in *A tour to London; or, new observations on England and its inhabitants*, trans. Thomas Nugent (Lockyer Davis, 1772). For Egremont's loss of £500, see G. Holman, *The Good Old Times; or Sussex 100 Years Ago* (Sussex Express, 1887).

Ogden's claims as the first recognisable bookmaker feature in Carl Chinn, *Better Betting with a Decent Feller: A Social History of Bookmaking* (Aurum, 2004). Sir John Lade's description comes from the *Sporting Magazine* (1793); some of his other behaviour from Lewis Melville, *Some Eccentrics and a Woman* (Martin Secker, 1911).

Chapter 8: The Regeneration Gap

For Henry Mellish, most attractive of the Turf's many wastrels, see Thomas Raikes, *A Portion of the Journal Kept by Thomas Raikes, Esq., from 1831 to 1847: Comprising Reminiscences of Social and Political life in London and Paris during that period* (Longman Brown, 1858); and, a consistently fertile source, J. S. Fletcher in *The History of the St Leger Stakes 1776–1901* (Hutchinson, 1902). Sancho's match at Lewes is in the *Sporting Magazine* (1806). For the naked duellist Howorth, see Alfred Spencer (ed.), *The Memoirs of William Hickey* (Hurst & Blackett, 1948).

For Egremont's benevolent regime at Petworth, see H. A. Wyndham, *A Family History 1688–1837: The Wyndhams of Somerset, Sussex, and Wiltshire* (OUP, 1950); D. B. Brown, C. Rowell and I. Warrell (eds.), *Turner at Petworth* (Tate Publishing, 2002); Martin Butlin, *Turner at Petworth: Painter and Patron* (Tate Publishing, 1989); Alun Howkins, 'J. M. W. Turner at Petworth: Agricultural Improvement and the Politics of Landscape' in John Barrell (ed.), *Painting and the Politics of Culture: New Essays on British Art 1700–1850* (Oxford University Press, 1992). See also Alexander Penrose (ed.), *The Autobiography and Memoirs of Benjamin Robert Haydon 1786–1846* (G. Bell, 1927); C. R. Leslie, *Autobiographical Recollections* (John Murray, 1860); and Sir H. Maxwell (ed.), *The Creevey Papers, a Selection from the Correspondence and Dairies of Thomas Creevey* (John Murray, 1903). Thormanby also draws an affectionate portrait of Egremont in *Kings of the Turf* (Hutchinson, 1898).

Grafton's reformation is attested by his own hand in *Hints Etc Submitted to the serious attention of the clergy, nobility and gentry by 'a layman'* (White & Debrett, 1789, 2nd edition) and *The serious reflections of a Rational Christian* (1797); and by his vicar in Thomas Belsham, *Uncorrupted Christianity unpatronised by the great* (Johnson, 1811).

The Druid's evidence regarding the training methods of the younger Chifneys is backed up in H. C. Howard and W. G. Craven, *Racing and Steeple-chasing* (Longmans Green, 1886).

Chapter 9: Nobblers, Broken Heads and the 'artful dodger of the corps'

Many of the rogues and worthies contesting in this chapter (and Chapter 11) have been in familiar circulation since first appearing in the work of *Nimrod*, *Sylvanus* and *The Druid*. Daniel Dawson's denouncement of the Jockey Club from death row made the *Sporting Magazine* (1812) and the rout of the thimbleriggers at the 1829 St Leger meeting gave a martial quality to all this class warfare. The Duke of Cleveland is identified as one of the victorious generals in the *Spectator's* account of 19 September 1829, but otherwise the episode is one of many borrowed from a four-volume kaleidoscope by the priceless John Fairfax-Blakeborough, *Northern Turf History* (J. A. Allen, 1948).

The fake Polish countess is from E. Neale, *Whychcotte of St John's; or, The Court, the Camp, the Quarter-deck and the Cloister* (Effingham Wilson, 1833). For the reach of Jemmy Bland's tentacles, see Rev. James Pycroft, *The Cricket-Field* (Longman Green, 1854, 2nd edition); the immortal notion of Bland 'eating birds' nests in Pekin with chopsticks' is from Bernard Darwin, *John Gully and His Times* (Cassell, 1935).

The detailed description of the St Leger comes from the *Sporting Magazine* (1829) and the *Oriental Sporting Magazine* (1830).

Chapter 10: The West Awake

John Welcome essays a thorough review in *Irish Horseracing: An Illustrated History* (Macmillan, 1982); while Fergus D'Arcy provides plenty of original material in *Horses Lords and Racing Men: The Turf Club 1790–1990* (Turf Club, 1991) – not least regarding the Ruthven affair. Contemporary sources for this include the *New Sporting Magazine* (1836) and Maurice O'Connell (ed.), *The Correspondence of Daniel O'Connell* (Irish University Press, 1973).

The Irish sport's early administration is explored in James Kelly, 'The Pastime of the Elite: Clubs and Societies and the Promotion of Horse Racing', in J. Kelly & M. J. Powell (eds), *Clubs and Societies in Eighteenth-Century Ireland* (Four Courts Press, 2010). The modest first advertisement for Birdcatcher at stud is from Tony and Annie Sweeney, *The Sweeney Guide to the Irish Turf 1501–2001* (Edmund Burke Publisher, 2002); and his corresponding obscurity, at first, from the *Bloodstock Breeders Review* of 1915. See also M. F. Cox, *Notes of the History of the Irish Horse* (Sealy, Bryers & Walker, 1897); S. J. Watson, *Between the Flags: A History of Irish Steeplechasing* (A. Figgis, 1969); Harry R. Sargent, *Thoughts Upon Sport* (Simkin Marshall, 1895); and Noel Phillips Browne, *The Horse in Ireland* (Pelham, 1967).

The remarkable family of Mrs George Watts is chronicled by Rev. Donald D. Mackinnon, *Memoirs of Clan Fingon* (Lewis

Hepworth and Co., 1899). His outlandish claims about Napoleon and Harriet's sister are supported by Robert Southey in his *History of the Peninsular War, Vols I & II* (John Murray, 1823) and in Rev. C. C. Southey, *The Life and Correspondence of Robert Southey, Vol. IV* (Longman, 1850).

The German prince's memorable day at the races comes from Hermann Pückler-Muskau's *Tour in England, Ireland, and France in the Years 1828, 1829, with remarks on the manners and customs of the inhabitants* etc (Library of Congress, 1833).

Chapter 11: 'I see a rum set in my day . . .
But these beat all calculation.'

Another chapter grown largely from the seeds sown by *Sylvanus*, *Nimrod* and *The Druid*.

For John Scott's conservative methods, see John B. Radcliffe, *Ashgill, or the Life and Times of John Osborne* (Sands, 1900); and for the financial rewards that confirmed his status, see M. J. Huggins, *Kings of the Moor: North Yorkshire Trainers 1760–1900* (University of Teeside, 1991).

The key appraisal of Bentinck is by Michael Seth-Smith, *Lord Paramount of the Turf: Lord George Bentinck, 1802–1848* (Faber & Faber, 1971). John Kent, the trainer, preserves his patron in a brine of sycophancy in his *Racing Life of Lord George Cavendish Bentinck, M. P. and other Reminiscences* (Blackwood, 1892); in the opposing camp is the mendacious author of *Reminiscences of William Day of Danebury* (R. Bentley, 1886). If Day fails to mention his attempt to cripple a Derby favourite, it is not overlooked by the *Sporting Magazine* (1845).

The Running Rein scandal has been well set in context by Nicholas Foulkes, *Gentlemen and Blackguards: Gambling Mania and the Plot to Steal the Derby of 1844* (Weidenfeld & Nicolson, 2010); and M. J. Huggins, 'Lord George Bentinck and Racing Morality in Mid-Nineteenth Century England: The "Running Rein" Derby Revisited' in the *International Journal of the History of Sport* (1996, 13:3). For the allegation that Little Wonder was also a ringer, see Sir John D. Astley, *Fifty Years of My Life in the World of Sport at Home* and *Abroad* (Hurst & Blackett, 1894). See also Henry Blyth's *Hell and Hazard* (Weidenfeld & Nicolson, 1969) and Thormanby's *Sporting Stories* (Mills & Boon, 1909).

A Day at the Races: Doncaster, 17 September 1845

Besides contemporary accounts, notably in the *Sportsman* (1845), The Baron's St Leger was reviewed over a decade later in the *Sporting Review* (1857); and the objection received by the stewards over dinner later still in *Baily's Magazine* (1883).

Chapter 12: 'Mr Palmer passes me five times in five minutes.'

The story of Sidney Herbert and his disenchantment with both Caroline Norton and the Turf so aptly condensed the mid-century evolution of what came to be known as 'Victorian values' that Norton, described by Sydney Smith as 'that superb lump of flesh', consecutively provided Trollope, Disraeli and Meredith with a model so thinly disguised that the latter was obliged, following legal action by her family, to preface later editions of *Diana of The Crossways* (Chapman & Hall, 1889) with a note disowning the calumnies he had revived. See Diane Atkinson, *The Criminal Conversation of Mrs Norton* (Preface Publishing, 2012), and Alan Chedzoy, *A Scandalous Woman* (Allison & Busby, 1992).

For Herbert himself – a man described by Richard Monckton Milnes as 'just the man to rule England . . . birth, wealth, grace, tact, and not too much principle' – see Tresham Lever, *The Herberts of Wilton* (John Murray, 1967); also, though heavily sanitised, Arthur H.-G. Stanmore, *Sidney Herbert, Lord Herbert of Lea: A Memoir* (Dutton, 1906).

Herbert's role in the repeal of the Corn Laws made an enemy of Bentinck, whose outrage was preserved in Benjamin Disraeli's *Lord George Bentinck: a Political Biography* (Colburn, 1852). For the reference to Bentinck hoisting Disraeli into the saddle, see Lady Gregory (ed.), *Sir William Gregory: An Autobiography* (John Murray, 1894).

For contrasting responses to the 1845 St Leger see the *Sportsman* of that year: indignation on behalf of George Watts in October; and perplexity over the success of Irish breeders in November. For a proud compatriot's claims on behalf of 'Irish Birdcatcher' see R. H. Copperthwaite, *The Turf and the Racehorse: Describing Trainers and Training, the Stud-farm, the Sires and Brood-mares of the Past and Present* (Day, 1865).

The spectacular burnout of Jack Mytton was recorded at first hand by his friend Nimrod in *Memoirs of the Life of the Late John Mytton* (Ackermann, 1837, 2nd edition); see also Richard Darwall in *Madcap's Progress: The Life of the Eccentric Regency Sportsman John Mytton* (Dent, 1938); and, best and briefest, Edith Sitwell in *English Eccentrics* (Faber & Faber, 1933).

At the opposite end of the spectrum of Victorian cautionary tales looms Dr Palmer. Looking back over his Turf career in *Kingsclere* (Chatto & Windus, 1896), the great John Porter remembered how, in his youth, he was given a note by the family doctor to tell their mutual trainer that his friend Cook had died. The seventeen racehorses owned by the Rugeley poisoner prompted a plethora of such moralising books and pamphlets as *The doings of William Palmer, the alleged wholesale poisoner: his public frauds and private trickeries; with a glance at his career in connection with the Turf and betting men* (F. Mitchell, 1860); *Illustrated life and career of William Palmer of Rugeley: containing details of his conduct as a school-boy, medical student, racing-man, and poisoner* etc (Ward & Lock, 1856). See also Anthony Hunt and John Griffiths, *Hednesford's Horse Racing History* (Mount Chase Press, 2010). For a modern perspective on the Palmer case, see Ian Burney, *Poison, Detection and the Victorian Imagination* (Manchester University Press, 2006).

Chapter 13: Full Steam Ahead

Roy Church provides a comprehensive background to the rise of James Merry in *The History of the British Coal Industry, Vol. III, 1830–1913* (OUP, 1986); while Alan Campbell illuminates life below ground in 'Honourable Men and Degraded Slaves: A Comparative

Study of Trade Unionism in Two Lanarkshire Mining Communities 1830–1874' and, with Fred Reid, 'The Independent Collier in Scotland', both in Royden Harrison (ed.), *Independent Collier: The Coal Miner as Archetypal Proletarian Reconsidered* (Palgrave Macmillan, 1978); and *The Lanarkshire Miners: A Social History of their Trade Unions 1775–1874* (John Donald, 1979). See also: R. P. Arnot, *A History of Scottish Miners from the Earliest Times* (Allen & Unwin, 1955); Andrew Miller, *The Rise and Progress of Coatbridge and surrounding neighbourhood* (D. Robertson, 1864). For the self-taught poet Janet Hamilton, see *Poems, Essays and Sketches* (J. Maclehose, 1880).

On the 'Cottage Countess' see Elisabeth Inglis-Jones, *The Lord of Burghley* (Faber & Faber, 1964). Family historian G. Ravenscroft Dennis does not dress up the bigotry of her son, Lord Exeter, in *The House of Cecil* (Constable, 1914).

Merry and Exeter feature among several useful portraits in T. H. Bird, *Admiral Rous and the English Turf* (Putnam, 1939). For the admiral's determination to get his leaking frigate home in time for Newmarket, see Lady Augusta Fane, *Chit Chat* (Thornton Butterworth, 1926).

For the impact of the railways see Wray Vamplew, *The Turf: A Social and Economic History of Horse Racing* (Viking, 1976). The experiences of Dickens in Doncaster are recorded in Charles Dickens and Wilkie Collins, *The Lazy Tour of Two Idle Apprentices* (Hesperus Press, 2011). As for the case that may have inspired *Jarndyce v. Jarndyce*, see Herbert Barry, 'Mr Thellusson's Will' in the *Virginia Law Review* (1936 22:IV).

Chapter 14: Old Sweats and New Money

Despite the brass-necked claims of William Day in *The Racehorse in Training; with Hints on Racing and Racing Reforms* (Chapman & Hall, 1880), it was John Dawson who first 'astonished the old hands' at Newmarket by renouncing the 'sweats' regime – as Fairfax-Blakeborough attests in *Sporting Days and Stories* (P. Allan, 1925). The spectacular career of his brother is recorded in E. M. Humphris, *The Life of Mathew Dawson* (Witherby, 1928), while Henry Custance recalls winning the Derby for Dawson and Merry in *Riding Recollections and Turf Stories* (Edward Arnold, 1894).

For very useful insights into the life of stable staff see M. J. Huggins, 'Nineteenth-Century Racehorse Stables in their Rural Setting: A Social and Economic Study' in *Rural History* (1996, 7:2). For Thomas Ward, see Jesse Myers, *Baron Ward and the Dukes of Parma* (Longmans Green, 1938) and Alexander, Lord Lamington, *In the Days of the Dandies* (Eveleigh Nash, 1906). The culture of stable secrecy is confirmed in Charles Alderson, *Selections from the Charges and other Detached Papers of Baron Alderson* (John W. Parker, 1858); see also A. E. T. Watson, *The Racing World and its Inhabitants* (Macmillan, 1904).

Londesborough (Lord Albert Denison as he then was) emerges as a civilised product of his class and time in *Wanderings in Search of Health* (priv. 1849). He also makes a cameo appearance in *Left Hand, Right Hand!* (Macmillan, 1945) by his grandson, Osbert Sitwell.

For the humble origins of Merry's rivals, see Andrew MacGeorge, *The Bairds of Gartsherrie* (Glasgow University Press, 1875); for Richard Naylor's antecedents, John Hughes, *Liverpool Banks and Bankers 1760–1837* (Henry Young, 1906). Leyland's violations of slaving regulations are suggested in J. E. Inikori, 'Market Structure and the Profits of the British African Slave Trade' in *Journal of Economic History* (1981, 41:4); see also Katie McDade, 'Liverpool Slave Merchant Entrepreneurial Networks 1725–1807' in *Business History* (2011, 53:7); and Richardson, Schwarz and Tibble (eds), *Liverpool and Transatlantic Slavery* (Liverpool University Press, 2010).

A Day at the Races: Epsom, 20 May 1863

For the inspiration to his masterpiece, see William Powell Frith, *My Autobiography and Reminiscences* (Richard Bentley, 1887). Descriptions of the day are otherwise based on material in *Baily's Magazine* (1863).

The despair of Fordham is recorded in George Hodgman, *Sixty Years on the Turf* (G. Richards, 1901), while William Day's opinion of Johnstone's 'plunging' is in a *Sporting Life* compendium: *The British Turf and the Men who Have Made It* (Biographical Press, 1906).

Chapter 15: 'She is my brood mare.
The others are my hacks'

The chapter's title quote is from Jane Ridley's fine biography, *Bertie: A Life of Edward VII* (Vintage, 2013); others include Philip Magnus, *King Edward the Seventh* (E. P. Dutton, 1964); E. F. Benson, *Edward VII: An Appreciation* (Longmans, 1933); Sidney Lee, *King Edward VII: A Biography* (Macmillan, 1927); Christopher Hibbert, *Edward VII: The Last Victorian King* (Palgrave Macmillan, 2007). Elizabeth Hamilton puts the flesh on the bones of the Mordaunt divorce saga in *The Warwickshire Scandal* (Michael Russell, 1999).

Henry Chaplin, who introduced Bertie to the Turf, is central to a little gem in Henry Blyth, *The Pocket Venus: A Victorian Scandal* (Walker, 1966) – containing much that the Marchioness of Londonderry could hardly, as his daughter, submit to the public in *Henry Chaplin: A Memoir* (Macmillan, 1926).

For Christopher Sykes and his family, see his nephew and namesake in the minor classic *Four Studies in Loyalty* (Collins, 1946); and his grandson C. S. Sykes in *The Visitors' Book* (Putnam, 1978). Fairfax-Blakeborough must for once be counted an also-ran with *Sykes of Sledmere* (Philip Allan, 1929).

For Westminster see Gervas Huxley, *Victorian Duke: The Life of Hugh Lupus Grosvenor, First Duke of Westminster* (OUP, 1967); also F. B. Smith, *The Making of the Second Reform Bill* (CUP, 1966); Maurice Cowling, *1867: Disraeli, Gladstone and Revolution* (CUP, 1967). Sources regarding Rosebery are listed under Chapter 17, though his dowry can be judged from Richard Davis, *The English Rothschilds* (Collins, 1983) and George Ireland, *Plutocrats: A Rothschild Inheritance* (John Murray, 2007).

The early careers of Robert Peck and Jem Snowden are stitched together by Fairfax-Blakeborough in *Malton Memories and l'Anson Triumphs* (Truslore & Bray, 1925). Peck's preparation of Doncaster to win the Derby for Merry features in Sydenham Dixon, *From Gladiateur to Persimmon: Turf Memories of Thirty Years* (Grant Richards, 1901); so does the nerve of Merry's favourite jockey 'Speedy' Payne.

Doncaster's Epsom success was played out against a grim background at the pithead, explored in Fred Reid, 'Alexander Macdonald and the Crisis of the Independent Collier 1872–74' in Royden Harrison (ed.), *Independent Collier: The Coal Miner as Archetypal Proletarian Reconsidered* (Palgrave Macmillan, 1978). See also Gordon M. Wilson, *Alexander McDonald: Leader of the Miners* (Elsevier Science, 1982).

For an entertaining account of Richard Naylor in cranky old age, and much else besides, see Lord Rossmore *Things I Can Tell* (Eveleigh Nash, 1912); and, for Stockwell's own last years, a rare interview with a celebrated stud groom in John Griffiths in the *Bloodstock Breeders' Review* of 1915.

A Day at the Races: Alexandra Palace, 1 July 1868

This draws heavily on a horrifying description in James Greenwood, *The Seven Curses of London* (Stanley Rivers, 1869). For the elderly man beaten up by a welshing gang and the revenge of the gentry see Dyke Wilkinson, *Rough Roads* (Sampson Low Marston, 1912). The race meeting advertisement is from the *Saturday Review*, 20 June 1868. See also Ron Carrington, *Alexandra Park and Palace: A History* (GLC, 1975).

Chapter 16: 'The lad rode as well as any could'

John Welcome's biography *Fred Archer: His Life and Times* (Faber & Faber, 1967) is worthy of its great subject; see also *The Three Archers* (S. H. Brookes, 1885) by 'A Cheltonian' and E. M. Humphris, *The Life of Fred Archer* (Brentano's, 1923). For an insight into the privations of earlier jockeys, see the *Sporting Magazine* (1806).

A royal tip for Lillie Langtry appears in Caroline Ramsden, *Ladies in Racing* (S. Paul, 1973), while Bertie's first investments in a stud are charted by A. E. T. Watson in *King Edward VII as a Sportsman* (Longmans, 1911).

For the burnout of the Bairds' fortune, see Richard Onslow, *The Squire: Life of George Alexander Baird, Gentleman Rider 1861–1893*

(Harrap, 1980); while the resolution of the Bend Or identity crisis is in M. A. Bower et al., 'Truth in the Bones: Resolving the Identity of the Founding Elite Thoroughbred Racehorses' in *Archaeometry* (2012, 54:5).

Chapter 17: 'My God, Berkeley, this is too hot!'

Rosebery was a Charles James Fox for his times, a radical at home on the Turf and in great houses, witty, erudite and cynical. The standard biography by Robert Rhodes James, *Rosebery* (Weidenfeld & Nicolson, 1963), captured the enigma well but Leo McKinstry has made fine use of fresh material in *Rosebery: Statesman in Turmoil* (John Murray, 2005). Two fine contemporary portraits, expressing disappointment and adoration respectively, can be found in A. G. Gardiner, *Prophets, Priests and Kings* (Dent, 1914) and John Buchan, *Lord Rosebery, 1847–1930* (H. Milford, 1931); Winston Churchill managed to find the middle ground in *Great Contemporaries* (Thornton Butterworth, 1937). An official biography by the Marquess of Crewe, *Lord Rosebery* (John Murray, 1931), was hopelessly asphyxiated by the wariness of a son-in-law. For a focus on his Turf career, see Edmund Heathcote Thruston, *Earl of Rosebery, Statesman and Sportsman* (Tavistock Press, 1928).

McKinstry is persuasively dismissive of conspiracy theories connecting Rosebery's putative homosexuality and the prosecution of Oscar Wilde but these are placed in enlightening context by Brian Roberts in *The Mad Bad Line: The Family of Lord Alfred Douglas* (Hamilton, 1981); and Linda Stratmann, *The Marquess of Queensberry* (Yale, 2013).

Anita Leslie's *Edwardians in Love* (Hutchinson, 1972) is essential background to the bounders of the Marlborough House set, though something of their better side comes through in *The Memoirs of Admiral Lord Charles Beresford* (Methuen, 1914); and in Geoffrey Bennett, *Charlie B* (Dawnay, 1968). See also the Countess of Warwick, *Life's Ebb and Flow* (Hutchinson, 1929) and *Afterthoughts* (Cassell, 1931). For Baron Hirsch, see Anthony Allfrey, *Edward VII and His Jewish Court* (Weidenfeld & Nicolson, 1991); and for a review of the

Tranby Croft affair, see Michael Havers, Edward Grayson and Peter Shankland, *The Royal Baccarat Scandal* (Souvenir Press, 1988).

Though hardly the autobiography it might have been, Lillie Langtry recorded her visit to the Kisber Stud in *The Days I Knew* (Hutchinson, 1925). The development of the Hungarian Turf is explored in Miklos Zeidler, 'English Influences on Modern Sport in Hungary', in *Hungarian Quarterly* (2006, Vols 181 and 182); and John Pinfold, 'Foreign Devil Riders', *Hungarian Quarterly* (2008, Vol. 192).

A Day at the Races: Ascot, 17 June 1897

Especially useful here was Richard Marsh's autobiography, *Trainer to Two Kings* (Cassell, 1925). For Bertie's letter, see Theo Lang, *My Darling Daisy* (Sphere, 1968). General Williams encounters the tip of a parasol in J. B. Booth, *Old Pink 'Un Days* (Grant Richards, 1924).

Chapter 18: 'He is far ahead of the lot, even with all his faults'

This period falls within the ageless compass of George Lambton, *Men and Horses I Have Known* (Thornton Butterworth, 1924). Background to his life, and that of his brother, can be found in John Colville, *Those Lambtons! A Most Unusual Family* (Hodder & Stoughton, 1988).

James Lambie, *The Story of Your Life: A History of the Sporting Life Newspaper* (Matador, 2010) is illuminating throughout, and for the Lambtons' heyday in particular – their anti-doping crusade placed memorably in context by a 1900 report that the Jockey Clubs of Austria and Hungary had prohibited all doping except with whisky, sherry and champagne.

See also George Plumptre, *The Fast Set* (Andre Deutsch, 1985); Stuart Menzies, *Lord William Beresford: Some Memories of a Famous Sportsman, Soldier and Wit* (Herbert Jenkins, 1917); C. R. Acton,

Silk and Spur (Richards, 1935); and John Dizikes *Yankee Doodle Dandy: The Life and Times of Tod Sloan* (University of Nebraska Press, 2004). This excellent biography is underpinned by its subject's own words in *Tod Sloan by Himself* (Grant Richards, 1915).

For a portrait of McCalmont see A. E. T. Watson, *A Sporting and Dramatic Career* (Macmillan, 1918). See also the Duke of Portland, *Men, Women and Things* (Faber & Faber, 1937) and *Memories of Racing and Hunting* (Faber & Faber, 1935); *John Porter of Kingsclere, an Autobiography* (Grant Richards, 1919); and, a dismal disappointment considering his prominence in scandal, Sir George Chetwynd in *Racing Reminiscences, and Experiences of the Turf* (Longmans, Green & Co., 1891).

Sir Charles Rose's loss of two sons in South Africa is recorded by Captain Sir George Arthur in *The Story of the Household Cavalry*, Vol. II (Archibald Constable, 1909). His kinship with Mr Toad, along with the tale of another tragic son, is dealt with in Josceline Dimbleby, *A Profound Secret: Mary Gaskell, her daughter Amy, and Edward Burne-Jones* (Doubleday, 2004).

For Rosebery's son-in-law, see James Pope-Hennessy, *Lord Crewe 1858–1945: The Likeness of a Liberal* (Constable, 1955). Quentin Crewe's recollections of his grandfather in *Well, I Forget the Rest* (Hutchinson, 1991) are not terribly warm, but another side to the man can be heard directly in *Stray Verses 1889–1890* (John Murray, 1891).

For Disraeli's conversation with Bismarck, see William Monypenny and George Buckle (eds), *The Life of Benjamin Disraeli, Earl of Beaconsfield* Vol. VI (John Murray, 1920); and for speculations about the new king's style, see Randolph S. Churchill, *Winston S. Churchill: Youth 1874–1900* (Heinemann, 1966). The ever interesting Regy Brett's reflections on the transformation in Bertie, after winning the Derby, come from Lord Esher, *Cloud-Capp'd Towers* (John Murray, 1927).

Chapter 19: Jewels in the Crown

The Big Hole at Kimberley could almost be filled with the books it has yielded, invaluably condensed in Geoffrey Wheatcroft, *The Randlords: The Men Who Made South Africa* (Weidenfeld & Nicolson,

1985). Brian Roberts sifts a rich seam of newspaper reports in *The Diamond Magnates* (Hamish Hamilton, 1972) and *Kimberley: Turbulent City* (David Philip, 1976). Martin Meredith's *Diamonds, Gold and War* (Simon & Schuster, 2007) is an enjoyable primer to the geopolitical background. For the diamond magnates' second rush on the Rand, which made Solly Joel's reputation, see A. P. Cartwright, *The Gold Miners* (Purnell, 1962).

Early biographers tended to ignore or dismiss the rumours about the family's rise, understandably so in Stanhope Joel's *Ace of Diamonds: The Story of Solomon Barnato Joel* (F. Muller, 1958). Harry Raymond's *B. I. Barnato: A Memoir* (Isbister, 1897) is a hagiography, and it is not until Stanley Jackson's *The Great Barnato* (Heinemann, 1970) that more colour begins to intrude.

Barnato's first partner, Louis Cohen, must be treated as more entertaining than reliable in *Reminiscences of Kimberley* (Bennett, 1911); which still puts him one step ahead of Sir David Harris, Barnato's cousin, in *Pioneer, Soldier and Politician* (Low Marston 1931). It is a relief to find a compassionate witness of the early days of Kimberley in J. S. Matthews, *Incwadi Yami, or Twenty Years' Personal Experience of South Africa* (Rogers & Sherwood, 1887) ; for a taste of expansionist attitudes before the Jameson Raid, see Lord Randolph Churchill in *Men, Mines and Animals in South Africa* (Sampson, Low Marston & Co., 1892); and for treatment of native workers John M. Smalberger, 'IDB and the Mining Compound System in the 1880s' in the *South African Journal of Economics* (1974, 42:4).

For Barnato's great rival see Robert I. Rotberg, *The Founder: Cecil Rhodes and the Pursuit of Power* (OUP USA, 1988), though John Flint's *Cecil Rhodes* (Little, Brown & Co., 1974) remains a succinct gem.

The Autobiography of Robert Standish Sievier (1906) was published before he had achieved the peak of his fame, or notoriety, but that fine storyteller John Welcome fills the gaps in *Neck or Nothing: The Extraordinary Life and Times of Bob Sievier* (Faber & Faber, 1970). See also Charles Morton, *My Sixty Years of the Turf* (Hutchinson, 1930).

For general background to the Argentinian Turf see Roy Hora, *The Landowners of the Argentine Pampas: A Social and Political History 1860–1945* (OUP, 2001). Its governing body is chronicled by Jorge Newton and Lily de Newton in *Historia del Jockey Club de Buenos*

Aires (Ediciones LN, 1966); and its patriarch in Douglas W. Richmond, *Carlos Pellegrini and the Crisis of the Argentine Elites, 1880–1916* (Praeger, 1989). A rewarding indulgence is Maria Saenz Quesada's *Estancias: The Great Houses and Ranches of Argentina* (Abbeville Press, 1992). See also W. H. Hudson, *Far Away and Long Ago* (Dent, 1918); and a feature in the *Bloodstock Breeders' Review* of 1923, where the ageing Cyllene is found 'alive and yet dead'.

Memories of electoral intimidation and violence in Rose's constituency can be found in Mary Chamberlain, *Fenwomen: A Portrait of Women in an English Village* (Virago, 1975).

Chapter 20: 'All their young men are killed'

For this chapter's title quote, see C. Percy and J. Ridley (eds), *The Letters of Edwin Lutyens to his Wife Lady Emily* (Collins, 1985).

Whatever the failings of the society that produced and destroyed Raymond Asquith, our own can only seem diminished by the timeless scintillation of John Jolliffe (ed.), *Raymond Asquith: Life and Letters* (Collins, 1980).

His enchanted circle lives on through its own words in John Buchan, *Memory Hold the Door* (Hodder & Stoughton, 1940); Diana Cooper, *The Rainbow Comes and Goes* (Hart-Davis, 1958); Frances Horner, *Time Remembered* (Heinemann, 1933); Duff Cooper, *Old Men Forget* (Hart-Davis, 1953); Laurence Jones, *An Edwardian Youth* (Macmillan, 1956); Edward Marsh, *A Number of People* (Heinemann, 1939); Artemis Cooper (ed.), *A Durable Fire: Letters of Duff and Diana Cooper 1913–1950* (Collins, 1983). Others to have kept the flame alive since include Jeanne Mackenzie in *The Children of the Souls: A Tragedy of the First World War* (Chatto & Windus,1986); Angela Lambert, *Unquiet Souls: The Indian Summer of the British Aristocracy 1880–1918* (Macmillan, 1984); Philip Ziegler in *Diana Cooper* (Hamish Hamilton, 1981).

Randolph S. Churchill is commendably even-handed in *Lord Derby, 'King of Lancashire': The Official Life of Edward, Seventeenth Earl of Derby 1865–1948* (Heinemann, 1959). Likewise Michael Seth-Smith in *A Classic Connection: The Friendship of the Earl of Derby and the*

Hon George Lambton 1893–1945 (Secker & Warburg, 1983). See also, Quintin Barry in *Lord Derby and His Horses: A Tory Grandee and the Turf* (Helion & Co., 2012).

David Dutton's useful appraisal opens *Paris 1918: The War Diary of the British Ambassador, the 17th Earl of Derby* (Liverpool University Press, 2001). The contempt of Derby's wartime boss is given free rein in *War Memoirs of David Lloyd George* (Ivor Nicholson & Watson, 1933-6); For the men recruited by Derby for the front, see Graham Maddocks, *Liverpool Pals: 17th, 18th, 19th and 20th (Service) Battalions, the King's (Liverpool Regiment)* (Cooper, 1991); and F. C. Stanley, *The history of the 89th brigade, 1914–18* (Daily Post, 1919).

The Commons exchange over Rickaby is recorded in *Hansard*, 21 November 1917, Vol. 99, cc1193–4, while the description of its instigator is from his son, Harry Watt, in *Don't Look at the Camera* (Elek Books, 1974). For the lasting disgust of Joe Childs, see *My Racing Reminiscences* (Hutchinson, 1952).

The luxury of modern trainers' residences is noted in Charles Richardson, *The English Turf: A Record of Horses and Courses* (Methuen, 1901).

A Day at the Races: Epsom, 6 June 1923

Aside from the sources on Lord Derby see *Donoghue Up! The Autobiography of Steve Donoghue* (Scribner's, 1938); and Tommy Weston, *My Racing Life* (Hutchinson, 1952). For the claim that George Lambton rejected the winner as a yearling see *The Memoirs of Aga Khan: World Enough and Time* (Cassell, 1954).

Lambton himself gives an account of the dam of Pharos in *Scapa Flow: A Great Brood Mare* (Curwin Press, 1937), while the influential pedigrees established by Lord Derby are charted by Clive Graham in *Hyperion* (J. A. Allen, 1967). (Graham records how the Duchess of Montrose's French maid, incensed by the sacking of her boyfriend, quietly plaited her mistress's long, flaming hair to the chair, curtseyed, and left the house for good.)

Chapter 21: 'I have no method.
Method is imitation. I invent.'

Though we can read his own words in *Breeding the Racehorse* (J. A. Allen, 1958), Federico Tesio is arguably best understood through his business partner, Mario Incisa della Rochetta, in *The Tesios as I Knew Them* (J. A. Allen, 1979). Don Mario is as affectionate as he is mischievous, his style as elegant as his spirit is humane.

See also Franco Varola, *The Tesio Myth* (J. A. Allen, 1984); Ken McLean's *Tesio: Master of Matings* (Horwitz Grahame, 1984), not least for the nugget that Gubellini incensed the Parisian crowd with a fascist salute. For the first leg of Italy's great sporting double in Paris, see Simon Martin, *Football and Fascism: The National Game under Mussolini* (Berg, 2004).

For Tesio's young rival, see Gaia Servadio's excellent Luchino Visconti (Weidenfield & Nicolson, 1982); Laurence Schifano, *Luchino Visconti: The Flames of Passion* (HarperCollins, 1990); Gianni Rondolino, *Luchino Visconti* (UTET, 1981; Italian); and fascinating first-hand testimony from his former assistant Ubaldo Pandolfi in *La Repubblica*, 18 July 1985.

For the capers shared by the sons of Lambton and his ill-fated stable jockey, see *First to Finish* (Souvenir, 1969) by Bill Rickaby.

Chapter 22: 'Chuck, what I tol' you?'

The title quote for the chapter is from Jay Hovdey, *Whittingham: A Thoroughbred Racing Legend* (The Blood-Horse, 1993).

There seems to have been no middle ground about Horatio Luro, worshipped by some, deeply mistrusted by others. A personal view is that the show was so obviously worth the price of admission that the small print becomes irrelevant. The full spectrum of opinion is available between Joe Hirsch, *The Grand Senor: The Fabulous Career of Horatio Luro* (The Blood-Horse, 1989); Gael Elton Mayo in *A Man in a Panther Skin: The Life of Prince Dimitri Djordjadze* (Kensal Press, 1985); and Muriel Lennox, *Dark Horse: Unravelling the Mystery of Nearctic* (Cormorant Books, 2001). The story that Luro could end a quarrel by tethering a horse on its owner's lawn is from Arnold Shrimpton, 'He Won Them Both' in *The Canadian Horse* (1963). See also Alfred Wright, 'The Continental Touch of Senor Horatio Luro' in *Sports Illustrated*, 5 April 1964; and Cot Campbell's recollections in the *Blood Horse*, 26 April 2013.

For Bill Hartack see an outstanding self-examination, with Whitney Tower, 'A Hard Ride All the Way', in *Sports Illustrated*, 27 March 1967. When Hartack made the cover of *Time* (10 February 1958) his father boasted of beating him as a boy. See also 'Whatever Happened to Bill Hartack?' in *Sports Illustrated*, 24 June 1963.

Those who knew E. P. Taylor only on the Turf might be surprised by John Virtue, *Fred Taylor: Brother in the Shadows* (MQUP, 2008). They will feel more at home with Richard Rohmer, *E. P. Taylor* (McClelland & Stewart, 1978), whose description of Taylor's rescue at sea was supplemented by Leslie Roberts, *C.D.: The Life and Times of Clarence Decatur Howe* (Clarke, Irwin & Co., 1957) and William Kilbourn, *C.D. Howe: A Biography* (McClelland & Stewart, 1980).

For a broader context, see Peter C. Newman, *The Canadian Establishment* (McClelland & Stewart, 1976). See also a couple of features in *McLean's* magazine: 'E.P. Taylor and His Empire' by Pierre Berton (February 1950) and 'The Table Talk of E.P. Taylor' (November 1971) by Peter C. Newman.

For his Turf career, see Muriel Lennox in *E. P. Taylor: A Horseman and His Horses* (Burns & MacEachern, 1976); Edward L. Bowen, *Legacies of the Turf: A Century of Great Thoroughbred Breeders*, Vol. II (Eclipse Press, 2004); John P. Sparkman, *Foundation Mares* (Thoroughbred Times, 2008); also Robert Boyle, 'Millionaire's Brew', *Sports Illustrated*, 2 April 1962.

Finally, for some of the cameos around Luro: J. C. Perry and C. Pleshakov, *The Flight of the Romanovs: A Family Saga* (Basic Books, 1999). E. J. Kahn Jr., *Jock: The Life and Times of John Hay Whitney* (Book Sales, 1981); Amy Owens, 'Liz and her Llangollen' in the *Blood Horse*, 27 August 1988; Whitney Tower, 'Lady Liz of Llangollen', in *Sports Illustrated*, 9 June 1958; John H. Clark, *Trader Clark* (Thoroughbred Press, 1991).

A Day at the Races: Churchill Downs, 2 May 1964

The race that changed everything for the stallion that changed everything is described by Muriel Lennox, *Northern Dancer: The Legend and His Legacy* (Mainstream, 2002); Avalyn Hunter, *The Kingmaker* (Eclipse, 2006); Kevin Chong, *Northern Dancer: The Legendary Horse that Inspired a Nation* (Viking, 2014); Trent Frayne, *Northern Dancer and Friends* (Funk & Wagnalls, 1969).

Hunter S. Thompson's seminal 'The Kentucky Derby is Decadent and Depraved', was published in *Scanlan's Monthly*, June 1970, and included in *The Great Shark Hunt: Strange Tales from a Strange Time, Gonzo Papers*, Vol. I (Picador, 2010).

Chapter 23: 'Bang him on the nose early, Bobby. Make his eyes water.'

The first phase of John Magnier's Coolmore adventure, with Robert Sangster, is slickly drawn in Patrick and Nick Robinson, *Horsetrader: Robert Sangster and the Rise and Fall of the Sport of Kings* (HarperCollins, 1993) – source of the title quote for the chapter. See also Roy David, *Robert Sangster: Tycoon of the Turf* (Heinemann, 1991); Steven Crist, *The Horse Traders* (W. W. Norton, 1986); and Clive Gammon, 'Horses for His Kingdom' in *Sports Illustrated*, 13 November 1978.

There is natural authority to Jacqueline O'Brien and Ivor Herbert's *Vincent O'Brien: The Official Biography* (Bantam, 2005), but see also Raymond Smith, *Vincent O'Brien: The Man and the Legend* (Sporting Books, 1997) – not least for a terrier with a cigar in its mouth, perched on a barstool in Fermoy, his recollections conceivably more reliable than those vouchsafed by Billy McDonald – and Tim Fitzgeorge-Parker, *Vincent O'Brien: A Long Way from Tipperary* (Pelham, 1974).

For Claiborne Stud, see Bill Nack's peerless 'Blood Brothers and Bluegrass' in *My Turf: Horses, Boxers, Blood Money and the Sporting Life* (Da Capo Press, 2003).

Chapter 24: 'They'd run through a wall for you.'

For the rise of Michael Tabor, see Peter Cunningham, *The Story of Thunder Gulch* (Orion, 1996); also Julian Muscat, 'Life's a Gamble', *Thoroughbred Owner & Breeder Magazine*, 2 July 2012.

For a sense of the spirit animating Godolphin, see Mohammed bin Rashid al Maktoum, *My Vision* (Motivate, 2012), while the tragedy that hit the stable even as Galileo began his rise is in Rachel Pagones, *Dubai Millennium: A Vision Realised, a Dream Lost* (Highdown, 2007). For background to Urban Sea, see Anne Holland, *Sea the Stars: The World's Best Racehorse* (W&N, 2009); Neville Callaghan gave a retirement interview to Peter Thomas, 'Not So Nasty', in *Racing Post*, 20 November 2007.

Chapter 25: 'I'd be surprised if there's ever been a better horse'

Various author interviews over the years with Bobby Frankel and Henry Cecil include: 'I don't like to be defeated – beat depression, get on', *Independent*, 24 July 2011.

Henry Cecil *On the Level* (Harrap, 1983) was a light-hearted memoir; for an unabashed examination of his subsequent troubles see Brough Scott, *Henry Cecil: Trainer of Genius* (Racing Post Books, 2014). Cecil's stepfather is remembered in Bill Curling, *The Captain: A Biography of Captain Sir Cecil Boyd-Rochfort* (Barrie & Jenkins, 1970).

See also Steve Haskin, 'Hall of Famer Bobby Frankel Dies at 68', *Blood Horse*, 16 November 2009; and Joe Drape, 'Frankel Says His Horse is a Natural', *New York Times*, 8 June 2000.

Index